U0648098

中华译学馆立馆宗旨

以中华为根　译与学并重
弘扬优秀文化　促进中外交流
拓展精神疆域　驱动思想创新

丁酉年冬月许钧撰　罗卫东书

罗卫东

中華譯學館·中华翻译研究文库

许　钧◎总主编

文本内外

戴乃迭的中国文学外译与思考

辛红娟　刘园晨◎编著

ZHEJIANG UNIVERSITY PRESS
浙江大学出版社

总　序

改革开放前后的一个时期,中国译界学人对翻译的思考大多基于对中国历史上出现的数次翻译高潮的考量与探讨。简言之,主要是对佛学译介、西学东渐与文学译介的主体、活动及结果的探索。

20 世纪 80 年代兴起的文化转向,让我们不断拓宽视野,对影响译介活动的诸要素及翻译之为有了更加深入的认识。考察一国以往翻译之活动,必与该国的文化语境、民族兴亡和社会发展等诸维度相联系。三十多年来,国内译学界对清末民初的西学东渐与"五四"前后的文学译介的研究已取得相当丰硕的成果。但进入 21 世纪以来,随着中国国力的增强,中国的影响力不断扩大,中西古今关系发生了变化,其态势从总体上看,可以说与"五四"前后的情形完全相反:中西古今关系之变化在一定意义上,可以说是根本性的变化。在民族复兴的语境中,新世纪的中西关系,出现了以"中国文化走向世界"诉求中的文化自觉与文化输出为特征的新态势;而古今之变,则在民族复兴的语境中对中华民族的五千年文化传统与精华有了新的认识,完全不同于"五四"前后与"旧世界"和文化传统的彻底决裂与革命。于是,就我们译学界而言,对翻译的思考语境发生了根本性的变化,我们对翻译思考的路径和维度也不可能不发生变化。

变化之一,涉及中西,便是由西学东渐转向中国文化"走出去",呈东学西传之趋势。变化之二,涉及古今,便是从与"旧世界"的根本决裂转向对中国传统文化、中华民族价值观的重新认识与发扬。这两个根本性的转变给译学界提出了新的大问题:翻译在此转变中应承担怎样的责任?翻译在此转变中如何定位?翻译研究者应持有怎样的翻译观念?以研究"外译中"翻译历史与活动为基础的中国译学研究是否要与时俱进,把目光投向"中译外"的活动?中国文化"走出去",中国要向世界展示的是什么样的"中国文化"?当中国一改"五四"前后的"革命"与"决裂"态势,将中国传统文化推向世界,在世界各地创建孔子学院、推广中国文化之时,"翻译什么"与"如何翻译"这双重之问也是我们译学界必须思考与回答的。

综观中华文化发展史,翻译发挥了不可忽视的作用,一如季羡林先生所言,"中华文化之所以能永葆青春","翻译之为用大矣哉"。翻译的社会价值、文化价值、语言价值、创造价值和历史价值在中国文化的形成与发展中表现尤为突出。从文化角度来考察翻译,我们可以看到,翻译活动在人类历史上一直存在,其形式与内涵在不断丰富,且与社会、经济、文化发展相联系,这种联系不是被动的联系,而是一种互动的关系、一种建构性的力量。因此,从这个意义上来说,翻译是推动世界文化发展的一种重大力量,我们应站在跨文化交流的高度对翻译活动进行思考，以维护文化多样性为目标来考察翻译活动的丰富性、复杂性与创造性。

基于这样的认识，也基于对翻译的重新定位和思考，浙江大学于 2018 年正式设立了“浙江大学中华译学馆”，旨在“传承文化之脉，发挥翻译之用，促进中外交流，拓展思想疆域，驱动思想创新”。中华译学馆的任务主要体现在三个层面：在译的层面，推出包括文学、历史、哲学、社会科学的系列译丛，“译入”与“译出”互动，积极参与国家战略性的出版工程；在学的层面，就翻译活动所涉及的重大问题展开思考与探索，出版系列翻译研究丛书，举办翻译学术会议；在中外文化交流层面，举办具有社会影响力的翻译家论坛，思想家、作家与翻译家对话等，以翻译与文学为核心开展系列活动。正是在这样的发展思路下，我们与浙江大学出版社合作，集合全国译学界的力量，推出具有学术性与开拓性的“中华翻译研究文库”。

积累与创新是学问之道，也将是本文库坚持的发展路径。本文库为开放性文库，不拘形式，以思想性与学术性为其衡量标准。我们对专著和论文(集)的遴选原则主要有四：一是研究的独创性，要有新意和价值，对整体翻译研究或翻译研究的某个领域有深入的思考，有自己的学术洞见；二是研究的系统性，围绕某一研究话题或领域，有强烈的问题意识、合理的研究方法、有说服力的研究结论以及较大的后续研究空间；三是研究的社会性，鼓励密切关注社会现实的选题与研究，如中国文学与文化“走出去”研究、语言服务行业与译者的职业发展研究、中国典籍对外译介与影响研究、翻译教育改革研究等；四是研究的(跨)学科性,鼓励深入系统地探索翻译学领域的任一分支领域,如元翻译理论研究、翻译史研究、翻译批评研究、翻译教学研究、翻译技术研究等,同时鼓励从跨学科视角探索翻译的规律与奥秘。

青年学者是学科发展的希望,我们特别欢迎青年翻译学者向本文库积极投稿,我们将及时遴选有价值的著作予以出版,集中展现青年学者的学术面貌。在青年学者和资深学者的共同支持下,我们有信心把"中华翻译研究文库"打造成翻译研究领域的精品丛书。

许　钧

2018 年春

目　录

第二编　戴乃迭民间文学英译

第三编 戴乃迭散文、寓言式杂文英译

第四编　戴乃迭乡土文学英译

第五编　戴乃迭女性文学英译

导　言

1919 年 1 月 19 日，戴乃迭(原名格莱迪斯・玛格丽特・泰勒，Gladys Margaret Tayler，戴乃迭是其与杨宪益结婚后的中文名字)出生在北京的一个英国传教士家庭。七岁时，她在母亲和姐姐希尔达的陪同下，返回英国接受教育，此后在柴郡读了一年女子小学，在肯特郡教会女校沃森斯道・霍尔(Walthamstow Hall)学校度过了十年寄宿生涯。1937 年秋，她以优等生身份获得国际奖学金，进入牛津大学攻读法国文学。

戴乃迭的父亲约翰・伯纳德・泰勒(John Bernard Tayler，中文名戴乐仁)是一位传教士，大学毕业以后参加伦敦传教士会社，被派到中国，在天津新学书院和燕京大学执教十多年后，前往当时十分贫穷的中国甘肃地区发起社会改良运动，收容无家可归的孤儿，为他们提供免费教育。父亲戴乐仁的理想主义情怀和对贫困中国发展的关怀，无形中影响了戴乃迭后来对世界的认识和对中国的同情与理解。戴乃迭进牛津大学时，正值日本大肆侵略中国，战火蔓延到了中国的大部分土地上。英国人的正义感加上她的中国情愫使戴乃迭成了一个坚定的抗日派。当时，留学英伦的杨宪益担任牛津大学中国学会主席，戴乃迭担任学会秘书。她帮助杨宪益组织中国学会的会议，记录下每次会议的重要内容。这些活动迅速拉近了两位年轻人之间的距离，这对异国青年很快陷入热恋。儿时北京生活的美好回忆，加上父亲在社会价值观方面的影响，戴乃迭决定为了“才华横溢的杨”放弃法国文学专业，改学中国文学。

当时，牛津大学刚刚开始设置中国文学荣誉学位，戴乃迭是攻读该学位的第一个学生。戴乃迭的中文导师休斯(Ernest Richard Hughes)①是一位仁慈、开明,具有绅士风度的老先生,虽然中文口语水平并不十分高,但他对人文主义特别是中国儒家学说怀有浓厚兴趣,致力于向英国及西方社会系统介绍儒家思想发展史、著名儒学家和主要儒家经典,对西方了解孔子及其思想起到一定作用。休斯的中文名字叫修中诚,原是英国伦敦会教士,1911 年到中国福建汀州传教十八年,后在上海中华基督青年会任职,1933 年回母校牛津大学任中国哲学和宗教教师。戴乃迭跟随休斯教授学习儒家的“四书五经”,杨宪益推荐她读中国古典诗歌和传奇故事以及晚近的古典散文。在休斯和杨宪益的共同指导与影响下,戴乃迭在中国文学方面进步非常迅速,以优异的成绩获得二等荣誉学位毕业。

1940 年夏天,戴乃迭随杨宪益辗转来到战火中的中国,在此后长达半个多世纪的时间里,她通过独译或合译(杨宪益是其最主要合作者)将逾千万字的中国文学作品译介到英语世界,为中国翻译事业、中西文化交流做出了卓越贡献。

一、戴乃迭中国文学英译与译介贡献

戴乃迭对中国文学作品的译介以 1938 年牛津求学期间与杨宪益合译《离骚》为发端,到 1989 年患病卧床搁置译笔,持续了整整半个世纪。其译作按翻译主体可分为两大类:一类是与杨宪益合译(含少量与他人合译)的作品,另一类是个人独立译作。其中,合译作品以古典文学为主,譬如《红楼梦》《老残游记》《史记选》《宋明评话选》《唐代传奇》等,兼及部分现当代文学作品,如《鲁迅选集》(四卷)、丁玲的长篇小说《太阳照在桑干河上》、郭沫若的话剧《屈原》(五幕剧)等。戴乃迭的独立译介活动最早可

---

① 1939 年,在牛津大学汉学讲座教授空悬的情况下,时任中国哲学和宗教讲师的休斯主持开展牛津大学汉学发展史上的一次重大改革,创立汉学科(Chinese Honour School),确定本科四年制的课程内容和考试方法,设置正式学位,戴乃迭为牛津大学汉学科荣誉学位第一人。后来,因翻译《红楼梦》饮誉世界的英国汉学家大卫·霍克思在休斯指导下专攻中文,是牛津汉学科招收的第二位学生。

追溯到1950年出版的《原动力》(*The Moving Force*),第一部署名独立译作则是外文出版社1953年出版的《李家庄的变迁》(*Changes in Li Village*)。戴乃迭一生独立译品体裁丰富多样,以现当代小说为最大宗,诗歌次之,兼及部分散文、剧本、文论、童话、寓言等。

在中国生活半个多世纪,戴乃迭的中文水平相当出色,"会写一笔正楷小字,能仿《唐人说荟》,用文言写小故事,写得文字简秀"①。汉学家詹纳尔(William John Francis Jenner)称"戴乃迭是当世寥寥可数的中文外译大家。她的译作一部分是独立完成的,一部分是跟她丈夫杨宪益合作完成的,其数量和质量都令人叹为观止"②。通过考证"熊猫丛书"系列和外文出版社杨、戴译作信息,爬梳《中国文学》(*Chinese Literature*)1951—2000年的全部刊次,统计发现,戴乃迭独译作品总计430篇(部)③,含现当代小说115篇(部),散文55篇,诗歌60首,剧本、寓言、童话、相声等200篇(则)。其中独立成册的译著20余部(不包括收录其作品的合集译著,且不计再版)。她译介的作家、诗人120人次,几乎囊括了所有现当代名家。

基于文献梳理,我们试将戴乃迭的译介贡献总结为如下三方面:

(1)对中国现代文学的译介贡献。自20世纪50年代起,戴乃迭在《中国文学》杂志上相继翻译了艾青、巴金、老舍、吴组缃、萧红、殷夫、朱自清等众多现代作家作品,其中最值得关注的是她对沈从文作品的译介。1962年,戴乃迭翻译了沈从文的代表作《边城》④。1981年,"熊猫丛书"以首发之作的形式推出戴乃迭独译的沈从文中短篇小说选集《边城及其它》(*The Border Town and Other Stories*)。翌年,她独译的沈从文散文选集《湘西散记》(*Recollections of West Hunan*)出版。虽然沈从文重新进入

---

① 李辉. 杨宪益与戴乃迭:一同走过. 郑州:大象出版社,2001:3.

② 杨宪益. 我有两个祖国——戴乃迭和她的世界. 桂林:广西师范大学出版社,2003:153.

③ 由于历史原因,很长一段时期外文出版社发行的译作,以及《中国文学》刊载译文没有译者署名,不少译作的译者无从考证,此处梳理的皆为戴乃迭独立署名的译作。

④ 刊载于《中国文学》1962年第10—11期。

文学圈层中心更多得益于夏志清在《中国现代小说史》中的评价与金介甫(Jeffrey C. Kinkley)、马悦然(Goran Malmqvist)、王德威等人的推崇，而戴乃迭彼时的选择与译介，无疑在一定程度上推动了沈从文作品的域外传播与重新评估。沈从文研究专家金介甫评价戴乃迭英译《边城》“优美动人”[①]，他在自己的译本中沿用戴乃迭对《边城》书名的翻译——Border Town，并在译序中专门提到“我的翻译格外感谢沈从文的朋友戴乃迭1981 年的译本”[②]。

(2)对中国当代文学的译介贡献。当代文学占戴乃迭独立译作选材的绝大部分，其中最为瞩目的是她对新时期女性作家作品的译介。20 世纪 80 年代，受西方女性主义思潮影响，戴乃迭大量翻译了“文革”中成熟起来的中国当代女作家的作品。[③] 她主要通过三种渠道推介这些女作家作品：一是通过《中国文学》杂志、“熊猫丛书”，以合集或单行本的方式对外译介新时期女作家作品，如新凤霞自传《新凤霞回忆录》、张洁《爱，是不能忘记的》、谌容《玫瑰色的晚餐》、王安忆《人人之间》等。二是凭借自身中英双重文化身份和良好的国际声誉，通过参与文化交流、学术交流和发表演讲促进西方世界对中国新时期女作家的了解。1983 年，她在英国利兹大学发表题为“中国女作家”(Chinese Women Writers)的演讲，“堪称20 世纪 80 年代英语地区新时期女作家研究的学术起点”，“其中涉及的女作家及其作品渐次获西方世界青睐并得到译介”。[④] 三是身体力行带动学者参与对女作家作品的译介，“汉学家吴芳思(Frances Wood)因与戴乃迭熟悉而接触到女作家戴厚英的《人啊！人!》，进而产生兴趣并译成英

---

① Kinkley, Jeffrey. English Translations of Shen Congwen's Masterwork, *Bian Cheng* (*Border Town*). *Asian and African Studies*, 2014 (1): 45.

② Congwen, Shen. *Border Town*: *A Novel*. Jeffrey Kinkley (trans.). New York: Harper Collins Publishers, 2009: vii.

③ Davin, Delia. Gladys Yang. *The Guardian*, 1999-11-24.

④ 付文慧. 中国女作家作品英译(1979—2010)研究. 北京: 对外经济贸易大学出版社, 2015: 16.

文”①。

(3)对中国英语教育事业的支持和青年译者的扶持。20 世纪 60 年代初,应商务印书馆邀请,戴乃迭以北京为背景,为当时的英语学习者编写了口语会话教材《学习讲英语》(*Learn to Speak English*),该教材 1963 年首印出版,1964 年再次印刷,总印数逾 10 万册②。作为外文出版社的外籍专家,戴乃迭经常为社内的青年译者润色、修改译文,特别注重对年轻人的扶持。原《中国文学》副主编王明杰先生回忆说,“我翻译的巴金的作品《春天里的秋天》,就是戴乃迭帮助修改的”,“当时给我改稿最多的是戴乃迭,她给我改得非常好”。③ 被夏志清称为“公认的中国现当代文学之首席翻译家”的葛浩文正是在戴乃迭举荐下才翻译了张洁代表作《沉重的翅膀》④,该作的出版“标志着葛氏翻译事业的转型”⑤。

可以说,戴乃迭为中国现当代文学在英语世界的译介与传播做出了不可磨灭的贡献。这样一位对中国现当代文学外译有奠基之功的翻译大家,国内译学界对其研究现状如何?存在哪些不足?未来研究潜势如何?我们拟通过对文献数据的可视化呈现,佐以文本细读,回答上述问题。

二、戴乃迭翻译研究可视化呈现与潜势剖析

我们运用科学计量学工具 CiteSpace 软件绘制知识图谱并结合文献查证与文本细读,对当前戴乃迭翻译研究的研究热点和发展演化历程进行了分析。在中国知网数据库(CNKI)中,我们首先以“戴乃迭”为检索项,以“篇名”“主题”“关键词”为检索条件开展三轮联合检索(检索时间:

---

① 付文慧. 中国女作家作品英译(1979—2010)研究. 北京:对外经济贸易大学出版社,2015:17.

② 戴乃迭. *Learn to Speak English*(学习讲英语). 陆钦颐,张祖德,注. 北京:商务印书馆,1963:i.

③ 参见吴自选.《中国文学》杂志和中国文学的英译——原《中国文学》副总编王明杰先生访谈录. 东方翻译,2010(4):55.

④ 赋格,张健. 葛浩文:首席且惟一的“接生婆”. 南方周末,2008-03-27.

⑤ 张丹丹. 葛浩文中国文学英译脉络及表征扫描. 中国翻译,2018(4):52.

2019 年 8 月 1 日，分别获得文献 192 篇、505 篇、531 篇；继而在高级检索中以“戴”并含“译”、“杨”并含“译”对“篇名”进行两轮检索，分别获文献 311 篇和 58 篇。通过对文献标题、摘要、关键词以及具体内容的细读进行逐条筛选，人工剔除重复或无关文献后，最终得到 521 篇文献作为本研究的对象和 CiteSpace 图谱绘制的数据来源。中国知网可查获最早一篇戴乃迭翻译研究论文《〈红楼梦〉西文译本序跋谈》出现在 1979 年，故我们将该年度设定为研究起始节点。

1. 戴乃迭翻译研究热点分析

“某一领域的研究热点是指在一个具体时间维度内，有着内在关联、一定数量的论文集中探讨的科研问题。”[①]关键词是论文核心内容的高度概括与浓缩，对某一研究领域高频关键词的统计和分析可在一定程度凸显该领域的研究热点。基于检索到的 521 篇论文文献，我们利用 CiteSpace 软件绘制出关键词聚类图谱，即研究热点视图，图中每一个节点代表一个关键词，关键词字号越大，说明相关文献越多(如图 1 所示)。

基于研究热点视图，结合对该领域的文献细读，我们发现 1979—2019 年国内戴乃迭翻译研究的热点主要集中在如下三个方面：

(1)对戴乃迭与杨宪益合译作品《红楼梦》的关注

杨、戴合译的《红楼梦》英文版自 1978 年问世以来，一直是翻译学界研究的热点。关注点多在对诗词、字句、习语、修辞等翻译策略与方法的比较研究，[②]研究成果虽丰，却存在“研究方法单一、剖析不够深刻、选题重复”[③]等现象。此外，图 1 中关键词“杨译”“杨译本”的出现也从一个侧面反映出，不少研究者在论及杨宪益、戴乃迭合译的《红楼梦》或其他作品时，往往会忽略戴乃迭作为合译者的独特贡献。

(2)对戴乃迭独译作品《边城》《阿诗玛》和《沉重的翅膀》的关注

《边城》是沈从文最负盛名的作品，共有 4 个英文全译本。对戴乃迭

---

① 金胜昔，林正军. 国内翻译认知研究的文献计量分析. 外语教学，2016(5)：98.

② 刘迎姣.《红楼梦》英译研究回顾与展望. 湖南科技大学学报(社会科学版)，2013(3)：151.

③ 辛红娟，等. 杨宪益翻译研究. 南京：南京大学出版社，2018 年，第 83 页.

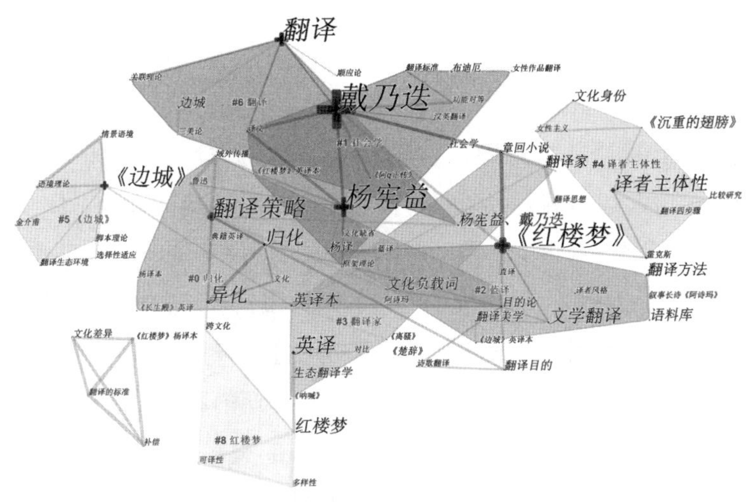

图 1　戴乃迭翻译研究关键词聚类

《边城》译本的研究论文数量虽多(文献统计显示有 80 余篇),却同样存在明显的选题重复、研究同质化倾向,论者多从“翻译美学”“文化负载词”等视角切入。在知网“高级检索”中“篇名”条目以“翻译美学”并含“边城”进行检索,显示结果为 11 篇学术论文。其中被引频次最高的是发文时间最早的刘小燕《从翻译美学观看戴乃迭对〈边城〉中美学意蕴的艺术再现》。该文通过对比金隄、白英(Robert Payne)合译本与戴乃迭《边城》译本,分析指出戴乃迭译本更为流畅自然,再现了原文的美学意蕴①。

《阿诗玛》是彝族撒尼人的口传叙事长诗,通过塑造阿诗玛这一善良勇敢的女性形象,歌颂了撒尼人“断得弯不得”的民族精神,2006 年入选第一批国家级非物质文化遗产名录。自 1953 年云南省文工团圭山工作组将《阿诗玛》搜集、整理、翻译为汉语文本后,《阿诗玛》相继被译成多国语言,是成功走出国门的少数民族典籍。美国加州大学戴维斯分校女性资源研究中心主任、女性与性别研究项目兼职教授司佩姬(Margaret Byrne

---

① 刘小燕. 从翻译美学观看戴乃迭对《边城》中美学意蕴的艺术再现. 北京交通大学学报(社会科学版), 2005(2): 74.

Swain，彝名诗薇）盛赞《阿诗玛》的世界性意涵，"'阿诗玛'的传说已经成为与现代性及全球主义有关的地方文化的一部分。不管从地理形象还是文化形象来说，'阿诗玛'都与撒尼人的传统文化有关，同时，也与中国乃至世界有关"①。戴乃迭英译的《阿诗玛》作为迄今为止唯一的英文全译本，在《阿诗玛》走向世界的过程中发挥了关键作用。王宏印、崔晓霞从翻译诗学和民族典籍翻译视角，对戴乃迭《阿诗玛》英译本做了体制、格律及语言方面的分析，肯定了戴乃迭以诗译诗，运用英国民谣体形式翻译汉语叙事长诗的创举。② 崔晓霞的专著《〈阿诗玛〉英译研究》从撒尼数字文化、撒尼特色比喻、撒尼民风民俗等五方面的翻译对戴乃迭《阿诗玛》译本进行了全面、深入的研究，盛赞译本是"诗歌翻译的典范"③。

《沉重的翅膀》是女作家张洁的第一部长篇小说，完稿于 1981 年 4 月，1983 年 12 月第四次修改后走上中国文学最高奖茅盾文学奖的领奖台。1987 年，戴乃迭译本 *Leaden Wings* 在英国出版发行。原作聚焦"四化"建设与工业改革，而戴乃迭译本则主要聚焦改革洪流中的女性情感与女性生存状况，"在一定程度上甚至可以被当作女性文本解读"④。这种带有明显改写性质的翻译行为引起研究者关注，目前学界对戴译《沉重的翅膀》的研究较为多元。张生祥、汪佳丽以《沉重的翅膀》为例，从翻译文本的选择、译序的撰写、具体翻译策略等方面分析了戴乃迭翻译活动中所体现出的女性主义倾向⑤。辛红娟、唐宏敏通过分析戴译《沉重的翅膀》的内副文本与外副文本，剖析戴乃迭译介行为中彰显的"文化融合意识、女性

---

① 李竞立. 世界的"阿诗玛"——《阿诗玛》国际学术研讨会侧记. 云南日报，2004-09-15.

② 王宏印，崔晓霞. 论戴乃迭英译《阿诗玛》的可贵探索. 西南民族大学学报(人文社会科学版)，2011(12)：202-206.

③ 崔晓霞.《阿诗玛》英译研究. 北京：民族出版社，2013：210.

④ 付文慧. 多重文化身份下之戴乃迭英译阐释. 中国翻译，2011(6)：18.

⑤ 张生祥，汪佳丽. 女性译者主体性探究——析戴乃迭英译《沉重的翅膀》. 当代外语研究，2015(8)：63.

主义意识与读者接受意识”①。

(3)对戴乃迭文化身份的研究

在“文化身份(认同)”研究领域,西方翻译理论家关注的焦点在于翻译对族群文化身份的构建意义,②而对戴乃迭这样一位反向“离散者”(diasporas),国内学者更关注她的个体文化身份对译介文本选择、译介策略的影响。付文慧指出,宏观层面的中英双重文化身份使戴乃迭的翻译拥有深厚的中国情怀,而微观层面的女性文化身份则使戴乃迭的译介带有浓厚的女性主义倾向。③ 王惠萍基于后殖民主义理论对文化身份的论述,探讨文化身份的流动性对戴乃迭译介选择的影响,考察了戴乃迭不同时期翻译风格的嬗变,认为戴乃迭在 20 世纪 50—60 年代的“翻译方法以直译为主,辅以意译和套译,译文完整保留原文的内容,少有删略”,在 80 年代的翻译方法则“以意译和套译等方法为主,而以直译为辅……进行了较多的删略”。④

2. 戴乃迭翻译研究热点演变分析

为梳理 1979—2019 年戴乃迭翻译研究的历时发展动态,分析研究热点随时间的演变与迁移,洞察该领域的研究潜势,我们使用 CiteSpace 软件绘制时间线视图(timeline view),以 1 年为一个时间分区,总计 40 个时间分区,选取每个时间分区内被引频次最高的文献引用数据,生成戴乃迭翻译研究历时变化图,能够较为直观地显示出高频关键词及其对应的年份,如图 2 所示。

1979—1999 年,国内戴乃迭翻译研究论文仅 44 篇,论文主题多关于杨、戴合译作品《红楼梦》译本的赏析,及其翻译策略、翻译方法以及翻译

---

① 辛红娟,唐宏敏.从副文本解读戴乃迭的翻译观——以《沉重的翅膀》英译本为例.外国语言与文化,2019(2):131.

② 高胜兵,王娟.利玛窦的文化身份与其翻译策略和效果.中国翻译,2019(3):63-74.

③ 付文慧.多重文化身份下之戴乃迭英译阐释.中国翻译,2011(6):16-20.

④ 王惠萍.后殖民视域下的戴乃迭文化身份与译介活动研究.北京:新华出版社,2014:143.

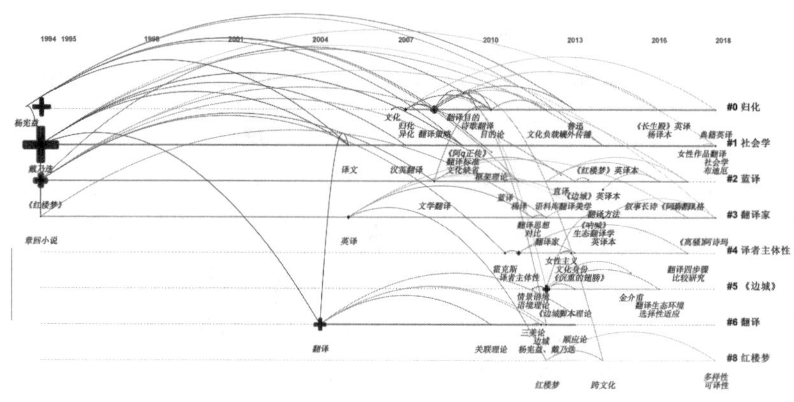

图 2　戴乃迭翻译研究历时变化图

技巧的归纳总结，如韩忠华从书名、人名、习语的翻译等方面归纳杨、戴《红楼梦》的翻译技巧。① 刘壮冲所撰《〈湘西散记〉英译文的一些失误》在肯定戴乃迭译文纯正流畅的基础上，指出因译者不熟悉湘西方言而出现的一些误译。② 此外，许渊冲在《喜读〈鲁迅诗歌〉英译本》一文中，比较戴乃迭独译的鲁迅诗歌与杨、戴合译版本，指出"戴译重'意似'"、"杨译精练"。③ 这一阶段尚处于翻译研究的文化转向初期，译者研究处于相对边缘状态，学界较少对译者主体进行研究，素以合作者身份出现的戴乃迭所引起的关注自然就更少。

随着翻译学界研究范式的变化，研究者开始借助翻译功能学派、翻译文化学派、翻译哲学学派等诸多学派理论解读现当代译品，"目的论""操控论""翻译规范""阐释学""关联理论"等开始成为切入戴乃迭译文分析的理论视角。"信达雅""化境论""三美论""翻译美学""生态翻译学""适应/选择"等关键词在图 2 中的出现能够在一定程度上显示中国传统译论的继承与创新。随着翻译学研究疆域的拓展与本体研究的深化，"人们越

---

① 韩忠华．评《红楼梦》杨氏译本．红楼梦学刊，1986(3)：279-302．

② 刘壮冲．《湘西散记》英译文的一些失误．中国翻译，1994(2)：36．

③ 许渊冲．喜读《鲁迅诗歌》英译本．外语教学与研究，1981(3)：42．

来越清醒地认识到,在翻译这个以人的思考和创作为中心的艺术活动中,最不应该忽视的恰恰就是对这个活动的主体——译者的研究和重视"①。此后,戴乃迭作为独立译者的身份、其独译作品中所展现的主观能动性开始引发关注,"译者主体性""文化身份""女性主义"成为研究戴乃迭译介活动的新视角。研究方法不仅有传统的定性研究方法,还开始采用"语料库"的定量研究方法,研究者多基于同一文本的多译本建立平行语料库,据以分析各译本的文体特色或译者风格,如赵秋荣、郭旭基于《边城》四译本的平行语料库,考察译者关于报道动词"说"的译介策略,研究指出戴乃迭翻译报道动词时用词最为丰富,并且有意减少使用过去时。②

线视图显示的戴乃迭翻译研究关键词频率变化,与国内翻译学研究的轨迹几乎同步,可以说,戴乃迭丰沛的译作为研究者提供了验证各类中外翻译学理论的语料。

3. 戴乃迭翻译研究可拓展空间

基于1979—2019年戴乃迭翻译研究状况,不难看出,目前学界对戴乃迭与杨宪益合译之外的译作、翻译思想、翻译风格、译作传播与接受情况等方面的研究相对较少,研究深度与广度也十分有限。我们尝试在前文研究现状展示的基础上,剖析当下研究的可拓展空间,以期推动戴乃迭译介研究向更全面、深刻的维度发展。

(1)全面梳理戴乃迭独立译作,深化对其独立译者身份的研究

目前,学界对戴乃迭译作的研究集中于她的合译作品《红楼梦》与独译作品《边城》《沉重的翅膀》《阿诗玛》等,较少涉及其他数百种长短不一、题材各异的译作。主要原因在于,学界对戴乃迭独译作品以及她作为独立译者的身份缺乏应有的重视。我们发现,不少论文在列举、分析戴乃迭译作时甚至出现张冠李戴现象:一是混淆戴乃迭合译与独译作品,尤以沈从文的《边城》为甚;二是弄错戴乃迭和其他译者的译作。

---

① 张柏然,许钧.面向21世纪的译学研究.北京:商务印书馆,2002:397-398.

② 赵秋荣,郭旭.译者的明晰化策略研究——基于《边城》四译本报道动词"说"的考察.解放军外国语学院学报,2019(5):117.

戴乃迭英译的《边城》初刊在《中国文学》杂志 1962 年第 10 期和第 11 期上，1981 年与沈从文三部短篇小说《萧萧》《丈夫》《贵生》，以及黄永玉回忆性散文《太阳下的风景——沈从文与我》汇编成册，作为“熊猫丛书”系列首发之作《边城及其它》推出，以上译者署名皆为 Gladys Yang。然而，文献检索显示，不少研究者误认为《边城》为杨、戴合译作品。我们在回溯查证这些论文的参考文献时发现，此类论文的信息讹误，多因译林出版社 2009 年出版中英对照版《边城》版权页误将译者定为杨宪益、戴乃迭所致。同类讹误还有："熊猫丛书"系列的《湘西散记》为戴乃迭独译作品，并非合译；李恍、张风一等人创作的话剧《赤道战鼓》(*War Drums on the Equator*)为戴乃迭独译作品，也非合译。此外，戴乃迭与其他译者的译作也常常被混淆。以下略举几例：古华的《爬满青藤的木屋》(*The Log Cabin Overgrown with Creepers*)译者为詹纳尔，谌容的《人到中年》(*At Middle Age*)为喻璠琴、王明杰合译，王安忆的《流逝》(*Lapse of Time*)译者为葛浩文(Howard Goldblatt)，以上常被误认为戴乃迭译作。李英儒的《野火春风斗古城》(*In an Old City*)译者为戴乃迭，却被不少研究者归入沙博理(Sidney Shapiro)译作。

有鉴于此，学界亟须严格依照文献学规范梳理《中国文学》杂志、"熊猫丛书"系列及 20 世纪 50—80 年代外文出版社发行的各类现当代文学作品英译本，对杨宪益、戴乃迭合译作品以及他们的独译作品进行认真考证，以第一手的资料还原他们的翻译贡献。不仅考证译者署名，对译作的中文题名也应当予以重视，我们发现研究论文中弄错戴乃迭译作中文题名的情况不在少数，如她独译的话剧《赤道战鼓》在不少研究中被误写为《赤壁战鼓》，《长江上的白鸥》常被误写为《长江上的白鸽》等等不一而足。

(2)系统归纳、提炼戴乃迭的翻译思想

译者的翻译思想体现在原文本选择、翻译过程和翻译风格等各个方面，是翻译家研究的重要内容，缺少对译者翻译思想的体察势必会造成译文评价的偏颇。在我们搜集的 521 篇文献中，仅一篇专文探讨戴乃迭的翻译思想。戴乃迭毕生致力于翻译实践，极少提及自己对翻译的见解，在一定程度上给研究者的系统梳理与归纳带来了挑战。我们试提出如下四方面途径:一是从她本人撰写的为数不多的文章中找寻其对翻译的论述,如她在评价霍克思《红楼梦》英译本时说“大卫·霍克思的杰出成就是让西方读者能用优美的英语来阅读这部中国名著”①,文中能够看出她对读者接受的关注。二是梳理杨宪益以及《中国文学》编辑部同事接受访谈时对戴乃迭翻译的评述,比如,王明杰曾提到戴乃迭对人名翻译的见解,“小说中的人名,戴乃迭说,一般可采用意译,不要音译。因为音译外国人读不出来又记不住”②。三是从她撰写的译序、译本注释、增添的附录等副文本资源中提炼出她的翻译见解。四是深入译本内部,开展文本细读,从中西思维差异中探究戴乃迭秉持的跨语际实践原则。

在对戴乃迭翻译思想的研究中,应重视她与杨宪益翻译思想的异与同。目前在戴乃迭翻译研究中,一旦论及合译作品,研究者几乎一边倒地谈论杨宪益的翻译思想。事实上,合译涉及译者之间的对话、斡旋与妥协,仅仅论及一人,所得结论失之片面。1980 年 3 月,应澳中理事会、澳大利亚文化委员会文学部邀请,戴乃迭与杨宪益、作家俞林、学者王佐良组成中国作家协会代表团赴澳大利亚参加文化交流活动。在接受当地报纸《时代日报》等多家媒体的采访,被问及“你是否认为译者应改写原文?”这一问题时,杨宪益的观点是,译者应尽量忠实于原文的形象,过分强调创造性是不对的,必须非常忠实于原文;而戴乃迭却回答说,“应该更富有创造性。翻译家应大致做到这样。然而,我们长期以来一直受过去工作环境的限制,以致现在我们的翻译家比较拘泥于原文”③。可以看出,戴乃迭与杨宪益关于翻译的见解不尽相同。戴乃迭倡导的“创造性”实则涵盖了对译入语诗学和读者接受的体察。但由于她和杨宪益都具有高度的文化自觉,都以传播中华文化为宗旨,虽然“忠实”并非她所信奉的首要翻译标

---

① Yang, Gladys. Review of David Hawkes' *The Story of the Stone. A novel in five volumes by Cao Xueqin. Vol. I: The golden days. Vol. II: The crab-flower club. Bulletin of the School of Oriental and African Studies*, 1980 (43): 622.

② 胡牧,朱云会. 英文版《中国文学》杂志生产传播机制中的译者群体与人文精神——王明杰先生访谈录. 燕山大学学报(哲学社会科学版),2019(4):30.

③ 肯尼思·亨德森. 土耳其挂毯的反面//王佐良. 翻译:思考与试笔. 北京:外语教学与研究出版社,1997:84.

准,她的译文也始终带有明显的忠实色彩,较之新生代汉学家、翻译家葛浩文,更注重与原文保持一致。①

(3)加强对戴乃迭译作底本的史料考证

"在描述翻译学的体系中,确定译本所依据的原本是必不可少的环节。只有确定了原本,才能探寻译本与原本在语篇层面的相互关系。"②未确定译者所依照的原本就对译本进行评论,如原文系版本较多,差别较大的文本,所得翻译研究结论很难站得住脚。作为一名严谨的译者,戴乃迭的不少独立译作在再版、重印时根据不同原本多次修改,因此在对戴乃迭译作进行分析时,应具备充分的版本学意识。

确定译本所据底本最直接的方法是查证译本的版权页,并参阅译序或后记。譬如,戴乃迭与杨宪益合译的《牡丹亭》译序写明,底本来源于明代徐日曦(笔名硕园)删订本《还魂记》,收录于毛晋所编《六十种曲》③,并非市面常见的各类版本。如果译作中没有提供明确的底本信息,研究者可以通过文本细读,结合译本诞生的情境甚或译本刊印后的最早评述性文献去推证底本信息。譬如,戴乃迭独译的《阿诗玛》(*Ashma*)初刊于《中国文学》1955 年第 3 期,1957 年由外文出版社出版,译序注明原文为 1955 年人民文学出版社发行的云南圭山工作组整理本。1981 年外文出版社再版时,不仅英文书名更改为 *Ashima*,译文内容较初版也有不同,然而译序却并未对此进行说明。通过比对译本与《阿诗玛》各类整理本,我们发现,再版的 *Ashima* 底本为 1960 年中国作家协会昆明分会重新整理本,即李广田整理本。译作底本考证不仅能够给予译本及译者公正评价,分析、推证的过程也能成为新的学术生长点。描述翻译学代表人物吉迪恩·图里(Gideon Toury)指出,"在好几种情况下,原本可能存在众多版本。一旦遇到这种情况,任何证明研究者所选择的原本是正确的尝试都将至少部分取决于译本所展现的特点,而这使得确定原本的身份成为比较分析本

---

① 孟令子. 文学翻译中的性别建构——以强势语为例. 中国外语,2015(6):87.

② 王金波. 乔利《红楼梦》英译本的底本考证. 明清小说研究,2007(1):279.

③ Tang, Hsien-tsu. The Peony Pavilion. Yang Hsien-yi and Gladys Yang(trans.). *Chinese Literature*, 1960(1):43.

身的一部分”①。

三、副文本视角下戴乃迭翻译思想探究：以《沉重的翅膀》英译为例

戴乃迭与杨宪益的合作贯穿了两人译介生涯的始终，两人的基本合作模式为杨宪益翻译初稿，戴乃迭加工润色。戴乃迭作为译者的主观能动性相对受到囿限。因此，对戴乃迭翻译思想的研究应当更多关注其独立翻译的诸多文本，“将戴乃迭从杨宪益妻子、助手的身份中剥离开来，在历史背景中还原和考证其译者主体的身份”②。戴乃迭独译实践主要分为两个阶段，第一个阶段为 20 世纪 50 年代初至 60 年代中期，第二个阶段为 20 世纪 70 年代末至 80 年代末，其中第二阶段是她翻译生涯的高峰期和集大成期。这一时期，由于社会历史语境和我国外宣政策的变化，女性主义思潮以及个人际遇的影响，戴乃迭自主选择不少自己喜欢的作家、作品进行翻译与推广，语言文字中跃动着译者之思，呈现出较明显的译者风格。当其时，中国涌现出一批具有性别立场的女作家，她们的主体意识逐渐走向自觉与自在。戴乃迭通过《中国文学》杂志、“熊猫丛书”，以合集或单行本的方式对外译介张洁、新凤霞、张辛欣、桑晔、王安忆等女性作家的作品，而她翻译的张洁作品《沉重的翅膀》(*Leaden Wings*)因语言优美、风格鲜明广获赞誉，译文与“副文本”成为提炼戴乃迭翻译思想的典型素材库。

1. 戴译《沉重的翅膀》副文本分析

法国叙事学理论家热奈特(Gérard Genette)在其 1987 年的法文专著《界限》(*Seuils*)中首创“副文本”(paratext)概念，十年后该书英文版《副文本：阐释的门槛》(*Paratexts: Thresholds of Interpretation*)面世，引发世

---

① Toury, G. *Descriptive Translation Studies and Beyond*. Amsterdam: John Benjamins, 1995: 74-75.

② 黄勤，刘晓黎. 从幕后到台前：翻译家戴乃迭研究综述. 外语与翻译，2017(2):7.

界范围内文论研究者的关注。他后来解释说，“我当时在其他地方苦于找不到更好的术语而称作‘副文本性’的东西，如标题、副标题、互联型标题；前言、跋、告读者、序；插图；磁带、护封以及其他许多附属标志，它们为文本提供了一种(变化的)氛围，它大概是作品实用方面即作品影响读者方面的优越区域之一”①。在热奈特看来，副文本在文本－作者－出版商－读者之间起着复杂的调节作用。虽然副文本研究最初主要是针对文学作品，并非指涉翻译/译著的副文本，却为文化转向视角下的翻译研究拓展了空间，增添了新的研究维度。戴乃迭英译《沉重的翅膀》作为其独立翻译的女性作家作品，具有鲜明的副文本特质：用长达1700多个词的译者序代替原作中的序言，邀请学者为译本作跋，通过添加主要人物列表为读者构建有效理解场域等。接下来我们将通过分析戴译《沉重的翅膀》的副文本因素，揭示这些副文本与译文本之间何以形成对话关系，于寂然无声处凸显戴乃迭的文字转换、文学译介、文明对话的准则。

从副文本与文本的位置角度而言，可分为“内副文本”和“外副文本”。前者主要包括标题、副标题、序言、后记、献辞、插图、注释等有助于读者理解正文本信息的文本形式；而“外副文本”则包括诸如媒体刊载的相关访谈、评论或作为私人交流性质的书信、日记，甚至包括磁带、护封以及其他许多附属性标志等。内、外副文本对于全面阐释作品意义具有不可或缺的作用，是译者对目标读者进行引导的语言文化场。戴乃迭省译《沉重的翅膀》原文序言，从女性身份出发，撰写长达16个段落的译者序，系典型的“原创性序言”(the original preface)②。序言除对詹纳尔和达文(Delia Davin)帮助润色译文表示致谢外，主要包括：(1)作者张洁的生平以及创作背景简介，呈现作者张洁作为女作家所经历的坎坷，突出张洁作品的女性维度；(2)张洁早期作品的内容、主题和社会影响，以作品《爱，是不能忘记的》说明这一时期作者围绕“爱和婚姻”展开创作；(3)《沉重的翅膀》的内容和主题，将读者的注意力从原作工业改革主题转移到作品中所披露

---

① 热拉尔·热奈特．热奈特论文集．史忠义，译．天津：百花文艺出版社，2001：68.

② Genette, G. *Paratexts: Thresholds of Interpretation*. Cambridge: Cambridge UP, 1997: 1.

的现代社会婚姻体制问题，将关注点转向女性话题和中国女性的情感生活状况；(4)张洁另外两部知名作品《方舟》和《条件尚未成熟》，前者被视为女性主义色彩浓厚的小说，后者则继续《沉重的翅膀》的经济改革主题，以凸显作者的创作主题——以社会现实为基础，探求个人，尤其是女性的价值与幸福感；(5)翻译过程中采用的省略译法和人物译名方法介绍。

戴乃迭邀请好友、女性主义翻译家达文为译本作跋，聚焦中国女性社会地位和面临的生存困境。达文的跋涵盖如下三方面内容：(1)对文中的女性人物给予特别关注，对主要女性人物的性格、形象以及生活状态进行分析；(2)简要介绍作者张洁的个人婚姻生活，解释张洁作品缺乏更多积极女性角色的原因；(3)对张洁作品做出积极评价，称其有助于西方读者了解中国当代社会。戴乃迭本人所作的序言并未直指中国女性的地位及现状，她的这一观点经由他人之口——达文的跋得以完美外化。对于译文本而言，译者序与请人所作的跋两种内副文本，是译者与赞助人实施翻译“共谋”的平台，共同引导译文读者的“前景化”(foregrounding)阅读。

此外，戴乃迭还增加译前注释，帮助译语读者理解小说中的复杂人物关系。在此，“译前注释”是指译本中位于译序之后、正文本之前的主要人物列表。译本中添加的人物列表呈现出三方面特征：(1)赋予主要女性人物美丽的英文名字，男性人物名则直接用汉语拼音表示；(2)以女性为中心对主要男性人物的社会关系进行介绍；(3)添加主要女性人物的婚姻状况介绍。[①] 中国小说中繁杂的人物关系往往会给英语读者造成困扰，译文前的人物列表能够为读者解读文本、理解小说情节提供重要帮助。

《沉重的翅膀》英译本由英国维拉戈出版社(Virago Press)刊印发行，出版社的选择堪称是一个非常典型的外副文本。作为全球首家专门针对女性读者的出版社，创建于1973年的维拉戈出版社以出版女性作家和女性文学的代表作为主，具有良好的市场反响。这一发行渠道让译本在走向流通之初就打上了明确的女性主义烙印，将读者的阅读期待引向对文

---

① 张生祥，汪佳丽．女性译者主体性探究——析戴乃迭英译《沉重的翅膀》．当代外语研究，2015(8)：65．

中女性话题的关注。

戴乃迭作为女性离散者的独特身份使其《沉重的翅膀》英译外副文本有特殊的表现形式。通常意义上的"离散者"多指那些由第三世界国家流动和移居至第一世界国家的人群，反方向的流动和迁移则因未形成规模效应而较少受到关注。第三世界国家向第一世界国家"离散"的驱动力多为政治和经济，如意识形态阵营的对垒、宗教矛盾、武装冲突和"契约劳工"的大规模流动等，而反向"离散"的驱动力则或为对"他者"文化的兴趣和热爱或为个人情感因素。反向"离散者"往往不会以疏离的姿态面对新环境或刻意保持对故国的"幻想或神话"，而是以十分积极的态度了解和适应居住国的民族和文化传统。戴乃迭正是这样一位出于个人情感原因以及对中国文化的热爱，主动来到中国的反向"离散者"。她深爱英国，也热爱中国，她生前常对来访的记者和朋友说"我觉得我有两个祖国！"①如果说幼年在中国的经历是被动接受，那么成年之后不顾母亲的激烈反对做出选择，跟随杨宪益重返并长居中国则是听从内心声音做出的主动决定。她终生保持着对中国和中国文化的热爱，数十年如一日兢兢业业完成的门类繁多、数目庞大的译作就是明证。②

此外，学者对戴乃迭及其译作的相关评论，以及戴乃迭本人针对翻译刊发的文章，也是戴译作品外副文本的重要组成部分。李欧梵(Leo Lee)在论及中国文学外译效果时曾说，"……我个人的印象是，在阅读了'熊猫丛书'的一些译本后，最好的翻译还是出自戴乃迭之手"③。戴乃迭译《中国当代七位女作家选》引起西方女性主义研究者的浓厚兴趣。澳大利亚外交事务部官员魏登豪(Irene Wettenhall)读后说，"这些故事间接为我们提供了关于现代中国女性地位的大量信息，……这些故事质朴而不陈腐，令人耳目一新，值得一读。作品文学性强，且翻译整体上能为西方读

---

① 杨宪益. 我有两个祖国——戴乃迭和她的世界. 桂林：广西师范大学出版社，2003：序2.

② 付文慧. 多重文化身份下之戴乃迭英译阐释. 中国翻译，2011(6)：19.

③ Lee，L. Contemporary Chinese Literature in Translation—A Review Article. *Journal of Asian Studies*，1985(3)：566.

者接受。选集适合作为高中及大学中文学习者和跨文化女性研究者的教材"①。此外,戴乃迭在 1985 年 9 月《中国季刊》(*China Quarterly*)刊发题为《女作家》(*Women Writers*)的文章,着重介绍张洁的几部作品——《爱,是不能忘记的》《沉重的翅膀》和《方舟》,对英国读者了解此期中国女性作家、女性婚姻、生活状况也有着非常明显的文本外引导意义。

2. 戴乃迭英译《沉重的翅膀》彰显的翻译观

戴乃迭《沉重的翅膀》英译内、外副文本丰富,内容涵盖作品产生的社会文化语境、翻译动因、翻译选材、翻译策略、翻译标准、心中的目标读者以及翻译过程中遇到的种种跨越。这些文字承载着译者的翻译态度和翻译观念,是梳理译者翻译思想的重要一手资料。对《沉重的翅膀》英译本开展副文本分析,有助于揭示戴乃迭在翻译中秉持的文化融合意识、女性主义意识与读者接受意识。

(1)文化融合意识

通过上文对戴乃迭"离散"经历、译作自评及他评等外副文本的分析,不难看出,戴乃迭在文化融合意识与文化融合能力方面较之本土译者有着得天独厚的优势。她在语言操作层面具有较高驾驭能力,能够采用灵活多样的翻译方法增强译文的可读性,她还能够精确预判西方读者的审美期待和文化领悟能力。她对中国文化的认同与尊重,在《沉重的翅膀》英译本中体现为彰显中华文化之"异",译本中呈现着的文学、文化"杂合性"正是其文化融合意识在语言层面的修辞体现。

东西方两种语言文化之间不存在完全的对应关系,文化之间的接触必然带来思想的杂合。就文化交流而言,"杂合"是不同文化在接触与交流过程中自然形成的现象,是不同语言和文化相互交流、碰撞,最后形成的具有多种语言文化特点但又自成一格的混合体。译文杂合是指译文不可避免地会包含一些来自原文的语言、文化或文学的成分,而且这些成分都是译入语文化中所缺少的,如新异的词汇和句法、具有异国情调的文化

---

① Wettenhall, I. Review of *Seven Contemporary Chinese Women Writers*. *The Australian Journal of Chinese Affairs*, 1983(10): 175-178.

意象和观念以及译入语文学中所缺乏的文体和叙事手法等等。[①] 戴译本中男女人物名字的具体翻译方式典型地体现出文本的"杂合"特质。文中主要的女性人物名字采用意译,承载一定的文化含义,如叶知秋译为Autumn,夏竹筠译为Bamboo,刘玉英译为Jade,郁丽文译为Radiance,万群译为Joy,何婷译为Grace等。相比之下,译本中的男性人名均直接以汉语拼音形式呈现,构成译本中的异质成分。译本的语言杂合是其作为反向离散译者,外化文化融合意识的体现。

戴乃迭在译者序中细致介绍了她在翻译过程中对原文某些信息与表达的删减与裁切,是出于对接受国主流诗学的体认,为达成文学、文化融合的修辞操作。一般而言,单一文化身份的译者,在兼顾双语文化的"异"与"同"时,鉴于自身的主客观因素,总会不由自主地造成对某一文化的"偏颇"。在翻译策略选取方面,戴乃迭具备一种世界性的眼光,以文化间的交流和互动为旨归,她的双重民族文化身份使她能够跳出单一文化的囿限,以一种更敏锐、中立的视角去审度两种文化,通过翻译活动促进两者的对话。

(2)女性主义意识

20世纪60年代中后期,西方妇女解放运动进入强调性别的社会建构时期。"社会性别"概念得以彰显,性别研究受到空前关注,"女性主义"成为此后通过语言和社会实践表述出来的最强有力的文化身份表达形式。"妇女通过语言获得解放"成为70年代的口号。在后现代文化视域中,人们清晰地意识到,语言是意义争夺的场所,是主体检验自我和证明自我的竞技场,"语言不仅是交流的工具还是操纵的工具"[②]。在女性主义者看来,传统的语言是男性定制的,反映男性的生活、现实和观念,命名了男性的世界,女性的世界隐而不现。针对这一弊端,唯一的出路就是"使女性

---

① 韩子满. 文学翻译与杂合. 中国翻译,2002(2):56.

② Flotow, L.V. *Translation and Gender: Translating in the "Era of Feminism"*. Manchester: St. Jerome Publishing, 1997: 8.

在语言中清晰可见"①,确保语言体现对女性世界的关怀。

《沉重的翅膀》英译本中,戴乃迭使用译者序、跋和人物列表等内副文本,凸显原作的女性主题和女性角色,使小说的女性维度得以呈现与拓展。戴乃迭的女性关照意识在具体的词汇、句法、篇章层面都可以找到佐证。张生祥、汪佳丽撰文分析该英译本在词汇层面的动词、形容词、副词与句法层面的疑问句、转化句法的省译、增译,以及语篇层面的缩减、省略和顺序调整,指出戴乃迭在文本翻译中彰显出来的女性主义意识,不同于西方女性主义者的"僭越"或"颠覆",采用的"是一种不同于西方女性主义者的翻译策略"②。

戴乃迭在翻译中体现出来的女性主义意识独具特色。"一方面,它不同于加拿大女性主义者的激进策略,没有对原文作过多的干涉,而是忠实于原作的精神。通过个别地方适度的变通,戴乃迭凸显了作品中女性的地位,增加了文本的女性主义色彩。另一方面,戴乃迭的女性主义策略也不同于斯皮瓦克生硬拗口的异化翻译,而更加注重文本的可读性。"③在文本本身的措辞选择和语篇转换方面,戴乃迭通过使用具有女性特质的措辞,使原文的女性气息清晰可感,戴乃迭通过序、跋、人物对照表及相关英文评述,使原文的女性话题立体可见,内、外副文本的呼应,极大地提高了《沉重的翅膀》作为女性文本在海外的识别度和接受度。

(3)读者接受意识

从戴乃迭译作的内副文本和相关外副文本中,我们可以清楚地捕捉到译者对读者接受的关照。戴乃迭认为,译者的读者意识很重要,"我们不仅在为美国人或者澳大利亚人做翻译,也在为亚非国家中懂英语的读

---

① Gauvin, L. *Letters from an Other*. Susanne de Lotbinière-Harwood (trans.). Toronto: Women's Press, 1989: 9.

② 张生祥,汪佳丽. 女性译者主体性探究——析戴乃迭英译《沉重的翅膀》. 当代外语研究, 2015(8): 69.

③ 王惠萍. 后殖民视域下的戴乃迭文化身份与译介活动研究. 北京: 新华出版社, 2014: 158.

者而工作”[①]，为此她主张译者要“更富有创造性”，在一定程度上改写原文，以适应读者。

《沉重的翅膀》原文长达 28 万字，戴乃迭在英译时进行了大幅删减，改动大致可分为两类：一类是有关政治、经济体制改革问题的冗长叙述，通常以人物对话或讲话的形式出现，与小说的情节推进和风格塑造关系不大，比如郑子云关于行为科学的一处讲话，计 1500 余字。对于此类删减，戴乃迭在序言中做过明确解释，认为中国的出版社在敦促作家压缩、删减作品方面做的努力不够，而上述内容除非对中国 1980 年前后的经济背景有相当了解的内行人士，很难为读者所欣赏。[②] 这是她基于对中西文学创作规范（即诗学）的体认实施的翻译行为。

另一类删减涉及小说的语言艺术风格。张洁早期作品的一大特色是强烈的参与性，作者或借作品人物之口或直接出面发声，表达对具体事件的看法或评论，文本呈现出一种全知叙事的多声道特色。此类书写在《沉重的翅膀》中俯拾皆是，[③]这一叙事特色被李欧梵评价为“煽情、描述上的陈词滥调和夸张的抒情”[④]。戴乃迭在处理此类内容时往往删繁就简。戴乃迭在译者序中虽然没有详细交代，对此类文本的删减原因，但可以肯定的是无论是删减还是改造，都是以目标读者为导向，是为了趋向英语世界的诗学与读者阅读习惯而实施的文本改写。

戴乃迭毕生勤勉，专注于中国文学英译实践，并无专门的翻译理论著述，她在独立翻译过程中赋予文本的大量副文本资源弥足珍贵，是全面、系统刻画戴乃迭翻译思想的宝贵史料。为便于学界窥见戴乃迭的译事思考或文学推介，本书搜集了戴乃迭几乎所有独立发行译作的“序言”/“前

---

① 文明国．杨宪益对话集：从《离骚》开始，翻译整个中国．北京：人民日报出版社，2010：11．

② Zhang，J. *Leaden Wings*. Gladys Yang（trans.）. London：Virago Press，1987：xii.

③ 付文慧．多重文化身份下之戴乃迭英译阐释．中国翻译，2011(6)：20．

④ Lee，L. Under the Thumb of Men. *The New York Times Book Review*，1987-01-18.

言”,按照译著出版发行先后顺序排列,力图向读者呈现出比较文学视域中的戴乃迭翻译思考与书写。在这一大的研究前提下以及出于对此前所言学界对戴乃迭翻译文本了解的不足,本书选择戴乃迭有代表性的民间文学英译、散(杂)文英译、乡土文学英译和女性文学英译数十篇(片段),以期呈现戴乃迭中国文学英译实践与思考的全貌。此外,本书附录部分还附有根据大量第一手资料查证、整理出来的戴乃迭译作单行本列表和1955—1991 年间发表在《中国文学》上的全部戴乃迭译文篇目,希望有更多学界同仁能够加入到对戴乃迭英译资料的梳理、对比分析和理论提升,共同汲取戴乃迭毕生积淀的翻译智慧。

第一编

戴乃迭翻译思考文存

一

《雪峰寓言》译序①

Preface to *Fables by Feng Xuefeng*

The fable is a form of Chinese folklore which dates back to the very beginnings of Chinese prose literature. Traditionally it has been a means of imparting moral lessons, and the modern fable has developed and adapted this tradition to meet the needs of the modern world.

Most of Feng Xuefeng's fables were written during the 1930s and 1940s. Like his close friend and colleague, Lu Xun, that giant of modern Chinese literature, Feng was obliged to use veiled language and parables to expose the evils of that time. The fable was a form of literature peculiarly suited to the period of White Terror in China when Kuomintang censorship forced writers to turn to satire and other kinds of oblique writing.

The fables selected here can be divided into two main categories: those written to encourage and guide the people in their struggle for independence and a new society, and those to attack their enemies. In the latter category, many of the tales are directed against specific abuses of power by the Kuomintang government, while others ridiculed the greed, stupidity and cruelty of imperialism. China has overthrown the reactionary government of the past and no longer fears imperialism, but these fables still have their

---

① 选自：Feng, X. F. *Fables by Feng Xuefeng*. Gladys Yang (trans.). Beijing: Foreign Languages Press, 1953/1983.

significance today.

To take a few examples: "The Monkeys and the Corpse" exposes the hypocrisy of the Kuomintang in their talk of morality and such spurious gestures as the new life movement. "The Fox's Trumpet" describes Kuomintang press censorship, which forced readers to look between the lines to get the news from the daily papers: one way of learning the truth was from the clumsy denials put out by government spokesmen.

Only one fable in this collection was written since Liberation: "The Snake's Strangling Tactics", which puts in a nutshell the truth about the imperialist blockade of China in the 50s.

The wisdom gained by the Chinese people in the course of their struggles is passed on to us by Feng Xuefeng in these fables. And along with the revolutionary message of a new China are combined the humanism, love of nature and sense of humour characteristic of the Chinese people, which give the fable its special poetic quality.

二

《阿诗玛》译序①

Preface to *Ashma*

"Ashma"is a long and colourful narrative poem which has been handed down orally for generations by the Shani people in Yunnan. The poem describes a young village girl, Ashma, and her brother Ahay. In simple, unadorned language, it relates Ashma's determined struggle against the despotic landlord who has carried her off. With their vitality and their longing for freedom and happiness, young Ahay and Ashma epitomize the whole Shani people.

A branch of the Yi, one of the minority peoples in Southwest China, the Shani live in Kueishan District, southeast of Kunming, the provincial capital of Yunnan. They have their own spoken language, and a simple written script. They love music and dancing, and can express their feelings and wishes with a simple musical instrument made of bamboo—the mô-sheen.

From the age of twelve till the time of their marriage, young Shani people live away from home in special hostels for girls and boys, where, every evening, they can enjoy themselves by singing, playing flutes or

---

① 选自：*Yunan People's Cultural Troupe Ashma*. Gladys Yang (trans.). Beijing: Foreign Languages Press, 1957/1981. 1957 年版的书名在 1981 年再版时更名为 Ashima，此处收录的为 1957 年版的译序。

stringed instruments, or making love. In the past, however, although they could love freely, they could not marry whom they pleased but had to abide by their parents' choice. This explains why, for many generations, through "Ashma" the Shani people have expressed their longing for freedom and happiness.

In the past the Shani peasants were exploited by the feudal landlords who seized the fruits of their labour every year, leaving them to live in misery. This explains why "Ashma" voices the Shani's fierce hatred for oppressors.

"Ashma" is the most popular poem of the Shani people. Whenever a marriage takes place, old folk will squat on stools to sing "Ashma"; and the young people will shed tears over Ashma's sufferings and rejoice at her victory. Those who are unhappily married will sing "Ashma" again and again, drawing strength and courage from the poem. Girls working in the fields will sing "Ashma" too, and they often used to say: "Ashma's sufferings are the sufferings of all Shani girls."

Though this long poem has been handed down for many generations, there has never yet been a standard Shani text. In 1953, some writers and artists in Yunnan sent a work team to the mountainous district where the Shani live, to compile as complete a version of "Ashma" as possible. By living and working with the Shani for a long period of time, they became good friends with them and gradually came to understand their social system, customs, thoughts and feelings. After a careful study of many different versions of the poem, the work team compiled "Ashma" and translated it into Chinese. In 1954, when this long poem was published in the "*Yunnan Daily*" in Kunming and "People's Literature" in Peking, it received a warm welcome. Later it was published in book form by the People's Literary Publishing House, and the English translation has been made from this book.

China is a multi-national country. Under the cruel rule of reactionaries in the past, the minority people suffered all manner of hardships and their cultures were attacked and to some extent destroyed; yet, even so, the vernacular literature was preserved and enriched by the labouring people. In New China all the minority peoples are equal members of one big family, and their national cultures are respected and appreciated. The discovery, compilation and publication of "Ashma" form but one instance of the way in which the fine literature and art of the minority peoples are valued today.

三

《无声的中国——鲁迅作品选》前言[①]

Introduction to *Silent China*: *Selected Writings of Lu Xun*

Lu Xun (Lu Hsun) is the great writer of modern China. His life spanned several decades of the prolonged revolution, led in its later stages by Mao Tsetung, that remade China. Dying in 1936, on the eve of the Sino-Japanese War[②], he did not see his country's liberation and emergence as a modern state. However, his writings reflect the trend of history, foretelling the Chinese people's choice of socialism and the resurgence of China as a great nation.

Lu Xun, whose real name was Zhou Shuren, was born in 1881 in Shaoxing, south of the Yangtse Valley. His grandfather held a minor official post, and his father was a scholar. In 1893 his grandfather was imprisoned on a charge of bribery, and the sharp decline in the family fortunes was accelerated by his father's long illness followed by his death in 1896. Lu Xun later classified himself as the son of a family which had come down in the world. He paid many visits to pawnshops while still a boy only 'half the height' of the pawnshop counter.

---

① 选自：Yang, G. (ed. & trans.). *Silent China—Selected Writings of Lu Xun*. London: Oxford University Press, 1973.

② 编者注："抗日战争"现已规范表达为：the Chinese People's War of Resistance Against Japanese Aggression (the War of Resistance)。

During his boyhood Lu Xun also spent some time with relatives in the country. Here he made friends with the villagers' children, saw something of the impoverishment of the countryside as China's natural economy was destroyed by capitalism, and developed a sympathy with the peasants that was to stay with him.

This was during the declining years of the Qing dynasty. Earlier in the century the once powerful and self-sufficient Chinese empire, outstripped by the capitalist countries of the West, had been forced to open up treaty ports and foreign settlements and grant foreigners extra-territorial rights. The corrupt Manchu government, with the backing of the imperialist powers, was able to crush revolts aimed at changing the political and social system. In all its long history the great Middle Kingdom had never been reduced to such straits. China had become the sick man of Asia, a 'dish of loose sand'.

Patriotic scholars sought for some means to make China independent and strong. As the traditional ideological weapons had failed, they borrowed the theories of the West, such as evolution, bourgeois republicanism, and democracy. Western-style schools were opened, and many students were sent to study abroad.

Lu Xun's education combined the traditional with the modern. Confucian schooling in childhood gave him a good grounding in the Chinese classics. But his family had no money. So in 1898, at the age of eighteen, he entered one of the new institutions teaching Western science and technology, the Naval Academy in Nanking, a free, state-run school of naval engineering. The next year he transferred to the School of Railways and Mines. Upon his graduation in 1901, he was awarded a government scholarship for further study in Japan.

At Kobun College, Tokyo, where he first studied Japanese, he read voraciously in Western philosophy, political science, and literature. China's backwardness and low international status were brought home to him ever more keenly. He met Chinese political refugees in Japan and took his stand with the most radical of these, joining the Guangfuhui (Resurgence Society) which aimed at setting up a republic. He wrote a short poem at this time expressing grief over his country's oppression and vowed to sacrifice himself to the cause of China's regeneration.

In 1904 Lu Xun went to Sendai to study medicine, in the hope of later popularizing modern science and overcoming the old superstitions which, as he describes in his reminiscences, had cut short his father's life. However, in 1906 he saw a slide of the execution of a Chinese during the Russo-Japanese War, and was staggered by the apathy of the Chinese onlookers. To cure disease now seemed less important than to arouse his fellow-countrymen; and he felt that literature was the best tool for this purpose. Thus from the start his aim in writing was political: to awaken and enlighten the Chinese people. He wrote articles on progressive trends in culture and on the poetry of revolt, and translated stories from countries of eastern Europe under Tsarist rule, where conditions had much in common with those of China.

Lu Xun had originally intended to go to Germany for further study. In 1909, however, his younger brother Zhou Zuoren, who was also studying in Japan, married a Japanese wife, thus increasing the family's financial burden, and Lu Xun had to return to China to support his mother and two younger brothers.

Lu Xun's first job in China was teaching biology and chemistry in Chekiang Normal School, the teacher-training college in his native province. He then became dean of studies of a school in his hometown. After the 1911 Revolution which established the Chinese Republic under Sun Yatsen, Lu Xun became the principal of Shaoxing Normal School. Early in 1912 he was invited to work in the Ministry of Education in Nanking, seat of the provisional government of the new Republic, and when the capital moved that same year to Peking, Lu Xun accompanied the ministry to the north.

The 1911 Revolution had toppled the Qing dynasty, but because it did not mobilize the people it failed to overcome the foreign and feudal domination of China. The old reactionary forces retained power, as Lu Xun describes in 'The True Story of Ah Q'. The ambitious ex-Manchu official

Yuan Shikai ousted Sun Yatsen, made himself president, and in 1916 tried to restore the monarchy. Although he failed, power remained in the hands of northern militarist cliques. China was a republic in name only. In reality it was a semi-feudal, semi-colonial country fought over by contending warlords each of whom had the backing of a different foreign power.

Lu Xun was deeply disillusioned by the failure of the 1911 Revolution. For several years, while working in the Ministry of Education in Peking, he immersed himself in old books, studied Buddhist philosophy, and collected stone-rubbings. The Western school system, natural sciences, and social and political theories which he had helped to introduce had done much to discredit China's traditional ideology, but these had now been proved powerless in the face of the alliance between imperialist and feudal forces. What was the way out?

The answer for many Chinese intellectuals came with the October Revolution of 1917 and the establishment in Russia of the first socialist state. Chinese whose dreams of achieving a Western-style democracy had been shattered now saw in Russia a model for a more thoroughgoing revolution. In the cultural field this involved a revolution in the written language. The classical Chinese written by scholars was unintelligible to the common people, most of whom were illiterate; and if 'silent' China's millions were to be enlightened the written language had to be brought much closer to the vernacular. In 1918 Lu Xun began to write poems, short stories, and essays in colloquial Chinese. His story 'A Madman's Diary', an impassioned call to fight against the man-eating old culture, was published in April that year in *New Youth*, the most influential progressive journal of the day. He followed this up with the essay 'My Views on Chastity'. This was the real start of his literary career, and the time when he began using the pen-name Lu Xun.

In 1919 Lu Xun helped to launch the May Fourth Movement, which started as a student movement against imperialism and feudalism and gradually enlisted the support of wide sections of Chinese society. Among its slogans were: 'Down with the old ethics and up with the new!' 'Down with the old literature and up with the new!' Lu Xun through his writings acted as the standard-bearer of this movement, and did all he could to support the student vanguard. In 1920 he began lecturing at Peking University and other colleges. His influence on young intellectuals was growing, although many of his stories and prose poems of these years reveal a deep sense of personal isolation and anguish. But being Lu Xun, he never gave up fighting. In 1925 he championed the students of the Peking Women's Normal College who opposed their reactionary president. Later one of them, Xu Guangping, became his wife.

In March 1926, the Peking warlord government killed or wounded more than two hundred unarmed patriots, mostly students, for demonstrating against imperialism. Lu Xun, who spoke up for them, had to go into hiding. In August that year, to avoid persecution in Peking, he went south to Amoy University; but finding the place a stagnant backwater, he resigned at the end of the year. In January 1927 he accepted a post in the Sun Yatsen University in Canton, storm centre of the second democratic revolution.

Since 1924 the progressive wing of the Kuomintang Nationalists had been co-operating with the Communists to combat the northern warlords. In 1926 their joint forces set out from Canton on the Northern Expedition and within a few months had control of southern and central China. But Sun Yatsen had died by then, and his successor Chiang Kai-shek suddenly turned against the Communists and the Kuomintang's own left wing, and in April 1927 initiated a reign of white terror.

The years 1927-37 saw the first civil war between the Nationalists and the Communists. Chiang Kai-shek organized two series of 'encirclement and suppression' campaigns, military ones to wipe out the Communist base in the Jinggang Mountains of central China, and cultural ones to suppress democratic opinion. Both ended in failure. In 1934 the Red Army broke through encirclement and set out on the Long March, while popular demands for democracy steadily grew, drawing inspiration from Lu Xun's fearless polemical writings.

Lu Xun never joined the Communist Party, but during these stormy years he came to believe that Communist leadership was the only way to save China. In October 1927 he had moved to Shanghai, where the next year his only son was born, and where he remained till the time of his death. He studied and worked indefatigably. In 1928 he joined the Chinese Revolutionary Mutual-Aid Society. In 1930 he was a founding member of the China Freedom League and the China League of Left-Wing Writers. In 1933 he joined the China League for Civil Rights. A patriot and an internationalist, he opposed not only Chiang Kai-shek's fascist rule and Japanese aggression in China, but was against all imperialist wars and strongly condemned Nazi persecution of the Jews.

The Kuomintang murdered progressive writers, and Lu Xun living under this reign of terror was often forced to go into hiding, as he writes in his poem 'Long Nights'. He had to resort to over a hundred different pen-names and to the use of innuendo and allusion to get his work passed by the censor. In his later years he gave up writing stories in favour of essays dealing with topical issues. Some of his friends deplored the fact that he spent so much time on ephemmeral political writing, but Lu Xun replied that his essays were daggers and darts hurled at the reactionaries to expose abuse and falsehood, and write them he must.

Lu Xun had hoped to collect material for a full-length novel about the epic Long March, but he died before this book could be written. At the end of 1935, when he heard that the Red Army had successfully reached the north-west, he sent a telegram of congratulations to the Central Committee of the Party in which he wrote: 'In you lies the hope of China and all humanity.' And when, in 1936, after Mao Tsetung called for a united front with Chiang Kai-shek against Japan, some Chinese Trotskyites accused the Communists of betraying the revolution, Lu Xun stated his position explicitly: 'I count it an honour to have as my comrades those who are now doing solid work, treading firmly on the ground, fighting and shedding their blood in the defence of the Chinese people.'

In spite of ill health, persecution, and the pressure of work, Lu Xun gave generously of his time to help young writers and artists. Friends who knew him in the thirties recall him as a short, emaciated, haggard figure, well aware that his tuberculosis was incurable, but refusing to be hospitalized as long as he could stand up to fight. Striding along in his shabby old white silk gown, he retained his almost boyish exuberance and mordant sense of humour to the last. At a reception at the Russian Consulate in Shanghai to commemorate the October Revolution, Lu Xun's disreputable felt hat fell behind the hat-stand. When he retrieved it he kicked it down the stairs and pummelled it before putting it on. 'This is a rickshaw-puller's hat,' he said. 'And that's all I am—a rickshaw-puller.'

As he had written earlier:

Fierce-browed I coolly defy a thousand pointing fingers.
Head bowed, like a willing ox, I serve the children.

Lu Xun defied the reactionaries and worked for the people all his life. Mao Tsetung has called him "The chief commander of China's cultural revolution... not only a great man of letters but a great thinker and revolutionary"; and elsewhere, "the bravest and most correct, the firmest, the most loyal and the most ardent national hero, a hero without parallel in our history".

As the dates at the end of the selections indicate, Lu Xun's writings were originally published in magazines and newspaper supplements, 'The True Story of Ah Q' appearing as a serial. The majority of his stories and reminiscences, including the first four stories in this selection, were written between 1918 and 1926. After 1927, polemical articles and essays formed his main output, but in addition he wrote some historical tales with a topical significance such as 'Leaving the Pass', written in 1935. Besides two collections of short stories, one of *Old Tales Retold*, a volume of prose poems, one of reminiscences, and over 600 essays, Lu Xun wrote a history of Chinese fiction, made many translations of foreign literature and literary criticism, and edited and published albums of Chinese and foreign art. He also left diaries and a large number of letters to friends and to his wife.

To make a selection from all this wealth of material is difficult. I have tried to indicate something of Lu Xun's versatility, the causes he championed and the abuses he attacked; but considerations of space and the difficulty of understanding certain of his writings without a knowledge of their historical background, have forced me to omit many important works—the essays dealing with the relationship between literature and revolution, for instance. Lu Xun's brilliant writing in the vernacular helped to shape modern Chinese prose, and I have included a number of prose poems written in the vernacular, as well as poems in the classical style.

The List of Sources at p. 195, compiled by W. J. F. Jenner, gives the Chinese volume from which each of the selections is taken. Mr. Jenner has also provided the Note on Pronunciation at p. 196, for Chinese names which are romanized in this volume according to the Hanyu Pinyin system. This book owes much to his assistance and advice. I am also very grateful to Miss Catharine Carver of the Oxford University Press for her expert and understanding editorial help in the later stages of preparing this book.

Most of the writings in this selection are revised versions of translations from the 1957 edition of *Lu Xun quan ji* done with the help of my husband and published by the Foreign Languages Press, Peking. I am grateful for the permission to use this material and am alone responsible for any errors in the new versions.

四

霍克思《红楼梦》英译评论[①]

Review of David Hawkes' *The Story of the Stone*. *A novel in five volumes by Cao Xueqin*. *Vol*. Ⅰ: *The golden days*. *Vol*. Ⅱ: *The crab-flower club*

The Story of the Stone is one of the great translations of this century. No other single book tells us so much about Chinese civilization.

Although *Hong lou meng*, Cao Xueqin's mid eighteenth-century masterpiece, is the most highly-esteemed classical Chinese novel, it is only recently that complete English translations of it have been made. Various excerpts and abridged English versions of what was called *The dream of the red chamber* have been published in the last century and more, but these were a poor shadow of the original, for much of its immensely rich content and subtle characterization was inevitably lost.

At about the same time that Yang Xianyi and I were asked by the Foreign Languages Press in Beijing (Peking) to translate the *Dream*, Chinese scholars were delighted to hear that David Hawkes, having resigned his chair as Professor of Chinese at Oxford, was to translate the first eighty

---

① 选自：Yang, G. Review of David Hawkes' *The Story of the Stone*. *A novel in five volumes by Cao Xueqin*. *Vol*. Ⅰ: *The golden days*. *Vol*. Ⅱ: *The crab-flower club*. *Bulletin of the School of Oriental and African Studies*, 1980(43): 621-622.

chapters, consigning the supplement to a collaborator. Such is the cult of *Hong lou meng* in China that there this news invested him with a halo. And the appearance of Vol. I of *The story of the stone* in 1973 probably caused even more of a stir in Hong Kong and mainland China① than in the West.

The first comment I heard from a Chinese academician was, 'Excellent. Very readable. But from a scholar of Professor Hawkes' stature I had hoped for a definitive translation. This doesn't conform to any single edition.' This strikes me as cavilling. There are many texts of the first eighty chapters of *Hong lou meng* and Chinese scholars are still collating them to compile what may become a definitive edition. David Hawkes explains that he has based his translation mainly on the 120-chapter Gao E edition, with the first eighty chapters by Cao Xueqin and the last forty by Gao E, sometimes adopting readings from other early texts and occasionally making his own emendations in line with his sense of responsibility to readers, author and text. I think he has made an excellent job of this and is fully justified.

Since the novel abounds in textual problems, 'Redologists'—as students of *Hong lou meng* are called—often disagree with each other's interpretations. Although my husband and I had the benefit of the advice of Redologists and colleagues while making our translation, *A dream of red mansions*, various cases of mistranslation have been pointed out. And so it is with some of David Hawkes' renderings. But the consensus is that his is a scholarly and brilliant translation. Thus when a new journal on *Hong lou meng* was launched in Beijing last summer, he was the first foreign sinologist to be invited to contribute to it.

All classical Chinese novels pose certain problems to modern Western readers: the alien social, historical and religious background; the juxtaposition of supernatural elements with realistic narrative; the welter of confusing names and courtesy names ... David Hawkes smooths the reader's

---

① 编者注:戴译 mainland China 作为“中国大陆”的英文对应表达,现规范表达多为 mainland of China 或 China's mainland。

way by providing essential background information in his admirable prefaces and appendices.

He partly solves the nomenclature confusion by following the earlier tradition of giving the bondmaids translated names such as Aroma and Nightingale. Purists have pointed out that some of these are inaccurate and certain of the names defy translation; therefore, my Chinese colleagues outvoted me when I proposed doing the same. But to my mind Western readers need this assistance, and the practice helps to remind us that the slave girls' names were given them arbitrarily by their mistresses.

Where *Hong lou meng* differs from other Chinese novels and presents a special problem to the translator as well as to foreign readers, is in its uniquely literary quality. It abounds in classical allusions, references to literary and historical figures, quotations from poems and puns incomprehensible to most Westerners. Moreover, the young hero and his girl relatives are steeped in literature and spend much time competing at versifying, incidentally revealing their characters in the verses they write. It has been said that poetry is the only art form unable to cross national barriers. David Hawkes displays his supreme skill as a translator by carrying into English the literary flavour of the original, dispensing as far as possible with footnotes by unobtrusively amplifying the text to make quotations or allusions intelligible. By about the time that he reached chapter IX, he told me that he felt his brain was shrivelling and to combat this he had begun learning Welsh. This conveys some idea of the arduousness of making a one-man translation of *Hong lou meng*, but there is not the least evidence of this in his felicitous English version which seems a sheer labour of love.

Mao Zedong advised young Chinese to read *Hong lou meng* in order to understand Chinese feudalism, and foreign readers can learn more from this novel than from many volumes of history. To get into it needs perseverance, but the effort required is well rewarded; for in this complex story of the daily life and decline of a noble household and the vicissitudes of its hangers-on we see not only countless facets of Chinese civilization but also the corruption of the Qing bureaucracy, the growing decadence of the landed gentry and the impoverishment of the peasantry, which led eventually to the collapse of the Manchu dynasty.

On another level, of course, this is a sophisticated story of adolescent love, tragic, yet illumined by humour; and Cao Xueqin's portrayal of his protagonists is by any standard masterly in its psychological insight and subtlety. Here he broke with the method of earlier novelists who based their work on story-cycles or histories, drawing instead on his own experience to show how his characters developed and reacted to each other. This marvellous novel creates a world of its own. So engrossing is it, for all its slow tempo, that many Chinese re-read it every year and frequently quote from it, and its chief characters are household words. David Hawkes' superb achievement is to have made this Chinese masterpiece available to Western readers in excellent English. Our translation *A dream of red mansions* is by comparison I fear a mere crib.

五

谌容和她的小说《人到中年》[①]

A New Woman Writer Shen[②] Rong and Her Story "At Middle Age"

There is still a dearth of good new novels in China, but in 1979 more novelettes appeared than in any previous year since Liberation. Better fitted than short stories to introduce a wide range of characters and explore a subject in depth, they have proved popular. Some deal with different aspects of the Cultural Revolution; others, now arousing more interest, with social problems since the fall of the "gang of four". "At middle Age", published in January this year in the Shanghai bi-monthly *Harvest*, is one of these.

The concept of age is relative. In the early fifties, I translated a story about village life in which one peasant was constantly referred to as the "old man" or "old fellow". He was only thirty-nine but nearly decrepit, owing to back-breaking toil and malnutrition. In the West, the threshold of old age has been pushed back, but Chinese consider thirty-five as the start of middle age. And, like most professionals of her generation, Dr Lu has aged

① 选自：Yang, G. A New Woman Writer Shen Rong and Her Story "At Middle Age". *Chinese Literature*, 1980(10): 64-77.

② 编者注：谌容，当代女作家，虽然大众常将其姓氏读作"chén"，戴乃迭音译为 Shen，与作家本人的陈述一致。在 2019 年 9 月作家出版社推出的《谌容文集》中，谌容关于自己的姓氏读音，写了一段话："我这个姓，《百家姓》上就没有。谌，这个字《新华字典》上只有一个音：chén。我们家祖祖辈辈却念'甚'……"

prematurely.

Today's "middle-aged" intellectuals were educated after Liberation. Brought up in a time of great revolutionary enthusiasm, by and large they had high ideals and studied hard to equip themselves to serve the people well. They work long hours, often under poor conditions, and their sole holidays are a few festivals. Whereas the position of the workers and peasants has improved vastly since Liberation, the new intellectuals' salary is still very low. Living quarters in China's big cities are fearfully cramped, and in this respect intellectuals are worse off than peasants.

It is true that prices in China are relatively low. Professionals have security as well as free medical attention. Still, they are on a very tight budget. And in the absence of labour-saving devices, housework is wearisome and time-consuming, as is child-minding and queueing for vegetables. After doing a day's hardwork as well as the household chores, it requires real dedication to sit down at night and study to keep abreast with developments in your own field. It is admirable how many intellectuals make this effort day after day. But inevitably this takes a toll of their health.

During the Cultural Revolution, to be an intellectual was to be suspect. Many had their homes raided, their books seized and burnt. There had previously been Eight Categories of Bad Characters: landlords, rich peasants, reactionaries, criminals, Rightists, renegades, spies and capitalist-roaders. Now the intellectuals were labelled Stinking Number Nine, ignominiously assigned to the bottom of this list. Some were given menial tasks, such as cleaning out lavatories. Others were sent to the countryside, unable for years to use their special skills.

In 1976, the arrest of the "gang of four" elated intellectuals. Surely, spring had come back to China! Only later did we gain some idea of the havoc that had been caused and the problems resulting from the wrecking of the economy, the tremendous wastage of talent, the spread of bureaucracy.... Chinese woke up to the fact that they had fallen years behind and must catch up, must modernize the country.

The older cadres are doing their best, valiantly working on long after they should have retired; but their strength is falling. The younger college graduates or technicians in their twenties or early thirties often speak of themselves as the "lost generation". Their education was totally disrupted by the Cultural Revolution, and however hard they try to study now it is difficult to make up for those lost years. They will make their contribution eventually, but it will take time for them to become proficient.

That is why the middle-aged professionals have the key role to play in China's modernization. They have taken up this heavy responsibility, overworking and sacrificing their health, considering themselves as expendable. The old experts have been honoured, given public recognition; but there is not enough recognition of the great contribution made by the middle-aged, which is out of all proportion to the meagre remuneration they receive. Shen Rong is one of the first writers to have called attention to this serious problem. Her readers' reaction is: Society should devote as much care to safeguarding the middle-aged professionals as Dr Lu devotes to curing her patients.

Shen Rong, a native of Wushan County in Sichuan, was born in 1935. Like Dr Lu, she did not have a "good class origin". Her parents were neither workers, peasants nor revolutionaries, her father being a judge in the Beiping Court of the Kuomintang's Supreme Court, her mother a teacher and an amateur artist.

After Liberation, at the age of fifteen, stirred by the revolutionary changes around her, she left junior middle school after only one year to be a salesgirl in a bookshop set up for workers. "We were full of enthusiasm," she recalls. "We youngsters, with packs of books on our backs, marched along the banks of the Jialing River to mines and factories. I remember a woman worker who ordered a copy of our magazine *Learn Culture*. 'I can't read yet,' she said, 'but I'm buying this because our Party has liberated us and wants us to study.'... This experience was a class education for me."

In '52, Shen Rong transferred to the *Southwest Workers' Daily* in Chongqing. During the next two years she studied Russian by following broadcast lessons, doing so well that in '54 she was admitted to the Russian

Language Institute in Beijing. Just before graduation she married a journalist.

In '57 she started work as a translator in the Radio Station. She drove herself too hard, and in '63 started having dizzy spells and fell seriously ill. She went to a people's commune in Shaanxi to convalesce, and stayed in the home of a woman brigade leader. When she talks about village cadres, her face lights up. She considers them the salt of the earth. In'64 she returned to Beijing. Not yet fit enough to go back to her job, she did some writing and painting. Her first works were plays, and one was being rehearsed when the start of the Cultural Revolution quashed it.

Between '69 and '73, when most cadres were sent down to the country, she went with her colleagues to Tongxian. There, again, she lived with a peasant family and joined in the field work. "I got the highest work-points allocated for transplanting rice shoots," she told me. "It was hard. When the others knocked off I went on working, as otherwise I couldn't have finished my quota. But I enjoyed it. And that work improved my health. Then I joined a team which went from village to village explaining the Party's policies at that time. We were called in to settle all kinds of disputes. It was a rare chance to get to know the peasants."

In Tongxian she finished writing her first novel *Perpetual Youth*, published in '75. In '76 she went to Anhui to collect material for her second novel *Light and Dark*, published in '78. She took her little daughter and younger son, but left her elder son behind.

"Do you feel, like Dr Lu, that you've been a bad wife and mother?" I asked.

"Yes, I do. Like Dr Lu, I feel we must make sacrifices to get work done."

She has also written two other novelettes, *Eternal Spring* and *White Snow*.

Shen Rong is reluctant to talk about herself. "There was nothing remarkable about my youth," she says. However, it is clear that she has remarkable application, tenacity and powers of observation.

The problems of middle-aged professionals were in her mind for some time. I asked why she decided to make her central characters doctors instead of, say, schoolteachers who also perform a vital social service and are desperately overworked and under-paid. She said it was because doctors cure the sick and come into contact with people of all walks of life. She familiarized herself with Tongren Hospital in Beijing. "The sacrifices our middle-aged professionals make are no less than those made on the Long March," she told me vehemently.

Dr Lu is refreshingly different from the general run of heroines in Chinese writing. She is typical of the first generation of professionals trained in New China, expressing her patriotism by means of hard work and expecting little reward. To make the best possible contribution to the country, she even neglects her children—she has no time to plait her small daughter's hair. Outwardly so mild, she has iron determination, a high sense of responsibility, great technical skill and a thoroughly humanitarian attitude to her patients, showing the same concern for an old peasant as for a high official.

I asked Shen Rong, "Is Dr Lu typical, or have you idealized her?"

"She is typical," was the immediate reply.

I told her I personally disliked the meekness with which Dr Lu puts up with the insinuations and arrogant officiousness of Qin Bo, Vice-minister Jiao's wife. To me this smacked of the Christian exhortation to turn the other cheek.

"No," Shen Rong said. "It's because she has more important things on her mind. And, as Lu Xun wrote, 'The highest contempt is wordless.'"

The relationship between Dr Lu and her husband is tender and comradely. Indeed, this story should be read by members of the Women's Liberation Movement who wonder why there is no feminist movement in China. Chinese men do not stand in the way of their wives' careers, and they help with the housework and children. Men and women share the same problems. Many Westerners think the Chinese an inscrutable people who conceal their feelings, but most writers in China today are more akin to

Dickens than to his hard-boiled 20th-century successors in their unabashed display of emotion. Thus Shen Rong evokes the poetry in Dr Lu's austere life by quoting the Hungarian poet Petöfi.

Qin Bo is brilliantly drawn, a perfect foil to unassuming, admirable Dr Lu. At first she strikes us as an experienced old cadre, principled, concerned for others and conscientious. Her costume of good material is plain but well cut, her hair dyed and stylishly waved. She keeps mouthing Marxist precepts, but on her lips they are empty platitudes. We soon realize that she judges other people by their titles, status and appearances. She expects, because of her husband's high position, to receive privileged treatment. China is plagued with too many old "revolutionaries" of this kind who no longer have any revolutionary feeling. Entrenched in leading positions, they do no useful work and make things difficult for other people. We cannot ascribe Dr Lu's heart attack to Qin Bo's harassment, but undoubtedly it was a contributing factor.

Two controversial characters in this story are Dr Jiang and her husband, who are leaving for Canada. In addition to the hard conditions of intellectuals, they have had to put up with political discrimination on account of their connections overseas. When the ultra-Left line prevailed, many patriotic overseas Chinese who had come back to China to help build up the country were treated as suspects, as second-class citizens. Now that the government has relaxed the restrictions on emigration, a number of well-qualified doctors have left. Dr Jiang and her husband, after a mental struggle, feeling rather guilty about it, decide to leave. Today, when this country is desperately short of trained personnel, a brain drain is deplorable. Some readers have therefore criticized Shen Rong for portraying this couple so sympathetically. When I asked her about this she defended her stand, and also said that most readers side with her. She wanted to highlight the shocking living conditions which make patriotic professionals go abroad in the hope of giving their children a better education and of coming back, later on, better qualified themselves.

"How can it be solved, this problem of the middle-aged?" I asked.

"Surely China just doesn't have the funds or the housing to improve their living conditions much in the near future."

"I can't give you any solution. But the Central Party Committee has issued certain directives calling on administrative heads to show more concern for this group of low-paid technical personnel. In my story I simply tried to draw public attention to their predicament, and to pay my tribute to them." Then she told me that the newspaper *Health* had published an article urging the heads of the Ministry of Health to read this story.

六

《新风霞回忆录》译序[①]

Preface to *Xin Fengxia Reminiscences*

The appearance of Xin Fengxia's *Reminiscences* has caused a considerable stir. Not simply because of her immense popularity as an actress and singer, but because these reminiscences have literary and historical value—they give us a vivid picture of the life of the working people before Liberation and their vicissitudes in the course of China's tumultuous revolution.

In China, one of the revolutionary changes brought about by Liberation was in the status of actors. In the past, although a virtuoso like Mei Lanfang, the renowned Beijing opera actor, might make a fortune and win a world reputation, actors and actresses came from poor families and were by and large considered little better than pimps and prostitutes.

Xin Fengxia's life illustrates the change in their fortunes.

Her family came originally from Suzhou, a city known for the beauty of its girls; but she was born in 1932 in a Tianjin slum. Her real name was Yang Shuming; Xin Fengxia is her stage name. She was the eldest of seven children, and her father who peddled sugar-coated haws was unable to feed or clothe them adequately. So small Fengxia had no schooling. Barefooted

---

① 选自：Xin，F. X. *Xin Fengxia Reminiscences*. Gladys Yang (trans.). Beijing: Chinese Literature Press，1981.

she scrounged for cinders, cooked, washed and helped mind the babies. Her clothes were made of dyed sacking, padded with cotton in winter, worn with a lining in autumn, and without a lining in summer. Outgrown, they were handed down to the younger children, and when in rags they were used to make cloth shoe-soles. Such a family, under Japanese occupation and the KMT regime, had to struggle just to survive.

Fengxia's uncle was a fiddler in an opera company, and his daughter was an actress. At the age of seven Fengxia started learning from her, and by the time she was ten was acting minor Beijing opera parts. She received no pay for this, only a free meal of porridge.

A little later she joined a *pingju* troupe. *Pingju* is a form of opera which originated in the countryside of northeast Hebei around the turn of the century and has always had close ties with the peasants and workers. Many of its themes were romantic, and its language, being more colloquial than that of Beijing opera, made it easily understood. Small townsfolk enjoyed it, although before Liberation the literati thought it crude, preferring Beijing opera or *kunqu* opera. In the last forty years, however, *pingju* has enriched itself by absorbing certain features from other operas, films and plays, and it is now popular throughout the country.

By the time Fengxia was fourteen her father was ill, leaving her as the family's mainstay. She worked for a pittance in a textile mill all day and in the evening performed with the *pingju* troupe. Her mother, still suckling a baby, took her there, helped dress her and make her up, then accompanied her home. When hooligans barred her way in the street, her mother kowtowed to them, begging them not to beat her. Her mother helped her make and embroider her costumes. Watching different types of opera, she learned avidly from the performers, soon becoming a fine actress and excellent singer with a remarkably clear enunciation. To make extra money after the performance she would go to sing in brothels. She saw the seamy side of life in the old society, yet retained her innocence and integrity. From the operas she saw and from a blind minstrel, their neighbour, she learned the feudal concepts of justice, and chastity. At the risk of beatings she refused to play erotic parts.

At fourteen she began to be cast in leading roles. When eighteen she acted in the opera *Return One Snowy Night* by Wu Zuguang. She sang the songs in the film *Don't Waste Your Youth*, for which he had written the script, but at that time she did not know him. And then came Liberation, when Fengxia's name was already widely known.

Her mother had hoped that this talented daughter of hers would become a rich man's concubine, the best fate most actresses in the old days could hope for. And friends now offered to arrange her a marriage with a man with official status. But Fengxia had other ideas. Popular among Chinese for centuries, despite the rigid feudal marriage system, has been the theme of a romance between "a talented scholar and a beauty". Fengxia wanted to marry a scholar who would be both her husband and teacher, a man who could write and direct operas, film-scripts and plays. She and Wu Zuguang first met when she was a star of twenty whose gramophone records were in great demand, and he was thirty-four, a brilliant playwright treated as an equal by senior dramatists such as Cao Yu, Tian Han and Xia Yan. The magazine *New Observer* asked Wu to interview her. He invited her out to a meal because she had no other spare time.

"He appreciated my frankness and naivety," Fengxia told me. "I admired his good looks, sincerity and learning. He seemed so good, so gentle, compared with the brutal types of men I'd known."She fell in love with him.

Later that year, having been made a representative of the Youth Federation, she went to ask Wu to help her write a speech. He encouraged her to study and lent her books.

"I've something to tell you," said Fengxia.

"Go ahead."

"I'd like to marry you. How about it?"

Speechless with surprise at first, Wu finally said, "I must think it over."

"Why?"

"I'd need to be responsible for you for life."

In January '51, in spite of certain opposition, they married. Ouyang Yuqian and Lao She presided at the wedding, which was attended by Guo Moruo, Mei Lanfang and many other eminent figures in cultural circles.

They were immensely busy, blissfully happy. Fengxia, apart from acting and rehearsing, liked to cook for her husband and make his clothes. She would sit up at night sewing, knitting, practising writing. She contracted TB that year and coughed blood, but the private company to which she belonged would not let her rest or go to hospital. So in '52 she joined the PLA *Pingju* Troupe, spent half a year in hospital and recovered, then went to Korea to perform for the Chinese People's Volunteers. By then she had an extensive repertoire of traditional operas as well as new ones. Some of her best performances were in *Xianglin's Wife*, *The Cowherd and the Weaving Maid* and *Liu Qiaoer*, an opera to popularize the new Marriage Law and preach equality for women. Although she wrote no scripts herself she had become adept in improving the dialogue and inventing a new style of singing, so she became the founder of a new school. For two years she attended a literacy school in the mornings. She kept a diary and started writing essays. Chinese characters are difficult to master, especially for grown-ups; but she studied tenaciously, and when unable to write a character would sketch what she meant instead. In '57 the *People's Daily* published two of her essays "New Year" and "My Aunt", and this brought her almost as great a sense of achievement as her spectacular stage success.

Then, in '57, Wu Zuguang was unjustly labelled a Rightist and sent the next year to the Great North Waste for labour reform. His salary was terminated. Fengxia had to support their three children and old parents. An official urged her to divorce Wu or the consequences would be serious. She refused. She had promised him, "I'll never leave you, never let you down." "Lady Precious Stream in the opera waited for eighteen years for her husband," she declared. "I'll wait twenty-eight years, for ever!" The next three years were her most creative ones. In addition to supporting the family she economized to send Wu food parcels.

In'58, the year of the "Big Leap", she gave as many as six performances a day, so tired that "I could sleep on my feet," she recalls. Her audiences loved her. "Sackfuls of fan mail" from workers and intellectuals helped to keep up her morale. Every day she made time to write to her husband about the children's development and her work. Wu wrote back giving advice. "Each of his letters was a lesson for me," she says. "Each of mine was an exercise in composition." In 1961 when at last he came back he brought all Fengxia's letters carefully stacked in chronological order. Unfortunately they were later destroyed by Red Guards.

Wu Zuguang went on writing and Fengxia acting till the "cultural revolution". Then the family was split up. Husband and wife were sent to different cadre schools, unable to correspond, away from the children. For six years Fengxia, although she had high blood pressure, had to dig air-raid shelters, clean toilets and push barrows. "That was the hardest time," she says. "How I missed my family!"

In '75, she was cleared and returned to her troupe, not to act but as a stage hand. But after rough treatment by the thugs of the "gang of four" she fell ill with cerebral artery thrombosis, which was wrongly diagnosed as apoplexy. Her left side was paralysed. Not for three years did she get the right treatment; hence her recovery has been very slow. Now she can walk painfully with a stick. She writes and paints plum-blossom, vines, gourds and peaches in the style of Qi Baishi. She also has many students and is often asked to go out and give reports. She receives many letters every day from all parts of the country, as well as from Hong Kong and Singapore where her films *Liu Qiaoer* and *Flowers As Go-between* are well-known. If she goes to the theatre applause bursts out, and she has to be carried up to the stage to say a few words before the show can start. A member of the People's Political Consultative Council, she is also on the executive committee of the Dramatists' Association. Because the political climate has changed, traditional opera is flourishing, and she can make a useful contribution by passing on her experience to young actresses, she is happy and optimistic about China's future.

Wu Zuguang, now in the Ministry of Culture, devotes his time to writing. His recent five-act play *Itinerant Players* is set in Tianjin, based on Fengxia's early life.

Fengxia started to write her reminiscences in '77. Over eighty of them have appeared, and she plans to write more.

Fengxia's reminiscences show her keen powers of observation and eye for detail, her amazing memory and gift of total recall, her insight into a wide range of characters, and her genuine concern for other people—qualities needed to reach the top of her profession. With her vivid, frank and unaffected style, she is a born story-teller who sketches unforgettable vignettes of her family and colleagues, loyal friends, grasping managers, rich men and scoundrels... the blood, tears and revolt in the old society and the changes in the new, all based on her own first-hand experience.

It is indeed a tragedy that this brilliant actress has been so long unable to perform. However, the doctors say that eventually she should recover completely. Her life is still rich and full. Her two sons and daughter live with them, and theirs is a very happy family. One source of particular satisfaction to her is that her daughter Wu Shuang is one of the best students at the National Conservatory of Music. Fengxia believes that she will become another outstanding singer.

七

《当代女作家作品选》序[①]

Preface to *Seven Contemporary Chinese Women Writers*

"Women scientists and writers are few in our country," states Huang Zongying in "The Flight of the Wild-geese." True, compared with men they are few, but their number is growing. There are 220 women in the Writers' Association who, while drawing regular salaries from the editorial board, film studio or writers' association to which they are attached, spend most of their time on creative work. In this volume we introduce seven representative women writers, whose stories and reportage present a good cross-section of life in China.

Although the writers selected vary considerably in age, experience and background, all show a strong sense of social responsibility. In China, literature is not viewed as a form of entertainment or simply as a source of aesthetic enjoyment, but as an effective means of education, of inspiring readers with high ideals and the belief that these can be attained. This revolutionary idealism is a feature of all seven pieces presented here.

At the same time these stories reflect reality. China's relaxed political climate and growing democracy in the last few years have resulted in more truthful writing and a wider range of themes. Love, social injustice, the

---

① 选自 Ru，Z. J. et al. *Seven Contemporary Chinese Women Writers*. Gladys Yang (trans.). Beijing：Chinese Literature Press，1982/1983/1985/1990.

value of the individual, humanism and other subjects formerly taboo are now being fearlessly tackled—often with an unabashed display of emotion. Social problems dating from or arising after the "cultural revolution" are the themes chosen by most women writers.

However, one problem not dealt with explicitly is that of the status of women in China today. There is no militant writing about the issue of women's emancipation. According to the constitution, women and men have equal rights in China; but this cannot be fully carried out in practice yet, although the position of women is now vastly improved. These stories tell us indirectly a good deal about their status.

It is significant that the heroines of "At Middle Age" and "The Flight of the Wild-geese" are skilled professionals, the surgeon Dr Lu and the botanist Qin. After the founding of the People's Republic intellectuals were seldom cast in leading roles in literature, for emphasis was placed on presenting workers and peasants as the heroes of our times. Lu and Qin are devoted to their work and serve the people with great technical skill, but neither receives official recognition for her contribution. Indeed Qin is under a cloud because she has been labelled as a landlord's daughter and has offended certain bureaucrats. Her Party secretary, who should have a high ideological level and give political guidance, makes the revealing male-chauvinist remark, "Although she has her faults, we must make allowances for her being a woman."

Dr Lu works overtime in the hospital and at home bears the brunt of housework and minding the children, yet feels guiltily that she is a bad wife and mother. Many Chinese professional women have this sense of guilt. All women, even those with small children, work after their 56-day maternity leave. In a materially backward country like this, there are few labour-saving devices, housework is wearisome and time-consuming, and in the cities people often spend hours queuing up to buy vegetables. Many women age prematurely trying to be good housewives while at the same time improving their technical skills. Zhang Jie has said to me on several occasions, "To be a woman is hard!" But there is no women's liberation movement in China, partly because women's position is infinitely better than before, partly because they see their problems in the general social context and are working for modernization to lighten their burdens. This explains why their difficulties are presented as something peripheral, not as the central theme of most of these stories.

What concerns our women writers most is the younger generation. Zong Pu describes the generation gap between certain old intellectuals attacked during the ten years of chaos and the younger generation who suffered on account of their parents. These young people seem cynical, flippant, materialistic, but they have their ideals too. "Melody in Dreams" shows some of them risking arrest by denouncing the feudal fascism of the "gang of four" during the Tiananmen Incident in 1976, and scoffing at their elders who urge them to play safe.

Other problems of young people are frankly presented: their disrupted education; lack of interesting employment; the difficulties met with by boys and girls sent from town to the countryside; the low incomes and overcrowding which threaten to break up young couples' marriages; their mental confusion after the turbulent years in which revolutionary traditions were thrown overboard and bureaucracy, nepotism and corruption were rampant.... Women writers are truthful spokesmen for the youth. If they have not experienced for themselves the problems of the young, they do their homework conscientiously. Thus before writing "The Path Through the Grassland" Ru Zhijuan went to live for a period in the Daqing oilfield.

Shen Rong, before writing "At Middle Age" about the difficulties of middle-aged intellectuals, familiarized herself with a hospital in Beijing. Embarking on a story like this took courage, because there is still some uncertainty about the dividing line between positive exposure of problems and abuses and anti-socialist writing. This work aroused attention to problems for which there can be no rapid solution—how to improve the material conditions of overworked professionals.

Courage of the same kind is shown in Huang Zongying's sensitive reportage "The Flight of the Wild-geese". The woman botanist Qin has the same high sense of responsibility, professional expertise and idealism as Dr Lu. But for years she has been considered politically backward. A reporter following up her case to establish the truth might well offend the higher authorities.

Zhang Jie's "Love Must Not Be Forgotten" aroused considerable interest as well as much controversy. It has been included in this selection because she considers it one of her most representative works. Boldly unconventional, idealistic and intensely romantic, it sheds interesting light on the changes in the attitude to love in socialist China, still strongly influenced by feudal ideas about marriage.

Many of the stories here stress human sympathy or love and friendship even during sharp class struggles. This is a positive feature following a period during which relations between individuals were affected by the current political line—a man in trouble might be divorced by his wife and repudiated by his children, even if they believed that he had done nothing wrong. The botanist Qin, for example, is not a black or white stereotype, but a complex human being, principled and dedicated to serving the people, yet over-sensitive and liable to lose her temper. Although she is labelled as the daughter of a landlord, the mountain villagers love her for her concern for them and her selfless work to improve their livelihood.

The ultra-Left line in literature in the past encouraged writing according to set formulas, and the ten years of turmoil deprived young would-be writers of a good education and the access to classical Chinese and foreign literature needed to raise the quality of their work. This is evident from the immaturity, lack of sophistication and verbosity of certain stories. But the last few years have been a period of experimentation in finding fresher forms and styles, and women writers are paying attention to this. However, their works are above all significant because of their subject matter and the honest picture they present of life in China today.

八

《北京的传说》译序[①]

Preface to *Beijing Legends*

These folk-tales are translated from *Beijing Legends*, compiled by Jin Shoushen, a Manchu gentleman whose family lived for many generations in Beijing. Based on the tales told him by people from many walks of life in the capital, they were first published in 1957 by the Beijing Publishing House. What they lack in literary polish is made up for by the genuine folk flavour with which they carry us back to the building of Beijing as the Ming capital in 1421. They deal with the city's layout, some of its chief monuments, place names and different legends, and give us fascinating glimpses of the life of rulers as well as ordinary people.

The front cover, the painting of Nezha, was done for Panda Books by the well-known cartoonist Ding Cong. Nezha plays a prominent part in these tales and has a special place in Chinese legend; but his pedigree can be traced back to India. An Indian Buddhist legend describes a young god Nalakuvara or Nalakubala, who was the third son of the Heavenly King Vaisravana, one of the twenty devas. During the Ming Dynasty, this boy's name was transliterated as Nezha, first in Wu Cheng'en's *Pilgrimage to the West* and then in *The Canonization of the Gods*; and his father became Li

---

① 选自 Jin, S. S. *Beijing Legends*. Gladys Yang (trans.). Beijing: Chinese Literature Press, 1982.

Jing, an early Tang general who won renown by defeating the Eastern Turks. Because Li Jing helped to build up the Tang Dynasty he became a guardian god.

The Canonization of the Gods attributed great ability to Nezha, who was said to have killed the son of the Dragon King. In revenge, the Dragon King tried to flood the country. In order to clear his father of blame, Nezha disembowelled himself and cut off all his flesh which he derived from his parents; but after his death his divine teacher made him a new body out of a lotus flower, and he became a god. The *Pilgrimage to the West* presents him as one of the gods who defended Heaven and fought with the Monkey King. Because of his supernatural powers and his defiance of the Dragon King, Nezha was a well-loved figure and the people of Beijing were proud to claim his patronage.

Unfortunately many of the temples and pagodas described in these tales have now fallen into ruins. China had such a wealth of old relics, and such limited funds for their upkeep, that they were not carefully treasured. Thus the capital's city wall and most ornamental archways were pulled down after Liberation to facilitate traffic and, for a lover of history, the face of old Beijing is sadly changed. All the more reason then, to preserve these legends describing its past; and it is heartening to see that today the People's Government is taking steps to restore old monuments.

Half a million years ago, in the days of Beijing Man, this area was largely underwater. This old folk memory seems to be embodied in the name Bitter Sea Waste. Beijing knows climatic extremes, a blazing summer and a freezing winter. Its people were never accustomed to the softer ways of living in the south, for drought, high winds and sandstorms constantly threatened the city. Hence the many stories of wicked dragons—the lords controlling water—who are presented as trying to take over Beijing.

Emperors, their advisers and ministers figure in some of these stories, seen from the viewpoint of the man in the street as a grasping, tyrannical, incompetent lot. They have no idea, for instance, how to design the corner towers of the Forbidden City: the plan for these is copied from a pedlar's cricket cage. And so, as in most folk stories of other lands, the real heroes are there sourceful working people who retain their self-respect and sense of humour through natural calamities, man-made disasters and countless political changes.

九

《单口相声故事选》译序[①]

Preface to *Traditional Comic Tales*

These comic tales are a form of *xiangsheng* (pronounced "she-ang sheng"), literally "face and voice", the satirical, laughter-evoking performing art with the largest audience in China. *Xiangsheng* artists can dispense with a stage or stage props, but they must be good singers, elocutionists, comedians and mimics. There are usually two performers. However, the stories presented here are "single-mouth *xiangsheng*"—solos.

It is claimed by some that the ancestors of *xiangsheng* were the court jesters of old who told stories or cracked jokes to amuse their masters. But *xiangsheng* are not designed to entertain the aristocracy; like music-hall they are for the man in the street. The skills required for them were being perfected between the 11th and 13th centuries when populous mercantile cities grew up in south China with a host of merchants, small tradesmen, artisans and apprentices, all avid for amusement. By the end of the 13th century, Hangzhou, the capital of Southern Song, had over one million inhabitants. Marco Polo described it as "the greatest city which may be found in the world, where so many pleasures may be found that one fancies himself to be in Paradise". To cater to the urban lower class, story-tellers,

---

① 选自 Zhang, S. C. et al. *Traditional Comic Tales*. Gladys Yang (trans.). Beijing: Chinese Literature Press, 1983.

ballad-singers and many other folk artists performed daily in the streets, parks and tea-houses. To compete with rival showmen and capture an audience they had to be virtuosos. The story-tellers usually specialized in different subject matter: ghost stories, romances, tales of shrewd and upright judges, or Buddhist legends.... Moreover these stories were distinguished by their humour, their delight in puns and playing upon words, their mockery without malice, all of which are features of our modern *xiangsheng*. There were no *xiangsheng* then. But popular entertainers practised their arts through all the vicissitudes of Chinese history. And centuries later *xiangsheng* were able to draw on these earlier performing skills and some of the traditional repertory.

Xiangsheng took shape in the second half of the 19th century, in such north China cities as Baoding, Beijing and Tianjin where, significantly, *pingju* opera also evolved to satisfy those townsfolk who found it easier to appreciate than Peking Opera. One pioneer in this art form, Zhu Shaowen, trained first as a clown in Peking Opera. To start with, *xiangsheng* artists played in streets or market-places, some concealing themselves behind curtains to mimic the sounds of animals, children crying, a house on fire.... They then came into the open to crack jokes and perform *xiangsheng* drawn from traditional plays, tales and ballads, or based on topical events. In their efforts to raise a laugh they included not a few bawdy jokes—in those days their audiences were restricted to men. Their social status was low. They had no security, and to make a living often performed in brothels. Most illiterate apprentices learned their craft by imitating their masters' performances.

A *xiangsheng* artist of the second generation, Li Deyang, refined on the art form and gained such popularity that he was given the nickname "Everyone's Idol". Thanks to his influence and that of his confrères, *xiangsheng* now moved from the streets into theatres.

An outstanding comedian of the third generation was Zhang Shouchen (1898-1970), who compiled this collection of stories. A native of Beijing, at fifteen he was apprenticed to the *xiangsheng* performer Jiao Dehai, and he collaborated with "Everyone's Idol". He appreciated the artistic skills of the best traditional *xiangsheng* and opposed the vulgarity of certain items, which he edited and improved, although our readers are likely to find the humour in some of his stories rather crude. Well-known in Beijing, Tianjin, Jinan and Nanjing, he performed in duologue, solo and trio *xiangsheng*, creating original stories of his own to satirize the old society. After Liberation he concentrated on performing solo *xiangsheng*, training young artists, and compiling a collection of comic stories. Here we present only a selection of them, as the puns in many others defy translation.

As Zhang's stories evolved in the cities of north China in a semi-feudal context, most of them reflect the ideas of the urban lower class. They ridicule and expose the corruption, miserliness and ineptitude of old-time officials and landlords, the hypocrisy of feudal ethics, the foibles and strange adventures of small townsfolk and artisans. Akin to yet different from standard jokes and short stories, they have better characterization and fuller plots than the former and are more humorous than the latter, their jokes being an integral part of the recital, designed to bring out the main theme and reveal contradictions. The different incidents form a logical sequence without undue elaboration, and much is left to the listeners' imagination including, often, the conclusion and moral. For all their exaggeration they present a vivid and basically truthful picture of those bygone days. Some of them remind us of a Chaplin film in which the underdog, in spite of his quirks and apparent stupidity, gets a rise out of those with high position and power.

Since Liberation a host of new *xiangsheng* artists, both professional and amateur, has emerged. They received encouragement and help from such scholars as Luo Zhangpei and Wu Xiaoling, and the great writer Lao She who himself wrote *xiangsheng*. No other art form can compete with *xiangsheng* in the speed with which they reflect new topical issues. And the artists' social status is vastly improved; for as their performances go on the air to all parts of the country, helping to popularize the standard Beijing dialect, many of them are national celebrities—"Everyone's Idols".

十

《芙蓉镇》译序①

Preface to *A Small Town Called Hibiscus*

Hunan, this hinterland province larger than France, is essentially a region of hills and mountains apart from the plain around the Dongting Lake. It has a very ancient civilization. During the Warring States Period (403—221 BC) the kingdoms of Yue and Chu had their distinctive cultures here, and in subsequent centuries the central authorities found it hard to control its independence-loving people, owing to the difficulties of communication. Hunan has produced a great many talented writers. Outstanding among its twentieth-century authors are veteran woman novelist Ding Ling, Shen Congwen, and Zhou Libo who won fame after Liberation. Since the 80's a group of talented younger writers has emerged. One of them is Gu Hua, whose style is somewhat influenced by Shen Congwen.

In the thirties and forties Shen Congwen wrote brilliant idyllic stories and essays about west Hunan, conjuring up its countryside, folk customs and old way of life, to dispel the illusion that this was a "bandit area" shrouded in mystery. (see Panda Books "*The Border Town and Other Stories*" and "*Recollections of West Hunan*") Now Gu Hua is doing the same for south Hunan, a good example being his long story *A Log Cabin Overgrown with*

---

① 选自：Gu, H. *A Small Town Called Hibiscus*. Gladys Yang (trans.). Beijing: Chinese Literature Press, 1983/1987/1990.

Creepers (see "*Chinese Literature*" 1982, No. 12). However, his work has an added significance, as readers will see from *A Small Town Called Hibiscus*.

Gu Hua, whose real name is Luo Hongyu, was born in 1942 in a village of about a hundred households at the foot of the Wuling Mountains in south Hunan. His father, a small KMT functionary and accountant, died when Gu Hua was five, leaving his elder brother to support his mother and four younger children. Like other village boys, Gu Hua went barefoot, minded water-buffaloes, gathered firewood and carried charcoal to market. At the same time he attended the primary school in the little town of Jiahe.

Jiahe, so cut off in the past from the outside world that the local dialect is incomprehensible to people from elsewhere, was known as a centre of folk-songs, notably the cycle of songs to "accompany the bride" sung before a girl left home to get married. And Jiahe had an excellent middle school at which Gu Hua studied. Because he showed a flair for writing and won prizes for composition, he was put in charge of the blackboard bulletin; and if classmates failed to hand in contributions he would improvise poems to fill up the space. He read all the literature that he could lay his hands on, and longed to see something of the outside world. As his brother could only allow him one yuan a month as pocket-money, he failed to realize his dream of saving up fifteen yuan to hike to Chenzhou, the administrative centre 130 kilometres away.

After finishing junior middle school Gu Hua taught for a year in the Jiahe primary school. He then entered a technical school to study agriculture, after which he spent fourteen years, from 1962 to '75, in the Agricultural Research Institute in Qiaokou, formerly a waste land, where he learned to grow rice, vegetables and fruit and repair farm implements. There he married Yujuan, a lively, pretty fellow worker. And there in the early sixties he wrote his first short story.

In those days it was not easy for unknown writers to get into print. Editors would first investigate their political record and class origin. However, after some of the Party cadres in Chenzhou vouched for Gu Hua, his first story *Sister Apricot* was published in 1962.

At Qiaokou, Gu Hua took part in the various political movements of that period, including the Four Clean-ups Movement and the unprecedented "great cultural revolution". He recalls, "Ingenuous and stupid, I followed along blindly. I was criticized from time to time, but never got into big trouble. However, I saw my contemporaries, colleagues and friends playing different parts as they were tossed up or down by tempestuous movements, and that distressed and revolted me. A few years ago I even felt that life was a kind of Vanity Fair..."

The heads of the Agricultural Research Institute encouraged Gu Hua's literary leanings and gave him time off to indulge them. In 1970 he went for the first time to a forestry station in the mountains to write. In 1975 he was transferred to the Chenzhou Song and Dance Ensemble to give him more time for writing.

After the fall of the "gang of four" his dream of travelling to broaden his horizons and see more of life came true. In 1980 he became a member of the Chinese Writers' Association, attended a writers' conference in Beijing, went to lectures on literature and met many well-known authors. In his spare time he wrote his prizewinning *A Log Cabin Overgrown with Creepers*, published in 1981, as well as other short stories. He resolved to write a novel about characters he knew in a small community which could mirror the turbulent age. Although he feared he was hardly up to this, he received encouragement from the editors of the Hunan People's Publishing House. And when the young writers taking the literary course were given a month off to do some writing, he went back to the forest in the Wuling Mountains and wrote a first draft of over 100,000 characters, which he tentatively entitled *A Remote Mountain Town*. In August he went back to Beijing to continue his studies, and in September handed in his incomplete manuscript. He expected it to be put on the shelf. Instead he was very soon told by the editors that they approved of it. They kept him in Beijing to revise and complete the novel. He was most impressed by the concern of these editors and older writers who encouraged him and made constructive suggestions.

It was Qin Chaoyang, an eminent literary critic, who changed the novel's title to *A Small Town Called Hibiscus*. And it was published in the monthly *Modern Times* (*Dangdai*) 1981, No. 1. It created a furore, for readers all over the country instantly related to it. To a great extent this was because it made a breakthrough in tackling a new theme. It is a devastating denunciation of the ultra-Left political line which prevailed in China from the late nineteen-fifties till the fall of the "gang of four". By presenting the ups and downs of seven or eight major characters in a small town in Hunan during this period, it shows us a microcosm of all China in those twenty stormy years. Gu Hua pulls no punches but writes forcefully with profound understanding based on first-hand experience. He exposes horrors, travesties of justice and the ultra-Leftists' denial of human kindness as well as other traditional Chinese virtues. At the same time he writes not with bitterness but with wry humour, which is how most Chinese who went through those terrible years tend to describe their experiences today. So this heart-rending novel also has many laughter-evoking scenes.

As early as '66, the first year of the "cultural revolution", Gu Hua in his remote agricultural research institute sensed "something rotten in the state of Denmark". Increasingly he grew more and more aware of the dangers of the ultra-Left line and the cult of the individual. To have voiced this at the time, of course, would have landed him in gaol. Then in 1979 the Third Plenary Session of the Party made a preliminary summing up of the Party's mistakes. The first genuine criticism of Leftism made by the Chinese Party, it marked a major historical turning-point, the start of a nationwide righting of wrongs and of condemning the cult of the individual. This reinforced Gu Hua's convictions and provided them with a theoretical framework. It also gave editors the courage to publish *Hibiscus*.

This novel has its detractors. A few local cadres complain that Gu Hua has treated them shabbily. Yet the record shows that grassroots cadres who resisted the lunacies of the ultra-Left line very quickly lost power and landed themselves—and their families—in serious trouble. Others object: Why make a positive character like Gu Yanshan, "the soldier from the north", an impotent drunkard? And would it not be more edifying, more effective in pointing out the dangers of ultra-Leftism, if the cadres who followed this line were portrayed as impeccably moral instead of leading loose lives like Li Guoxiang and Autumn Snake Wang?

I think such critics are still influenced by the idea of a clear-cut distinction between "goodies" and "baddies", black and white, which for so long was the bane of Chinese writing. In this country too many stories, plays and film-scripts have been written to formula, describing stereotyped characters in stereotyped situations. How refreshing it is, then, when Gu Hua shows us real flesh-and-blood human beings with weaknesses as well as fine qualities. His characters are brilliantly drawn and convincing.

In 1982, *Hibiscus* was one of six novels to receive the first Mao Dun Literary Prize.

When Gu Hua heard that Panda Books intended to publish *A Small Town Called Hibiscus*, he induced the Cultural Bureau of Chenzhou to invite my husband Yang Xianyi and me, as well as one of our editors, to visit south Hunan for a week to absorb something of the local atmosphere. It was a fascinating experience. We visited a primeval forest in the mountains and the forestry station below it where Gu Hua wrote most of *Hibiscus* and where he gathered the material for *A Log Cabin Overgrown with Creepers*. We discovered that the little town Hibiscus is a composite of three places. Its natural setting is Qiaokou, where a jade-green river, East River, flows gently past the orchard where Gu Hua sowed, grafted and pruned tangerine trees at the foot of the Wuling Mountains majestic in the distance beyond green foothills. The flagstone street is based on Old Street in Jiahe, where Gu Hua went to school and his family still lives. And the size of Hibiscus at the start of the novel is approximately that of his childhood village.

As with the setting, so with the characters. Gu Hua does not write about real people in real life, as a number of Chinese writers tend to do, but invents characters on the basis of his observation of many individuals in different periods of recent Chinese history.

Gu Hua's output is impressive. By the end of 1981 he had to his credit two novels, four novellas, and over thirty short stories and essays, as well as songs. He is not a fast writer, however. He revises all his work four or five times, paying careful attention to technique and style.

A word now about this translation. An English translation is almost always longer than the Chinese original. As Gu Hua's narrative moves at a brisk pace, to convey this in English I have, with the author's permission, made certain abridgements, telescoped some passages, cut down on mixed metaphors which the Chinese delight in, or shortened lists of names or events such as the Three Anti or Five Anti Movements which would require footnotes or need to be paraphrased to make them intelligible to foreign readers. For instance, Gu Yanshan tells the children of Hibiscus stories about famous drunkards of old, listing six heroes and their exploits in their cups. I have retained one only, Wu Song who killed a tiger, who appears in the novel *Outlaws of the Marsh*.

Owing to the limitations of my English, now out of date after over forty years in China, I have failed to convey the raciness and earthiness of Gu Hua's language, which draws heavily on Chenzhou colloquialisms. I hope some younger sinologists will before long make new translations to do justice to his graphic, pungent style.

Gu Hua says: What times we have lived through! There cannot be many countries whose writers have such a wealth of material at their disposal. He is planning to write another full-length novel about the years of turmoil.

十一

《古华小说选》译序[①]

Preface to *Pagoda Ridge and Other Stories*

Gu Hua, born in 1942 in a small mountain village in South Hunan, took up writing in his spare time while working on a farm and published his first story in '62. There was pressure in those days on Chinese writers to gear their writing to the current political line, and his earliest works were fairly stereotyped. In the late seventies, after the fall of the "gang of four", Gu Hua like other writers felt free to express himself more truthfully and to deal with a much wider range of subject matter, to attack social abuses, describe backward superstitious practices and to introduce romance.

Gu Hua has written two novels, ten novellas and over fifty short stories as well as articles on writing and accounts of his travels in Egypt and Morocco. The four stories in this collection were written between '81 and' 83. "The Log Cabin Overgrown with Creepers" was voted one of the best short stories of 1981, while his outstanding novel *A Small Town Called Hibiscus* won a Mao Dun Literary Award in 1982. "Pagoda Ridge", though not a prize-winner, is one of his representative works. Its theme is not too original. Many Chinese writers have written about the hardships of the peasants during the "cultural revolution" and how, to survive, they defied

---

① 选自：Gu, H. *Pagoda Ridge and Other Stories*. Gladys Yang (trans.). Beijing: Chinese Literature Press, 1985.

the ultra-Left policies in agriculture. But Gu Hua's handling of this theme is gripping because of the local colour which pervades all his work. "Ninety-nine Mounds" and the other stories presented here also illustrate his familiarity with the folk-lore and customs of his native place.

We have amalgamated and slightly abridged Gu Hua's two articles "How I Became a Writer" and "About Pagoda Ridge" to help our readers understand the background of these stories.

Gu Hua is too modest to say much about his language, a treat for Chinese readers but losing much of its flavour in translation. He tells us that his Chinese teacher at school was always critical of his compositions because he kept straying from the subject, being interested in everything under the sun, and because he flouted conventions. In this respect some purists may still fault him. Born and bred in the Wuling Mountains, unlike some writers from cities who go to the countryside to experience life and enrich their vocabulary, Gu Hua comes out naturally with the idioms, local sayings, graphic figures of speech and crude swear words of the Hunan mountaineers. But he refines them to some extent and also uses classical expressions. He has made a study too of such Chinese stylists as Zhao Shuli and Shen Congwen. The result is a fresh, distinctive style of his own, colloquial and popular yet literary. Hunan has some of the loveliest landscapes in China, and so evocative are his descriptions of the Hunan countryside and the characters peopling it that film and TV producers reading his stories at once visualize them as pictures. Six films based on his work are being made.

Gu Hua has been called the Hardy of Hunan. He has not attained Hardy's stature. But though a century apart and living in totally different societies at opposite ends of the world, both men are regional novelists with a passionate love for their native place, its people and folk customs. They evoke these sometimes lyrically, sometimes with caustic humour, describing stark reality with deep feeling or with romantic or burlesque exaggeration. Both like to comment on the social scene. Both have given us unsurpassed portraits of country women, seemingly gentle yet strong enough to rebel against convention. Gu Hua has been criticized for dwelling unduly on the physical charm of some of his alluring heroines and for certain suggestively sensual passages, though Western readers are unlikely to take exception to this.

Where he differs completely from Hardy is in his approach to life. The English novelist generally saw human life as an inevitable tragedy, while Gu Hua is an optimist able to describe the nightmare of the "cultural revolution" with flashes of earthy humour in the best tradition of Chinese satire. He has infinite faith in ordinary people, convinced that sanity will prevail, and they will win through to the better life they deserve.

Gu Hua, now a well-known and popular novelist, has recently left his old home and moved to Changsha, the capital of Hunan. As a professional writer, attending many conferences and meetings and able to travel widely, his horizons are broadening. It will be interesting to see what effect this new style of life will have on his work.

十二

《邓友梅小说选》译序[①]

Preface to *Snuff-Bottles and Other Stories*

Deng Youmei, the son of a poor peasant, was born in Pingyuan County, Shandong in 1931. As a child he lived in Tianjin, in the same compound as the destitute yet arrogant concubine of a Manchu noble, and his interest in Manchu Bannermen dates from that time. He had little formal education but a very chequered career, caught up while a boy in the resistance to Japanese aggression. At eleven he delivered messages for the 8th Route Army. In his early teens he was carried off to Japan to work in a factory; then he joined a cultural troupe in the New Fourth Army and was a reporter attached to the People's Liberation Army.

After Liberation Deng came to Beijing. In 1951 he started writing. He received encouragement from Zhao Shuli, the popular author of *Rhymes of Li Youcai* who used traditional forms and colloquial language enjoyed by illiterate peasants. Zhao's advocacy of popular literature had a strong influence on him. Another important mentor was the writer Zhang Tianyi, his tutor in '52 when he studied in the Literary Institute of the Writers' Association. In '57 his story *On the Cliff* won an award. But Deng considers his early writings too simple and stereotyped with their contrived happy

---

① 选自 Deng, Y. M. *Snuff-Bottles and Other Stories*. Gladys Yang (trans.). Beijing: Chinese Literature Press, 1986.

endings. "My stories had a tiger's head and snake's tail," he says.

After he was made a Rightist in'57 Deng worked for twenty years as a manual labourer in Beijing and the provinces. In'62 he went to the Northeast to work in a clock factory. As it had no dormitory he bought a shelter which he shared for six years with a Manchu. From this man and a Manchu actor he learned a great deal about old Beijing and the life of Manchus there.

After the fall of the "Gang of Four" he went on writing. *Our Army Commander*, which deals with Marshal Chen Yi, won an award in '78.

In 1979 Deng tried his hand at fiction with more local colour. The Gang had tried to stamp out old customs, an intrinsic part of the cultural heritage, but some of these were reappearing and Deng believed that young people should learn about them. His *Taoran Pavilion Park*, set in Beijing, won a short story prize, increasing his confidence. He followed it up with *Black Cat*, *White Cat*, *Han the Forger*, *Na Wu*, *Snuff-Bottles* and other tales about life in Beijing past and present with obscure townsfolk as the main characters. This illustrates a new trend in Chinese writing. For years writers here were fettered, required to write about workers, peasants and soldiers. Intellectuals were not eligible as heroes, let alone effete Bannermen at the turn of the century. In the fifties even Lao She's superb play *Teahouse*, dealing with the lives of ordinary citizens in three historical periods in Beijing, was criticized in some quarters as unhealthy. Now writers can face up to reality and tackle any theme—provided they make no attack on the socialist system.

There has been an upsurge of popular literature, both indigenous and imported, with translations ranging from Jules Verne and Dumas to Agatha Christie and Arthur Haley. Deng's Beijing stories have the best qualities of popular literature, as they are compulsive reading with unforgettable characters and packed with information. Indeed, one of his reasons for writing about old Beijing is to fill in a gap in young people's general knowledge. Ironically, for a country with such a long history which has produced brilliant historians, history teaching in Chinese schools tends to be excessively dull. For generations most Chinese learned their history from classical novels, the theatre or story-tellers, and few novelists in recent years have tackled historical themes. Deng's work is thus much to be welcomed. And he was bold to enter this field, inevitably inviting comparison with one of the greatest writers of this century—Lao She, Beijing born and bred.

Deng recalls that after the "Gang of Four" was toppled new fiction appeared like mushrooms after rain, and he wondered how best he could make his contribution. Comparing his qualifications with those of other writers, he decided that many ex-Rightists could write about their painful experiences, and he was less skilled than Wang Meng or Liu Binyan in highlighting social problems. His forte was an extensive knowledge of Beijing and its history, people of all walks of life there and their social customs. During the "cultural revolution" when there was a dearth of novels, he had bought some works on antiques and Buddhism, and the knowledge so acquired became grist to his mill, as did the anecdotes he picked up from actors, bird-fanciers and old Beijing residents who went each morning with him to Taoran Pavilion Park to practise Chinese boxing.

Deng's wife in her article introducing *Snuff-Bottles* explains her misgivings when he chose this new line. She was reassured by the glowing reviews he received. He has been compared with Balzac because he writes the history that many historians omit, the history of social conventions and everyday life. Others have compared his work with genre paintings, for he covers a broad canvas, achieves a rich texture, and graphically conjures up bygone times researched in detail.

Many Chinese writers today are drawing on Western techniques. Deng, however, has developed traditional story-telling. *Snuff-Bottles* has a lead-in about snuff-bottles before the action starts, a practice dating back to the stories told in market-places in 11th-century China. Similarly, it ends with a hint that there is more to come. Deng also has the old story-tellers' mastery of thumbnail sketches and dramatic dialogue. His characters come to life, each one unique, each completely convincing, and their setting is unmistakably old Beijing, arousing nostalgia in senior citizens.

The complex characters created by Deng are a far cry from the stereotyped heroes and villains common in the first thirty years after Liberation. They are more reminiscent of those drawn by Lu Xun, some being failures or outcasts with few redeeming features. Na Wu, the incompetent son of a bankrupt Manchu family, is arrogant, dishonest and easily fooled. His decadence is tragic. Like him affable, timid Wu Shibao, descended from martial Bannermen, has been brought up with no trade to live on his pension. He sets great store by "face". When his pension stops he is willing to work for a living only if he cannot be seen demeaning himself in this way. He fails to take up arms to resist the imperialist troops, but refuses to disgrace China by painting foreign invaders inside his snuff-bottles. He is lucky to be taken in hand by the potter's strong-minded daughter.

Not long after Liberation Zhou Enlai warned the children of high-ranking cadres to learn a lesson from the degeneracy of the descendants of Manchu Bannermen, and not to live as parasites cashing in on the achievements of their parents. Deng's message to the younger generation today is somewhat similar. He wants them to understand that China had reached a dead end, could only be revitalized by revolution; to realize how New China has evolved from the old, and work hard to build up the country.

Deng decided to write about snuff-bottles after reading an account of Wang Xisan, a painter of snuff-bottle interiors, and his trials during the "cultural revolution". Wang painted bottles for his brigade to sell to finance their water conservancy project. He was training apprentices and doing well till the Red Guards attacked him for his "decadence". Deng then read up on snuff-bottles and made friends with old craftsmen, including Wang Xisan. While collecting material he was struck by the patriotism and strong sense of self-respect of Chinese craftsmen. In a temple in Foshan he saw a bronze incense-burner cast during the Boxer Uprising, with four legs planted on four foreign aggressors. The man who made that did so at the risk of his life. This helped Deng to visualize an honest, high-minded craftsman who would never stoop to flattery or deceit, and so he created the memorable potter Xie.

We look forward to reading more of these characters' adventures. Unfortunately Deng's output has been slowed down by his duties in the secretariat of the Writers' Association. However, he plans to write a sequel describing the fate of snuff-bottle painters from the founding of the Republic in 1911 to the invasion of China by Japan. A further sequel is planned to deal with the post-Liberation period.

十三

《张洁小说选》序[①]

Preface to *Love Must Not Be Forgotten*

"I once thought I was like a darting dragonfly, with no goals in life and no substantial pursuits. Only through literature did I discover myself. Successful or not, I am still very persevering... Some people spend a whole lifetime and still do not find or understand themselves. Others, of course, have a much easier time of it. For me, it took all of forty years." So writes Zhang Jie in an essay about writing, an essay titled *My Boat*.

She was born in 1937. During the Anti-Japanese War[②] her parents separated and her mother, a teacher, brought her up in a village in Liaoning Province. She had a passion for music and literature, but was persuaded to study economics as being of more use to New China. Upon graduating from the People's University she worked for some years in an industrial bureau, then in a film studio where she got a chance to write two film scripts, *The Search* and *We Are Still Young*. She is now a full-time writer, one of China's most popular authors.

Zhang Jie did not start to write until after the fall of the "Gang of

---

① 选自 Zhang, J. *Love Must Not Be Forgotten*. Gladys Yang (trans.). Beijing: Chinese Literature Press/ San Francisco: China Books & Periodicals Inc., 1987/ 1989.

② 编者注:"抗日战争"的规范表达参见前文,此不赘。

Four" and end of the Cultural Revolution. She was then forty years old. In 1978, her story *The Music of the Forests* won a prize as one of the best short stories of that year. Since then she has written many stories, essays, novellas and a novel, *Leaden Wings*, which recently won China's prestigious Mao Dun Literary Prize. She is a member of the Chinese Writers' Association and now works for the Beijing branch of the China Federation of Literary and Art Circles. She has visited West Germany and some other European countries, and participated in the seminar of Chinese and American writers held in Beijing in October, 1984.

Her earlier themes were mainly the problems of youth and love. She had divorced her husband because he maltreated her, and in a society still influenced by traditional ideas that was considered a stigma. She thus bitterly experienced the discrimination against women about which she writes so pungently.

Zhang Jie's later themes cover a wide range. Whether writing satirically or in a romantic vein she tackles current social problems with deep insight, lashing out at male supremacy, hypocrisy, corruption, bureaucracy, nepotism and other malpractices holding up China's advance. Some Westerners on the look-out for dissidents find it strange that she exposes the seamy side of China so ruthlessly, yet defends the socialist system as that best suited to China. Zhang Jie herself sees no contradiction here. Her responsibility as a writer, she feels, is to educate her readers and inspire them to eradicate social evils. As she puts it in *The Ark*, writing of a woman her own age: "She possessed neither the unshakeable optimism of previous generations, nor the blind pessimism of the younger generation. Her generation was the most confident, the most clear-minded and the most able to face up to reality."

From her teens on Zhang Jie took part in many political movements. A firm believer in socialism, she joined the Chinese Communist Party at an early age. But during the Cultural Revolution she was fiercely criticized and had to write a self-criticism in which she cited her own weak sense of class struggle and her individualism. Collegues attributed this "weakness" to the influence of the western novels she loved to read, novels of the 18th and 19th centuries. Now Zhang Jie recalls with some pride that she behaved decently in the Cultural Revolution, never betraying or slandering other people, because she loved the humanism in classical literature.

She finds it stimulating to be under fire. I have watched her several times being interviewed: she welcomes provocative questions and swiftly rebuts them or skillfully evades them.

Zhang Jie deserves credit as a pioneer who highlighted women's problems before authorities fully recognized them or took official action. As a consequence some of her stories have been most controversial. The first story in this collection, *Love Must Not Be Forgotten*, caused quite a furor when it was published in 1979. It justified love outside marriage, albeit of the most platonic kind, implying that the only moral marriages were those based on love. It also suggested that a girl should remain single unless she could find a man she loved and respected. Because of this, critics accused Zhang Jie of undermining social morality—most Chinese take it for granted that everyone must marry. She received anonymous letters attacking her. But she also received letters approving her stand and her courage.

The Ark proved no less controversial. This novella describes three women who are divorced or live apart from their husbands, and how hard it is for them to find suitable work and retain their self-respect in a male-dominated society. Some readers applauded Zhang Jie's fearlessness and acclaimed this as China's first feminist novel, though she denies that she is a feminist—she writes on all manner of themes. Certain detractors denounced her for encouraging women to let their resentment against men embitter them, so that they behave in an unwomanly way and are not really happy. Others claimed that she distorted socialism by painting too black a picture of women's difficulties. Yet others took an opposite line, objecting that most of the characters in this story were recognizable as living individuals. In this connection Zhang Jie wrote in *My Boat*: "Characters in literary works are perhaps composites of many people in real life, but they are still fictitious, something created by the author through logical reasoning."

The other stories in this collection gave rise to less public discussion than *The Ark* and *Love Must Not Be Forgotten*. All are sensitively written with feeling and insight. Their detailed descriptions of everyday life and the thoughts and hopes of widely differing characters should shed light on Chinese reality for foreign readers. For although China has opened up for some years now, to many westerners the Chinese are still an inscrutable people. Zhang Jie presents them as credible human beings. During her recent visit to Europe she was reported on in all the main West German papers, and the title of one feature article was: "A Far-away Country Gradually Moves Nearer." This delighted Zhang Jie, who believes that most of the world's troubles arise from misunderstanding—from lack of communication—and modern Chinese writers are best fitted to introduce their country abroad.

Her important novel *Leaden Wings*, not included in this collection, has as its central theme the modernization of industry. The publication of this book aroused further controversy. Exposing various abuses and man-made obstacles to modernization, it came under fire for "attacking socialism." But many readers welcomed it as painting a truthful picture of modern Chinese society. Her fan mail included the assurance, "If ever you're in trouble, come to me."

Zhang Jie is physically frail, mentally tough. She has heart trouble and easily grows tired. One evening she called when we were having a party at which some young people were dancing. She exclaimed, "I can't stay, I might have a heart attack."

Another visit was equally typical. Zhang Jie appeared, the light of battle in her eye and a tape-recorder in her handbag. She had been confronting someone who had passed on to her the accusations that *Leaden Wings* was "anti-Party, anti-socialism." Taping the interview, Zhang Jie refuted these charges, declaring, "I wrote that book precisely because I'm for socialism and China's modernization." Then, on her way to our flat, she passed the free market outside our gate and felt it her duty as a Party member to intervene so as to stop a peddler from charging exorbitant prices.

Because Zhang Jie is thoroughly militant, with a strong sense of social responsibility, she will no doubt continue to tackle sensitive issues with disregard for her own welfare. While affirming her complete faith in socialism she will go on exposing its present shortcomings, thus courting criticism from her more conservative readers. In *My Boat* she envisages herself putting out to sea and braving angry waves.

> ... I renovate my boat, patch it up and repaint it, so that it will last a little longer. I set sail again. People, houses, trees on shore become smaller and smaller and I am reluctant to leave them. But my boat cannot stay beached for ever. What use is a boat without the sea?
>
> In the distance I see waves rolling towards me. Rolling continuously. I know that one day I will be smashed to bits by those waves, but this is the fate of all boats—what other sort of end could they meet?

十四

《冯骥才小说选》序[①]

Preface to *The Miraculous Pigtail*

Feng Jicai was born in 1942 in Tianjin, the north China city which forms the background to many of his stories. As a boy Feng had wide interests: novels and classical Chinese poetry, classical Western music, history, sport and, above all, traditional Chinese art and folk art. After leaving middle school, while painting in his spare time he became a professional athlete playing centre in the Tianjin Basketball Team till he broke some bones and had to give up the game. Even today he looks like a tall athlete and is known to his friends as Big Feng. For over a dozen years Feng worked in the Tianjin Painting and Calligraphy Studio; but this peaceful period of his life was shattered by the "cultural revolution". His house was raided by Red Guards who drove him out so that he and his wife had to live in a small shabby room with no furniture but two "beds" made of bricks and boards. The studio was converted into a printing-mill and he became a travelling salesman, coming into contact with workers, clerks, peasants and handicraftsmen. He was appalled by the heart-breaking experiences of these ordinary people. Near where he lived, for instance, was a river where almost every day suicides drowned, some women tying

---

① 选自：Feng，J. C. *The Miraculous Pigtail*. Gladys Yang（trans.）. Beijing: Chinese Literature Press，1987.

small children to their waists before plunging to their death. He tried to imagine the horrors that had driven them to this, and made up stories about them. This was the start of his urge to write. For it seemed to him that the tragedies being enacted had never been described in books, that they laid bare people's true characters, and if he could record them this would be of value to later generations. So he locked himself in to write. If there came a knock on the door he hid his manuscripts away, sometimes panicking and taking them out to burn them. In this way he wrote about a million unpublished words which, he says, had only two readers: "God and myself." Nonetheless this was useful training besides showing his strong sense of social responsibility. He recalls with satisfaction that in those years he never wrote for money or to please those in power.

In 1973 Feng started collecting folktales and studying the local customs and history of Tianjin. The next year he transferred to the Tianjin Industrial Arts College to teach traditional painting.

Feng made a special study of the Boxer Movement at the turn of the century, a movement maligned by the Manchu rulers as well as most foreigners. Towards the end of the Qing Dynasty part of Tianjin had been divided up into foreign concessions where imperialist consuls, businessmen and missionaries were a law unto themselves. By 1900 such foreigners in many parts of China had aroused the opposition of the Society of Righteousness and Harmony, known in the West as The Boxers because many of its members drilled in the traditional martial arts. Feng collaborated with Li Dingxing to write *The Boxers*, a historical novel with strong local colour and sense of period, praised for its exposure of imperialism. After its publication in 1977 he became a professional writer in the Tianjin branch of the Writers' Association. He is now its vice-chairman.

Feng is a prolific and versatile writer, interested in social problems, in history, the history of painting, the theory of art and folk art. Apart from his fiction he often writes several articles on different themes at the same time. His subject matter and style are original. His short story "The Carved Pipe" and his novella *Ah!* both won national awards.

The Miraculous Pigtail, which won an award for the best novelette of 1984, is representative of Feng's historical works, giving a vivid picture of old Tianjin and its underworld, of the foreign concessions and the Boxers who tried to overthrow them. Folk legends have found their way into this story, sometimes introducing a note of melodrama. Another work of this genre is his *Three-Inch Golden Lotus*. This rather harrowing story about the cruel practice of foot-binding is also interspersed with descriptions of local customs, delicacies, entertainments and strange tales. Tianjin used to be thought a drab place compared with Beijing. Feng shows how colourful it really was and is the city's best spokesman.

However, he also addresses himself to subjects of nationwide significance. His new work *A Decade According to a Hundred People* records the nightmares of the "cultural revolution" as revealed by a hundred ordinary people. He believes that it is wrong to forget such horrors, than we must probe into their cause to prevent any repetition of those nightmares. Realizing that many atrocities were committed out of loyalty to a wrong political line and because humanism was considered bourgeois or revisionist, he concludes that if humanitarian values were to be swept aside again it would lead to fresh tragedies. Thus this book about the past serves to light the way forward.

十五

《沉重的翅膀》译序[①]

Preface to *Leaden Wings*

Zhang Jie is one of China's most interesting and controversial writers. She was born in 1937 in Beijing. Her father, a minor civil servant, and her mother, a teacher, separated when she was a child. She read voraciously at school and wanted to specialize in literature, but like many idealistic youngsters of her generation was induced to study a subject 'of more use' to the building of socialism, and graduated in 1960 from the Economics Department of the People's University. For some years she worked in the National Bureau of Mechanical Equipment, where she gained considerable knowledge about industry as well as human nature. But literature continued to be her main interest.

She did not begin to write till she was forty, just after the fall of Jiang Qing's Gang of Four. In 1978 she joined the Writers' Association; in 1980 she joined the Chinese Communist Party; and in 1982 she became a salaried member of the Beijing Branch of the China Federation of Literary and Art Circles, able to devote all her time to writing.

Between 1949 and 1977 there had been pressure on Chinese writers to gear their writing to the current ultra-Left political line, and subjects such as

---

① 选自：Zhang, J. *Leaden Wings*. Gladys Yang (trans.). London: Virago Press, 1987.

democracy, love unrelated to revolution, or the value of the individual were virtually taboo. The Third Plenary Session of the Party in 1978 condemned the previous ultra-Left line and called for a realistic approach to China's problems. It was said that practice was the criterion of truth, which should be sought from the facts. This encouraged writers to write more honestly and tackle a wider range of themes. It was under these circumstances that Zhang Jie began to write, addressing herself to a number of social problems.

The story that brought her into the public eye was 'Love Must Not Be Forgotten'. The Chinese media often imply that an individual's highest fulfilment comes from serving the people and making a contribution to the country. In 'Love Must Not Be Forgotten' Zhang Jie argues that this is not enough. The quality of life depends to a great extent on personal relations, and marriage is crucially important. In China all men and women are expected to marry. But what if you cannot find a congenial partner? The narrator of Zhang Jie's story is in this dilemma. At thirty she is practically 'on the shelf', yet has no potential husband she can love and respect. She finally decides to remain single if no kindred spirit appears despite social disapproval. Chinese moral values today are a mixture of socialist ethics and traditional conventions. And nowhere is the influence of tradition stronger than in the field of marriage. The mother of the narrator was a divorcee who till the end of her life was passionately though platonically in love with a married man, who returned her love at a distance. Her daughter therefore questions the current marriage conventions which inhibit genuine personal affection, and hopes that they will have changed by the time socialism is fully realized. These sentiments aroused enthusiastic support from many young readers. Some critics, however, accused Zhang Jie of a 'petty-bourgeois mentality', of attacking the moral basis of society and of being unduly influenced by such western writers as Chekhov and Hardy. She also received anonymous letters accusing her of immorality because of her defence of love—even in the purest form—outside marriage, and because she is a divorcee.

Leaden Wings, published in 1980, is a novel which has as its central theme the modernization of Chinese industry. This is a topic of vital importance. For many years China's industrial growth was distorted and hampered by policies that paid too little attention to economic realities and were highly suspicious of allowing market forces much play. The results included unnecessarily low living standards for the people and appalling waste and inefficiency. Since the late 1970s a drastic reform programme has begun with the aim of bringing China's industry up to world standards, but at the time the novel is set it was facing formidable obstacles from officials who had made their careers under the old system.

In the Ministry of Heavy Industry are two opposing camps, the old guard and the reformists. There are officials concerned only with clinging to power; genuine followers of the ultra-Left line who believe that any other way of running industry except 'putting politics in command' is revisionist; men devoted to the people's interests, determined to end corruption and inefficiency; others who see the need for reform but are not prepared to stick their necks out to achieve it; and cynics who take no side, waiting to see who gains the upper hand.

In addition to the struggle between these officials, Zhang Jie presents junior members of the ministry, factory workers, the wives and children of the protagonists, and other peripheral characters. The story is open-ended, and it is tantalizing not to know what becomes of all the individuals who have aroused our interest. The aim of the novel, however, is not to tell their story but to give a picture of a society in a state of flux and to serve as a vehicle for Zhang Jie's views on the need for more democratic and scientific approaches, recognition of the value of the individual, understanding of the generation gap, and an overhauling of social morality by throwing out vestiges of feudalism.

Thus the inadequacy of the present marriage system is highlighted, this time mainly from the viewpoint of men. Out of six married couples described only one is happy. In China men hold power and are the ones who formulate moral values. Yet where love is concerned they too, if they want to retain their social positions, are victims of the ethics they themselves have created or condoned. Vice-minister Zheng has no love for the wife who has been unfaithful to him, yet in public he plays the part of a devoted husband in order not to spoil his political image. This hypocrisy is the main flaw in an otherwise admirable character dedicated to reform, and as a result his personal life is empty and meaningless. Fang, another advocate of modernization, when sent down to the countryside during the Cultural Revolution had fallen in love with a young widow after his wife had left him. He did not marry her though, thinking that once he was rehabilitated such a marriage would count against him; so he too has thrown away his chance of personal happiness. In accounts like these Zhang Jie makes clear her belief that men and women must together overthrow the outdated aspects of traditional moral values and establish genuine socialist ethics if they are to find fulfilment and happiness in their personal relations.

Zhang Jie is reflected in several characters, among them the uncompromising woman reporter Autumn, who tackles problems she is incapable of solving. But the author admits that the character who speaks most for her is Ho Jiabin, a minor official in the ministry whose unorthodox and outspoken views are used by his enemies to keep him out of the Party.

The publication of *Leaden Wings* sparked off conflicting reactions. Young people in industrial ministries commented that it painted a true picture. Some officials, outraged by Zhang Jie's barbed satire, accused her of making a slanderous attack on the Party and socialism. Her Party secretary called her in to answer their accusations. Zhang Jie denied the charges and insisted that she wrote this novel because she was a communist who supported socialism and the modernization of China.

With so many problems inherited from the past, so many man-made obstacles, will China's modernization programme succeed in rising on its leaden wings and soaring ahead to efficiency and affluence? Only the future can show. Zhang Jie is optimistic, putting her faith in the government's realistic policy and the efforts of China's millions.

'The Ark', her next major work, is about the difficulties of three divorcees trying to live independent and dignified lives in a man's world. It has been acclaimed as an original and important feminist novella. It has also been criticized on the grounds that the three central figures let their resentment against men embitter them and make them unwomanly.

Another of Zhang Jie's recent works, 'The Time Is Not Yet Ripe', won the National Best Story Award for 1984. Its theme is not unlike that of *Leaden Wings*. To facilitate China's modernization, elderly administrators are being required to retire and younger, abler men are being given leading posts. This story satirizes a bureaucratic Party secretary who schemes—but fails—to sabotage the promotion of a capable young engineer. Here again Zhang Jie expresses her conviction that in spite of all obstructions China's economy will forge ahead.

This translation of *Leaden Wings* is based on the version published in 1980 by the People's Literature Publishing House, which is rather long-winded and diffuse. In my opinion Chinese publishers do not do enough to encourage writers to compress and cut their work. Many of Zhang Jie's detailed descriptions and interior monologues are effective and subtle, giving fascinating insights into contemporary Chinese life and ways of thinking. But in places the arguments about politics and economic policy go on for far too long. The detailed accounts of procedure to streamline production, of behaviourism and the methods used by advanced countries to make industry more efficient, are skipped by most Chinese readers. As appreciation of these arguments requires an inside knowledge of the Chinese economy around 1980 they bear the main cuts that have been made with the author's permission.

Because so many characters appear in *Leaden Wings*, it is difficult for foreign readers to differentiate between their names. In general these are written according to the Chinese phonetic alphabet; but I have changed the surname 'He' to 'Ho' to avoid confusion with the pronoun 'he'. I have also given some of the main women characters English names.

Finally I would like to thank Bill Jenner who spent his spare time in the sweltering Beijing summer improving my translation and Delia Davin who polished it once more, arranged its publication and checked the proofs for me.

十六

《龙的传说》译序[①]

Preface to *Dragon Tales: A Collection of Chinese Stories*

For all that it has never been seen, references to that mystic creature of ancient legend the dragon abound in the Chinese classics, and besides the *Book of Changes*' "dragon flying in the sky", folk legends such as that of the flood dragon's journey to the sea have prompted speculation that the dragon was in antiquity a tribal totem whose image has over the centuries been enriched and taken on new guises to the point where it has a diversity of forms, each with its appropriate designation.

Described in legend as unique, miraculous and protean, the dragon has the ability to raise floods, bring thunder and lightning, summon up storms and transform itself at will; its mighty power is seen as the embodiment of all that is imposing and majestic. And the sovereigns of old China, no doubt in a bid to enlist the creature's limitless awe, likened themselves to embodiments of the dragon, clothing themselves in its almighty dignity. Thus the dragon became the symbol of princely power, acquiring by a deal of spurious analogy a concomitant sanctity proof against all blasphemy.

Yet to the minds of the common people it suggested, far from dread, an omen of good luck and fortune, an object of love and praise and the

---

① 选自 Yang, Gladys. *Dragon Tales: A Collection of Chinese Stories*. Beijing: Chinese Literature Press, 1988.

matter of many an excellent tale and legend down the ages.

The thirty-five stories collected here, drawn partly from classical literature and partly from traditional popular legend, include the tale of the ascent to heaven on a dragon's back of Huang Di, the race ancestor of the Chinese, a legend hoary enough to have been quoted in the first century BC in Sima Qian's *Records of the Historian* and one which was to exert a far-reaching influence on the dragon's position in after ages. Yet the genre which endeared itself most and spread farthest was that of the dragoness, and this has been much pored over by folklorists and students of popular literature. Current among many of the peoples of China in variations according to their several manners and customs, this has provoked immortal pieces from the brushes of the past, prominent among them Li Chaowei's "The Dragon King's Daughter" in the Tang Dynasty. Pu Songling's "The Rakshas and the Sea Market" is a powerful Qing Dynasty reworking of this theme, where the writer attacks the iniquities of the feudal system via the medium of a weird narrative of the dragon palace beneath the waves, where the dragon woman is a picture of oriental charm, virtuous in her beauty, urbane in her passion and punctilious towards love. "Li Jing" here ingeniously tells how man took over the function of the legendary dragon as a bringer of rain; "Short-Tailed Old Li" with its fight between the black dragon and the white dragon is a prime example of the many myths linking the names of mountains and rivers with dragons: these and many others, like the legend still current among the Dai that the dragon is the guardian of the village, are thought-provoking stories with a strong and curious appeal.

This volume may help to probe the mystery of how and why the dragon, through all the natural accretions of cultural history millennia long, came to symbolize the spirit of the Chinese people.

第二编

戴乃迭民间文学英译

一

柳毅传(唐·李朝威)[①]

柳毅传

李朝威

仪凤中,有儒生柳毅者,应举下第,将还湘滨。念乡人有客于泾阳者。遂往告别。去至六七里,鸟起马惊,疾逸道左。又六七里,乃止。

见有妇人,牧羊于道畔。毅怪视之,乃殊色也。然而蛾脸不舒,巾袖无光,凝听翔立,若有所伺。毅诘之曰:"子何苦而自辱如是?"妇始笑而谢,终泣而对曰:"贱妾不幸,今日见辱问于长者。然而恨贯肌骨,亦何能愧避,幸一闻焉。妾,洞庭龙君小女也。父母配嫁泾川次子,而夫婿乐逸,为婢仆所惑,日以厌薄。既而将诉于舅姑,舅姑爱其子,不能御。逮诉频切,又得罪舅姑。舅姑毁黜以至此。"言讫,歔欷流涕,悲不自胜。又曰:"洞庭于兹,相远不知其几多也?长天茫茫,信耗莫通,心目断尽,无所知哀。闻君将还吴,密通洞庭。或以尺书,寄托侍者,未卜将以为可乎?"毅曰:"吾义夫也。闻子之说,气血俱动,恨无毛羽,不能奋飞。是何可否之谓乎!然而洞庭,深水也。吾行尘间,宁可致意邪?唯恐道途显晦,不相通达,致负诚托,又乖恳愿。子有何术,可导我邪?"女悲泣且谢,曰:"负载

---

① 中文选自:卢冀野.唐宋传奇选.上海:商务印书馆,1947:21-31;英译文选自:Li, C. W. The Dragon King's Daughter. In *Dragon Tales: A Collection of Chinese Stories*. Gladys Yang (trans.). Beijing: Chinese Literature Press, 1988: 14-30.

珍重，不复言矣，脱获回耗，虽死必谢。君不许，何敢言。既许而问，则洞庭之与京邑，不足为异也。"毅请闻之。女曰："洞庭之阴，有大橘树焉，乡人谓之社橘。君当解去兹带，束以他物。然后叩树三发，当有应者。因而随之，无有碍矣。幸君子书叙之外，悉以心诚之话倚托，千万无渝！"毅曰："敬闻命矣。"女遂于襦间解书，再拜以进，东望愁泣，若不自胜。毅深为之戚。乃置书囊中，因复问曰："吾不知子之牧羊，何所用哉？神祇岂宰杀乎？"女曰："非羊也，雨工也。""何为雨工？"曰："雷霆之类也。"毅顾视之，则皆矫顾怒步，饮龁甚异。而大小毛角，则无别羊焉。毅又曰："吾为使者，他日归洞庭，幸勿相避。"女曰："宁止不避，当如亲戚耳。"语竟，引别东去。不数十步，回望女与羊，俱亡所见矣。

其夕，至邑而别其友。月余到乡。还家，乃访于洞庭。洞庭之阴，果有社橘。遂易带向树。三击而止。俄有武夫出于波间，再拜请曰："贵客将自何所至也？"毅不告其实，曰："走谒大王耳。"武夫揭水指路，引毅以进。谓毅曰："当闭目，数息可达矣。"毅如其言，遂至其宫。始见台阁相向，门户千万，奇草珍木，无所不有。夫止毅，停于大室之隅，曰："客当居此以伺焉。"毅曰："此何所也？"夫曰："此灵虚殿也。"谛视之，则人间珍宝，毕尽于此。柱以白璧，砌以青玉，床以珊瑚，帘以水精，雕琉璃于翠楣，饰琥珀于虹栋。奇秀深香，不可殚言。然而王久不至。毅谓夫曰："洞庭君安在哉？"夫曰："吾君方幸玄珠阁，与太阳道士讲《火经》，少选当毕。"毅曰："何谓《火经》？"夫曰："吾君，龙也，龙以水为神，举一滴可包陵谷。道士，乃人也。人以火为神圣，发一灯可燎阿房。然而灵用不同，玄化各异。太阳道士精于人理，吾君邀以听焉。"

语毕而宫门辟。景从云合，而见一人，披紫衣，执青玉。夫跃曰："此吾君也！"乃至前以告之。君望毅而问曰："岂非人间之人乎？"毅对曰："然。"毅即设拜，命亦拜，命坐于灵虚之下，谓毅曰："水府幽深，寡人暗昧，夫子不远千里，将有为乎？"毅曰："毅，大王之乡人也。长于楚，游学于秦。昨下第，闲驱泾水之涘，见大王爱女牧羊于野，风环雨鬓，所不忍视。毅因诘之。谓毅曰：'为夫婿所薄，舅姑不念，以至于此。'悲泗淋漓，诚怛人心。遂托书于毅。毅许之，今以至此。"

因取书进之。洞庭君览毕,以袖掩面而泣曰:"老父之罪,不诊鉴听,坐贻聋瞽,使闺窗孺弱,远罹搆害。公,乃陌上人也,而能急之。幸被齿发,何敢负德!"词毕,又哀咤良久。左右皆流涕。时有宦人密侍君者,君以书授之,令达宫中。

须臾,宫中皆恸哭。君惊谓左右曰:"疾告宫中,无使有声,恐钱塘所知。"毅曰:"钱塘,何人也?"曰:"寡人之爱弟。昔为钱塘长,今则致政矣。"毅曰:"何故不使知?"曰:"以其勇过人耳。昔尧遭洪水九年者,乃此子一怒也。近与天将失意,塞其五山。上帝以寡人有薄德于古今,遂宽其同气之罪。然犹縻系于此,故钱塘之人,日来候焉。"语未毕,而大声忽发,天拆地裂。宫殿摆簸,云烟沸涌。俄有赤龙长千余尺,电目血舌,朱鳞火鬣,项掣金锁,锁牵玉柱,千雷万霆,激绕其身,霰雪雨雹,一时皆下。乃擘青天而飞去。毅恐蹶仆地。君亲起持之曰:"无惧。固无害。"毅良久稍安,乃获自定。

因告辞曰:"愿得生还,以避复来。"君曰:"必不如此。其去则然,其来则不然,幸为少尽缱绻。"因命酌互举,以款人事。俄而祥风庆云,融融怡怡,幢节玲珑,箫韶以随。红妆千万,笑语熙熙,中有一人,自然蛾眉,明珰满身,绡谷参差,迫而视之,乃前寄辞者。然而若喜若悲,零泪如丝。须臾红烟蔽其左,紫气舒其右,香气环旋,入于宫中。君笑谓毅:"泾水之囚人至矣。"君乃辞归宫中。须臾,又闻怨苦,久而不已。

有顷,君复出,与毅饮食。又有一人,披紫裳,执青玉,貌耸神溢,立于君左。君谓毅曰:"此钱塘也。"毅起,趋拜之,钱塘亦尽礼相接,谓毅曰:"女侄不幸,为顽童所辱。赖明君子信义昭彰,致达远冤。不然也,是为泾陵之土矣。飨德怀恩,词不悉心。"毅扮退辞谢,俯仰唯唯。然后回告兄曰:"向者辰发灵虚,巳至泾阳,午战于彼,未还于此。中间驰至九天,以告上帝。帝知其冤,而宥其失。前所谴责,因而获免。然而刚肠激发,不遑辞候。惊扰宫中,复忤宾客。愧惕惭惧,不知所失。"因退而再拜。君曰:"所杀几何?"曰:"六十万。""伤稼乎?"曰:"八百里。""无情郎安在?"曰:"食之矣!"君怃然曰:"顽童之为是心也,诚不可忍。然汝亦太草草。赖上帝灵圣,谅其至冤。不然者,吾何辞焉。从此已去,勿复如是。"钱塘复再拜。

是夕，遂宿毅于凝光殿。明日。又宴毅于凝碧宫。会友戚，张广乐，具以醪醴，罗以甘洁。初，笳角鼙鼓，旌旗剑戟，舞万夫于其右。中有一夫前曰："此《钱塘破阵乐》。"旌鉦杰气，顾骤悍慓。坐客视之，毛发皆竖，复有金石丝竹，罗绮珠翠，舞千女于其左。中有一女前进曰："此《贵主还宫乐》。"清音宛转，如诉如慕，坐客听之，不觉泪下。二舞既毕，龙君大悦，锡以纨绮，颁于舞人，然后密席贯坐，纵酒极娱。酒酣，洞庭君乃击席而歌曰："大天苍苍兮，大地茫茫。人各有志兮，何可思量，狐神鼠圣兮，薄社依墙。雷霆一发兮，其孰敢当。荷贞人兮信义长，令骨肉兮还故乡。齐言惭愧兮何时忘！"洞庭君歌罢，钱塘君再拜而歌曰："上天配合兮，生死有途。此不当妇兮，彼不当夫。腹心辛苦兮，泾水之隅。风霜满鬓兮，雨雪罗襦。赖明公兮引素书，令骨肉兮家如初。永言珍重兮无时无。"钱塘君歌阕，洞庭君俱起，奉觞于毅。毅踧踖而受爵，饮讫，复以二觞奉二君。乃歌曰："碧云悠悠兮，泾水东流。伤美人兮，雨泣花愁。尺书远达兮，以解君忧。哀冤果雪兮，还处其休。荷和雅兮感甘羞。山家寂寞兮难久留，欲将辞去兮悲绸缪。"歌罢，皆呼万岁。洞庭君因出碧玉箱，贮以开水犀；钱塘君复出红珀盘，贮以照夜玑；皆起进毅。毅辞谢而受，然后宫中之人，咸以绡彩珠璧，投于毅侧，重叠焕赫，须臾埋没前后。毅笑语四顾，愧揖不暇。洎酒阑欢极，毅辞起，复宿于凝光殿。

翌日，又宴毅于清光阁。钱塘因酒，作色，踞谓毅曰："不闻猛石可裂不可卷，义士可杀不可羞邪？愚有衷曲，欲一陈于公。如可，则俱履云霄；如不可，则皆夷粪壤。足下以为何如哉？"毅曰："请闻之。"钱塘曰："泾阳之妻，则洞庭君之爱女也。淑性茂质，为九姻所重。不幸见辱于匪人。今则绝矣。将欲求托高义，世为亲戚。使受恩者知其所归，怀爱者知其所付，岂不为君子始终之道耶？"毅肃然而作，欻然而笑曰："诚不知钱塘君孱困如是！毅始闻跨九州，怀五岳，泄其愤怒。复见断锁金，掣玉柱，赴其急难。毅以为刚决明直，无如君者。盖犯之者不避其死，感之者不爱其生，此真丈夫之志。奈何箫管方洽，亲宾正和，不顾其道，以威加人？岂仆之素望哉！若遇公于洪波之中，玄山之间，鼓以鳞须，被以云雨，将迫毅以死,毅则以禽兽视之,亦何恨哉。今体被衣冠,坐谈礼义,尽五常之志性,穷百行之微旨,虽人世豪杰,有不如者。况江河灵类乎?而欲以蠢然之躯,悍然之性,乘酒假气,将迫于人,岂近直哉!且毅之质,不足以藏王一甲之间。然而敢以不伏之心,胜王不道之气。惟王筹之!"钱塘乃逡巡致谢曰:"寡人生长宫房,不闻正论。向者词述疏狂,妄突高明。退自循顾,戾不容责。幸君子不为此乖间可也。"其夕,复饮宴,其乐如旧。毅与钱塘,遂为知心友。

明日,毅辞归。洞庭君夫人别宴毅于潜景殿。男女仆妾等,悉出预会。夫人泣谓毅曰:"骨肉受君子深恩,恨不得展愧戴,遂至睽别。"使前泾阳女当席拜毅以致谢。夫人又曰:"此别岂有复相遇之日乎?"毅始虽不诺钱塘之请,然当此席,殊有叹恨之色。宴罢,辞别,满宫悽然。赠遗珍宝,怪不可述。毅于是复循途出江岸,见从者十余人,担囊以随,至其家而辞去。毅因适广陵宝肆,鬻其所得,百未发一,财已盈兆。故淮右富族,咸以为莫如。

遂娶于张氏,亡,又娶韩氏。数月,韩氏又亡。徙家金陵。常以鳏旷多感,或谋新匹。有媒氏告曰:"有卢氏女,范阳人也。父名曰浩,尝为清流宰。晚岁好道,独游云泉,今则不知所在矣。母曰郑氏。前年适清河张氏,不幸而张夫早亡。母怜其少,惜其慧美,欲择德以配焉。不识何如?"毅乃卜日就礼。既而男女二姓,俱为豪族,法用礼物,尽其丰盛。金陵之士,莫不敬仰。居月余,毅因晚入户,视其妻,深觉类于龙女,而逸艳丰厚,则又过之。因与话昔事。妻谓毅曰:"人世岂有如是之理乎?"

经岁余,有一子,毅益重之。既产,逾月,乃秾饰换服,召亲戚,相会之间,笑谓毅曰:"君不忆余之于昔也?"毅曰:"夙为洞庭君传书,至今睽忆。"妻曰:"余即洞庭君之女也。泾川之冤,君使得白。衔君之恩,誓心求报。洎钱塘季父论亲不从,遂至睽违,天各一方,不能相问。父母欲配嫁于濯锦小儿某。惟以心誓难移,亲命难背,既为君子弃绝,分无见期。而当初之冤,难得以告诸父母,而誓报不得其志,复欲驰白于君子,值君子累娶,当娶于张,已而又娶于韩。迨张韩继卒,君卜居于兹,故余之父母乃喜余得遂报君之意。今日获奉君子,感喜终世,死无恨矣。"因呜咽,泣涕交下。

对毅曰:“始不言者,知君无重色之心。今乃言者,知君有感余之意。妇人匪薄,不足以确厚永心,故因君爱子,以托相生。未知君意如何? 愁惧兼心,不能自解。君附书之日,笑谓妾曰:‘他日归洞庭,慎无相避。’诚不知当此之际,君岂有意于今日之事乎? 其后季父请于君,君固不许。君乃诚将不可邪,抑忿然邪? 君其话之!”毅曰:“似有命者。仆始见君于长泾之隅,枉抑憔悴,诚有不平之志。然自约其心者,达君之冤,余无及也。以言慎勿相避者,偶然耳,岂有意哉。洎钱塘逼迫之际,唯理有不可直,乃激人之怒耳。夫始以义行为之志,宁有杀其婿而纳其妻者邪? 一不可也。某素以操真为志尚,宁有屈于己而伏于心者乎? 二不可也。且以率肆胸臆,酹酢纷纶,唯直是图,不遑避害。然而将别之日,见君有依然之容,心甚恨之。终以人事扼束,无由报谢。吁,今日,君,卢氏也,又家于人间。则吾始心未为惑矣。从此以往,永奉欢好,心无纤虑也。”妻因深感娇泣,良久不已。有顷,谓毅曰:“勿以他类,遂为无心,固当知报耳。夫龙寿万岁,今与君同之。水陆无往不适。君不以为妄也。”毅嘉之曰:“吾不知国客乃复为神仙之饵。”

乃相与觐洞庭。既至,而宾主盛礼,不可具纪。后居南海,仅四十年,其邸第舆马珍鲜服玩,虽侯伯之室,无以加也。毅之族咸遂濡泽。以其春秋积序,容状不衰,南海之人,靡不惊异。

洎开元中,上方属意于神仙之事,精索道术。毅不得安,遂相与归洞庭。凡十余岁,莫知其迹。

至开元末,毅之表弟薛嘏为京畿令。谪官东南。经洞庭,晴昼长望,俄见碧山出于远波。舟人皆侧立,曰:“此本无山,恐水怪耳。”指顾之际,山与舟相逼,乃有彩船自山驰来,迎问于嘏。其中有一人呼之曰:“柳公来候耳。”嘏省然记之,乃促至山下,摄衣疾上。山有宫阙如人世,见毅立于宫室之中,前列丝竹,后罗珠翠,物玩之盛,殊倍人间,毅词理益玄,容颜益少,初迎嘏于砌,持嘏手曰:“别来瞬息,而发毛已黄。”嘏笑曰:“兄为神仙,弟为枯骨,命也。”毅因出药五十丸遗嘏,曰:“此药一丸,可增一岁耳,岁满复来,无久居人世,以自苦也。”欢宴毕,嘏乃辞行。自是已后。遂绝影响。

嘏常以是事告于人世。殆四纪,嘏亦不知所往。

陇西李朝威叙而叹曰：五虫之长，必以灵者，别斯见矣。人，裸也，移信鳞虫。洞庭含吐大直，钱塘迅疾磊落，宜有承焉。嘏咏而不载，独可邻其境。愚义之，为斯文。

The Dragon King's Daughter

Li Chaowei

During the Yi Feng period (AD 676—678), a scholar named Liu Yi failed in the official examination and, as he was returning to the Xiang River Valley, decided to go and take his leave of a fellow provincial who was staying at Jingyang. He had ridden about two miles when a bird flying up from the ground startled his horse and made it bolt, and it galloped two miles before he could stop it. Then he caught sight of a girl herding sheep by the roadside. She was amazingly beautiful but her finely arched eyebrows were knit, her clothes were soiled, and she was standing there listening intently as if awaiting someone's arrival.

"What has brought you to such a wretched state?" Liu asked.

The girl first expressed her gratitude with a smile; then, unable to restrain her tears, replied, "Unhappy creature that I am! Since you ask me the reason, how can I hide the deep resentment I feel? Listen then! I am the youngest daughter of the Dragon King of Dongting Lake. My parents married me to the second son of the Dragon King of the Jing River; but my husband, devoted to pleasure and led astray by his attendants, treated me more unkindly every day. I complained to his parents, but they were too fond of their son to take my part. When I persisted in complaining, they grew angry and banished me here." Having said this, she broke down and sobbed.

"Dongting Lake is so far away," she went on. "It lies beyond the distant horizon, and I can get no word to my family. My heart is breaking and my eyes are worn out with watching, but there is no one to know my grief or pity me. Since you are going south and will pass near the lake, may I trouble you to take a letter?"

"I have a sense of justice," answered Liu, "and your story makes my blood boil. I only wish I had wings to fly there—why talk of trouble? But the lake is very deep, and I can only walk on land. How am I to convey your message? I fear I may be unable to get through, proving unworthy of your trust and failing in my own sincere wish to help you. Can you tell me how to make the journey?"

"I cannot say how I appreciate your kindness," said the girl, shedding tears. "If ever I receive a reply, I shall repay you even if it costs my life. Before you promised to help me, I dared not tell you how to reach my parents; but actually, to go to the lake is no harder than going to the capital."

Asked for directions, she told him, "South of the lake stands a big orange tree which is the sacred tree of the village. Take off this belt, put on another, and knock on the trunk three times. Someone will come to your call, and if you follow him you will have no difficulty. I have opened my heart to you as well as trusting you with my letter. Please tell my parents what you have heard. On no account fail me!"

Liu promised to do as she said. Then the girl took a letter from her pocket and handed it to him with a bow, all the while looking eastwards and weeping in a way that touched his heart.

When he had put the letter in his wallet, he inquired, "May I ask why you herd sheep? Do deities also eat cattle?"

"No," she answered. "These are not sheep, but rain-bringers."

"What are they?"

"Thunder, lightning, and the like."

Liu looked at the sheep closely, and saw that they moved proudly with heads held high. They cropped the grass differently too, although they were the same size as ordinary sheep and had the same wool and horns.

"Now that I am going to act as your messenger," he said, "I hope in future, when you get back to the lake, you won't refuse to see me."

"Certainly not!" she exclaimed. "I shall treat you as a dear relative."

Then they bid each other goodbye, and he started east. After a few dozen yards he looked back, but both girl and sheep had disappeared.

That evening he reached the county town and said goodbye to his friend. It took him over a month to get home, and he went without delay to

Dongting Lake. He found the orange tree south of the lake, changed his belt, faced the tree and knocked three times. A warrior came out of the water, and bowed to him. "Why have you come here, honourable sir?" he asked.

Without telling him the story, Liu simply answered, "To see your king."

The warrior parted the waves and pointed the way, saying to Liu as he led him down, "Close your eyes. We will be there in no time."

Liu did as he was told, and soon they reached a great palace where he saw clustered towers and pavilions, millions of gates and arches, and all the rare plants and trees of the world. The warrior asked him to wait at the corner of a great hall.

"What place is this?" asked Liu.

"The Palace of the Divine Void."

Looking round, Liu saw that this palace was filled with every precious object known to man. The pillars were of white jade, the steps of jasper; the couches were of coral, the screens of crystal. The emerald lintels were set with cut glass, while the rainbow-coloured beams were inlaid with amber. And the whole created an impression of strange beauty and unfathomable depth which defied description.

The Dragon King was a long time in coming, and Liu asked the warrior, "Where is the Lord of Dongting?"

"His Majesty is in the Dark Pearl Pavilion," was the reply. "He is discussing the Fire Canon with the Sun Priest, but will have finished soon."

"What is the Fire Canon?" Liu wanted to know.

"Our king is a dragon," was the reply, "so water is his element, and with one drop of water he can flood mountains and valleys. The priest is a man, so fire is his element, and with one torch he can burn down a whole palace. Since the properties of the elements differ, they have different effects. As the Sun Priest is expert in the laws of men, our king has asked him over for a talk."

He had barely finished speaking when the palace gate opened, a mist seemed to gather and there appeared a man in purple holding a jasper sceptre. The warrior leaped to attention, crying, "This is our king!" Then he went forward to report Liu's arrival.

The Dragon King looked at Liu and asked, "Are you not of the world of men?"

Liu replied that he was, and bowed. The king greeted him in return and asked him to be seated.

"Our watery kingdom is dark and deep, and I am ignorant," said the Dragon King. "What has brought you, sir, from such a distance?"

"I am of the same district as Your Majesty," replied Liu. "I was born in the south, but have studied in the northwest. Not long ago, after failing in the examination, I was riding by the Jing River when I came upon your daughter herding sheep in the open country. Exposed to wind and rain, she was a pitiful sight. When questioned, she told me she had come to such a pass because of her husband's unkindness and his parents' neglect. I assure you, her tears as she spoke went to my heart. Then she entrusted this letter to me and I promised to deliver it. That is why I am here." He took out the letter and passed it to the king.

After reading the missive, the king covered up his face and wept. "Though I am her old father," he lamented, "I have been like a man blind and deaf, unaware that my child was suffering far away, while you, a stranger, came to her rescue. As long as I live, I shall never forget your kindness." He gave way to weeping, and all the attendants shed tears.

Presently a palace eunuch approached the king, who handed him the letter with orders to tell the women in the inner palace. Soon wailing was heard from within and in alarm the king bade his attendants, "Quickly tell the women not to make so much noise, or the Prince of Qiantang may hear them!"

"Who is this prince?" asked Liu.

"My younger brother," said the Dragon King. "He used to be the Prince of the Qiantang River, but has now retired."

"Why must you keep it from him?"

"Because he is overbold," was the reply. "The nine years of flood in the time of the ancient sage King Yao was due to one of his rages. Not long ago he quarrelled with the angels in heaven and flooded the five mountains. Thanks to a few good deeds I had to my credit, the heavenly emperor pardoned him; but he has to be kept here. The people of Qiantang are still waiting for his return."

He had scarcely finished when there came a great crash, as if both heaven and earth had been torn asunder. The palace shook and mist seethed as in burst a crimson dragon more than a thousand feet long, dragging after it a jade pillar to which its neck had been fastened by a gold chain. Its eyes were bright as lightning, its tongue red as blood, and it had scarlet scales and a fiery mane. Thunder crashed and lightning flashed around it, then snow and hail fell thick and fast, after which it soared up into the azure sky.

Panic-stricken, Liu had fallen to the ground. But now the king himself helped him up, urging, "Have no fear! All is well."

After a long time, Liu recovered a little. And when calm enough he asked leave to withdraw. "I had better go while I can," he explained. "I couldn't survive another experience like that."

"There's no need to leave," said the king. "That's the way my brother goes, but he won't come back that way. Do stay a little longer." He called for wine, and they drank to pledge their friendship.

Then a soft breeze sprang up, wafting over auspicious clouds. Amid flying pennons and flags and the sound of flutes and pipes, in came thousands of brightly dressed, laughing and chattering girls. Among them was one with beautiful, arched eyebrows who was wearing bright jewels and a gown of the finest gauze. When she drew near, Liu saw that she was the girl who had given him the message. Now she was shedding tears of joy, as she moved through a fragrant red and purple mist to the inner palace.

The king said with a laugh to Liu, "Here comes the prisoner from the Jing River!" He excused himself and went inside, and from the inner palace happy weeping was heard. Then the king came out again to feast with Liu.

Presently a man in purple strode up to stand by the king. He was holding a jasper sceptre and looked vigorous and full of spirit. The king introduced him as the Prince of Qiantang.

Liu stood up to bow, and the prince bowed in return. "My unhappy niece was insulted by that young blackguard", he said. "It was good of you, sir, with your strong sense of justice, to carry the news of her wrongs so far. If not for you, she would have pined away by the Jing River. No words can express our gratitude."

Liu bowed and thanked him. Then the prince told his brother, "I reached the river in one hour, fought there for another hour, and took another hour to come back. On my return journey I flew to high heaven to report to the Heavenly Emperor; and when he knew the injustice done he pardoned me. In fact, he pardoned my past faults as well. But I am thoroughly ashamed that in my indignation I did not stop to say goodbye, upsetting the whole palace and alarming our honourable guest." He bowed again.

"How many did you kill?" asked the king.

"Six hundred thousand."

"Did you destroy any fields?"

"About three hundred miles."

"Where is that scoundrel, her husband?"

"I ate him."

The king looked pained.

"Of course that young blackguard was insufferable," he said. "Still, that was going rather far. It is lucky that the Heavenly Emperor is omniscient and pardoned you because such a great injustice had been done. Otherwise what could I have said in your defence? Don't ever do that again!" The prince bowed once more.

That evening Liu was lodged in the Hall of Frozen Light, and the next day another feast was given at the Emerald Palace. All the royal family gathered there, music was played, and wine and delicacies were served. Then bugles, horns and drums sounded as ten thousand warriors danced with flags, swords and halberds on the right-hand side, while one came forward to announce that this was the triumphal march of the Prince of Qiantang. This spectacular and awe-inspiring display impressed all who saw it.

Then to an accompaniment of gongs and cymbals, stringed and bamboo instruments, a thousand girls dressed in bright silks and decked with jewels danced on the left-hand side, while one came forward to announce that this music was to celebrate the return of the princess. The melodies were poignant and sweet, breathing such grief and longing that all who heard were moved to tears. When the two dances were over, the Dragon King in high good humour made the dancers presents of silk. Then the guests sat down together to feast, and drank to their hearts' content.

When they had drunk their fill, the king rapped on the table and sang:

Wide the earth and grey the sky,
Who can hear a distant cry?
The fox lies snugly in his lair,
But thunderbolts can reach him there.
A true man, who upholds the right,
Restored my daughter to my sight.
Such service how can we requite?

After the king's song ended, the prince made a bow and sang:

Life and death are fixed by fate,
Our princess found a worthless mate.
By River Jing she had to go,
In wind and frost, in rain and snow.
This gentleman her letter bore,
Then we restored her to this shore.
This we'll remember ever more!

After this song, the king and prince stood up and each presented a cup to Liu, who hesitated bashfully before accepting, then quaffed off the wine, returned the cups and sang:

Like a blossom in the rain,
The princess longed for home in vain,
I brought back tidings of her plight,

And all her wrongs were soon set right,
Now we feast, but soon must part,
For home again I needs must start.
Bitter longing fills my heart!

This song of his was greeted by loud applause.

The king brought out a jasper casket of rhinoceros horn which could part the waves, and the prince an amber dish bearing jade that shone at night. They presented these to Liu, who accepted the gifts with thanks. Then the inmates of the palace started piling silk and jewels beside him, until gorgeous materials were heaped up all around. Laughing and chatting with the company, he had not a moment's quiet. Sated at last with wine and pleasure, he excused himself and went back to sleep in the Hall of Frozen Light.

The next day he was feasting again in the Pavilion of Limpid Light when the Prince of Qiantang, heated with wine and lounging on the couch, said insolently, "A hard rock can be smashed but not made to yield, and a gallant man can be killed but not put to shame. I have a proposal to make. If you agree, all will be well between us. If not, we can perish together. How about it?"

"Let me hear your proposal," said Liu.

"As you know, the wife of the Lord of the Jing river is our sovereign's daughter," said the prince. "She is an excellent girl with a fine character, well thought of by all her kinsmen but unlucky enough to have suffered indignities at the hands of that scoundrel. However, that's a thing of the past. We would like to entrust her to you, and become your relatives for ever. Then she who owes you gratitude will belong to you, and we who love her will know she is in good hands. A generous man shouldn't do things by halves. Don't you agree?"

For a moment Liu looked grave. Then he rejoined with a laugh, "I never thought the Prince of Qiantang would have such unworthy ideas. I have heard that once when you crossed the nine continents, you shook the five mountains to give vent to your anger; and I have seen you break the golden chain and drag the jade pillar after you to rescue your niece. I thought there was no one as brave and just as you, who dared risk death to right a wrong, and would sacrifice your life for those you love. These are the true marks of greatness. Yet now, while music is being played and host and guest are in harmony, you try to force me to do your will in defiance of honour. I would never have expected this of you! If I met you on the angry sea or among dark mountains, with your fins and beard flying and mist and rain all around, though you threatened me with death I should consider you a mere beast and not count it against you. But now you are in human garb. You talk of manners and show a profound understanding of human relationships and the ways of men. You have a nicer sense of propriety than many gallants in the world of men, not to say monsters of the deep. Yet you try to use your strength and temper—while pretending to be drunk—to force me to agree to your proposal. This is hardly right. Although small enough to hide under one of your scales, I am afraid of your anger. I hope you will reconsider your proposal."

Then the prince apologized. "Brought up in the palace, I was never taught etiquette," he said. "Just now I spoke wildly and offended you—your rebuke was well deserved. Don't let this spoil our friendship." That night they feasted together again as merrily as ever, and Liu and the prince became great friends.

The day after, Liu asked permission to leave. The queen gave another feast for him in the Hall of Hidden Light, which was attended by a great throng of men and women, maids and servants. Shedding tears, the queen said to him, "My daughter owes you so much, we can never repay you. And we are sorry to have to say goodbye." She told the princess to thank him.

"Shall we ever meet again?" asked the queen.

Liu regretted now that he had not agreed to the prince's request. His heart was very heavy. After the feast, when he bid them farewell, the whole palace was filled with sighing, and countless rare jewels were given him as parting gifts.

He left the lake by the way he had come, escorted by a dozen or more attendants who carried his bags to his home before leaving him. He went to a jeweller's at Yangzhou to sell some of the jewels, and though he parted with about one hundredth only he became a multi-millionaire, wealthier by far than all the rich men west of the Huai River.

He married a girl called Zhang, but soon she died. Then he married a girl called Han; but after several months she died as well, and Liu moved to Nanjing.

Loneliness tempted him to marry again, and a go-between told him, "There is a girl called Lu from Fanyang County, whose father, Lu Hao, used to be magistrate of Qingliu. In his later years he studied Taoist philosophy and lived by himself in the wilderness, so that now no one knows where he is. Her mother was named Zheng. The year before last the girl married into the Zhang family at Qinghe, but unfortunately her husband died. Because she is young, intelligent and beautiful, her mother wants to find a good husband for her. Are you interested?"

So Liu married this girl on an auspicious day, and since both families were wealthy, the magnificence of their gifts and equipage impressed the whole city of Nanjing.

Coming home one evening about a month after their marriage, Liu was struck by his wife's resemblance to the Dragon King's daughter, except that she was in better health and more lovely. Accordingly, he told her what had happened.

"I can't believe it," She replied. Then she told him that she was with child, and Liu became more devoted to her than ever.

A month after the child was born, Liu's wife dressed herself in fine clothes, put on her jewels, and invited all their relatives to the house. Before the assembled company she asked him with a smile, "Don't you remember meeting me before?"

"Once I carried a message for the Dragon King's daughter," he replied. "That is something I have never forgotten."

"I am the Dragon King's daughter," she said. "Wronged by my former husband, I was rescued by you, and I swore to repay your kindness. But when my uncle the prince suggested that we marry, you refused. After our separation we lived in two different spheres, and I had no way of sending word to you. Later my parents wanted to marry me to another river god—that stripling of the Zhuoqin River—but I remained true to you. Although you had forsaken me and there was no hope of seeing you again, I would rather have died than stop loving you. Soon after that, my parents took pity on me and decided to approach you again; but you married girls from the Zhang and Han families, and there was nothing we could do. After those girls had died and you came to live here, my family felt the match was possible. But I never dared hope that one day I might be your wife. I shall be grateful and happy all my life, and die without regret." So saying, she wept.

Presently she went on: "I did not disclose myself to you before, because I knew you did not care for my looks. But I can tell you now that I know you are attached to me. I am not good enough to keep your love, so I'm counting on your fondness for the child to hold you. Before I knew you loved me, I was so anxious and worried! When you took my letter, you smiled at me and said, 'When you go back to the lake, don't refuse to see me!' Did you want us to become husband and wife in future? Later when my uncle proposed the marriage and you refused him, did you really mean it or were you just offended? Do tell me!"

"It must have been fated," said Liu. "When first I met you by the river, you looked so wronged and pale, my heart bled for you. But I think all I wanted at the time was to pass on your message and right your wrong. When I said I hoped you wouldn't refuse to see me in future, that was just a casual remark with nothing behind it. The prince's attempt to force me into marriage annoyed me because I object to being bullied. Since a sense of justice had motivated my action, I could hardly marry the woman whose husband's death I had caused. As a man of honour I had to do what I thought right. So during our drinking I spoke from my heart, saying only what was just, with no fear of him. Once the time came to leave, however, and I saw the regret in your eyes, I was rather sorry. But after I left the lake, the affairs of this world kept me too occupied to convey my love and gratitude to you. Well, now that you belong to the Lu family and are a woman, I find my former feelings towards you were more than a fleeting passion after all! From now on, I shall love you always."

His wife was deeply moved and replied with tears, "Don't think human beings alone know gratitude. I shall repay your kindness. A dragon lives for ten thousand years, and I shall share my span of life with you. We shall travel freely by land and sea. You can trust me."

"I never thought you could tempt me with immortality!" laughed Liu.

They went to the lake again, where the royal entertainment once more given them beggars description.

Later they lived at Nanhai for forty years. Their mansions, equipage, feasts and clothes were as splendid as those of a prince, and Liu was able to help all his relatives. His perennial youth amazed everybody. During the Kai Yuan period(AD 713—741), when the emperor set his heart on discovering the secret of long life and searched far and wide for alchemists, Liu was given no peace and went back with his wife to the lake. Thus he disappeared from the world for more than ten years. At the end of that period, his younger cousin, Xue Gu, lost his post as magistrate of the capital and was sent to the southeast. On his journey Xue crossed Dongting Lake. It was a clear day and he was looking into the distance when he saw a green mountain emerging from the distant waves. The boatmen shrank back in fear, crying, "There was never any mountain here—it must be a sea monster!"

As they were watching the mountain approach, a painted barge came swiftly towards them and the men on it called Xue's name. One of them told him, "Master Liu sends his greetings." Then Xue understood. Invited to the foot of the mountain, he picked up the skirt of his gown and went quickly ashore. On the mountain were palaces like those on earth, and Liu was standing there with musicians before and bejewelled girls behind him, more splendid than in the world of men. Talking more brilliantly and looking even younger than formerly, he greeted Xue at the steps and took his hand.

"We have not been separated long," he said, "yet your hair is turning grey."

"You are fated to become an immortal and I to become dry bones," retorted Xue with a laugh.

Liu gave him fifty capsules, and said, "Each of these will give you an extra year of life. When you have finished them, come again. Don't stay too long in the world of men, where you must undergo so many hardships." They feasted happily, and then Xue left. Liu was never seen again, but Xue often related this story. And fifty years later, he too vanished from the world.

This tale shows that the principal species of each category① of living creatures possesses supernatural powers—for how otherwise could reptiles assume the virtues of men? The Dragon King of Dongting showed himself truly magnanimous, while the Prince of Qiantang was impetuous and straightforward. Surely their virtues did not appear from nowhere. Liu's cousin, Xue Gu, was the only other human being to penetrate to that watery kingdom, and it is a pity that none of his writings have been preserved. But since this account holds such interest, I have recorded it here.

---

① 原译文注释：The ancient Chinese divided the animal kingdom into five categories：feathered，furred，hard-shelled，scaly and hairless. The chief species of these categories were phoenix，unicorn，tortoise，dragon and man. From man，the most intelligent of all，these others derived some of their virtues.

二

羊角哀舍命全交(明·冯梦龙)[①]

羊角哀舍命全交

冯梦龙

背手为云覆手雨,纷纷轻薄何须数?
君看管鲍贫时交,此道今人弃如土。

昔时齐国有管仲,字夷吾;鲍叔,字宣子,两个自幼时以贫贱结交。后来鲍叔先在齐桓公门下,信用显达,举荐管仲为首相,位在己上。两人同心辅政,始终如一。管仲曾有几句言语道:"吾尝三战三北,鲍叔不以我为怯,知我有老母也;吾尝三仕三见逐,鲍叔不以我为不肖,知我不遇时也;吾尝与鲍叔谈论,鲍叔不以我为愚,知时有利不利也;吾尝与鲍叔为贾,分利多,鲍叔不以我为贪,知我贫也。生我者父母,知我者鲍叔。"所以古今说知心结交,必曰"管鲍"。今日说两个朋友,偶然相见,结为兄弟,各舍其命,留名万古。

春秋时,楚元王崇儒重道,招贤纳士。天下之人闻其风而归者,不可胜计。西羌积石山,有一贤士,姓左,双名伯桃,幼亡父母,勉力攻书,养成济世之才,学就安民之业。年近四旬,因中国诸侯互相吞并,行仁政者少,

---

① 中文选自:冯梦龙. 古今小说(上册). 许政扬,校注. 北京:人民文学出版社,1979:114-120;英译文选自:Feng, M. L. Yang Jiaoai Gives His Life to Save His Friend. Gladys Yang (trans.). *Chinese Literature*, 1982(10): 110-120.

恃强霸者多，未尝出仕。后闻得楚元王慕仁好义，遍求贤士，乃携书一囊，辞别乡中邻友，径奔楚国而来。迤逦来到雍地，时值隆冬，风雨交作。有一篇《西江月》词，单道冬天雨景：

习习悲风割面，濛濛细雨侵衣。
催冰酿雪逞寒威，不比他时和气。
山色不明常暗，日光偶露还微。
天涯游子尽思归，路上行人应悔。

左伯桃冒雨荡风，行了一日，衣裳都沾湿了。看看天色昏黄，走向村间，欲觅一宵宿处。远远望见竹林之中，破窗透出灯光。径奔那个去处。见矮矮篱笆围着一间草屋。乃推开篱障，轻叩柴门。中有一人，启户而出。左伯桃立在檐下，慌忙施礼曰："小生西羌人氏，姓左，双名伯桃。欲往楚国，不期中途遇雨，无觅旅邸之处，求借一宵，来早便行，未知尊意肯容否？"那人闻言，慌忙答礼，邀入屋内。伯桃视之，止有一榻，榻上堆积书卷，别无他物。伯桃已知亦是儒人，便欲下拜。那人云："且未可讲礼，容取火烘干衣服，却当会话。"当夜烧竹为火，伯桃烘衣。那人炊办酒食，以供伯桃，意甚勤厚。伯桃乃问姓名。其人曰："小生姓羊，双名角哀，幼亡父母，独居于此。平生酷爱读书，农业尽废。今幸遇贤士远来，但恨家寒，乏物为款，伏乞恕罪。"伯桃曰："阴雨之中，得蒙遮蔽，更兼一饮一食，感佩何忘！"当夜二人抵足而眠，共话胸中学问，终夕不寐。

比及天晓，淋雨不止。角哀留伯桃在家，尽其所有相待；结为昆仲，伯桃年长角哀五岁，角哀拜伯桃为兄。一住三日，雨止道干。伯桃曰："贤弟有王佐之才，抱经纶之志；不图竹帛，甘老林泉，深为可惜。"角哀曰："非不欲仕，奈未得其便耳。"伯桃曰："今楚王虚心求士，贤弟既有此心，何不同往？"角哀曰："愿从兄长之命。"遂收拾些小路费粮米，弃其茅屋，二人同望南方而进。

行不两日，又值阴雨，羁身旅店中，盘费罄尽。止有行粮一包，二人轮换负之，冒雨而走。其雨未止，风又大作，变为一天大雪，怎见得？你看：

风添雪冷，雪趁风威。
纷纷柳絮狂飘，片片鹅毛乱舞。

团空搅阵，不分南北西东；
遮地漫天，变尽青黄赤黑。
探梅诗客多清趣，路上行人欲断魂。

二人行过歧阳，道经梁山路，问及樵夫，皆说：从此去百余里，并无人烟，尽是荒山旷野，狼虎成群，只好休去。伯桃与角哀曰：“贤弟心下如何？”角哀曰：“自古道：‘死生有命。’既然到此，只顾前进，休生退悔。”又行了一日，夜宿古墓中，衣服单薄，寒风透骨。

次日，雪越下得紧，山中仿佛盈尺。伯桃受冻不过，曰：“我思此去百余里，绝无人家；行粮不敷，衣单食缺。若一人独往，可到楚国；二人俱去，纵然不冻死，亦必饿死于途中，与草木同朽，何益之有？我将身上衣服，脱与贤弟穿了，贤弟可独赍此粮，于途强挣而去。我委的行不动了，宁可死于此地。待贤弟见了楚王，必当重用，那时却来葬我未迟。”角哀曰：“焉有此理！我二人虽非一父母所生，义气过于骨肉，我安忍独去而求进身耶？”遂不许。扶伯桃而行，行不十里，伯桃曰：“风雪越紧，如何去得？且于道旁寻个歇处。“见一株枯桑，颇可避雪。那桑下止容得一人，角哀遂扶伯桃入去坐下。伯桃命角哀敲石取火，爇些枯枝，以御寒气。比及角哀取了柴火到来，只见伯桃脱得赤条条地，浑身衣服，都做一堆放着。角哀大惊曰：“吾兄何为如此？”伯桃曰：“吾寻思无计，贤弟勿自误了，速穿此衣服，负粮前去，我只在此守死。”角哀抱持大哭曰：“吾二人死生同处，安可分离？”伯桃曰：“若皆饿死，白骨谁埋？”角哀曰：“若如此，弟情愿解衣与兄穿了，兄可赍粮去，弟宁死于此。”伯桃曰：“我平生多病，贤弟少壮，比我甚强；更兼胸中之学，我所不及。若见楚君，必登显宦。我死何足道哉？弟勿久滞，可宜速往。”角哀曰：“令兄饿死桑中，弟独取功名，此大不义之人也，我不为之。”伯桃曰：“我自离积石山，至弟家中，一见如故。知弟胸次不凡，以此劝弟求进。不幸风雨所阻，此吾天命当尽。若使弟亦亡于此，乃吾之罪也。”言讫欲跳前溪觅死。角哀抱住痛哭，将衣拥护，再扶至桑中，伯桃把衣服推开。角哀再欲上前劝解时，但见伯桃神色已变，四肢厥冷，口不能言，以手挥令去。角哀寻思：“我若久恋，亦冻死矣。死后谁葬吾兄？”乃于雪中再拜伯桃而哭曰：“不肖弟此去，望兄阴力相助。但得微名，必当厚葬。”伯桃点头半答，角哀取了衣粮，带泣而去。伯桃死于桑中。后人有诗赞云：

寒来雪三尺，人去途千里。
长途苦雪寒，何况囊无米？
并粮一人生，同行两人死；
两死诚何益？一生尚有恃。
贤哉左伯桃！陨命成人美。

角哀捱着寒冷，半饥半饱，来至楚国，于旅邸中歇定。次日入城，问人曰：“楚君招贤，何由而进？”人曰：“宫门外设一宾馆，令上大夫裴仲接纳天下之士。”角哀径投宾馆前来，正值上大夫下车，角哀乃向前而揖。裴仲见角哀衣虽褴褛，器宇不凡，慌忙答礼，问曰：“贤士何来？”角哀曰：“小生姓羊，双名角哀，雍州人也。闻上国招贤，特来归投。”裴仲邀入宾馆，具酒食以进，宿于馆中。

次日，裴仲到馆中探望，将胸中疑义，盘问角哀，试他学问如何。角哀百问百答，谈论如流。裴仲大喜，入奏元王。王即时召见，问富国强兵之道，角哀首陈十策，皆切当世之急务。元王大喜，设御宴以待之，拜为中大夫，赐黄金百两，彩段百匹。角哀再拜流涕。元王大惊而问曰：“卿痛哭者何也？”角哀将左伯桃脱衣并粮之事，一一奏知。元王闻其言，为之感伤，诸大臣皆为痛惜。元王曰：“卿欲如何？”角哀曰：“臣乞告假到彼处，安葬伯桃已毕，却回来事大王。”元王遂赠已死伯桃为中大夫，厚赐葬资，仍差人跟随角哀车骑同去。

角哀辞了元王，径奔梁山地面。寻旧日枯桑之处，果见伯桃死尸尚在，颜貌如生前一般。角哀乃再拜而哭，呼左右唤集乡中父老，卜地于浦塘之原。前临大溪，后靠高崖，左右诸峰环抱，风水甚好。遂以香汤沐浴伯桃之尸，穿戴大夫衣冠，置内棺外椁，安葬起坟。四周筑墙栽树，离坟三十步建享堂，塑伯桃仪容，立华表，柱上建牌额。墙侧盖瓦屋，令人看守。造毕，设祭于享堂，哭泣甚切。乡老从人，无不下泪。祭罢，各自散去。

角哀是夜明灯燃烛而坐，感叹不已。忽然一阵阴风飒飒，烛灭复明。角哀视之，见一人于灯影中或进或退，隐隐有哭声。角哀叱曰：“何人也？

辄敢夤夜而入!”其人不言。角哀起而视之,乃伯桃也。角哀大惊,问曰:“兄阴灵不远,今来见弟,必有事故。”伯桃曰:“感贤弟记忆,初登仕路,奏请葬吾,更赠重爵,并棺椁衣衾之美,凡事十全。但坟地与荆轲墓相连近,此人在世时,为刺秦王不中被戮,高渐离以其尸葬于此处。神极威猛,每夜仗剑来骂吾曰:‘汝是冻死饿杀之人,安敢建坟居吾上肩,夺吾风水?若不迁移他处,吾发墓取尸,掷之野外!’有此危难,特告贤弟。望改葬于他处,以免此祸。”角哀再欲问之,风起,忽然不见。角哀在享堂中一梦惊觉,尽记其事。

天明,再唤乡老,问此处有坟相近否。乡老曰:“松阴中有荆轲墓,墓前有庙。”角哀曰:“此人昔刺秦王不中被杀,缘何有坟于此?”乡老曰:“高渐离乃此间人,知荆轲被害,弃尸野外,乃盗其尸,葬于此地。每每显灵。土人建庙于此,四时享祭,以求福利。”角哀闻其言,遂信梦中之事。引从者径奔荆轲庙,指其神而骂曰:“汝乃燕邦一匹夫,受燕太子奉养,名姬重宝,尽汝受用。不思良策以副重托,入秦行事,丧身误国。却来此处惊惑乡民,而求祭祀!吾兄左伯桃,当代名儒,仁义廉洁之士,汝安敢逼之?再如此,吾当毁其庙,而发其冢,永绝汝之根本!”骂讫,却来伯桃墓前祝曰:“如荆轲今夜再来,兄当报我。”

归至享堂,是夜秉烛以待。果见伯桃哽咽而来,告曰:“感贤弟如此,奈荆轲从人极多,皆土人所献。贤弟可束草为人,以彩为衣,手执器械,焚于墓前。吾得其助,使荆轲不能侵害。”言罢不见。角哀连夜使人束草为人,以彩为衣,各执刀枪器械,建数十于墓侧,以火焚之。祝曰:“如其无事,亦望回报。”

归至享堂,是夜闻风雨之声,如人战敌。角哀出户观之,见伯桃奔走而来,言曰:“弟所焚之人,不得其用。荆轲又有高渐离相助,不久吾尸必出墓矣。望贤弟早与迁移他处殡葬,免受此祸。”角哀曰:“此人安敢如此欺凌吾兄!弟当力助以战之。伯桃曰:“弟阳人也,我皆阴鬼;阳人虽有勇烈,尘世相隔,焉能战阴鬼也?虽茑草之人,但能助喊,不能退此强魂。”角哀曰:“兄且去,弟来日自有区处。”次日,角哀再到荆轲庙中大骂,打毁神像。方欲取火焚庙,只见乡老数人,再四哀求,曰:“此乃一村香火,若触犯之,恐贻祸于百姓。"须臾之间,土人聚集,都来求告。角哀拗他不过,只得罢了。

回到享堂,修一道表章,上谢楚王,言:"昔日伯桃并粮与臣,因此得活,以遇圣主。重蒙厚爵,平生足矣,容臣后世尽心图报。"词意甚切。表付从人,然后到伯桃墓侧,大哭一场。与从者曰:"吾兄被荆轲强魂所逼,去往无门,吾所不忍。欲焚庙掘坟,又恐拂土人之意。宁死为泉下之鬼,力助吾兄战此强魂。汝等可将吾尸葬于此墓之右,生死共处,以报吾兄并粮之义。回奏楚君,万乞听纳臣言,永保山河社稷。"言讫,掣取佩剑,自刎而死。从者急救不及,速具衣棺殡殓,埋于伯桃墓侧。

是夜二更,风雨大作,雷电交加,喊杀之声闻数十里。清晓视之,荆轲墓上,震烈如发,白骨散于墓前,墓边松柏,和根拔起。庙中忽然起火,烧做白地。乡老大惊,都往羊左二墓前,焚香展拜。从者回楚国,将此事上奏元王,元王感其义重,差官往墓前建庙,加封上大夫,敕赐庙额,曰"忠义之祠",就立碑以记其事,至今香火不断。荆轲之灵,自此绝矣。土人四时祭祀,所祷甚灵。有古诗云:

古来仁义包天地,只在人心方寸间。

二士庙前秋日净,英魂常伴月光寒。

Yang Jiaoai Gives His Life to Save His Friend[①]

Feng Menglong

PAST counting are the fickle friends
Who blow now hot now cold;
But Guan and Bao were true through thick and thin,
And we should not despise these men of old.

Guan Zhong and Bao Shu in the state of Qi made friends as boys when both were poor. Later, Bao served under Duke Huan of Qi, won his trust and was given a high post. Then he recommended Guan Zhong for prime minister, ranking above him. In perfect accord the two of them assisted the government.

Guan said, "I withdrew from three battles, but Bao Shu never thought me a coward, knowing that I had an old mother. I was dismissed from three posts but he never thought me incompetent, knowing that circumstances were against me. In our talks together he never thought me a fool, knowing that some times are more propitious than others. When we did business together I took the lion's share of the profit, but he never thought me grasping, knowing my poverty. My mother bore me, but it is Bao Shu who knows me."

So, from of old, close friends are invariably compared to Guan and Bao. Our story today is about two friends who, having met by chance, became sworn brothers, each giving his life for the other. Their names will live for ever.

During the Spring and Autumn Period (770—476 BC), Prince Yuan of Chu revered scholars, followed the Way, and gathered worthy gentlemen around him. Countless men, hearing of this, flocked to him. In Jishishan in

---

① 原译者注：This story is taken from *Gu Jin Xiao Shuo* (*Ancient and Modern Tales*), a collection of Song and Ming popular stories written in the vernacular edited by Feng Menglong (1574—1646).

the western Qiang region lived a scholar called Zuo Botao who had lost his parents early and studied hard to be of service to the world and pacify the people. When he was approaching forty, China's barons were contending against each other, and benevolent rulers were far outnumbered by tyrants. So Zuo did not try to become an official.

Then, hearing of Prince Yuan's humanity, love of virtue and his search for worthy men, Zuo, carrying a bagful of books, took his leave of his friends and neighbours in the village and set out on foot for Chu. It was mid-winter by the time he reached Yong, and he ran into a rainstorm. A verse set to the melody *Moon on the West River* describes a downpour in winter:

Wind, wailing, cuts your face,
Your clothes are soaked by rain;
The bitter cold bodes snow and ice,
Winter is back again.
The hills are dark and drear,
Fitful and faint the sun;
Travellers long for home
And wish their journey done.

Braving the lashing rain, Zuo Botao pressed on until he was wet through. At dusk he reached a village where he hoped to find a lodging for the night. Far off in a bamboo grove, he saw a light shining through a broken window. Making his way there he found a thatched cottage inside a low fence. He opened the gate in the fence and knocked at the door. It was opened and someone came out. Standing below the eaves, Zuo made haste to greet him.

"I am from the west country," he said. "My name is Zuo Botao. I am on my way to Chu but got caught in the rain, and I have nowhere to put up tonight. Will you be so kind, sir, as to take me in? I shall leave first thing tomorrow."

The other made haste to greet him and ushered him in. Zuo saw that the cottage was bare except for one bed piled with books, and realizing that his host was also a scholar he was about to bow when the other said:

"Don't stand on ceremony. Let me light a fire to dry your clothes, then we can talk."

He made a fire of bamboo to dry Zuo's gown, then prepared food and drink, entertaining him most hospitably. Asked his name he replied, "I am Yang Jiaoai. My parents died when I was a boy, and I live here alone.... I love to study and have given up farming. Today I am delighted by this visit of a worthy gentleman from far away. I only fear you may take offence at my poor entertainment."

"I shall never forget your kindness in sheltering me from the rain, not to mention giving me this good meal," Zuo answered. They enjoyed each other's learned conversation, and did not sleep all night.

The next morning, as it was still raining, Yang kept Zuo there and entertained him as best he could. They swore brotherhood, and since Zuo was the senior by five years, Yang bowed to him as his elder brother. Three days later the rain stopped and the road dried.

Zuo said, "Brother, you have the talent of a prime minister and the aspiration to govern an empire. It would be a pity for you to spend all your life here in the countryside, instead of taking an official post."

Yang replied, "It is not that I don't want one, but no post has been offered to me."

"If that is how you feel," said Zuo, "the Prince of Chu is keen to find scholars. Why not come with me to his court?"

"I will gladly do whatever you say, Elder Brother."

So taking some rice and modest travelling expenses, Yang left his cottage and they set off together for the south.

They had not been two days on the road when it rained again, and they put up at an inn. Then their money ran out, and all they had left was a bag of rice which they took it in turns to carry. As they pressed on through the rain a high wind sprang up, and snow fell thick and fast. What was it like?

Wind freezes the snow,
Which makes use of the wind's might
To whirl like goose-feathers and catkins

To a great height;
Soon the flurrying snow has hidden
North, south, east and west from sight,
Covering earth and sky,
Turning all colours white.
Poets watch the plum blossom in high delight,
But travellers are ready to die of fright!

After the two men had passed Qiyang their way led through Liangshan. Woodcutters whom they questioned warned them, "It is over a hundred *li*, with not a soul living in those barren hills, and the wasteland is infested with wolves and tigers. Better not go."

Zuo asked Yang, "What do you think, worthy brother?"

Yang answered, "The proverb says: Life and death are fated. Since we've come so far, let's go on. We mustn't regret our decision."

They went on for another day, spending the night in an old tomb. They were thinly clad, and the cold wind pierced to the marrow of their bones.

The next day it snowed harder, and drifts lay deep in the mountains. Unable to stand the cold, Zuo said, "We've still over a hundred *li* to go through deserted country. Our food is running out, and our clothes are thin, one of us travelling alone has a chance to reach Chu; if the two of us try, we shall either starve or be frozen to death on the way. Why should we perish like grass? I'm going to take off my clothes and give them to you, brother, and you can take this grain to press on your way. I can honestly go no further; I'd rather die here. When the Prince of Chu sees you he is bound to give you an important post, and then you can come back to bury me."

"That's unthinkable!" protested Yang. "Although we had different parents, integrity matters more than one's own flesh and blood. How can I go off alone in search of advancement?" He would not hear of it, and helped Zuo along for several more *li*.

Then Zuo said, "A blizzard's blowing up. We'll have to stop. Let's find a roadside shelter."

They saw an old mulberry tree, under which there was room for just one man to shelter. Yang supported Zuo to sit down there, and Zuo told him to strike a light on a rock and make a fire of dead branches to keep off the cold. Yang went off to fetch faggots. On his return he found Zuo naked on the ground, his clothes folded up beside him.

"What does this mean, brother!" exclaimed Yang in horror.

"I can think of no other way out. Don't waste time, but put on these clothes and take the grain with you. I'll wait here to die."

Yang embraced him, sobbing, "We must live or die together, brother. How can we part?"

"If we both starve to death, who will bury our white bones?"

"In that case, you take my clothes and the grain, and let me die here."

"My health is poor, you are in your prime, stronger than I am; besides I lack your learning. The Prince of Chu is certain to make you a high minister. What does my death matter? Don't delay, make haste and go."

"If I left my elder brother to starve to death under this mulberry while I went to make my own name, I would be beneath contempt. No!"

"When I left Jishishan and went to your home you treated me like an old friend. I saw you have outstanding ability; that is why I urged you to look for advancement. It's a pity that we were held up by bad weather, but this must be my fate. If I let you perish here too, that would be criminal." With that he made for a stream in front, meaning to drown himself. Yang caught hold of him, weeping bitterly, then wrapped his clothes around him and helped him back to the mulberry tree; but Zuo threw off the clothes. Before Yang could remonstrate again, he saw that Zuo's expression had changed, his limbs were cold and he was unable to speak—he just signed to him to leave.

Yang thought, "If I wait here I shall freeze to death too. Then who would bury my brother?" He prostrated himself in the snow before Zuo and said with tears, "Your undutiful brother is leaving. I hope you will watch over me from the shades. If I make a name I shall give you a grand burial." Zuo nodded approval. Then, weeping, Yang took the clothes and grain and left him. Zuo breathed his last below the mulberry. Later men made this verse in his honour:

To journey far in winter
Over deep snow and ice
Is hard when you're perished with cold,
And harder without rice.
Two going together must die,
But the rice for one would suffice;
And one survivor could still be relied on —
Useless to make a double sacrifice.
Zuo Botao's loyalty we commend:
He gave his life to save his friend.

Half famished, Yang Jiaoai journeyed on through the bitter cold to Chu, where he put up at an inn. The next day he went into town and asked, "How can I obtain an audience with the Prince of Chu who is looking for worthy men?"

He was told, "There is a state hostel outside the palace gate. The first minister Pei Zhong receives scholars from all parts of the country there."

Yang made his way to this hostel, reaching it just as the minister alighted from his carriage. Yang stepped forward to bow and Pei Zhong saw that, although his clothes were ragged, his deportment was striking.

Hastily returning his greeting Pei asked, "Where are you from, sir?"

"My name is Yang Jiaoai, a native of Yongzhou. Hearing that your prince is recruiting men of worth I have come to offer him my services."

Pei Zhong invited him into the hostel, entertained him to a meal and put him up for the night there.

The next day Pei called on him and asked him probing questions to gauge his learning. Yang answered readily and fluently. Highly impressed, Pei went to report this to Prince Yuan. Then the prince promptly summoned Yang to ask how to make his state rich and strong, and Yang for a start made ten proposals to meet the urgent needs of the situation. Overjoyed, the prince feasted him, appointed him a minister of the second rank, and presented him with a hundred taels of gold as well as a hundred lengths of brocade. Yang prostrated himself with tears.

"Why are you weeping so bitterly, sir?" the prince asked in surprise.

Yang related in detail how Zuo Botao had stripped off his clothes and given them to him with the grain. The prince was deeply moved, and all his ministers grieved.

"What do you wish to do, sir?" asked the prince.

"Your subject begs leave to go back there. When I have buried Botao I will return to serve Your Highness."

Then the prince conferred a posthumous official title on Zuo, donated a handsome sum for his funeral and ordered mounted attendants to accompany Yang's carriage.

After leaving Prince Yuan, Yang travelled back to Liangshan to find the old mulberry tree. Zuo's corpse was still there, in appearance unchanged as in life. Yang prostrated himself, weeping, then ordered his attendants to assemble the local elders. For the site of the grave they chose a plain by Putang, with a stream in front and a high cliff behind, as this seemed an ideal locality, surrounded on both sides by hills. When Zuo's corpse had been washed with scented water, they laid him out in official robes and placed him in a coffin with an outer cover. This was interred and a gravemound heaped over it, round which they built a wall and planted trees. Thirty paces from the grave a sacrificial pavilion was erected, with a statue of Zuo and ornamental pillars from which a tablet was hung. By the wall a tiled house was built for a caretaker. When all this was completed, a sacrifice was made in the pavilion, where they mourned bitterly. Even the village elders and attendants shed tears. The sacrifice at an end, they all dispersed.

That night lanterns and candles were lit and Yang kept vigil, sighing. Suddenly a gust of cold wind made the candles flicker. In the shadows he saw a figure faltering at the threshold and heard a muffled sobbing.

"Who's there?" Yang challenged. "Who dares intrude at this hour of the night?"

The other said nothing. Yang stood up for a better look—it was Botao.

In amazement Yang exclaimed, "Elder Brother! Your spirit is not far away. What brings you to see me now?"

"Thank you for holding me in remembrance, brother," Zuo replied. "Newly appointed to a post, you asked leave to come and bury me. Moreover, a title has been conferred on me, as well as a fine coffin and funeral robes—what more could I desire? But my grave is close to the grave of Jing Ke, who was killed during his attempt to assassinate the King of Qin. He was later buried here by Gao Jianli. Every night his fierce spirit comes with a sword to curse me, 'You died of cold and hunger, how dare you build a tomb next to me, spoiling this fine locality of mine? If you don't move away, I shall break open your tomb and throw your corpse into the wilds!' I've come to tell you, brother, what danger I'm in. I hope, to avoid this calamity, you will move my grave elsewhere."

Before Yang could question him further, a wind sprang up and he vanished. Yang woke with a start from this dream in the pavilion, but remembered every detail.

Next day he sent once more for the village elders to ask if there was another tomb in the vicinity.

"In the shade of the pines is Jing Ke's tomb," they told him. "In front of it stands a temple."

"He was killed while trying to assassinate the King of Qin," said Yang. "Why should he be buried here?"

"Gao Jianli came from these parts, so when he heard that Jing Ke's corpse had been left lying in waste land, he carried it away and buried him here. His spirit often manifested itself. So the local people built a temple here, where sacrifices are offered in the four seasons to pray for good fortune."

This convinced Yang of the truth of his dream, and he took his attendants to Jing Ke's temple. Pointing at the image he swore, "You lout from Yan, the Prince of Yan treated you well, giving you famous singing-girls and rich jewels. But instead of devising a good way to carry out the great task entrusted to you, when you went to Qin, you lost your life and brought trouble on your country. Yet you came here to intimidate the villagers and demand sacrifices! My elder brother Zuo Botao is a famous scholar of our times, humane, just and incorruptible. How dare you threaten him? If you do this again, I shall pull down your temple, raze your grave and destroy you once and for all!" He then went to Zuo's tomb and announced, "If Jing Ke comes again tonight, let me know, brother."

That night in the pavilion he lit a candle and waited. Sure enough, Zuo entered groaning. "I am grateful for the action you took, brother," he said. "But Jing Ke has a host of retainers, all dedicated to him by the local people. If you make straw effigies dressed in coloured costumes with weapons in their hands, and burn them in front of my tomb, Jing Ke will be unable to storm in and destroy me." This said, he vanished.

That same night Yang had straw effigies made, dressed in motley colours and armed with swords and spears. He set up several dozen beside the tomb and burnt them. Then he prayed, "If all goes well, please let me know."

In the pavilion that night, the wind and rain sounded like contending armies. Yang went out to have a look, and saw Zuo rushing towards him.

"Those straw men you burnt have been no use, brother," he said. "Jing Ke has enlisted Gao Jianli's support. They're bound to disinter me before long. Please, brother, lose no time in moving away my grave to avert this calamity!"

"How dare he bully my elder brother like this!" swore Yang. "I'll do my best to defeat him."

"You are a mortal, we are ghosts," replied Zuo. "We inhabit different worlds. How can even the bravest man alive defeat ghosts in the underworld? Straw effigies can only raise a din—they can't repulse a powerful spirit like this."

"Go back, brother," said Yang. "I shall find some way out."

The next day Yang went back to the Temple of Jing Ke to curse him and smash his image. Just as he was about to burn the temple down, some village elders interceded, "Our whole village sacrifices to this spirit. If we offend it, we may all be destroyed." Soon other villagers gathered there too to dissuade him. Unable to win them over Yang had to abandon his plan.

Returning to the pavilion he composed a memorial to thank the Prince of Chu. He wrote, "Botao saved my life by giving me his share of grain, so that I was able to meet my sage lord. The honour conferred on me is sufficient for my lifetime; allow me to show my gratitude after death." He wrote this memorial from his heart and, having entrusted it to his attendants, went to lament bitterly by Zuo Botao's grave. He told his attendants, "My brother is menaced by Jing Ke's powerful spirit and has no way out—this is more than I can bear. Rather than distress the villagers by burning Jing Ke's temple and digging up his grave, I mean to die, so that as a ghost in the underworld I can help my brother to fight this powerful spirit. Bury me to the right of his tomb, that we may remain undivided in life and death to repay his goodness to me. On your return, report this to the Prince of Chu. I beg him to act on my advice, to safeguard our country for ever." This said, he drew his sword and cut his own throat. Before his attendants could stop him he was dead. They made haste to lay him out and bury him beside Zuo's tomb.

At the second watch that night there was a great storm. Thunder rolled, lightning flashed, and battle-cries could be heard for many *li* around. At dawn they saw Jing Ke's tomb gaping open, white bones scattered before it, while the pine and cypress trees beside it had been uprooted. The temple suddenly went up in flames and was razed to the ground. In consternation they went to the tombs of Yang and Zuo to burn incense and worship there.

The attendants on their return to Chu reported this to Prince Yuan. Deeply moved by Yang's integrity, he sent officials to erect a temple before his tomb, raised his rank and conferred a tablet for his temple inscribed "The Temple of Loyalty and Integrity". Another tablet was set up to record his story, and here incense has been burnt for him ever since. This was the end of Jing Ke's spirit. The local people sacrifice here in all four seasons, and their prayers are always answered. As an old verse testifies:

Humanity and justice embrace the earth and sky,
Yet in the small space of men's hearts they lie.
On the two worthies' temple the autumn sun shines bright,
And their brave spirits share the moon's cold light.

三

《阿诗玛》(10—13 章)[1]

10　比赛

阿支关起大铁门，
拦住阿黑不准进：
"小米做成细米饼，
我们比赛讲细话。
谷子做成白米花，
我们比赛讲白话。

"唱得赢，
就准你进，
唱不赢，
就不开门。"

"大路十二条，
小路十三条，
大路随你走，
小路也随你挑。

---

① 中文选自：云南人民文工团工作组搜集.黄铁，杨知勇，刘绮，公刘整理. 阿诗玛. 北京：人民文学出版社，1955；英译文选自：Yang，G.（trans.）. Ashma（a Shani ballad）. *Chinese Literature*，1955(3)：3-51.

“我作事不亏理，
定能唱赢你；
你作事理不正，
关不住这道门。”

阿支坐在墙头，
阿黑坐在果树下，
一个急开口，
一个慢回答。

“春天的季鸟，
什么是春季鸟？”

“布谷是春季鸟，
布谷一叫，
青草发芽，
春天就来到。”

“夏天的季鸟，
什么是夏季鸟？”

“叫天子是夏季鸟，
叫天子一叫，
荷花开放，
夏天就来到。”

“秋天的季鸟，
什么是秋季鸟？”

“阳雀是秋季鸟，
阳雀一叫，
天降白霜，
秋天就来到。”

“冬天的季鸟，
什么是冬季鸟？”

“雁鹅是冬季鸟，
雁鹅一叫，
大雪飘飘，
冬天就来到。”

唱了一天零一夜，
阿支脸红脖子大，
越唱越没劲，
声音就像癞蛤蟆。

唱了一天零一夜，
阿黑从容面含笑，
越唱越有神，
声音就像知了叫。

阿支唱得一句不剩，
阿黑才反过来问：

“山林果树上的刺，
是什么人儿生？
绵羊山羊的屎，
是什么人做成？”

阿支唱不过，
阿支答不上，
只得把门开，
把阿黑请进来。

阿黑一进屋，
就喊阿诗玛，

“阿诗玛，阿诗玛，
你在哪里？你快回答。”

热布巴拉赶紧说：
“软石磨斧亮闪闪，
我们比赛去砍树，
比得赢就准你见阿诗玛。”

“大路十二条，
小路十三条，
大路随你走，
小路也随你挑。

“我作事不亏理，
哥哥一定能见妹妹；
你们作事理不正，
手拿板斧心打颤。”

热布巴拉两父子，
两斧头砍下一小块，
勇敢的阿黑一个人，
一斧头砍下三大块。

热布巴拉砍不过，
心中想出坏主意：
“今天不是砍树天，
各人砍的各人接。”

勇敢的阿黑心中想：
“砍树接树都不怕，
看你还有什么新花样？
看你还有什么鬼办法？”

热布巴拉父子俩，
两人接了一小块，
勇敢的阿黑一个人，
一连接了三大块。

热布巴拉接不过，
心中又打坏主意：
“今天不是接树天，
细米看谁撒得快。”

勇敢的阿黑心中想：
“栽树撒种都不怕，
看你还有什么新花样？
看你还有什么鬼办法？”

热布巴拉两父子，
两人撒了一小块。
勇敢的阿黑一个人，
一口气撒了三大块。

热布巴拉撒不过，
心中又打坏主意：
“今天不是撒种天，
各人撒的各人拾起来。”

勇敢的阿黑心中想：
“撒种拾种都不怕，
看你还有什么新花样？
看你还有什么鬼办法？”

热布巴拉两父子，
两人拾了一小块。

勇敢的阿黑一个人，
一口气拾了三大块。

热布巴拉走过来，
一面假笑一面问：
“一个土塘三颗种，
你拾的细米怎么少三颗？”

“山上的青松，
不怕吹邪风，
三颗细米不难找，
勇敢的阿黑难不倒。”

天黑的时候，
叫天子不叫，
野狗也不咬，
阿黑找细米去了。

天色渐渐亮，
远远的地方，
有个老人犁荞地，
犁铧闪银光。

“好心的老大爹，
请你告诉我，
我丢失了三颗细米，
应该到哪里去找？”

犁地老人亲切的回答：
“丢失锄头田里找，
丢失黄牛山上找，
丢失细米要去树上找。

"山上叫三声，
山下叫三声，
山腰有一棵树，
树梢上站着三个灰斑鸠。

"两个头朝东，
中间那个头朝西，
射下中间那一个，
细米就在它膝子里。"

阿黑跑到树脚下，
弓满箭直射得准，
斑鸠扑的落下地，
膝子里吐出三颗米。

11　兄妹相见

阿黑装起三颗细米，
转身向热布巴拉家奔，
拉弓射出三箭，
人没到箭先射中大门。

三支箭都钉在热布巴拉家
大门、供桌、堂屋上，
好人轻轻拿，
坏人休想拔。

三箭穿过墙，
全院都震响，
热布巴拉家着了慌，
知道阿黑要来算账。

全家来拔箭，
好像生了根，
五条牛来拖，
也不见拔动半分。

所有的办法都用尽，
一点也不行，
只好打开黑牢门，
向阿诗玛求情。

“阿诗玛,阿诗玛，
求你哥哥把箭拔，
我认输来你家赢，
今后再不敢欺侮你们。”

阿诗玛知道哥哥来救她，
胆子更大更不怕!
她说:“你们有本事做坏事，
就该有本事把箭拔。”

热布巴拉说：
“阿诗玛呵,阿诗玛，
你家的箭听你家的话，
只要你把箭拔掉，
就让你和哥哥回家。”

“哥哥射的箭，
妹妹拔得起；
不是替你家拔箭，
是为了想和哥回家。”

阿诗玛一伸手，

三支箭都拔掉，
阿诗玛的手，
赛过五条牛。

12　打虎

用尽了多少坏办法，
都难不倒阿黑；
说尽了多少假意话，
也骗不了阿诗玛。

热布巴拉起坏心，
一心想把阿黑害，
不叫的黄蜂专叮人，
热布巴拉假殷勤。

话未出口先假笑：
“舅舅辛苦了，
好好睡一觉，
明天再送你们走。”

热布巴拉半夜商量的话，
阿诗玛都听见了，
聪明的阿诗玛，
口弦吹三调：

“哥哥阿黑呀！
你知道不知道？
他们比赛比不过，
今晚要放虎害哥哥。”

阿黑吹横笛，
回答阿诗玛：

“妹妹别担心，
弓箭藏在身。”

果然半夜老虎叫，
叫得地动山也跳，
张开口来小锅大，
胡须就像扇子摇。

山区人民爱打猎，
能手要数勇敢的阿黑，
豺、狼、虎、豹死他手，
少说也有九百九十九。

三只老虎冲上楼，
阿黑闪过楼梯口，
“嗖”“嗖”三箭射过去，
老虎立刻倒下地。

大力气阿黑，
脚踏虎身手撕皮，
剥下大虎皮，
又照样套上虎身。

脚趾夹着虎尾，
靠在老虎身边，
心里盘算周全，
假装睡得香甜。

热布巴拉家父子俩，
一夜不睡等天亮，
早起假意喊阿黑：
“舅舅家，下楼洗脸吃饭啦！”

使劲喊一回，
没有人答应，
使劲喊两回，
还是没有动静；

使劲喊三回，
依然没有响声，
只见楼梯口，
老虎摇尾巴。

热布巴拉家，
一家笑哈哈，
“人已经吃光了，
老虎才摇尾巴。”

话还没说完，
轰隆一声响，
三只死虎滚下楼，
阿黑在楼口伸懒腰。

“你家养虎不对我说，
吵得一夜睡不着，
今早起得晚，
对不起你家了。”

阿支吓得脸发白，
热布巴拉脸发青，
阿支浑身不停地抖，
热布巴拉抖不停。

“舅舅，对不起，
忘了告诉你，

赶快剥虎皮，
拿虎肉做菜请舅舅吃。”

阿黑说：
“你们剥大的，
还是剥小的？”
热布巴拉说：
“舅舅为大剥大的，
我们剥小的。”

热布巴拉两父子，
用尽全身力气，
一顿饭的时间，
还没有剥下半张皮。

阿黑手提虎尾巴，
左一甩，
右一甩，
就掉下一整张皮来。

“老虎的毛算多了，
你们的坏主意多过老虎毛，
老虎的肉我不吃了，
救阿诗玛比吃虎肉重要。”

热布巴拉两父子，
吓得全身流冷汗，
眼看阿黑兄妹往外走，
不敢上前去阻拦。

13　回　声

热布巴拉家心不甘，

商量办法来暗算，
眼看阿黑兄妹就回家，
回了家就更没办法。

忽然想起十二崖子脚，
阿黑兄妹一定要走过，
十二崖子脚，
有一条小河。

小河上面有个湖，
积满山洪水，
石堤四面围，
庄稼好收成。

热布巴拉一伙人，
决堤放尽湖中水，
用山洪卷走阿诗玛，
使他兄妹两离分。

马铃响来玉鸟叫，
兄妹二人回家了，
远远离开热布巴拉家，
爹妈从此不忧伤。

松树尖上蜜蜂不停留，
松树根下蜜蜂嗡嗡叫，
远远离开热布巴拉家，
爹娘从此眯眯笑。

哥哥吹笛子，
妹妹弹口弦，
哥哥说话妹高兴，

妹妹说话哥喜欢。

走到十二崖子脚，
走到河水边，
突然洪水滚滚来，
小河顷刻变大河。

哥哥前面走，
妹妹过不了河，
哥哥后面走，
妹妹过不了河，

阿黑拉着阿诗玛的手，
阿诗玛拉着阿黑的手，
迎着洪水，
一起往前走。

兄妹两人啊！
不管小河还是大河，
不管水浅还是水深，
都要一起过。

洪水滚滚来，
卷来一个大漩涡，
可爱的阿诗玛，
被漩涡卷走了。

留下了她的声音，
在水面上回转：
"哥哥阿黑呀！
赶快来救我！"

十二崖子上，

住着另一个姑娘，

她的名字叫诗卡都勒玛①，
她的命运和阿诗玛一样。

她是个勤劳美丽的姑娘，
大家都把她爱在心上，
偏偏她的公婆，
对她百般折磨。

天造老石崖，
石崖四角方，
她逃到十二崖子上，
把石崖当作家乡。

亲人怎样喊她，
她就怎样回答。
可爱的诗卡都勒玛，
从此就叫做“应山歌”。

听见阿诗玛的呼喊，
看见阿诗玛被洪水卷走，
“应山歌”姑娘呵！
她又是着急，又是难过。

瓦雀不离屋檐，
好人关心好人，
看见阿诗玛遇难，

---

① 原编选者注：诗卡都勒玛——撒尼族传说中她是一个很有名的美丽可爱的姑娘，出嫁后，由于忍受不了公婆的虐待，就跳崖自杀。她婆婆到处找她，到石崖前喊她，崖石那边就有同样的声音回答，以后，大家就叫诗卡都勒玛为“应山歌”姑娘。

哪能站在一边！

“应山歌”姑娘呵！
她投入漩涡，
排开了洪水，
把阿诗玛救活。

天空出彩霞，
红光照四方，
彩霞托着两个姑娘，
两个姑娘像姊妹一样。

两个姑娘在一个屋里住下，
两个姑娘亲热的说着知心话，
高高的十二崖子顶，
开出了一朵并蒂花。

哥哥阿黑呵！
在洪水中翻腾，
在漩涡中急转，
阿诗玛却早已不见！

他打平了漩涡，
制服了洪水，
焦急的高声叫喊：
“阿诗玛！阿诗玛！阿诗玛！”

十二崖子顶，
有人来答应，
同样的声音，
“阿诗玛！阿诗玛！阿诗玛！”

只见彩霞漫天边，

一道红，一道黄，
彩霞下面的崖顶上，
站着阿诗玛和“应山歌”姑娘。

可爱的阿诗玛呵！
耳环亮堂堂，
银镯带手上，
脸上笑眯眯，
眼睛放亮光。

“勇敢的阿黑哥哥呵！
天造老石崖，
石崖四角方，
这里就是我的住房。

“从今以后，
我们不能同住一家，
但还是同住一村，
同住一块地方。

“勇敢的阿黑哥哥呵！
每天吃饭的时候，
盛了金黄色的玉米饭，
你来叫我，
我就答应你。

“告诉亲爹妈，
每天做活的时候，
不管天晴还是下雨，
不管放羊还是犁地，
不管挑水还是煮饭，
不管绣花还是织麻，

你们来叫我，
我就答应你们。

“告诉我的小伴，
每次出去玩耍，
不论端午还是中秋，
不论是六月二十四还是三月初三①，
吹着清脆的笛子，
弹着悦耳的三弦，
你们来叫我，
我就答应你们。”

从今以后，
阿诗玛变成了回声，
你怎样喊她，
她怎样回应。

每天吃饭的时候，
阿黑盛着玉米饭，
对着石崖喊：
“阿诗玛，阿诗玛。”

石崖那边，
阿诗玛住的地方，
也照样回答：
“阿诗玛，阿诗玛。”

① 原编选者注：六月二十四，三月初三——六月二十四是“火把节”，是撒尼族最盛大的节日，在六月二十四的前后三天，在山野中举行盛大的斗牛及抬跤（即摔跤）大会；会后，青年男女即在山野中尽情欢乐，谈情说爱，一直到深夜。三月初三主要是青年的节日，每年逢这一天，路南附近几县的撒尼族青年，都穿着崭新的衣裳，到老圭山聚会，这是青年找寻爱人的好机会。

爹妈出去做活的时候，
对着石崖喊：
“爹妈的好囡呀，
好囡阿诗玛！”

对面，同样的声音，
回答亲爹妈：
“爹妈的好囡呀，
好囡阿诗玛！”

小伴们每次出去玩的时候，
都要来约阿诗玛，
他们弹着三弦，吹着笛子，
对着石崖大声欢笑。

对面，也传来同样的声音，
笛声悠扬，
歌声嘹亮，
笑声在山林中回荡。……

Ashma (Chapters 10—13)

X

Then Ajii barred the iron gate,
To shut Ahay outside.
"First let me see if you can guess
My riddles!" Ajii cried.

"If you sing best and pass the test,
You shall come in, Ahay.
But if you cannot answer me,
Then you must go your way."

"Twelve roads there are ahead of you,
And thirteen pathways too;
Then take your pick of any road,
The choice is left to you!

"My cause is just, so I shall win
In any bout of song;
You cannot shut your door on me,
For you are in the wrong."

Then Ajii sat upon the wall,
Beneath a tree, Ahay;
The one uneasy in his mind,
The other calm and gay.

And straightway Ajii asked Ahay:
"Which is the bird of spring?"

"The cuckoo is the bird of spring;
Spring comes when cuckoos sing."

"Which is the bird of summer then?"
Asked Ajii, sore downcast.
"The skylark is gay summer's bird,
When lotus blooms at last."

"Which is the bird of autumn, then,
That sings when leaves do fall?"
"The nightjar is rich autumn's bird;
The frost comes at its call."

"Which is the bird of winter cold,
Which comes when snowflakes fly?"
"The swift wild goose, for when it calls
We know that winter's nigh."

They sang for one whole day and night,
Till Ajii, like to choke.
Was breathing hard, his throat was hoarse,
His voice a feeble croak.

They sang for one whole day and night;
Ahay in smiling ease,
For all to hear outsang the clear
Cicadas in the trees.

When Ajii had no riddles left,
Ahay his questions tried:
"Who gave the hawthorn trees their thorns
Upon the mountain side?"

But Ajii could not answer him,
The coward's tongue was tied;
He had to open up the gate
And let Ahay inside.

And when the threshold he had crossed
He shouted joyously:
"Where are you, Ashma? Ashma, love!
Make haste and answer me!"

But straight Rabûbalor proposed:
"First whet your axe, Ahay!
If you can fell more trees than I,
Then you shall have your way."

"Twelve roads there are ahead of you,
And thirteen pathways too;
Then take your pick of any road,
The choice is left to you!"

Rabûbalor and Ajii plied
The axe with furious strokes;
But ere they felled a single tree,
Ahay felled three great oaks.

Rabûbalor saw they had lost,
And planned a third attack.
"This is no day for felling trees;
Now put the timber back!"

But felling trees or grafting trees

Left Ahay undismayed.
"Let's see what other tricks you have,
What other plans you've laid!"

While Ajii and Rabûbalor
Were grafting one small tree,
Our brave Ahay, with no man's help,
Had quickly grafted three.

Rabûbalor saw they had lost,
But countered in a trice:
"This is no day for grafting trees;
How fast can you sow rice?"

But grafting trees or sowing rice
Left Ahay undismayed.
"Let's see what other tricks you have,
What other plans you've laid!"

Rabûbalor and Ajii then
Threw rice by handfuls fast,
But three or four times more than they
The bold Ahay had cast.

When he perceived that they had lost,
Thus spoke Rabûbalor:
"This is no day for sowing rice;
Now pick it up once more!"

But scattering or picking rice
Left Ahay undismayed.
"Let's see what other tricks you have,

What other plans you've laid!"

While Ajii and Rabûbalor
Picked up a little rice,
Three times as much, with no man's aid,
Ahay picked in a trice.

Rabûbalor walked over then,
And crowed with wicked glee:
"Three grains of rice to every ditch,
But you are short of three!"

The young pine on the mountain side
Fears neither wind nor gale;
Although Ahay had lost three grains,
His courage did not fail.

And when the skylark ceased to sing,
And daylight left the plain,
And savage dogs no longer barked.
He went to find the grain.

When slowly, slowly rose the sun,
He saw, far far away,
An old man plough a buckwheat field,
His ploughshare bright as day.

"O good old man, I ask your aid,"
Up spoke our brave Ahay.
"Where can I find three grains of rice
That I lost yesterday?"

The kind old ploughman answered him:
"Lost hoes seek in the lea;
Lost herds seek on the mountain side;
Lost rice seek on a tree.

"Now give three shouts upon the hill,
And in the valley three;
Upon a branch half up the hill
Three turtle doves you'll see.

"The middle dove, it faces west,
But east the other twain.
Shoot down the dove that faces west;
Its crop contains your grain."

Then running to the tree, Ahay
His bow bent in a trice;
The turtle dove that he brought down
Spat out three grains of rice!

XI

Ahay picked up the grains of rice,
And ran to Ajii's door;
He strung his bow and aimed three times:
His shafts were swift and sure.

Three arrows struck that wicked house:
The shrine, the wall, the door.
Good men might pluck those arrows out,
But not Rabûbalor.

And as the arrows pierced the wall,

With fear those villains shook;
great their dismay, for now Ahay
Could bring them all to book!

The kinsmen gripped the arrows then,
And wrenched with might and main;
They yoked five buffaloes abreast,
But tugged and pulled in vain.

In vain all measures that he knew
Rabûbalor essayed;
He had to open Ashma's cell
And beg her for her aid.

"Oh, ask your brother, Ashma fair,
To pull these arrows out.
For we have lost, and he has won;
No more your will we'll flout."

With Ahay near, she had no fear,
But said: "With all your craft,
And all your skill in working ill,
You cannot pull one shaft?"

"Sweet Ashma," said Rabûbalor,
"Your shafts your words obey.
If you will pull them out, then home
We'll send you with Ahay."

"The arrows that Ahay has shot
Would yield to me, I know.
I'd sooner kill than lend my skill;

And yet I fain would go."

As soon as she put forth her hand,
Out came the arrows three;
Thus stronger than five oxen great
Did Ashma prove to be.

XII

They could not overcome Ahay
For all their wicked wiles;
Nor yet prevail on Ashma sweet
With their deceitful smiles.

Yet still that knave, Rabûbalor,
Resolved to have his way.
The silent wasps are those that sting:
He smiled upon Ahay.

And, swallowing his rage, he said:
"You must be tired, I know.
Then rest yourself before you leave;
Tomorrow you shall go."

But Ashma knew their wicked plot
To kill Ahay right soon;
And taking out her small mô-sheen,
She played a warning tune.

"Take care, Ahay! Now they have failed
In every contest fair,
They will let tigers out tonight
To kill you! Oh, beware!"

Then Ahay played upon his flute,
To answer Ashma dear.
"With bow and arrows I am armed;
Sweet sister, do not fear!"

That night they loosed great tigers three
Who prowled on velvet paws,
With baleful eyeballs all agleam,
And monstrous, slavering jaws.

The Shani folk all love to hunt,
But none excelled Ahay;
With knife and bow he had laid low
A thousand beasts of prey.

Three tigers climbed the tower stairs,
But from the stairway dark
Ahay shot three swift arrows down:
Each arrow found its mark.

The largest of these dreadful beasts
He deftly skinned anon,
Then put the skin back as before,
That none could see't was done.

But he had formed an artful plan;
His vigil he did keep,
His toe upon the tiger's tail,
He lay as if asleep.

Rabûbalor and Ajii too

Stayed wide awake all night,
Then called at dawn: "Arise, Ahay!
Come down to eat! It's light!"

They called as loudly as they could,
But no one made reply;
They called again a second time,
But heard no answering cry.

They called once more, both loud and long,
Yet all to no avail;
But noticed there, above the stair,
A tiger switch its tail.

The kinsmen of Rabûbalor
Both loud and long laughed they.
"We see a tiger switch its tail;
It must have killed Ahay!"

While yet the words were on their lips,
A crash disturbed the dawn!
As three dead tigers rolled downstairs,
Ahay stood up to yawn.

"I did not know you kept these cats.
Their howling was so great,
That I must ask your pardon now
If I have slept too late.

Rabûbalor turned grey with fear,
And Ajii he turned white;
Rabûbalor he quaked with dread,

And Ajii shook with fright.

"You must excuse us. We forgot
To tell you, dear Ahay.
We'll have these tigers skinned at once,
To feast you here today."

"And will you skin the largest first,
Or with the least begin?"
"You skin the largest: 'tis your due—
The smaller we will skin."

To skin the smaller tigers then,
They sweated, sire and son;
But in the time it takes to dine
Skinned only half of one.

Ahay he grasped the tiger's tail,
And pulled from left to right,
And then held up the skin entire
To their astonished sight.

"Your wicked schemes outnumber far
A tiger's hairs, I know.
I will not eat the tiger's meat,
For homeward I must go."

Then with cold sweat was Ajii wet,
And old Rabûbalor;
They saw sweet Ashma led away,
Yet dared not bar the door.

XIII

Rabûbalor was not content,
But swore to wreak his hate;
For when Ahay was far away,
Then it would be too late.

He called to mind the great ravine
Which lay upon their road;
In that ravine, twelve crags between,
A little brooklet flowed.

Upstream a mountain lake was dammed
With stony rampart good;
The crops around were safe and sound,
Protected from the food.

Rabûbalor and all his men
Would breach that dike of stone;
The flood should carry Ashma off
And leave Ahay alone!

The mare's bell rang, the jade bird sang,
They left Rabûbalor;
And now that they were riding home,
Their parents grieved no more.

Then Ashma sweet her small mô-sheen,
Ahay his flute did play;
With joy he heard his sister dear,
And she with joy Ahay.

They reached the foot of twelve steep crags,
The brook ran hard beside;
Then suddenly the banks gave way,
And flood spread far and wide.

Then Ashma could not cross the flood
While Ahay walked behind;
Yet when he led, or rode ahead,
No path could Ashma find.

The brother held his sister's hand,
And Ashma held Ahay;
To brave the waters of the food,
Hand clasping hand went they.

Ahay and Ashma did not fear,
Though loud the torrent roared;
The rushing tide they both defied,
Together they would ford.

But on the foaming water rolled,
To form a whirlpool great,
And lovely Ashma was caught up
And borne off by the spate.

Her voice alone was left to float
And hover on the wave:
"O brother, brother, save me now
From such a watery grave!"

Above the twelve crags in that place
Another maiden dwelt;

Her name Skadulma, and to her
The same fate had been dealt.

A lovely and a nimble girl,
Beloved of all was she;
But all her husband's kith and kin
Had wronged her cruelly.

Now Heaven had made a mighty rock,
An ancient boulder square;
And she had scaled those twelve great crags,
And made her dwelling there.

And whensoe'er her dear ones called,
She answer made the same;
So "Echo" ever afterwards
Became Skadulma's name.

When Echo heard sweet Ashma's call,
And saw her swept away,
The mountain maid was sore afraid,
And great was her dismay.

As sparrows to their eaves return;
Kind folk for kind folk sigh.
Echo, who saw sweet Ashma's plight,
Could not stand idly by.

While Ahay battled with the waves
And braved the torrent's might,
The whirlpool's vortex snatched away
His sister from his sight!

And Echo then, fair mountain maid,
The raging waters braved;
She clove the angry, foaming flood,
And Ashma's life she saved.

At last Ahay the whirlpool's spate,
And torrent overcame;
Then "Ashma! Ashma! Ashma dear!"
Three times he called her name.

And high above the twelve great crags,
An answer floated clear—
The selfsame accents as his own:
"O Ashma! Ashma, dear!"

He saw the bow that spanned the sky,
Half golden and half red;
Echo and Ashma radiant stood
Beneath it, high o'erhead.

With sparkling ear-rings Ashma stood,
And silver bracelets bright;
A soft smile played about her lips,
Her sweet, dark eyes alight.

"Oh, brother, see this ancient rock,
That rises square and sheer.
Heaven gave it as a refuge sure,
And my new home is here.

"From this day forward, never more

Together shall we stand;
But in one hamlet shall we live,
So far, yet close at hand.

"And daily when the meal is cooked,
And when your bowl you take,
If you will call me, brother dear,
An answer will I make.

"And brother, tell my parents dear,
Whatever may befall,
That though the day be fair or foul,
I'll answer at their call.

"As they tend sheep or plough the land,
Or cook or carry water.
Or sew or spin, I'll answer them,
Whene'er they call their daughter.

"And brother, bid my playmates dear
Remember as they sing,
That at the summer festival,
The festival of spring,

"As on the soft mô-sheen they play,
Or flute's clear echoes fall,
If they will come and call my name,
I'll answer at their call."

So Ashma spoke, and from that day
An echo she became.
Call her a thousand different ways,

She answers with the same.

Each day, his maize bowl in his hand,
Beneath the boulder high,
Before Ahay began to eat,
"Dear Ashma!" he would cry.

And then from Ashma's rocky lodge
That towered above the shore,
The words that he had called returned
"Dear Ashma!" ever more.

When Ashma's friends laid by their work
To roam through wood and glade,
Their songs and laughter filled the glen,
As on their flutes they played.

Then from the mountain echoed back
The flutes' soft piercing trills,
And merry songs and laughter spread
Through all the woods and hills.

And when her parents went to work,
They hailed the boulder sheer;
"O Ashma, daughter lost to us!
Oh, Ashma! Ashma, dear!"

And from the peak the selfsame sound
The good old folk could hear:
"O Ashma, daughter lost to us!
Oh, Ashma! Ashma, dear!"

四

单口相声故事四则[①]

看财奴

逢这种特别的事都出在我们那儿。我们那个村儿有这么一家子，这老头儿是个大地主，有仨儿子，三房儿媳妇。家里养活七十多匹牲口，种着八十多顷地，开着两个大粮行，可是家里吃饭老得掺糠，吃菜呀就是白水儿熬哇！一大锅菜，菜帮儿、菜根儿全有，搁一大把盐齁死爹！搁油的时候儿呀，得老头儿亲自搁油，别人搁油不成，上上下下五十多口子人吃饭，这一大锅菜呀搁多少油？搁四钱油。一天搁四钱，十天不就是四两吗？钱跟钱不一样，油罐儿里头搁一根筷子——筷子头儿上扎一个小钱儿，开锅的时候儿当家的搁油，这手托着罐子，这手拿着筷子往油罐儿里一蘸，提溜起来往锅里一控，这叫一钱。您说也纳闷儿，大年三十儿打来四两香油，吃到过年大年三十儿，一约哇七两五，吃了一年倒多出三两五来，它为什么多三两五哇？为什么？他把汤带回来啦！

一家子都得跟着他吃糠，他这仨儿媳妇儿娘家都趁钱，享受惯啦！吃那糠窝窝成吗？谁吃呀！要不怎么叫看财奴哪，老头儿吃！一顿好几个糠窝窝吃得挺饱。儿子、儿媳妇儿、孙子在旁边儿举着糠窝窝也得咬两口，咬两口搁那儿就算饱啦！一剩剩一大笸箩，他看着还挺欢喜，说：

---

① 中文选自：张寿臣，等. 单口相声传统作品选. 北京：中国曲艺出版社，1981；英译文选自：Zhang，S. C. *Traditional Comic Tales*. Gladys Yang（trans.）. Beijing：Chinese Literature Press，1983.

“我们起家运，都吃不多！”

吃完了饭他出去捡粪去，一出去就是二十多里，捡几泡马粪来回四十多里。赶上他一出去，家里是刀、勺乱响啊，肉山酒海，想吃什么吃什么！等到他也回来啦，这儿也吃完了，连家伙都拾掇起来啦！儿子、儿媳妇儿还能都睡个晌觉。晚上啊，还吃糠窝窝，一人咬一口就完啦！

有这时候儿，夏景天儿，吃完了早饭他出去捡粪去啦，家里刀、勺乱响，儿子、儿媳妇儿这儿作饭。嗯！赶上闹天儿，老头儿回来啦，眼瞧就要进门啦！好，要叫他进了门，一瞧肉山酒海，能玩儿命！这怎么办啊？不要紧哪，他绝对进不来，进了大门也进不了二门。哦，二门上着锁？没有！他这儿子、儿媳妇儿想出道儿来啦，这儿做着饭哪，要不正吃着哪，一瞧，闹天儿啦，出去一个人抓这么两、三把黄豆往门道里一撒就得，放心吃吧，老头儿就进不来啦！怎么？他揹着粪筐走到门道一瞧，地下净是黄豆，站在那儿就骂街：

“嗐！怎么这么糟践东西呀！啊？这是闹着玩儿的？”

骂一个够，没人理他，他蹲在那儿呀一个黄豆粒一个黄豆粒地捡。您算算，三把黄豆他一个不剩全得把它捡净了——里头连家伙都刷完啦！

后来怎么样哪？直顶到他死这钱不舍得花。临死的时候儿他不放心哪，怕儿子把家底儿给抖落了，把仨儿子叫到跟前，问他大儿子：

“我不行啦，我死之后你怎么料理我呀？”

大儿子这么想，他爸爸活着的时候儿趁那么些财产，没吃过没花过，太冤哪！哥儿仨赌受这份儿产业一分……唉！心里难过呀！

“爸爸，您只管放心，我们一定对得起您，您只管放心得啦！”

“不成啊，你们怎么个对得起我呀？怎么料理我呀？”

“怎么料理您的后事，都打点好啦，给您预备一个金丝楠的棺材，咱们出点儿产业，可着那俩大米庄发送您还不成吗？铺金盖银，陀罗经被，给您七个金钱压土，身上给您带七颗珠子，咱们搁七七四十九天，念僧、道、番、尼四棚经，出殡用六十四人扛……”

这话还没说完哪，老头儿就急啦：

“放屁，放屁！不像话，不像话呀！咱们家里趁多少哇？俩大米庄也不够哇！这么发送我！金丝楠棺材不是埋到地下也烂了吗？七颗珠子，七个金钱那得多少钱？你这么糟践哪！哎哟，搁四十九天，亲友一来得多大挑费呀！用我的钱弄饭让他们吃，我心疼啊！哎，滚！滚一边儿去，不成！”

大儿子碰啦！问二的：

“你怎么办哪？”

二的一听，哥哥那个谱儿是大点儿。

“老爷子您放心吧，我哥哥那个谱儿哇是大，咱们是不那么趁。再说我们还得过哪！给您来一个杉木的，杉木十三圆儿，装裹呢，七颗珠子不用啦，七颗金钱给您哪！铺金盖银，陀罗经被，满免。搁三七二十一天就成，接三念一棚经，平常日子不念经，也不办事。”

“不行，这也大，按你这么一说，哎，一个米庄也剩不了什么啦！不行，不行！三儿说！三儿，三儿，怎么办？”

他这三儿子聪明，知道他爸爸那个心思，心想：我说两句话呀，把老头儿骂死得啦，等他死了我们再慢慢儿办。

“您问什么，老爷子？”

“你怎么办哪？”

“我跟您的心思一样啊，我俩哥哥说的完全不对，他们不会过日子，您这一辈子克勤克俭来的钱，要这么一摆谱儿给花啦，多冤哪！再说，搁三七二十一天，亲友都来，天天不得给他们吃吗？犯不上啊！我有个办法，说出来您准能放心，您死之后我们一个子儿不花，不但不花钱，还要赚俩钱儿！”

看财奴哇这一辈子也没想到人死了还能赚钱！

“我死之后还要赚俩钱？哎呀，好，小子，你说说怎么赚法？我得听听你这道儿，看你怎么把我料理出去！”

“是呀，不但把您料理出去，料理出去之后还得赚钱哪！您哪虽说病了这些日子，可是膘儿没掉哇，您骨盘儿又大，这身肉怎么也得有一百多斤哪！就用二斤盐钱，来点儿糖色，把您卸剥卸剥拿糖色、盐水这么一煮，把五脏洗洗当杂碎，推着车这么一卖，满打跟羊肉、牛肉一个价儿吧！您这一百多斤肉我们得赚多少钱哪！这么着，把您也料理啦，我们还赚钱，您看怎么样？"

他大儿子、二儿子吓了一跳，准知道老头儿得急呀！嘿！你瞧怪不怪，不但没急，他倒乐啦！

"好，好小子，哎呀，你这才对我的心思，应当这么办！好小子，好小子！卖肉可是卖肉哇，推车出门儿往南，千万别上北边儿去！"

"北边儿怎么啦？"

"北边儿那几家街坊啊他们爱赊账！"

全想到啦！

（张寿臣口述）

The Miser

It happened in our village, the strange story you're going to hear.

A big landlord here had three sons and three daughters-in-law. They owned six dozen head of cattle, some two hundred acres of farmland and two grain shops, yet they always mixed bran with their rice and instead of frying their vegetables simply boiled them in water. A big pan of vegetables, outer leaves, roots and all, with a great handful of salt—ugh! If oil was added it had to be done by the old landlord himself. What with family and servants they had over fifty mouths to feed, so how much oil do you suppose was added to this pan of vegetables? Four tenths of an ounce a day. Four ounces in ten days, right? A chopstick was kept in the oil vat with a small scoop on one end. When the master added oil, one hand on the vat, the other holding the chopstick, he scooped it up and emptied it into the pan—that was four tenths of an ounce. But strange to say, four ounces of sesame oil bought on New Year's Eve would last for a whole year, and there'd be seven and a half ounces left over—he'd produced an extra three and a half ounces! How come? Each time he emptied his scoop he refilled it with the water in the pan!

The whole household had to eat bran with him. His three daughters-in-law came from rich families and were accustomed to living well. How could they eat bran muffins? Yet they couldn't just sit there watching the old man stuffing himself with bran muffins at each meal. His sons, daughters-in-law and grandchildren had to swallow a couple of mouthfuls of muffin too, after which they put them down saying they had had enough. There were always a lot left over, and he would say gleefully:

"We're none of us big eaters, that's why our family's thriving."

After breakfast he would go off to collect horse-dung, trudging forty *li* there and back. As soon as he left there was a great clatter of cleavers and ladles in the kitchen as the others prepared to gorge themselves. Masses of meat they had and lashings of liquor. By the time he came back they had finished, cleared everything away, and his sons and their wives had enjoyed a good siesta. In the evening, when bran muffins were served again, they ate only one mouthful each.

One summer day when the miser went out after breakfast to collect dung, they prepared their meal with a clatter of cleavers and ladles. But their luck had run out—the old fellow came back early. My, if he came in and saw all that meat and liquor, there would be the devil to pay! What could they do? Don't worry, he couldn't come in, or at least only through the main gate, not through the inner gate. Why, was the inner gate locked? No. But his sons and daughters-in-law thought up a dodge. One of them took two handfuls of soya beans and scattered these by the gate. Then they could cook and eat their meal in peace, and the old man wouldn't disturb them. Why not? When he stepped through the main gate with his crate of dung, he saw beans all over the ground and let out a bellow:

"Hell! What a waste! What fool did this?"

They let him curse and swear, paying no attention as he squatted down to pick up those beans one by one. Figure it out for yourselves. By the time he had picked up every single bean the people inside had washed up.

And afterwards? He hoarded his wealth right up to the time of his death. And on his death-bed what worried him was the fear that his sons would squander his property. He called them in and asked his eldest son:

"I'm done for. How will you manage my funeral?"

His eldest son thought it too bad that his father had made so much money yet never spent it. Now he and his brothers would each inherit a share—it didn't seem right.

"Don't you worry, dad," he said. "We'll give you a handsome funeral."

"That won't do. What do you mean by handsome? Tell me."

"We've got it all worked out. We'll give you a coffin of the best *nanmu* wood. We can sell those two grain shops to pay for the funeral, can't we? You'll have a gold bed sheet below, and a silvery quilt embroidered with charms above, seven gold coins to keep down the earth, seven pearls to wear. And for forty-nine whole days we'll get Buddhists, Taoists, lamas and nuns to recite masses for you. You'll have sixty-four pall-bearers...."

Before he could say any more his father cut in, "You silly ass! What rubbish you talk. Are we made of money? Selling two grain shops wouldn't raise enough to give me such a send-off. The *nanmu* coffin would only rot in the ground. And how much would seven pearls and seven gold coins cost? Want to ruin the family? Why, in forty-nine days our relatives and friends would eat you out of house and home! I can't bear you feeding them at *my* expense. Bah, get away, scram! Nothing doing."

After snubbing his eldest son he asked the second:

"How would *you* handle things?"

The second son thought his brother had overdone it.

"Don't worry, sir," he said. "My brother wanted more than we can afford, because we still have to live! We'll give you a fir-board coffin with no pearls inside, just seven gold coins. And there's no need for a gold bed-sheet and a silvery quilt embroidered with charms. We'll mourn for twenty-one days, with masses said every three days, not every day."

"No, that's still too much. Why, that would clean us out. No, no! Number Three! How would *you* handle it?"

His third son was clever and understood his father. He thought: I'll make the old fellow pop off with rage, then we can take our time arranging his funeral.

"What did you ask, sir?"

"How would you handle it?"

"I agree with you, my brothers were quite wrong. They don't know how to manage. The money you've worked so hard all your life to save, what a shame it would be if they squandered it like that! Besides, if we mourned for twenty-one days we'd have to feed all our relatives and friends. That would never do. I have a plan to set your mind at rest. We won't spend a cent on your funeral—we'll make some money instead!"

The miser had never imagined that money could be made out of a dead man.

"How will you do that, eh? Tell me, there's a good lad. I want to hear how you would handle the business."

"I'd handle it so as to make some money. Though you've been ill you haven't wasted away—your big carcass should weigh at least a hundred pounds. If we buy two pounds of salt and a little sugar, we can strip off your flesh and boil it with them, cleaning up your viscera to use as offal. Then we can push a barrow through the street, selling your meat for the same price as mutton or beef. We should make quite a tidy sum for over a hundred pounds. That way we'd dispose of you and make money too. What do you think of my plan?"

His elder brothers were horrified, but to their surprise the old man approved. Just imagine, instead of losing his temper he beamed!

"Fine, there's a good lad, you know me. Do it that way. Good for you, lad! But push your barrow of meat to the south of our gate. Be sure not to take it north."

"Why not north?"

"The families to the north like to buy on credit."

He thought of everything!

(Told by Zhang Shouchen)

糊涂县官

在旧社会有一句话:“同行是冤家。”有些人就相信了这句话,吃了不少亏,上了不少当。同行与同行之间闹对立,连出家的和尚老道都闹别扭,古书里有很多和尚与老道互相争斗的故事,他们念的经就有矛盾。

谁家死了人,请棚和尚来念经,超度亡魂,叫鬼魂到西方去,因为西方是极乐世界,西方接引。

可是老道一念经,叫鬼魂到东方去,因为东方是白阳世界。

要是换尼姑念经,就叫鬼魂到南方去,南海大士不是在南边儿吗?

可是喇嘛来念经,就叫鬼魂到北方去。世界上没有鬼,如果真有鬼,这就麻烦大啦。怎么哪?要是请和尚、老道、尼姑、喇嘛在一块儿冲这死人念经,叫鬼魂也为难哪,到底上哪方好呢?听谁的对呢?这鬼魂没准主意啦,只好站在那儿转吧。您看马路上刮的旋风,大概就是他们念经念的,不!这不像话啦。

从前有这么一段笑话,有一个和尚,四海云游,到处为家,指着化缘维持生活,有一天在茶馆里遇见一个老道,两位一边喝茶一边盘道,每人都在夸奖自己,互相都有点儿看不起对方,谈来谈去就谈到经卷和学问上了。

老道说:“出家最好当道士,打扮潇洒大方,我做一首诗,请你听听:头戴道冠,身穿蓝衫,手拿拂尘,亚似神仙。”

和尚说:“你不像神仙,神仙没有像你这样的,你看我才真像神仙呢,我也作一首诗:吃斋行善,常把经念,身披偏衫,好像罗汉。我看你是:发长不便(就是说老道的头发太长不方便),每天打扮,非男非女,实在难看。”

和尚说老道不像女的,不像男的。老道不乐意啦。当时给和尚也作了四句:“身披袈裟,头上无发,割掉耳朵,好像西瓜。”

嘎!这一句话可把和尚气急啦,俩人越说越恼,最后还真打起来啦。在那黑暗的社会里,什么稀奇古怪的事儿都能发生,和尚抓住老道的头发,左右开弓,打了十几个大嘴巴。老道也抓和尚,抓了半天什么也没抓着,因为和尚没有头发,老道七抓八抓把和尚的耳朵抓着啦,往上一提,一张嘴,喀哧!把和尚的鼻子咬下一块来。这一下子可坏了!和尚弄得满脸都是血,茶馆里看热闹的人都围满喽。七嘴八舌的说什么的都有。

这个说:"这是什么世道!"

那个说:"出家人真不像话,他们要是这样,我们俗家人该怎么办哪!"

正在这个时候,地方来了一看,两个出家人打架,还把鼻子咬下来啦。见血就归刑事案子,不能私休,一定要惊官动府。把和尚、老道带到县衙门,偏偏又碰上这位县官是用钱运动来的,上任日期不久,问了几件案子,一件也没问清楚,是一位糊涂县官;不但糊涂,并且还怕太太。

县官一听来了打官司的,马上吩咐升堂。三班六房齐声"威武"一喊,县官往堂上一坐,差人们列站两旁。县官一看堂下跪着一个和尚,一个老道。再看和尚满脸净是血。县官问和尚:"为什么打官司?"

和尚说:"他咬我的鼻子。"

县官又问老道:"你为什么咬他鼻子?"

这个老道不承认,说:"老爷,不是我,是他自己咬的。"

县官说:"和尚,你自己咬的,为什么反告人家?"

和尚一听,心里这个气就大啦。我自己怎么能咬自己的鼻子?忙说:"老爷,我自己咬鼻子够不着哇。"

老爷一听心说:对,对,对!自己是够不着咬。向老道说:"他自己够不着咬。"

老道说:"他站在板凳上咬的。"

老爷一听认为完全有理,自己咬自己的鼻子,如果够不着,一站高点儿,那准能够着。责问和尚说:

"好你大胆的和尚,站在凳子上把自己的鼻子咬下来,反要诬赖好人,来呀,拉下去重打四十!"

您看这和尚多倒霉,让人家把鼻子咬掉了,还挨了四十板子,挨了打不算,还给押起来啦,派差人跟老道上街找保释放,就这样马马虎虎退堂啦。县官回到内宅,太太就问:

“老爷,今天是什么案子,为什么这么快就退堂啦?”

县官说:“太太你不知道,是两个出家人打官司,一个狡猾的和尚,自己把鼻子咬下来,不说实话,反告老道,愣说是老道咬下来的,当时我把和尚打了四十板子押起来啦,老道找保释放。太太,我今天这件案子审得不错吧?”

太太一听,就知道又弄错啦。说道:

“老爷,自己咬自己的鼻子,天大的本事也够不着哇。”

老爷说;“我也是这样问的,可是老道说他站在板凳上咬的。太太请想,不论够什么够不着,一站高点儿,不就够着了吗?”

太太说:“站得再高也不能咬着自己的鼻子呀。我给你搬个凳子,你站上去咬咬自己的鼻子,试试怎么样?”

老爷有点儿怕太太,他真站在凳子上,够了半天,张着大嘴,怎么样也咬不着自己的鼻子,可是他还不明白,又问道:

“太太,这个凳子是不是太矮啦?”

太太说:“好吧,来,你上房去够够看。”老爷当时到了院里,登着梯子就上了房啦,站在房顶上够了半天,没够着,这才明白。

太太又生气又是乐,说:“你快给我下来吧,赶快派人把老道捉回来,重新过堂。把老道得重重的打一顿,给和尚出出气。不然的话,老百姓也不服,说不定你这个官儿做不长啦。可是我又怕你问不清楚。这可怎么办呢?干脆这样儿吧!过堂的时候我躲在旁边,我跟你打哑谜,到时候听我的,叫你对老道怎么样,就怎样。好不好?”

老爷一听,太高兴啦:

“就这么办吧!”马上派人把老道捉回来,二次升堂,老爷早早坐在堂上,太太蹲在老爷身后,三班六房站立两边。把老道带到堂上往那儿一跪,老道心想:这回要倒霉。

老爷一拍惊堂木说:“老道!和尚的鼻子是谁咬的?”

老道说:“您不是问过了吗,是他自己咬的。”

老爷说:“不对!他自己怎么能够得着?”

老道说:“他不是站在凳子上了吗。”

老爷说:“胡说,老爷我都上了房啦也没够着哇!”

太太心想:嗐!你跟他说这个干什么呀!用手一拉老爷的衣服,冲老爷伸了四个手指头,这意思是打四十板子。

老爷回头一看:“来呀,打老道四板。”

老道心想:老爷太恩典啦,闹了半天,才打我四板儿。自己往地下一趴,等着挨打。

太太心想:糟啦!我让他打四十,他怎么看成四板儿啦。噢,一个手指头算一板,要是伸五个手指头,那就是五板,要把手一翻,那就是十板,对。又一拉老爷的衣服,伸了五个指头,反来复去,一五、一十、十五……四十。

老爷回头一看太太的手翻来覆去的,当时吩咐:“把老道翻过来打。”

老道一听,这个气呀。打人还有翻过来打的吗?这是什么老爷,简直是糊涂虫嘛。站堂的也觉得不像话,可是老爷传下话来,不敢不翻,一拧老道脚脖子,真给翻过来啦。

太太拉住老爷直摆手。老爷心想:摆手是怎么回事?噢!明白啦。“来呀,给老道揉揉肚子。”

老道心想:我肚子又不痛,给我揉肚子干什么?

气得太太冲老爷直咬牙,老爷一看,太太咬牙是什么意思?噢!“来呀,把老道的鼻子咬下来!”

太太急得都出汗啦,冲老爷又咬牙又摆手,又指自己,这意思是:我说的不是这么回事儿。老爷更糊涂啦:“来呀,你们别咬啦,让太太来咬吧!”

(张永熙口述)

The Stupid Magistrate

In the old days there was a saying: Men in the same line are bound to be enemies. Those who believed this lost out or landed themselves in trouble. When people in the same walk of life gunned for each other, even Buddhist monks and Taoist priests fell out. There are plenty of old stories about their squabbles and how their canons contradicted each other.

When someone died his family would set up canopies and ask Buddhist monks to recite sutras to release his soul from purgatory and urge it to go west, to the Western Paradise.

But a Taoist priest would urge the spirit to go east, to the realm of the sun.

A nun would call upon it to go south, to where Guanyin had her abode.

As for a lama, he would direct it north.

There are no spirits, of course. If there were, that would really be troublesome. Why? Well, how would a spirit know where to go with Buddhists, Taoists, nuns and lamas chanting different directions to it at the same time? Which of them should it listen to? Not knowing what to do, it could only circle round. Most likely those whirlwinds you see in the street are caused by such incantations. No, what a ridiculous notion!

Once something ludicrous happened. There was a monk roaming the country, begging for alms. One day in a teahouse he met an old Taoist priest, and while sipping their tea the two of them started chatting. Each boasted about himself and rather looked down on the other, and they fell to discussing their canons and beliefs.

The Taoist said, "It's best to be a Taoist, with a dignified get-up like mine. Listen to a verse I've made:

> Blue robe and Taoist hat,
> What sanctity!
> A whisk in hand
> He seems a deity."

The Buddhist said, "You're no deity. Deities don't look like you, they look like me. I've made a verse too.

He does good works,
Abstains from meat and wine,
Chants sutras all day long
Like an arhat divine.

As for you:

Long hair gets in your way,
You dress up every day.
Are you a woman or a man?
A disgusting sight, I say!"

This put the Taoist's back up. He retorted:

"With that patchwork cape of yours
And head shaved like a felon,
If your ears were cut off
You'd look like a watermelon."

That enraged the monk. So both of them lost their tempers and came to blows. In those bad old days the strangest things could happen. The Buddhist grabbed hold of the Taoist's hair and boxed him on the ears a dozen times. The Taoist tried to grab hold of the Buddhist, but this was hard because he had no hair. Finally he grabbed his ears, yanked up his head and bit a hunk off his nose! That was the limit! The monk's face was streaming with blood. Everybody in the teahouse had crowded round to watch.

"What's the world coming to!" said one.

"Men in holy orders too!" another exclaimed. "If they carry on like this, what should we laymen do!"

Just then a bailiff came in and found them fighting, one with his nose bitten. Bloodshed made it a criminal case which couldn't be patched up in private but must be taken to court. So he hauled both the Buddhist and Taoist to the yamen. It so happened that the magistrate had got his post through bribery, and he hadn't been long in office or tried many cases. He had bungled every one. He was not only stupid but hen-pecked.

Hearing that there was a case to try, the magistrate held court. The yamen attendants raised an intimidating shout as he took his seat, flanked by his runners. He saw a Buddhist and a Taoist kneeling before him. The Buddhist's face was bloody. The magistrate asked him. "Why have you come to court?"

The monk said, "He bit my nose."

The magistrate asked the Taoist, "Why did you bite him?"

"I didn't, Your Honour," lied the Taoist. "He bit it himself."

The magistrate said, "You bit your own nose, monk, so why accuse someone else?"

That made the monk mad—how could he have bitten his own nose? He blurted out, "Your Honour, I couldn't reach it."

The magistrate thought: That makes sense. He told the Taoist, "He couldn't reach it."

The Taoist said, "He stood on a stool to bite it."

That convinced the magistrate. He bellowed, "You bold wretch of a monk, you stood on a stool to bite off your nose so as to put the blame on an innocent man. Here, give him a good beating—forty strokes!"

Poor monk! His nose was bitten off and after being beaten he was thrown into the lock-up, while a runner took the Taoist off to find someone to stand surety for him, then released him. And so in this offhand way the trial ended.

When the magistrate went back to his room his wife asked, "What was the case today that you settled so quickly?"

He told her, "It was a squabble between a priest and a monk. The rascally monk had bitten off his nose, but he wouldn't admit it and accused the Taoist of doing it. I gave him forty strokes and jailed him, and released the Taoist on bail. Not a bad day's work was it, madam?"

His wife knew he had muffed it again. She said, "No one, however clever, could reach his nose to bite it, sir."

"That's what I said," he answered. "But the Taoist told me he'd stood on a stool. You see, madam, by standing higher up he could reach it."

"However high you stand, you can't bite your own nose," she retorted. "Suppose I fetch a stool and you try for yourself?"

As the magistrate was rather afraid of his wife, he did as she suggested. He opened his mouth wide, but couldn't bite his nose. Not understanding why, he asked, "Isn't this stool too low, madam?"

"Very well," she said, "go up on the roof and see."

The magistrate at once went into the yard and climbed up a ladder to the roof. When he had stood there for a long time it dawned on him why he couldn't bite his own nose.

His wife, both pleased and exasperated, said, "Come down quick, and hurry up and get that Taoist arrested. You must try the case again, and give him a good beating to make it up to the monk. Otherwise the people here will hold it against you, and you may even be dismissed from your post. I'm afraid, though, you may botch the business again. How can we avoid that? Got it! I'll hide behind you in court and signal to you, so that you'll know what to do. What do you say?"

The magistrate was delighted.

"Right you are!" At once he had the Taoist brought back and took his seat in the court, his wife squatting behind him, attendants ranged on both sides. The Taoist knelt before him thinking: This time I'm for it.

The magistrate pounded his desk and demanded, "Old Taoist, who bit the monk's nose?"

"Didn't you ask me before? He did it himself."

"That's wrong—how could he reach it?"

"Didn't he stand on a stool?"

"Rubbish. I climbed up the roof and still couldn't reach it."

His wife thought: Why tell him that, you fool! She twitched the magistrate's gown and put out four fingers, meaning that the Taoist should be given forty strokes.

The magistrate seeing this said, "Give the Taoist four strokes."

The Taoist thought: How kind-hearted he is, just giving me four strokes after all this. He lay face down to be beaten.

The wife thought: Botheration! I meant forty strokes, not four. Well, if he takes one finger for one stroke, five fingers for five strokes, if I turn my hand that will make ten strokes. Right. She tweaked the magistrate's gown again, stretched out five fingers and turned her hand over four times to make forty strokes.

When the magistrate saw this he ordered, "Turn the Taoist over to beat him."

This annoyed the Taoist. Who ever heard of beating a man lying on his back? This magistrate was a real fool. The attendants were shocked too, but they had to obey orders, so they lugged the Taoist by the legs and turned him over.

The magistrate's wife waved her hand to make him stop. What did that waving mean, he wondered? Ah, he knew. "Rub the Taoist's belly," he said.

The Taoist thought: I haven't got stomach-ache, so why rub my belly?

The magistrate's wife ground her teeth with rage. What did that mean, he wondered? Ah! He gave the order:

"Bite off the Taoist's nose."

Sweating and frantic, his wife ground her teeth, waved her hand and pointed at herself to signal: That's not what I meant. The magistrate was completely foxed. He said, "No, don't you bite it, let my wife bite it off."

(Told by Zhang Yongxi)

贼说话

作贼的有说话的吗？这个贼上了房，等人睡着了他好偷哇，人家老不睡，他在房上着急啦："我说你们怎么还不睡呀？睡了我好偷哇！"没有那么一个。

闹贼，旧社会有这事，现如今可是没有贼啦！没有贼可是没有贼，您睡觉的时候对于门、窗户可也要留神。您要是不留神，丢了东西，您让我负责我也不负责！"张寿臣说的没有贼，我丢东西啦！"我不管这档子事。反正啊，该留神还得留神。到什么时候留神哪？下雨天儿，刮风天儿，睡觉的时候得特别留神。这一下雨，唏哩哗啦，"好，外头下雨啦，挺大的动静，在屋里忍了吧，早点儿睡，凉快！"天热，"嗬！今儿可凉快啦！"一觉睡得踏踏实实的，醒来一瞧：全没啦——下雨得留神。

刮风，外头有动静，呱喳一响，是下来人啦，屋里人这么想：这风大呀，把什么给刮下来啦？不出去啦——不出去丢东西啦！

"点灯人未睡"呀，"咳嗽心必虚"。这怎么讲哪？外头一有动静，屋里这位呀直咳嗽，贼不走啦！"咳嗽心必虚"，他知道你胆儿小哇，外头一有动静，你屋里一咳嗽，如同你告诉那贼："你可别闹哄啊，我可胆儿小，我这就睡觉，我睡着了就不管啦，东西全是你的！"醒了全没啦！外头有动静，你开开灯，坏啦！你这一开灯啊，你在明处他在暗处哪，你屋里是怎么个人，有几口儿，有什么防备，抵得住抵不住，他全知道啦。外头一有动静，我告诉您一个好法子：屋里这儿说着好好的话儿，不说啦，电门奔儿关啦，这贼抹头就跑，他知道您憋着算计他哪！

贼不说话，可也有说话的时候，这叫贼说话。怎么贼说话哪？嗬，什么事都特别！有一年哪，我们家闹贼，那位说："你们家还闹贼？"它分什么社会呀，这是在日本闹混合面儿那年，我们家里闹贼！那阵儿跟现在不一样，您瞧我们的生活，拿我张寿臣个人说吧，如今哪您瞧我这身肉，吃得饱，睡得着哇！穿什么衣裳都能上台呀，就穿这身制服，就能上台，见谁都成，制服就是礼服哇，就行啦。那年月不行，那年月要穿这么一件上来，台底下能嚷！你得架弄着！在旧社会，我们作艺的哪怕借加一钱哪，也得架弄着！夏天大褂儿就得有好几件儿，罗的，绸的。为什么哪？您想啊，上一场啊它就溻啦，再上一场，哎，溻了半截儿，您瞧多寒碜！干干净净，至少得有两件儿。到冬景天儿，皮袄，大衣，水獭帽子。一出来，人家不知道怎么回事，其实真着急，借加一钱来的！那是衣裳吗？那衣裳用处可大啦，这一件衣裳兼了好些差事，分到哪儿：走到街上，这就是便服；上哪儿去有应酬，这就是礼服；上台，这就是行头；睡觉，这是被卧；死啦，它就是装裹，全在身上哪！出来进去的就这一身呀。家里着急，光炕席，任嘛儿没有！

这贼呀，他瞧上我啦，“不怕贼偷，就怕贼惦记着”嘛！“张寿臣一定富裕，他要不富裕，出来能皮袄、大衣、水獭帽子吗？”嗯，他哪儿知道哇，我们家里住一间房，屋里四个旯旮空，一领炕席，睡觉压着，连被卧都没有！我是我那身儿呀浑身倒；我女人哪是她那身儿——棉裤、棉袄、大棉袍儿，浑身侧！枕头都没有哇，枕着我这双靴头儿，我一只呀，我女人一只。我女人那双靴头儿她得穿着，怎么？她那双袜子都没有袜底儿啦！就那么难。

哎，闹贼！我怎么知道闹贼呀？我们住一间北房，后山炕，头冲外睡，我哪，脑袋正对着个门，戴着我那帽子，把带儿一系，省得凉啊！这天后半夜儿，就觉着凉风一吹脑门子，我睁眼一瞧哇，蹭着进来一个人，又把门关上啦。我知道是闹贼，我可没嚷，因为什么没嚷？回头我一嚷，他这么一害怕，贼人胆虚，手里拿着家伙给我一下子，中伤啊！反正我没得可丢的，你屋里摸摸没有，你走啦，不惦记我就完啦。我这么瞧着他，他过来摸，一摸我这身儿呀全穿着哪，扒呀扒不下来；揪帽子，一揪我醒啦——其实我早醒啦——靴头儿，枕着哪！我女人也那身儿，炕上就有炕席。还摸。我心里说：你还不走吗？你走了就完啦，你走了我好睡觉哇！他摸来摸去呀摸到西南犄角儿去啦，吓我一跳！怎么回事？西南犄角儿哇那儿有我的存项，是我的粮台，那儿有一个坛子，里头装着四十多斤米。日本的时候不是买米买不着吗？托人哪弄了四十多斤。我这么一想啊：没有错儿，他绝不能抱着坛子上房，连坛子带米一百多斤，一来也笨，二来走街上准犯案。多一半儿贼都迷信，贼不走空，取个吉利——抓一把走，抓一把也就是熬碗稀饭,连干饭都吃不了,我何苦得罪你呀;你不惦记我就完啦!

我瞧他到那儿啦,一摸呀是个坛子,上头盖着一个秫秸秆儿锅盖,把锅盖搁地下啦,摸了摸里头是米,我心里说:你还不抓点儿吗?他站在我眼头里叉着腰想主意。贼可狠啦,狠心贼嘛!他这主意太损啦:他把他那二大棉袄脱下来啦,脱下棉袄往地下一铺哇,又抱坛子。我明白啦,我心说:好小子啊,你可损啦!你那意思把棉袄铺到这儿,把坛子抱来往那儿一倒,剩个坛子底儿,顶多给我留四两半斤的,你全弄走,这我可对不住你啦!他铺完棉袄一抱坛子,我这手顺炕边儿下来啦,把袄领子逮着啦,往上一拉哪,就压在我身底下啦。我喜欢啦:成啦,我身底下多一个褥子啦,我还瞧你的!

他不知道哇,抱着这坛子往我脑袋头里哗地这么一倒,我心里痛快啦,心说:小子,你算拿不了走啦!我吃的时候呀费点儿水!他把空坛子又搁那儿啦,他摸——他摸着大襟袖子一抻不就走了吗!一摸没摸着,他心里纳闷啊:怎么倒错地方啦?把米扒拉扒拉,一摸是地,他纳闷呀:一间屋子半拉炕,是铺这儿啦?又一摸,“嗯?”他出声啦!摸这头也没有,“咦?”

他这么一“嗯”、“咦”,声音挺大,我女人醒啦。女人胆小,拿脚直踹我:“快起来,快起来,有贼啦!”我沉住了气啦,我说:“睡觉吧,没有贼。”一说没有贼,贼搭碴儿啦:

“没有贼?没有贼我的棉袄哪儿去啦?!”

(张寿臣口述)

A Thief Talks

Do thieves talk? Would a thief climb on to a roof to wait for the people below to fall asleep, then lose patience and ask, "Why don't you turn in? Once you're asleep I can rob you!" No thief would do that.

There were plenty of thieves in the old days, not nowadays. Even so, you should shut your windows and door at night; otherwise, if you lose anything, don't expect me to take the responsibility. "Zhang Shouchen says there are no thieves, but I've lost something!" Well, that's nothing to do with me. Anyway, take care. Take care when? On wet or windy days, and especially before you go to bed. When the rain pelts down you say, "Listen to that downpour! Well, it cools things off—let's turn in early to sleep." In hot weather a cool spell helps you to sleep soundly. You wake to find yourself cleaned out—so watch out when it rains.

When the wind howls and someone thuds from the roof to the ground, the people indoors wonder: Has the high wind blown something down? But they don't go out—so the next day they find things missing!

"When lights are on the household's up" and "It's cowards who cough." What do these sayings mean? If someone indoors hears a noise outside and coughs, the thief won't go away. He knows that fellow's a coward. He's coughing to tell the thief, "Don't raise a rumpus. I'm nervous and I'm going to sleep; you can help yourself to anything you like." So he wakes to find everything gone!

If you hear movements outside and put on the light; you've had it! You're in the light, he's in the dark. He can see who you are, how many of you there are, what precautions you've taken against robbery. So here's my advice, if you hear movements outside: Stop talking and switch off the light, then the thief will skedaddle—he knows you're out to catch him!

Thieves don't generally talk, only on special occasions. One year we had a robbery in my place. You ask, "You had a robbery?" Well, that was under the Japanese occupation when the flour in the shops was mixed with dirt. You want to know what was stolen? In those days things were very different. Look at the way we live now. Take me for example. You can see I've plenty of flesh on my bones because I eat well and sleep soundly. I can come on stage wearing anything I like, that's why I'm wearing this tunic-suit. I pass muster anywhere in it, even on formal occasions. It wouldn't have done in the old days. If I'd worn this then on the stage, the audience would have booed me. You had to keep up appearances. In show business to do that we ran into debt. In summer we had to wear silk and satin gowns. Why? Two performances and you were drenched with sweat—you looked a sight! You needed at least two gowns to keep spruce and smart. In winter you had to have a fur jacket, an overcoat and an otter-skin cap. People seeing you couldn't tell that you were worried stiff about your debts! Why were clothes so important? They served many purposes. In the street they were casual clothes, at parties they were formal wear, on the stage they were costumes, in bed they were quilts, when you died they were shrouds—the same set of clothes. It was all I had. We had nothing else except for a mat on the *kang*.

That thief marked me out. He had his eye on me. "Zhang Shouchen must be rich with that fur jacket of his and an overcoat and otter-skin cap." He didn't know that we lived in one room without a stick of furniture, only a mat on the *kang*, not even a quilt! I covered myself with my clothes; my wife with her padded trousers, padded jacket and padded gown. We had no pillows. We both made do with one of my shoes. The wife had to keep hers on. Why? Her socks were worn through! That's how hard up we were.

Then a thief came. How did I know? We lived in a north room with the *kang* by the wall. I slept facing the door, with my cap on, its strings tied to keep out the cold. In the early hours I felt a draught on my head and opened my eyes. I saw someone creeping in, then closing the door. I knew it was a thief, but I didn't call out. Why not? If I'd startled him, he might have slashed me with the knife in his hand. Anyway I had nothing to lose; after groping around he could go and leave me in peace. I watched him grope around. He felt my clothes but couldn't tug them off. He didn't pull my cap off either for fear of waking me—though actually I was awake. And my shoes were under our heads. Apart from my wife and me, there was nothing on the *kang* but a mat. He went on groping. I thought: Why don't you leave? Clear off and let me sleep! Finally he groped his way to the southwest corner, and that gave me a fright. Why? That was where we kept our rice, over forty pounds of rice there in a vat. Under the Japs you couldn't buy rice, but I'd got a friend to get me this forty-odd pounds. Still, I knew he couldn't lug that vat on to the roof because with the rice it weighed over a hundred pounds, it was too heavy. Besides if he took it in the street he'd be arrested. Most thieves are superstitious, they won't go away empty-handed but must take a little something to bring themselves luck. All right, just take a handful to boil yourself some gruel, not enough for a bowl of rice. Why should I offend you? Just forget about me!

I watched him feel the vat, which had a lid on it made of sorghum stalks. He put the lid on the ground and fingered the rice. I thought: Why not take a bit? He stood there with his hands on his hips, thinking. Thieves are real devils. He hit on a way to fleece me. He took off his padded jacket and spread it on the ground before picking up the vat. I caught on. I thought: You rascal, you can't do that to me! He was going to empty the vat onto his jacket, leaving me at most a few ounces at the bottom. Well, I can't let you get away with that. When he turned to get the vat, I reached out for the collar of his jacket, pulled it on to the *kang* and lay on it. I gloated: Fine, an extra mattress for me. Let's see what you do now.

He didn't know. He picked up that vat and poured out the rice by my head. I chuckled to myself: You can't take that away, my lad! I shall just have to wash it clean before eating it. He put the empty vat back in the corner, then groped for his jacket to bundle it up and make off. When he couldn't find it that puzzled him. Did I empty out the rice in the wrong place? He scrabbled in the rice and felt the ground. He wondered: Where can I have put it?

"Eh?" he exclaimed. Couldn't find it anywhere. "Hell!"

His "Eh?" and "Hell!" were so loud that he woke my wife. She's easily scared, she kicked me. “Get up! Get up quick. There’s a thief!”

I just told her calmly, “Go to sleep, there’s no thief. But then the thief butted in:

“No thief? If there’s no thief, who’s taken my jacket?”

(Told by Zhang Shouchen)

三近视

今天这个节目叫什么？《三近视》。那位说："我们听过这出戏——《四进士》，没听说过三进士呀！"这"近视"跟那"进士"不一样，这个"三近视"是三位近视眼。这三个人都不是外人，都是我本家叔叔。我这三位叔叔都是近视，我大叔那种近视叫"清睛"。那位说："什么叫'清睛'啊？"一早儿哇什么也看不见，叫"清睛"眼。我二叔的近视也有名儿：叫"热涌"，一到晌午哇，哎呀！能叫骆驼绊一个大跟头。我三叔那叫"雀蒙"，一到晚上什么也瞧不见。

我这三位叔叔呀，嗬！闹的那笑话儿多啦！还是我小的时候儿哪，有一次我大叔上南顶——在北京永定门外头，五月初一开到五月十五，有庙会——逛去啦，走到半道儿他不知道还有多远，他要打听打听。一瞧，路西里站着个人。其实不是人，是什么哪？是坟地里的石头人——石人、石马嘛！我大叔跟石头人打听起道儿来啦：

"先生，劳驾劳驾，这儿离南顶还有多远啊？"

他问了四五句，那石头人能说话吗？还在那儿站着。

"哎！你是聋子？"

这石头人脑袋上落着个乌鸦，他这么一晃摇手哇：

"哎！聋子？"

乌鸦飞啦！他也乐啦：

"嘿嘿，这人多死呀，问你道儿你不告诉我，哼，你的帽子让风刮去啦，我也不告诉你！"

您瞧这眼睛耽误多大事，这是我大叔。

我二叔啊？也有笑话儿呀，有一天，我二叔走在街上，有一位老太太买了一只鹅——买鹅干吗呀？到我们北京是这个规矩：给儿子定亲啊，定亲之后要通信，男的这头儿给女的那头儿得送个鹅去，大白鹅——夹着。我二叔瞧着挺白呀，眼神儿不老强的：

"嗬，这棉花不错啊！我说，您这棉花多少钱一斤啊？"

他说棉花。这老太太还只当是别人买了棉花,他跟别人说话儿啊,没理他。我二叔走到跟前一边儿拿手摸,一边儿问:

"老太太,这棉花多少钱一斤?"

他顺着毛儿一摸,挺滑溜。

"哎哟,瞧错了,猪油哇!"

他又当是猪油啦。

"这猪油多少钱一斤啊?"

他往这头儿一摸呀,把鹅脖子攥住了,挺长。

"哎呀,藕哇!"

藕!他一使劲,鹅这么一叫唤,他撒手啦。

"啊,喇叭!"

什么他也没说对。

我三叔哪,有一次人家请他听夜戏回来,夏景天,才下过雨,有块炉灰地冲得挺干净,地里有根针,在地里头埋着半截儿,针尖儿在外头露着,电灯一照,挺亮。我三叔犯了财迷啦:

"钻石!钻石!哎呀!这玩意儿值钱!"

到跟前儿,伸手想捡起它来。一按,针尖儿冲上啊,扎了他一下子。

"哎呀嗬!蝎子!哎呀!蝎子!"

到电灯底下一瞧,流出一个血珠儿来,软忽忽。

"哎呀不是蝎子,珊瑚子,珊瑚子!"

他拿手一捻,一片血。

"嗐!臭虫!"

全没说对呀!

我这三个叔叔分家过,他们亲哥儿仨呀,一宅分三院,前后临街,大爷、二爷住在前头那趟街,我这三叔住在后边儿那趟街。夏景天儿,哥儿仨凑在一个院儿里,沏上茶,一块儿说话儿,凉快。说来说去呀就说到眼睛这儿来啦。怎么哪?一个人哪,他要是有个缺点,他就单护着这点儿,他不说这点儿差,老说这点儿比别人强。大爷坐在躺椅上:

"嗬!哎呀,老二、老三,你瞧我这眼睛啊近来好多啦,这蚊子在我眼前一飞呀，我就分得出这蚊子是公的是母的！”

我二叔一撇嘴：

“得啦您哪，得啦您哪，上回您出门儿让汽碾子给绊了一个跟头！这图吗儿？连汽碾子都瞧不见，还瞧得见蚊子哪？”

“我是夜眼哪，越到晚上越瞧得清楚！”

三爷说：

“大哥，二哥，你们也别吵，也别说谁眼神儿好，咱们这胡同口儿外头有一座关帝庙，这关帝庙明天挂匾，咱们上那儿瞧这块匾去，瞧瞧这匾什么词儿，咱们哥儿仨赌顿饭。瞧完了词儿，瞧清楚的吃饭白吃。谁瞧不清楚谁请客。二位哥哥，我这个主意怎么样？”

大爷、二爷说：

“好啦，就这么办啦，明儿咱们瞧匾去。”

哥儿仨定规好了。到十二点来钟凉风也下来啦，二爷、三爷都回家睡觉去啦。

我大叔躺在炕上睡不着：“不行，不行，明儿早晨一瞧匾，他们俩眼神儿都比我强，我一定瞧不清楚，请他们吃顿饭那没什么，还落个眼神儿不好，让他们留话把儿！”已经打赌了，怎么办哪？想了半天想起来啦：“关帝庙的和尚知道这匾是什么词儿啊，我事先跟和尚打听打听，问明白了怎么个词儿，心里有根，对！”起来呀，上和尚庙。到庙门口儿拍门。

“和尚，和尚！”

叫了两三声，和尚出来了。怎么哪？每天到十二点和尚要上回香，一听外头叫门，赶紧出来开门。

“哪位？”

开门一瞧：

“嗬，张大爷，您请里面！”

“不价，不价，给您添点儿麻烦！”

“什么事，您哪？”

“我听说明天是给关老爷挂匾吗？”

“对啦，施主给挂的。”

“跟您打听打听，这个匾文是什么词儿呀？”

和尚知道。和尚说：

“是给关老爷挂的，四个字：义气千秋。”

“噢噢噢，义气千秋！哈哈哈……劳驾劳驾！”

打听完了走啦，和尚也不知道是怎么回事，关门回去睡觉。

庙门口儿上我二叔来啦。我二叔跟我大叔一个心思，也怕瞧不清楚，饶着请人吃饭还落个话把儿，也上这儿打听来啦。他出胡同儿我大叔进胡同儿，哥儿俩走对脸儿会谁也没瞧见谁，您就知道眼神怎么样啦！到这儿叫门。

“当家的，和尚！”

和尚出来啦，开门一瞧是张二爷。

“嗬，施主，请里边坐！”

“不价不价，明儿这儿挂匾吗？”

和尚说：

“不错，给关老爷挂匾。”

“什么词儿呀？”

“义气千秋。”

“义气千秋！”

我二叔比我大叔心细：

“这匾是什么颜色呀？”

“蓝地儿金字。”

“噢噢，蓝地儿金字！哈哈哈……明儿见，明儿见！”

二爷走啦！和尚关门回去睡觉。庙门口儿上三爷又来啦。三爷也是睡不着觉哇，一个心思呀！打后街上这儿来啦！

“和尚，和尚！”

和尚说：

“今儿晚上别睡啦！”

和尚出来一瞧是张三爷。

“嗬，张三爷，您里边儿请！”

“不价不价，明儿您这儿……”

刚说到这儿，和尚就说：

“明儿这儿挂匾！给关老爷挂的，匾上是：‘义气千秋’。蓝地儿金字。”

就是我三叔年轻不是？他的心比谁都细。

“噢噢，有上下款儿吗？”

“有啊。”

“上下款儿是什么？”

“上款儿啊，是年月日，红字，下款儿是‘信士弟子某某某恭献’，那个‘献’字儿是红的，剩下的是金字。”

“是啦是啦，劳驾劳驾！”

他也走啦。他走啦，和尚也睡啦！

天一亮，大爷起来啦，漱口，正在攥着牙刷子漱口哪，二爷、三爷来啦：

“大哥！”

“啊，老二，老三，屋里去，喝水。”

“喝水？喝水干吗呀？回来再喝得啦嘛，咱们看匾去吧！”

“走走走。”

把牙刷子往这儿一放，哥儿仨手拉手儿奔关帝庙来啦。一出口儿，其实这庙啊，山门在这儿，我这位大叔往那儿指：

“得啦得啦，到啦到啦，别上跟前儿去，上跟前儿去谁都看得见，哈！赌这眼神嘛！你瞧！”

其实离着庙还远哪！

“这匾好啊，‘义气千秋’！‘义气千秋’！”

我大叔是文盲，他还要逞能：

“你瞧这‘秋’字儿写得多好！这‘秋’字儿的三点水儿多好！”

秋字儿哪儿有三点水儿？这不是瞎胡闹嘛！二爷说：

“大哥，你这眼神儿是好多了，原先瞧不清楚，现如今瞧得挺明白，‘义气千秋’。可有一节，大哥，那么大的字再看不见不是太难了吗！您瞧是什么颜色儿？您瞧字是什么颜色儿，匾什么颜色儿？”

大爷愣啦！心说:“坏啦！昨儿晚上忘了问啦!”

二爷说:

“你看不清了吧！蓝匾,字是金的！哎,我瞧得多清楚!”

三爷说:

“二哥比大哥眼神儿强,可是呀,‘义气千秋’那么大的字好看,蓝匾金字,叫太阳光一照,那再瞧不清楚,不是眼睛太坏啦！您把上下款儿念念吧,上下款儿您念念。”

二爷没词儿啦,没问哪！三爷说啦:

“你们哥儿俩都不成,我念给你们听听,上款儿呀年月日,红字,下款儿‘信士弟子某某某恭献’,那个‘献’字儿是红的,剩下的是金字。哎,怎么样您哪？一字不差！我瞧得最清楚,你们哥儿俩谁请客,反正我是白吃呀!”

大爷说:

“这么着吧,老三一定白吃,‘义气千秋’是我先瞧的,我也白吃,让你二哥花钱。”

二爷说:

“我不能花钱哪,我比您多瞧见点儿颜色啦,您得请客呀！这么着得啦,您拿八成啊,我拿二成,老三白吃!”

“我可不能拿,一定我得白吃。”

哥儿仨呀越说声音越大,差点儿打起来。

这时候儿和尚出来啦,和尚一瞧是张家哥儿仨。

“嗬,老三位来得挺早!”

“好,好,当家的,好啦好啦!”

把和尚揪过来啦。

“今儿您这儿挂匾对不对?”

和尚说:

“不错,挂匾。”

“给关老爷挂的?”

“是呀。”

大爷说：

"'义气千秋',对不对？"

和尚说：

"对呀。"

二爷说：

"蓝地儿金字儿,对不对？"

和尚说：

"对呀,没错儿。"

三爷说：

"上下款儿是什么什么,对不对？"

和尚说：

"全对呀。"

"成啦,我们仨人拿这事儿赌顿饭,和尚您也跟着吃,听您一句话,您说,谁输谁赢？"

和尚一听,乐啦！

"我说你们哥儿仨呀请客吧,全输啦,我一个人赢啦！我白吃,你们哥儿仨拿钱。"

"你怎么赢啦？"

"你们来得太早,我这匾还没挂哪！"

(张寿臣口述)

Three Short-Sighted Brothers

What's the title of this item? *Three Short-Sighted Brothers*. The three of them were my uncles, all short-sighted. First Uncle couldn't see a thing in the morning; Second Uncle would bump right into a camel at noon; and Third Uncle was as blind as a bat in the evening.

Ha, those three uncles of mine, they kept making fools of themselves. When I was a kid First Uncle set off for Nanding outside the Yongding Gate to go to the temple fair held from the first to the fifteenth of the fifth month. Halfway there he decided to ask how much farther he had to go. He saw a man standing west of the road. Actually it wasn't a man. What was it then? A stone statue in a graveyard—a stone man and a stone horse! First Uncle asked this statue the way:

"Excuse me, sir, how far is it to Nanding?"

He repeated his question five times, but how could a statue talk? It just stood there.

"Hey! Are you deaf?"

A crow had perched on the statue's head. First Uncle waved his hand.

"Hey! You deaf?"

The crow flapped off. First Uncle chuckled, "Ha, you pig-headed fellow, refusing to tell me the way. Now your hat's blown off and I shan't tell you either."

See how his short-sightedness had held him up. That was First Uncle.

Second Uncle? He made a fool of himself too. One day in the street he met an old lady who had just bought a goose. What for? It was the rule in Beijing that when you arranged a marriage for your son, after his betrothal you had to send a goose to the girl's family. The old lady had this big white goose under her arm. Second Uncle saw how white it was, but couldn't make it out clearly.

"Not bad, that cotton wool! How much a pound?"

Cotton wool! The old lady thought he was talking to someone else who had bought cotton wool, so she paid no attention. Second Uncle stepped forward to feel it, asking again, "How much a pound is this cotton wool, old lady?"

He stroked the goose's plumage, slick and slippery.

"Oh, my mistake, it's lard."

He took it for lard!

"How much is this lard a pound?"

He reached down and caught hold of the goose's long neck.

"Why, here's a lotus root."

A lotus root! He tightened his grip. The goose honked and he let go.

"No, it's a horn!"

He got it wrong each time.

As for Third Uncle, he was invited one evening to an opera. It was summer, and when he started home it had just rained. A patch of cinders had been washed very clean, and a needle was sticking out of it, pointing upwards. Its glitter in the lamplight made his palm itch.

"A diamond, aha! This is worth money!"

He stepped over to pick it up, but pricked himself.

"Dammit, a scorpion! A scorpion!"

Under the street lamp he saw a sticky drop of blood on his finger.

"Why, this isn't a scorpion, it's a lizard. Lizard!" he said.

He rubbed it and bloodied his hand.

"Bah, a bedbug!"

Wrong every time!

These three uncles lived separately in three different courtyards which opened on to two streets. First Uncle and Second Uncle had houses on the front street, Third Uncle on the back street. In summer they'd get together in First Uncle's courtyard, brew some tea and sit in the shade to chat. Somehow the conversation always came round to their eyesight. Why was that? Anyone with a physical defect always tries to cover it up, to make out that in this respect he's better than other people. One day First Uncle lolled back in a deck-chair.

"Well, Two and Three," he said. "My sight's improved so much recently that when a mosquito flies past I can see whether it's a male or a female."

Second Uncle looked at him scornfully.

"Come off it. Last time you went out you bumped into a steamroller. If you can't even see a steamroller, how can you see mosquitoes?"

"My sight's better at night. The later it is, the more clearly I can see."

Third Uncle said, "Quit squabbling, One and Two. Stop boasting about your eyesight. You know that the God of War's Temple outside this alley. Tomorrow it's going to have a tablet put up. Let's go and have a look at the inscription, and make a bet on it. Whichever of us sees it most distinctly will be treated to a meal by the other two. What do you say to that, brothers?"

First Uncle and Second Uncle said, "Fine. We'll go and see the tablet tomorrow."

At about midnight a cool wind sprang up, and Second and Third Uncle both went home to bed.

First Uncle lay on his *kang* but couldn't sleep. "This won't do. When we look at the tablet tomorrow they'll see it more clearly than I can. I don't mind treating them to a meal, but I don't want them to say my eyesight's no good." Still, he had agreed to the bet, so what could he do? At last he had an idea. "The monk in the God of War's Temple must know what's on the tablet, I'll go and ask him. I'll feel safer when I know the inscription!" He got up, went to the temple and knocked on the gate.

"Monk! Monk!"

The monk came out. So promptly? Well, at midnight he always got up to burn incense, so as soon as he heard knocking he opened the gate.

"Who is it?"

He looked out.

"Oh, Master Zhang, please come in."

"No, thank you, I've come to trouble you...."

"What can I do for you?"

"I hear you're putting up a tablet for the God of War tomorrow."

"That's right. Donated by one of our patrons."

"Can you tell me the inscription on the tablet?"

The monk of course knew it. He said, "It's 'Loyalty Everlasting'."

"Ha, 'Loyalty Everlasting!' Good.... Many thanks."

Having found this out he went off. The puzzled monk closed the gate and went back to bed.

Then Second Uncle arrived. Like First Uncle he was afraid he wouldn't be able to make out the inscription but would have to treat his brothers, who would make fun of him. He left the alley just as First Uncle turned into it, but neither saw the other—that's how good their eyesight was! He knocked at the gate.

"Hey there, monk!"

The monk came out and saw it was Second Master Zhang.

"Please come in and sit down," he said.

"No, thanks. You're putting up a tablet tomorrow?"

"That's right, to the God of War."

"What inscription?"

"Loyalty Everlasting."

Second Uncle had more foresight than First Uncle.

"What colour is the tablet?"

"Blue with gold characters"

"So, blue with gold characters. Fine.... See you tomorrow."

Second Uncle left and the monk went back to bed, but then along came Third Uncle. He couldn't sleep either for worrying. He'd come by the back street.

"Monk, monk!"

The monk said:

"No sleep for me tonight!"

He came out and saw Third Master Zhang.

"Oh, Third Master Zhang, come on in."

"No, thanks. Tomorrow...."

"We're hanging up a tablet to the God of War. The inscription

'Loyalty Everlasting' is in gold characters on a blue ground."

Third Uncle, being the youngest, was smarter than his brothers.

"Anything else written above or below?"

"Yes."

"What's written above?"

"The date in red. Down below is 'respectfully presented by a true believer', 'presented' is in red, the rest in gold."

"I see. Thank you very much."

He went off, and at last the monk could sleep.

First Uncle got up early the next morning. He gargled and was brushing his teeth when his two brothers arrived.

"Elder Brother!"

"Oh, Two, Three, come in, have a drink of water."

"Why drink water? We can drink when we get back. Let's go and see the tablet."

"Right you are."

The toothbrush was put down, and the three of them set off hand in hand to the temple. As soon as they were out of the alley, First Uncle pointed at the temple gate.

"Right, stay put, don't go any closer. Go any closer and anybody can see it. Ha! Now we'll test our eyesight. Look!"

In fact they were still some distance from the temple.

"A fine tablet, 'Loyalty Everlasting'. 'Loyalty Everlasting'."

First Uncle was illiterate, but now he tried to show off, "See how well the last character's written."

In fact he didn't know the first thing about calligraphy.

Second Uncle said, "Elder Brother, your sight's certainly improved. You can see 'Loyalty Everlasting' quite clearly. But those big characters aren't hard to make out. Can you see what colour they are, the characters and the tablet?"

That floored First Uncle. He thought, "Confound it, I forgot to ask that last night."

Second Uncle said, "Can't make it out, eh? The tablet's blue, the characters are gold. Ha, I can see more clearly!"

Third Uncle said, "Second Brother's sight is better than Elder Brother's. But those big characters 'Loyalty Everlasting' are easy to see. And gold characters on a blue ground are so clear in the sunlight, you'd have to have very poor eyesight not to see them. Can you read what's written above and underneath?"

Second Uncle was floored, he hadn't asked. Third Uncle said, "You can't, eh, either of you? I'll read it out to you. Above is written the date in red. Below is 'respectfully presented by a true believer', 'presented' in red, the other words in gold. Well, how about it? Not a word missing! My eyesight is the best. Which of you is going to treat me?"

First Uncle said, "Well, Three doesn't have to pay. But I was the first to see 'Loyalty Everlasting', so I don't have to pay either. Two must stand treat."

Second Uncle said, "That's not fair. I made out the colour, which is more than you did. You must stand treat. Or suppose you pay four fifths, I pay one fifth, and Three nothing."

"No, I'm not paying."

They were shouting now, about to come to blows.

Then the monk came out.

"Ha, you gentlemen are up early."

"Oh, good, here is the monk."

They tugged him over.

"Your tablet is to the God of War, right?"

"That's right."

First Uncle said, "'Loyalty Everlasting', isn't it?"

The monk said, "Right."

Second Uncle asked: "Gold characters on blue, eh?"

The monk said, "Quite right."

Third Uncle said, "And this is what's written above and underneath, right?"

The monk said, "You've got it all right."

"Good, we made a bet on this, the losers to stand the winner a treat. You come and join us, monk. You say who's won and who's lost. We'll take your word for it."

The monk laughed.

"I say you three brothers must treat me, because you all lost. I'm the only winner! You three will have to treat me to a meal."

"How can *you* be the winner?"

"You came too early. I haven't hung up the tablet yet!"

(Told by Zhang Shouchen)

五

《北京的传说》(五则)(金受申)[1]

八臂哪吒城[2]

人人都说北京城是个“八臂哪吒城”。人人都说只有八臂勇哪吒才能镇服得了“苦海幽州”的孽龙。北京城究竟怎么样修造的这一座“八臂哪吒城”呢？这在北京就传说下来一个民间故事。

皇帝要修一座首都北京城啦,就派了工部大官去修建。工部大官慌啦,赶忙奏明了皇帝,说:“北京这块地方,原来是个苦海幽州,那里的孽龙,十分厉害,臣子是降服不了的,请皇上另派军师们去吧!”皇帝一想,这话也有道理,没有上知天文,下知地理,上能知神,下能知鬼的“能人”,是不能修建北京城的。当时,皇帝就问这些军师们:“你们谁能去给我修建北京城呢?”好多军师们,都是你看着我、我看着你的不敢答话,时间长了,实在不好不答话啦,大军师刘伯温说:“我,我去吧!”二军师姚广孝紧接着也说:“我也去!”皇帝老儿高兴啦,准知道这两位军师是能“降龙伏虎”了

---

① 中文选自：金受申．北京的传说．北京：北京出版社，1981；英译文选自：Jin，S. S. *Beijing Legends*. Gladys Yang（trans.）. Beijing：Chinese Literature Press，1985.

② 原文注：北京内城是元朝至元四年(公元一二六七年)修建的。明朝洪武元年(公元一三六八年)把北面城墙拆掉，缩进五里，重建了北面城墙。永乐十七年(公元一四一九年)把原来的南面城墙拆掉，往南推展了一里多，重建了南面城墙，就成了现在北京内城的样子。北京外城是明嘉靖三十二年(公元一五五三年)修建的。

不起的人，就派了他们去修建北京城。

刘伯温、姚广孝领了“圣旨”，就到了现在北京城这块地方来啦。刘伯温、姚广孝到了北京这块地方，打下了公馆以后，就天天出去采看地形，琢磨怎么修建让孽龙捣不了乱的北京城。大军师刘伯温是看不起姚广孝的，二军师姚广孝是也看不起刘伯温的，刘伯温说：“姚二军师，咱们分开了住吧，你住西城，我住东城，各自想各自的主意，十天以后见面，然后坐在一起，脊背对脊背坐着，各人画各人的城图①，画好了再对照一下，看看两个人的心思对不对头。”姚广孝明知道刘伯温是要大显才能，独夺大功的，就冷笑了一声说：“好吧，大军师说得有理，就这么办！”当下，两个军师就分开住啦。起初两天，两个人虽然没住在一起，也没出去采看地形，可是两个人的耳朵里，都听见一句话：“照着我画，不就成了吗！”听这句话，象个孩子的声音，清清楚楚地说个没完，这是谁说话呢？怎么看不见人呢？照着你的“话”，你的“话”是什么“话”呢？刘大军师琢磨不透，姚二军师也琢磨不透。到了第三天上，两个军师都各自出去采看地形去啦，刘大军师走到哪里，他总看见有一个穿红袄短裤子的小孩子，在他前面走，刘伯温走得快，那小孩子也走得快，刘伯温走得慢，那小孩子也走得慢，刘伯温起初也没觉出特别来，后来他也有些疑心啦，就故意停住脚步，咦！真奇怪！那小孩子也站住啦，刘伯温琢磨不透这个小孩子是干什么的。另外，那姚二军师呢？也是碰见了这么样的一个小孩子，姚广孝也琢磨不透这个小孩子是干什么的。刘伯温、姚广孝各自回到各人公馆以后，耳朵里就又听见了那句话：“照着我画，不就成了吗！”刘伯温在东城想，姚广孝在西城也这么想：难道这个红袄短裤子的小孩，就是哪吒不成？不象啊！哪吒是八条膀臂呀！刘伯温在东城想：明天再碰见这个小孩子，我要细细瞧瞧他。姚广孝在西城也想：明天再碰见这个小孩子，我要细细瞧瞧他。

一夜过去了，是两个人约会的第四天啦，刘伯温吃完了早饭，带了一个随从出去遛达去了，他为什么今天要带随从呢？为的是：叫随从也帮助他看看是不是哪吒。在西城住的姚广孝，也是这个心思，也带了一个随从

① 原文注：北京人都知道，都传说：“刘伯温、姚广孝脊梁对脊梁画了北京城。”

出去找哪吒。两个军师,虽然一个住在东城,一个住在西城,可是心思都是一样,听见的话都是一样,碰见的孩子都是一样,今天他们又都碰见那红袄短裤子的小孩子啦。刘伯温、姚广孝今天碰见的小孩子,还穿的是红袄,还穿的是短裤子,只是红袄不是昨天那件红袄了,这件红袄很象一件荷叶边的披肩,肩膀两边有浮镶着的软绸子边,风一吹真象是有几条膀臂似的。刘伯温看了,心里一动:这不是八臂哪吒吗?赶紧往前就追,他想揪住这个小孩子,细细瞧瞧,没想到刘伯温追得快,那小孩子跑得更快,只听见一句:"照着我画,不就成了吗!"那小孩子就跑得没影没踪啦,再也瞧不见啦。刘伯温的随从,看见军师爷在大道上飞快地跑起来,他不知道是怎么回事,他在后面直喊:"军师爷!军师爷!您跑什么呀?"刘伯温听见了喊声,就停住了脚步,问他的随从:"你看见一个穿红袄短裤子的小孩了吗?""没有啊!咱们走了这么半天,不就是我跟军师爷吗!一个人也没瞧见呀!"刘伯温心里明白:这一定是八臂哪吒啦。那姚广孝呢?姚广孝也碰见了这么一个小孩子,也追那个小孩子来着,也听见了那么句话,他的随从也没看见有什么人,他也明白了这一定是八臂哪吒啦。

刘伯温回了他的东城公馆,姚广孝也回了他的西城公馆。刘伯温想:照着我画,画一定是画图的画字,不是说话的话字,八臂哪吒要我照他的样子画城图,那一定是能降服得住苦海幽州的孽龙啦,好!我看你姚广孝怎么办?我看你姚广孝画不出城图来,怎么配当军师爷!那在西城住的姚广孝,也是这么想来着:看你这个大军师,"大"字得搬搬家!在第九天上,刘伯温就通知了姚广孝:明天正午,在两城的中间,脊背对脊背画城图,请姚二军师准时到场。姚广孝答应啦。

第十天正午啦,在城中一个大空场上,摆下两张桌子,两把椅子,椅子背对椅子背,刘伯温来啦,姚广孝也来啦,刘伯温说:"二军师朝哪面坐呢?"姚广孝说:"大军师住在东城,就朝东坐,小弟朝西坐。"两个人落了座,有随从给摆好了纸、笔、墨、砚,两位军师拿起笔来,唰、唰、唰地一画,太阳刚往西转,两个人的城图就都画完啦。姚广孝拿起大军师画的城图来看,刘伯温拿起二军师画的城图来看,俩人都哈哈大笑起来,原来两张城图都是一样,都是"八臂哪吒城"。姚广孝请大军师给讲讲怎么叫八臂哪吒城？刘伯温说："这正南中间的一座门，叫正阳门，是哪吒的脑袋，脑袋嘛，就应该有耳朵，他的瓮城东西开门，就是哪吒的耳朵；正阳门里的两眼井，就是哪吒的眼睛；正阳门东边的崇文门、东便门，东面城门的朝阳门、东直门，是哪吒这半边身子的四臂；正阳门西边的宣武门、西便门，西面城门的阜成门、西直门，是哪吒那半边身子的四臂；北面城门的安定门、德胜门，是哪吒的两只脚。"姚广孝点了点头说："呕，是了。这个哪吒没有五脏，空有八臂行吗？"刘伯温红了脸，说："哪里有没五脏的哪吒呀！死哪吒镇服得了孽龙吗？"说着，急急地一指城图："老弟你看，那城里四方形儿的是'皇城'，皇城是哪吒的五脏，皇城的正门——天安门是五脏口，从五脏口到正阳门哪吒脑袋，中间这条长长的平道，是哪吒的食道。"姚广孝笑啦，慢条斯理地说："大军师别着急呀，我知道您画得挺细致，那五脏两边的两条南北的大道，是哪吒的大肋骨，大肋骨上长着的小肋骨，就是那些小胡同啦，是不是？大军师画得挺细致！"刘伯温叫姚广孝逗的急不得、恼不得的，反正"八臂哪吒城"的"北京城图"，是画出来啦，大军师刘伯温没夺了头功，二军师姚广孝也没夺了头功，刘伯温还不怎么在意，姚广孝是越想越难过，就出家当了和尚，专等看刘伯温怎么修造北京啦。

刘伯温这么一修造北京城不要紧，没想到惹得孽龙烦恼起来，这才又引起"高亮赶水"一大串故事来。

The Eight-Armed Nezha City

Everyone calls Beijing the Eight-armed Nezha City.① They say only eight-armed Nezha could have subdued the vicious dragons in the Bitter Sea Waste. Well, how did Beijing come to be built as an Eight-armed Nezha City? There's a folk-tale about this.

The Emperor decided to build a northern capital, Beijing,② and entrusted this task to the Minister of Works. That threw the minister into a panic. He promptly petitioned the throne: "Beijing was originally known as the Bitter Sea Waste, and the dragons are too vicious for your humble subject to overcome. I beg Your Majesty to send some military advisers instead!"

The Emperor saw reason in this. Beijing could only be built by a genius with knowledge of heaven and earth, who knew the ways of both the spirits above and the devils below. So he asked his advisers, "Which of you can go and build a northern capital for me?"

His advisers eyed each other, not daring to utter a word, until finally someone really had to answer and Chief Adviser Liu Bowen volunteered, "I'll go!"

At once Deputy Adviser Yao Guangxiao volunteered, "And so will I."

The Emperor was pleased, sure that these two outstanding advisers had the ability to overcome dragons and tigers. He forthwith sent them off to

---

① 译者注：Nezha, a mythical boy with supernatural powers, killed the son of the Dragon King. Later he disembowelled himself and cut the flesh from his bones; but his spirit took the form of a lotus, and he continued to battle with and overcome many evil spirits.

② 译者注：The inner city of Beijing was built in 1267 in the Yuan Dynasty. In 1368, when the Ming Dynasty was established, the north wall was pulled down and rebuilt five *li* to the south. In 1419, the south wall was pulled down and rebuilt more than a *li* farther south, forming the inner city as we know it today. The outer city wall was built in 1553.

build Beijing.

Liu Bowen and Yao Guangxiao took the imperial edict and travelled to the Waste where Beijing now stands. After putting up in a hostel, they went out every day to survey the terrain and figure out how to build the city in such a way that the dragons could not make trouble. However, Chief Adviser Liu and Deputy Adviser Yao had nothing but contempt for each other.

"Deputy Adviser Yao," proposed Liu, "let's live apart, you in the west city, I in the east. Each of us must think up a plan, then in ten days' time we'll meet and, sitting back to back, draw our plans for the city. Then we'll compare the two to see if they tally."

Yao Guangxiao knew perfectly well that Liu Bowen hoped to shine and hog all the credit.

"Very well," he said with a grim smile. "You're right, chief adviser, that's what we should do."

So the two advisers split up. For the first couple of days, although the two of them were staying apart and neither went out to survey the terrain, both heard a voice saying, "Just copy me and you'll do fine." The voice sounded like a child's, and the words were clearly repeated time and again. Who could the speaker be? There was no one to be seen. "Just copy me"—what did that mean? Neither adviser could make head or tail of this.

On the third day they both went out to survey the terrain again. Wherever Adviser Liu went he saw a child in a red jacket and short pants walking ahead of him. When Liu speeded up, so did the child; when he slowed down, so did the child. At first he paid no special attention to this, but then he started wondering about it. He deliberately stood still. Ah! How extraordinary! So did the child. Liu couldn't for the life of him think what the boy was up to.

How about Deputy Adviser Yao? He saw a child like that too, and couldn't for the life of him think what the boy was up to.

Back in their different hostels, again both advisers heard a voice in their ears. "Just copy me and you'll do fine." Liu in the east city and Yao in the west city wondered: Can this child in the red jacket and short pants be Nezha? Doesn't seem like him. Nezha was supposed to have eight arms. Liu in the east city and Yao in the west city came to the same decision: If I meet that boy tomorrow, I'll have a good look at him.

The next day, the fourth day after they had reached their agreement, Liu Bowen went out after breakfast for a stroll with an attendant. Why take an attendant today? So that the attendant could help him see if it was Nezha. Yao Guangxiao in the west city had the same idea. Both men had heard the same voice, seen the same child, and today they saw him again. Still wearing a red jacket and short pants, but not the same jacket as the previous day: this one was more like a cape with a lotus-leaf edge, and from the two shoulders dangled soft silken fringes which rustled in the windlike arms. At the sight of them Liu suspected that this must be Eight-armed Nezha. He hurried forward to catch hold of the child and have a closer look; but the faster he chased him the faster the child ran away, repeating, "Just copy me and you'll do fine!" Then he made off and vanished completely.

When Liu's attendant saw him chasing down the road, he did not know what was up. He called after him, "Commander! Commander! Why are you running?"

Liu stopped to ask him, "Did you see a child in a red jacket and short pants?"

"Not I," said the attendant. "All this time I've been following you I haven't seen a soul."

Then Liu Bowen knew for sure that it was Nezha.

As for Yao Guangxiao, exactly the same thing had happened to him.

The two commanders went back to their hostels. Liu thought: "Copy me" must mean draw a plan of a city like Eight-armed Nezha, so as to keep down the dragons in Bitter Sea Waste. Fine! Let's see how you handle this, Yao Guangxiao. If you can't produce such a plan, you're not fit to be imperial adviser! Yao in the west city was thinking at the same time: Now we'll soon see you lose your title "Chief Adviser"!

On the ninth day Liu sent word to Yao: "At noon tomorrow, in the centre of the city, we'll draw our plans back to back. Please be there on time." And Yao agreed to this.

At noon on the tenth day, in a big empty square in the centre of the town, two tables and two chairs were set out, the chairs back to back, and the two advisers arrived.

Liu asked, "Which way do you want to face, deputy adviser?"

Yao answered, "You live in the east city, chief adviser, so you should sit facing east. Your younger brother will sit facing west."

When they had taken their seats, attendants supplied them with paper, brushes, ink and inkstones. They picked up the brushes and stroke by stroke drew their plans. Just before sunset both finished their plans of the city, and each picked up the other's to examine it. Then both of them burst out laughing, because their plans were identical, each being an Eight-armed Nezha City.

Yao Guangxiao asked the chief adviser to explain his Eight-armed Nezha City.

Liu said, "This gate in the centre due south is *Zheng Yang Men*, Nezha's head. A head should have two ears, and those are the gates to its east and west. The two wells inside *Zheng Yang Men* are his eyes. On the east side, the *Cong Wen Men*, *Dong Bian Men*, *Chao Yang Men* and *Dong Zhi Men* are four of Nezha's arms. On the west side of the *Zheng Yang Men*, the *Xuan Wu Men*, *Xi Bian Men*, *Fu Cheng Men* and *Xi Zhi Men* are Nezha's other four arms. The *An Ding Men* and *De Sheng Men* in the north are his feet."

Yao Guangxiao nodded, saying, "Yes, of course. But does Nezha have only eight arms, no heart, liver, spleen, lungs or kidneys?"

Liu Bowen's face turned red. "Of course he has!" he retorted. "How could a dead Nezha keep down vicious dragons?" He pointed irately at his plan. "Look, brother. The rectangular Imperial City is Nezha's viscera, and *Tian An Men* at its entrance is the way into his viscera and leads in the other direction to *Zheng Yang Men*, his brain. The long, level road between them is Nezha's gullet."

With a laugh Yao Guangxiao drawled, "Don't get het-up, chief adviser. I can see your plan is most carefully worked out. The two roads running south and north on both sides of the viscera are Nezha's main ribs, and the alleys branching off are his lesser ribs—right? You've really worked it out to the last detail!"

Although provoked, Liu Bowen had to keep his temper. At any rate, the plan for an Eight-armed Nezha City had been drawn, and neither adviser could hog all the credit. Chief Adviser Liu did not mind about this, but Deputy Adviser Yao became so cast down that he went off to live as a monk, waiting to see how Liu would build Beijing.

What Liu Bowen did not foresee was that the building of Beijing would enrage the vicious dragons, which led to "Gao Liang's Race for Water" and many other stories.

三青走到卢沟桥[①]

“大青不动,二青摇,三青走到卢沟桥。”这又是刘伯温制造北京城的一个故事啦。北京人嘴里总是说:“刘伯温制造北京城”,我们就说是“刘伯温修建北京城”吧。刘伯温修建北京城,这又和大青、二青、三青有什么关系呢?这里就又有了一段民间传说。

刘伯温和姚广孝,打赌画北京城图以后,姚广孝心窄气量小,一赌气当和尚去啦,咱们不提姚广孝吧。单说大军师刘伯温,他是个另有心思的人,只是一心一意地修建这个“八臂哪吒城”样子的北京城。刘伯温想:修八臂哪吒城,这是一定的了,可是这苦海幽州的孽龙,究竟降得服降不服呢?这叫这位能掐会算的大军师为难啦。刘伯温盘算了一天又一天,后来知道了房山县上方山上,有三块得道一万年、五千年、一千年的大青石,专能降龙伏虎。刘伯温自己一个人想:如果把这三块“神石”弄一块来,一定能降服得了孽龙。他又想:这三块神石,如果把那得道一万年的“大青石”弄来,这苦海幽州的孽龙,就永远不会捣乱了,永远不会翻身啦。刘伯温又想:这么重的石头,又有这么大的“道行”,怎么弄到北京城来呢?这得想法子,得用软、硬两样方法才行。不说刘伯温想什么法子,单说上方山上的大青、二青和三青,弟兄三个在刘伯温想主意的时候,就知道刘伯温的计谋啦,大青说:“反正我不去,我在山里多么自在!”二青说:“我也不去,歪鼻子刘伯温支使不动我,我也不听他支使!”三青说:“谁愿意去呀?就怕歪鼻子弄什么厉害的手段哪!”大青愤愤地说:“歪鼻子来了再说!”

再说刘伯温盘算好了要搬这三块神石以后,就打点了两套主意:一套是预备了香花神礼,带上随从,去用“礼聘”的样子,请神石下山;另一套,是袖子里的计谋,他早搬来了许多“天”兵、“天”将,藏在袖子缝里,为的是

---

① 原文注:卢沟桥是金朝大定二十七年(公元一一八七年)开始修建,明昌三年(公元一一九二年)完工的。卢沟桥上石栏柱头的石狮,是明朝正统九年(公元一四四四年)重修卢沟桥的时候增加的。卢沟桥东边的肥城,正名“拱极城”,是明朝崇祯十三年(公元一六四〇年)修建的。

吓吓大青、二青、三青，让他们乖乖地下山。刘伯温打好这个主意，布置了一下，就带着一批随从，浩浩荡荡的去到上方山“请”神石，他们离开了北京城，直往西南，过了卢沟渡口，就直奔上方山啦。刘伯温这位大军师，到了上方山的山根底下，把平常的大军师威风收起来啦，老老实实地来到了三块神石的前面，摆好了香花神礼，恭恭敬敬地说：“三位神石在上，我刘伯温奉了皇帝的旨意，来请三位神石，驾临北京，少不得皇帝要封你们镇国大将军哩！”大青稳稳地躺在那里，一动也没动，二青、三青看了一眼大青，想：大哥既然没动弹，我们弟兄也就不用动弹啦。刘伯温一看，香花、神礼都送给你们啦，你们一动也不动，这真太叫人难看啦，叫你看看大军师爷的厉害！刘伯温低低地对袖缝里的“天”将说：“有劳诸位，把这三块混账石头，给赶到北京城去，皇帝一定要加封你们！”“天”兵、“天”将应了一声，就飞出了刘伯温的袖子缝，摆刀、枪、剑、戟，上前围住了三块神石，喝令三块神石，快快进北京！大青仍然一动不动；二青被这些“天”兵、“天”将威吓得不能不动弹一下，它摇了一摇；三青是抵抗不了刘伯温请来的这些助威的，只好分别两位哥哥，随刘伯温下山去吧。刘伯温知道自己也搬不动大青、二青的，有了三青，也就可以交了“皇差”啦，就带着随从，赶着三青，下了上方山，直奔北京去啦。

不提刘伯温赶着三青奔北京，单说刘伯温过卢沟渡口的时候，卢沟渡口的龙王，早接到苦海幽州龙王的儿子龙公的信啦，他们商量怎样拦阻三青进北京，他们商量妥了一条计策：在卢沟渡口上，修一座“蝎子城”，等刘伯温赶着三青过来的时候，就让蝎子把三青螫在这里，使它不能进北京。他们商量好啦，就先修蝎子尾巴——卢沟桥，一夜的功夫，卢沟桥修成了；他们再修蝎子身子，这就是在卢沟桥东面的“肥城”，肥城东门外的两口井，是蝎子的眼睛，再东边一点，南北有两座小土山，是蝎子的两只大前爪。蝎子城修成了，刘伯温赶着三青也到啦，他的随从报告他：“回禀大军师爷，卢沟渡口，咱们来的时候，还没有桥，现在不但有了长长的石头桥，桥东边还有一座城，请军师爷查看查看！”刘伯温听了这话，心里暗暗地吃了一惊，赶紧催马过桥查看，看出了这是蝎子城，这是对三青进京有妨碍的，可是没法子，走吧，刘伯温装出镇静的样子，说：“没什么，咱们过咱们的桥。”他又驱赶着三青往前走，三青刚走到桥西边，就一动也不敢动啦，刘伯温一方面暗地里叫“天”兵、“天”将催三青走路，一方面说：“三将军快点走吧，过了河就快到北京城啦！快受皇封啦！”三青没法子，只得哧溜哧溜地往前挪，好容易蹭过了卢沟桥。过了卢沟桥，刘伯温想：不要穿城，不要走蝎子脊背，那是危险的！他就驱赶着三青，绕走城南，刘伯温以为躲开了蝎子身子，三青就不至于被螫死了，没想到蝎子尾巴斜着甩过来，一钩子就把三青螫得永远不能动弹啦。刘伯温看了，叹了一口气：“嗐！北京城虽然不见得闹什么水灾，这卢沟渡口的两岸，可怕保不住啦！”他也就只好重新打算治孽龙的法子吧。

肥城南面，从打有了一块青石头以后，老百姓就传说了这么一个大青不动、二青摇、三青走到卢沟桥的故事。

How the Black Rock Went to Lu Gou Qiao

"The Big Black Rock made no move; the Second Black Rock would only budge; the Third Black Rock went to Lu Gou Qiao."① This is another story about how Liu Bowen built Beijing. The local people say he "created" Beijing, but we say he "built" the city. Still, what has this to do with the Black Rock? Another legend tells us.

After Liu Bowen and Yao Guangxiao each succeeded in drawing a plan of Beijing, Yao, being narrow-minded, went off in a huff to become a monk, so we can pass over him. Chief Adviser Liu was a wise man. He determined to build Beijing as an Eight-armed Nezha City. He thought: I can do this, that's certain; but will it really keep down the vicious dragons in this Bitter Sea Waste? This troubled the canny adviser. After thinking over the problem for two days, he learned that on Shangfang Mountain in the county of Fangshan there were three Big Black Rocks which had attained sainthood, one for ten thousand years, the second for five thousand years and the third for a thousand years; so they were able to subdue dragons and tigers. He thought: If I could get hold of one of those rocks with divine power, I'd surely be able to keep down the dragons. If I could get that Big Black Rock which has attained sainthood for ten thousand years, the dragons of Bitter Sea Waste would never be able to rampage again or stage another come-back. But how to get such a heavy rock, and one with such divine powers, down to Beijing? I must find some way by combining soft and hard tactics.

Before telling you what his tactics were, I should say that the three brothers the Big Black Rock, the Second Black Rock and the Third Black Rock on Shangfang Mountain knew what Liu Bowen was scheming.

---

① 译者注：The construction of Lu Gou Qiao, sometimes called Marco Polo Bridge, began in 1187 in the Jin Dynasty. The stone lions on the balustrades were added in 1444 under the Ming. The town of Fei east of the bridge was built in 1640.

The Big Black Rock said, "I'm not going—I'm sitting pretty here."

The Second Black Rock said, "I'm not going either. I'm not taking orders from Crooked Nose Liu Bowen."

The Third Black Rock said, "Who wants to go? I'm only afraid Crooked Nose may use violence to make me."

"Just let him try!" growled the Big Black Rock.

Liu Bowen, having made up his mind to shift these three sacred rocks, decided to use dual tactics. First he would prepare incense and offerings and, taking a retinue, would invite the three sacred rocks down with great pomp and ceremony. If that failed, he had another trick up his sleeve. He'd keep heavenly troops hidden in the seams of his sleeves to frighten the Big Black Rock, the Second Black Rock and the Third Black Rock into coming quietly down from the hill.

After making these preparations, Liu Bowen set out with an imposing retinue to invite the three sacred rocks down to the city. They went southwest from Beijing, crossed Lugou Ford and made straight for Shangfang Mountain. When they reached its foot, Liu Bowen dropped his chief adviser's swagger and went up very earnestly to the three sacred rocks. After lighting incense and presenting offerings, he said most reverently, "Respected Sacred Rocks, in accordance with the Emperor's edict, I, Liu Bowen, have come to beg you to honour Beijing with your presence. Then the Emperor will confer on each of you the title Commander of the Realm!"

The Big Black Rock lay there quietly and made no move. Seeing this, the Second Black Rock and the Third Black Rock thought: Since Big Brother hasn't moved, we needn't either.

When Liu Bowen saw that his incense and offerings had not done the trick, and the rocks had snubbed him like this, he decided to get tough. He whispered to the heavenly troops up his sleeve, "I shall have to trouble you to drive these three rascally rocks to Beijing. Then the Emperor is sure to ennoble you!"

With a cry of assent the heavenly troops flew out from the seams of his sleeves, brandishing swords, spears and halberds. They surrounded the three sacred rocks and yelled: "Get moving, quick, to Beijing!"

Still the Big Black Rock made no move. The Second Black Rock was scared into budging. The Third Black Rock, powerless to resist this show of might, had to leave his two elder brothers and go down the hill. Liu Bowen saw he could not shift the Big Black Rock and the Second Black Rock, but at least he had the Third Black Rock to show that he had carried out his imperial mission, and so he went down the mountain with his attendants to drive the Third Black Rock to Beijing.

Now for a slight digression. When Liu Bowen had crossed Lugou Ford, the Dragon King there had heard of his plan from Prince Dragon, son of the Dragon King of Bitter Sea Waste, and they had discussed how to block the Third Black Rock's way to Beijing. They decided to build a scorpion city at the ford, so that when Liu Bowen drove the Third Black Rock there the scorpion could sting him and stop him from going any farther. First they built the scorpion's tail, Lu Gou Qiao, which was finished overnight. Then they built its body, the town of Fei east of the bridge, with two wells outside its east gate as the scorpion's eyes. A little farther east stood two mounds, one north and one south, and these were the scorpion's front pincers. No sooner was this Scorpion City completed than Liu Bowen came along driving the Third Black Rock.

His attendants reported, "Adviser, when we came this way there was no bridge over Lugou Ford. Now there's not only a long stone bridge, there's a city as well to its east. Please take a look, sir."

Liu Bowen heard this with dismay, and spurred his horse to the bridge to investigate. He realized that this Scorpion City would try to prevent Third Black Rock from reaching Beijing. Still, there was nothing for it but to press on.

With a show of calm he said, "Never mind, let's cross this bridge of ours."

He drove the Third Black Rock on again. But the Third Black Rock stopped dead at the west end of the bridge. Then Liu Bowen secretly ordered his heavenly troops to drive the rock on, and told him, "Hurry up, Third

Commander. Once across this river we'll soon reach Beijing. Then the Emperor will grant you a title!"

Then the Third Black Rock had to trundle on till he had lumbered over Lu Gou Qiao. Liu Bowen decided not to go through the town over the scorpion's back—that was too risky! So he skirted south of it, driving the rock, to keep out of the scorpion's way so that the Third Black Rock would not be stung to death. Suddenly, however, the scorpion's tail lashed round and stung the Third Black Rock—he could never move again.

Liu Bowen sighed, "Confound it! Beijing may not be flooded, but both banks of this Lugou Ford quite likely will be!" So he had to think of another way of curbing those vicious dragons.

Ever since this black rock appeared south of the town of Fei, the local people have told this story describing how "the Big Black Rock made no move; the Second Black Rock would only budge; the Third Black Rock went to Lu Gou Qiao."

高亮赶水

不知道几百年、几千年啦，北京的老爷爷、老奶奶们都这么说：当初北京可苦啦，那时候，北京是一片苦海，谁都管它叫“苦海幽州”，苦海幽州的人，都躲在西面、北面的山上去住，把这片苦海让给了龙王。龙王和他的老婆龙母，带着儿子、儿媳、孙子、孙女，就占据了苦海，在苦海里自己称了王爷，闹得那时候的人，躲到山上去过苦日子。苦到什么份儿上呢？苦到用泥做锅，用斗量柴①，人们的日子过得苦极啦。也不知道又过了多少年，出来这么一个穿着红袄短裤，名字叫哪吒的小孩子，真有本事，来到苦海幽州，就跟龙王、龙子打起来啦，整整打了九九八十一天，哪吒拿住了龙王、龙母，逃跑了龙王的儿子、儿媳、孙子、孙女。龙王、龙母被拿住了以后，水就平下去啦，慢慢地露出陆地来，哪吒封闭了各处的海眼，把龙王、龙母封闭在一处顶大的海眼里，上面砌了一座大的白塔，叫龙王、龙母永久地看守白塔。苦海幽州的水平下去了，就不再叫苦海啦，光叫幽州啦。叫了幽州，就慢慢地有人在这里盖房子，在这里住起来。有了人家，就有村子，有了村子，就有集镇。逃跑了的龙子，这时也称了龙公啦，他的老婆也称龙婆啦，他们带着儿子、女儿躲在西山脚下一个海眼里，一声不响的过日子，他们越看苦海幽州的人家，一天比一天多，就一天比一天气闷，总想出来捣捣乱，总想出来发发水淹没那这时已然不叫“苦海”的“幽州”。

这一天，龙公听来了一个信息：幽州要盖北京城。他更气恼啦，他想：我们的龙宫，你们人给平啦，你们还要在这里盖城，真叫我好恼！后来，跟着又传来一个信息：刘伯温跟姚广孝，脊梁对脊梁画了北京八臂哪吒城图，并且北京正修八臂哪吒城哩！他跟龙婆说：“这可糟啦，这可恨透了人啦，幽州这地方，要修起来八臂哪吒北京城，咱们就甭想再翻身啦！”龙婆说：“算了吧，他盖他的城，咱住咱们的海眼龙宫，别找麻烦吧。”龙公一跺

① 原文注：“泥锅造饭斗量柴”，是北京流传很久的口语，泥锅指的是沙锅，斗量的柴指的是煤。

脚，说："这叫什么话？我不能瞧着他们过好日子！我得趁着八臂哪吒城没盖起来的时候，把城里头的水收回来，叫他们盖不了城，叫他们活活地渴死！"龙婆情知拦是拦不住啦，只好听她丈夫的话吧。

龙公、龙婆算计好了主意，第二天一清早，龙公、龙婆带着龙子、龙女，推着一辆独轮小车，小车上装满了青菜，扮做乡下进城卖菜的模样，龙公推着小车，龙婆拉着小绊儿，龙子、龙女在后面远远地跟着，就这样混进了北京城。龙公推着车子进了北京城，他哪有心情卖青菜呢？他找了个僻静地方，就把青菜全倒在地上啦。龙公、龙婆带着龙子、龙女，在城里转了一个圈儿，按着算计好了的法子：龙子把城里所有的甜水，都给喝净啦；龙女把城里所有的苦水，都给喝净啦；然后，龙子、龙女变成了两只鱼鳞水篓，一边一个，躺在车子上，龙公推着车子，龙婆拉着小绊儿，扬长地出西直门去啦。

这时候，刘伯温呢？他修造的八臂哪吒城，城是盖修齐啦，他正带着监工官、管工官修皇宫呢，忽然有人满头大汗地跑来回告他："回禀大军师，大事不好！现在北京城里的大大小小的水井，一齐都干啦，请大军师赶紧想主意！"刘伯温一听，也着了慌啦，他心里一琢磨：准知道这座八臂哪吒城，招了龙王、龙母的儿子龙公的嫉恨，本来嘛，八臂哪吒城修好了以后，一窝子大龙、小龙，就不能翻身了吗！刘伯温当下赶紧派人，分头到各城门查问，问问管门的门领官，今天有什么特别样子的人出门没有？许多人奉了大军师分派，都骑着快马，飞也似地到各城门查问去啦。不大功夫，全回来了，各门都没有差样的人出城，只有到西直门查问的人回来说："在西直门看见一个罗锅儿身子的老头儿，推着一辆独轮车，前边还有一个老婆婆拉小绊儿，车上放着水淋淋的两只鱼鳞水篓，前一个时辰，出西直门去啦。"门领官还说："因为这鱼鳞水篓很特别，所以多看了几眼，看着分量不大，可是那老汉推着车子还象很费劲呢！"刘伯温听了，点了点头，说："好一个狠毒的孽龙！现在的办法，就只有派人去把水追回来。"监工官说："怎么个追法呢？"刘伯温说："追回水来，也难也容易：难呢？是追的人如果被孽龙看出来，性命就保不住啦，就会叫他放出来的水给淹死！说容易呢？只要一枪两枪扎破鱼鳞水篓，不管后面有什么响动，千万不要回头，急忙跑回来，到了西直门就平安没事啦。”大伙儿都摇头说：“好玄！真不容易！”刘伯温急得直跺脚，说：“事情可紧急啊！等到孽龙把水送进海眼里，就追不回来啦！哪位去追呀？”大官小官你瞧着我，我瞧着你，谁也不搭腔，可把大军师急坏啦！这时候，只听一声清脆响亮的答话声：“大军师，我愿意追孽龙去，一定能赶上孽龙，一定能扎破他的鱼鳞水篓，一定能把水追回来！”刘伯温一瞧是一个二十多岁的年轻工匠，大眼珠子，脸上透着精神，刘伯温高兴啦，就问：“你叫什么名字？”这人说：“我叫高亮，是修皇宫的瓦匠。”刘伯温点了点头，马上打兵丁的兵器架子上，拿起一条红缨枪来，递给了高亮，说：“你一切要小心，我带着人在西直门城上给你助威。”高亮接过来红缨枪，答应了一声：“大军师放心吧！”头也不回，飞也似地追孽龙赶水去啦。

高亮跑出了西直门，可为难啦，往北是北关，通西北的大道，可以到玉泉山；往西是西关，通西南的大道，可以到西山“八大处”；往南是南关，通正南的大道，可以到西直门南边的那座阜成门，往哪里追呢？高亮想了想，这可是打闪认针的时间啊，高亮就想出主意来啦，他想：刘大军师不是说了吗？孽龙不是打算把水送进海眼里去吗？海眼，只有玉泉山有海眼，往西北追！高亮拔起脚来，往西北就追下去啦。高亮托着红缨枪，眼睛里冒出火似的光亮，往西北急急地追了下去，追了没有多大功夫，眼前出现了一道夹沟子，两旁高高的土坡，中间一道窄窄的夹沟，只能对对付付地通过一辆小车去，马拉大车都走不过去，两旁可是也有两条路，孽龙走哪一条路呢？这时候，土坡子上有几个种地的农民正说话呢，一个人说：“这两只水篓子很特别，怎么一闪一闪的象龙磷哪！”一个人说：“我真纳闷，玉泉山那边有多少甜水啊，为什么老天拔地的推着两篓子水往西北跑？”又一个人说：“真难为这老汉、老婆，推着这么两篓子水，这么快就过了咱们这个‘车道沟’，那么大年纪，真有把子力气！”高亮听了这个话，情知孽龙是过了夹沟子往西北去啦，他一声没响，托着红缨枪就穿过夹沟子，往西北一直追了下去。又追了不多远，眼前又出现了一片大柳树林子，树林子把路给岔成了两股小道，高亮不知道孽龙往哪条道儿去啦。他正发愣的时候，柳林子里有小孩子说了话：“咻！拿大扎枪的哥哥，你给我们练一趟呀!”高亮一瞧,大树底下有几个小孩子,拍着手朝他乐,高亮心里一动,马上高了兴,说:“小兄弟们,我回头给你们练枪,请你们先告诉我,有一个老大爷,一个老大娘,推着水车子,打这儿往哪条道儿去啦?”几个小孩子抢着说:“往西边那条道儿去啦!”高亮说了一声劳驾!就往这条道儿赶下去啦。后来,这个地方就叫了“大柳树”。高亮往前追着追着,发现了一片没有水的泥塘,四外水痕还显着湿漉漉的,泥塘中间有水车子印儿,高亮端详了一下,心里明白啦:这一定是池塘,孽龙车子误在这儿啦,真歹毒,他把这点水都不留,也给取了走啦,好可恨的孽龙!——这个地方,后来叫南坞。高亮扎枪点地,腾身越过了池塘,为了追回城里的水源,血奔心的直追了下去,不大功夫,又碰见了另外一处泥塘——这个地方,后来叫中坞——车子印儿也深了,脚印儿也多啦,高亮知道:孽龙一定是劳乏啦,不然哪会踩这么多、这么深的脚印儿,趁这时候快追,一定能追得上。高亮腿上使足了劲,往前直追,追了没有多远,玉泉山就在眼前啦。高亮仔细一瞧,远远果然有一辆装着两个鱼鳞水篓子的小车子,一个罗锅儿身子的老头儿,一个老婆婆,正坐在地上擦头上的汗呢,这一定是龙公、龙婆了,这龙公、龙婆显然是劳乏啦。高亮这时候,心里又高兴,又怦怦乱跳,他矮着身子,钻进了高粱地,绕到龙公、龙婆的后面,猛然一长身子,递枪就扎,一枪就扎破了一只鱼鳞水篓子,水哗的一下就流下来啦。高亮还要扎那一只水篓,哪里还有水篓,只见一个凸着肚子的小伙子,滋溜一下就钻进玉泉山海眼去啦。又瞧龙婆抱起来叫高亮扎破了的水篓,往北就飞过了北面的山头,投奔黑龙潭去啦。这都是同时的事,都是急如闪电的事,还没等高亮想:扎破一个水篓子,怎么交差,就听龙公大喝一声:“破坏我大事的小伙子,你还想走吗?”高亮打了一个机伶,转身提枪就跑,后面象涨潮一样的水声,就追下来啦。高亮紧跑水紧追,慢跑水慢追,眼看到西直门了,也能清清楚楚地看见西直门城墙上的刘伯温啦,他心里一高兴,没留神回头一看,水就把高亮卷走啦。打这儿,北京城里的井,又有了水,可大部分是苦水①，甜水呢？甜水叫龙子给带到玉泉山海眼里去啦。龙公呢？"北新桥"故事里再讲。后来，人们在高亮死的地方，修了一座桥，就叫高亮桥②。有人瞧见这座石头桥，就也会传说下这个故事来。

---

① 原文注：北京没有洋井、自来水以前，甜水井很少，大部分是苦水井，也有半甜半苦的二性子水井。那时候，一般人家都预备三种水：苦水洗衣服，二性子水做饭，喝茶才用甜水。由于那时候北京苦水多，所以"高亮赶水"的故事，说的也就比较普遍起来。

② 原文注：高亮桥在西直门外北关，水从玉泉山流出来，过了昆明湖，就到了长河，长河往东南流，经过动物园、北京展览馆的后面，往东就是高亮桥，水过了高亮桥，分别流入护城河、流入北京城里，在永定河引水工程没完成以前，几千年来就是北京地区的主要水源。长河古代叫"高粱水"，桥也叫"高粱桥"。从有了"高亮赶水"的民间传说，才有人叫它高亮桥。

Gao Liang's Race for Water

Hundreds of thousands of years ago, so the old folk in Beijing say, this place was in a bad way because it was a briny sea known as Bitter Sea Waste; and people had to live in the western and northern hills, leaving the Bitter Sea to the Dragon King. The Dragon King, his wife, son, daughter-in-law and grandchildren lorded it over the Bitter Sea so that the local people who had taken to the hills lived a wretched life. How wretched was their life? They used the earth as their cauldrons and weighed out their firewood in bushels.

Some years later a boy called Nezha appeared in a red jacket and short pants. He had real ability. Coming to the Bitter Sea he fought the Dragon King for nine times nine days, eighty-one days in all. He captured the Dragon King and his wife, while their son, daughter-in-law and grandchildren fled. After the capture of the Dragon King the water slowly ebbed away and soil emerged. Nezha sealed up the different outlets to the sea, sealing up the Dragon King and his wife in a large lake, then built a big white pagoda on top so that ever after they had to stay there to guard it.

Now that the water had ebbed away, the name Bitter Sea was changed to the Waste. As time went by people built houses there and settled down there. Villages sprang up, as well as market-towns. By now the dragon's son who had fled had become the king, and he and his wife took refuge with their son and daughter in a lake at the foot of the western hills. There they lay low, keeping quiet. When they saw the people of Bitter Sea Waste increasing from day to day, that increased their exasperation. They kept wanting to go out and rampage, to flood this Waste which was no longer called the Bitter Sea.

One day the new Dragon King heard that a city called Beijing was to be built in the Waste. That really enraged him. He thought: You people razed our Dragon Palace, and now you want to build a city there just to infuriate me! Then came word that Liu Bowen and Yao Guangxiao had back to back drawn a plan of Beijing—an Eight-armed Nezha City with eight gates—and its construction had already started.

The Dragon King told his wife, "Confound it! How maddening! If they build an Eight-armed Nezha City, we've no hope of making a comeback!"

"Never mind," said his wife. "Let them build their city. We'll stay here in our Dragon Palace and keep out of trouble."

The Dragon King stamped his foot. "That's no way to talk," he fumed. "How can I watch them sitting pretty! I must seize this chance, before their city is finished, to drain away all its water. Then before they can finish it they'll die of thirst!"

His wife, unable to talk him out of this, had to go along with him.

Having hatched their plot, the next day at dawn they set out with their son and daughter and a wheelbarrow loaded with vegetables. They had dressed like peasants going to the market in town. The Dragon King pushed the barrow, his wife pulled the loop in front, and with their children following some way behind they sneaked into Beijing. Of course the Dragon King had no intention of selling vegetables. He found an out-of-the-way spot and dumped them all there. Then he, his wife, Dragon Boy and Dragon Girl went round the town according to their plan. Dragon Boy drank all the sweet water there, Dragon Girl all the bitter water; then they changed themselves into two fish-scale water-panniers and lay down one on each side of the wheelbarrow. With the Dragon King pushing and his wife pulling it, they went out of *Xi Zhi Men* bold as brass.

Meantime what of Liu Bowen? Now that the Eight-armed Nezha City had been built, he had taken his inspectors to supervise the building of the imperial palace. Suddenly someone dashed over with sweat. "Report, chief adviser!" he shouted. "We're in big trouble. Every single well, large or small, in Beijing is dry. What's to be done!"

Liu Bowen was flabbergasted. Then he figured: Everyone knows that the Dragon King, his wife and their son Prince Dragon are jealous of this city. Because of course once it's built, that tribe of dragons can never make a come-back. He promptly sent subordinates to all the city gates to investigate and find out from the wardens if any suspicious characters had been through their gates that day. Horsemen galloped off to carry out his orders. Very soon they came back and reported that the only suspicious characters to leave the city had gone through *Xi Zhi Men*. One of them reported, "An old hunchback was seen at *Xi Zhi Men* pushing a wheelbarrow, with an old woman tugging in front. On the barrow were two dripping fish-scale water-panniers. They left by *Xi Zhi Men* an hour ago."

The warden added, "They were such strange fish-scale panniers that I had a good look at them. They weren't too big, yet that old fellow was sweating as he pushed the barrow."

Liu Bowen nodded. "The vicious old dragon!" he said. "We'll just have to send someone to catch him and bring back the water."

The chief inspector asked, "How can we do that?"

Liu told him, "It'll be hard or easy, depending on how you look at it. Hard, because if that damned dragon sees someone after him, he'll swamp him with water to drown him. Easy, because if our man spears the fish-scale panniers then dashes straight back without looking round no matter if all hell breaks loose behind, once he reaches *Xi Zhi Men* he'll be safe and sound."

His men shook their heads saying, "That's a tall order. Not easy."

Liu stamped impatiently. "There's no time to be lost! We can't wait for that damned dragon to empty all that water down his lake, or we'll never get it back. Who'll take this on?"

His officers, high and low, eyed each other in silence. The chief adviser was frantic! Then they heard a clear voice ring out:

"Let me go, sir. I promise to catch up with the damned dragon and to spear the fish-scale panniers. I guarantee to bring the water back."

Liu saw it was a builder in his twenties, big-eyed and alert-looking.

"What's your name?" he asked, very pleased.

"I'm Gao Liang, a mason working on the palace."

Liu nodded and promptly took a red-tasselled spear from the weapon rack. He handed it to Gao Liang, saying, "Be very careful. I'll take troops up the West Gate to back you up."

Gao Liang took the spear, promising, "You can count on me, sir." Then without one backward glance he flew off in pursuit of the dragon.

Once out of *Xi Zhi Men* a dilemma faced him. To the north was a road to the northwest, leading to Jade Spring Hill. To the west was a road to the southwest, leading to the western hills. To the south was a road south to *Fu Cheng Men*. Which way should he go? He must make a lightning decision. He thought: Didn't Liu Bowen say that damned dragon is taking the water to his lake? The only lake is at Jade Spring Hill. I'll catch him before he gets there. He sprinted off to the northwest, gripping his spear, his eyes flashing fire. Before long he came to a gully between two high banks, just wide enough for a wheelbarrow to pass through, but too narrow for a horsecart. There were roads on both sides, however. Would the dragons have taken one of them? On one bank some peasants were talking.

One said, "Very odd they were, those two water-panniers glinting like the scales of a fish or dragon."

"Beats me," said another. "With all that sweet water in Jade Spring, why lug those two panniers of water northwest?"

Another said, "That old fellow and his wife were puffing and blowing, lugging that barrow of water so fast through our gully. At their age too—they're really tough!"

Gao Liang knew then that the dragons had headed northwest. Without a word, gripping his spear, he hurried northwest through the gully. Before long the road forked in front of a willow copse. Which way had the dragons gone? He was at a loss when he heard some boys in the copse.

"Hey, big brother with the tasselled spear, give us a drill!" one called to him.

Gao Liang saw some small boys beneath the trees clapping their hands and grinning. His spirits rose. He told them, "Little brothers, I'll drill you presently. First tell me if an old man and old woman passed here pushing a wheelbarrow."

"They took that track to the left," the little boys chorused.

Thanking them, he set off again. Later on this place was given the name Big Willows.

Hurrying on in pursuit, Gao Liang came to a pool that had dried up. Its banks were spattered with water, and in the bed of the pool was a rut made by a barrow. At once he understood: This must have been a pond. That damned dragon's barrow stopped here and he didn't leave a single drop of water—he carried it all away! Later this place was given the name South Hollow.

Planting his spear in the ground, Gao Liang vaulted over the pond and hurried on, eager to get back the water for the city. Before long he came to another pond—later called Middle Hollow—with a deep rut made by the barrow and many footprints. He realized that the dragons must be tired; why else should they have left so many deep footprints? If he put on a spurt he could certainly catch up. He bounded forward, and very soon the Jade Spring Hill came into sight. Gao Liang strained his eyes. In the distance, sure enough, was a barrow loaded with two water-panniers. An old hunchback and an old woman were seated on the ground mopping their sweaty faces. They must be the Dragon King and his wife, quite worn out. Gao Liang exulted, his heart going pit-a-pat. He ducked into a field of sorghum to make a detour to the back of the dragons, then sprang up and speared one of the fish-scale panniers. Water came flooding out. But before he could spear the second, it changed into a pot-bellied youngster who dived into the Jade Spring. The dragon's wife picked up the pannier Gao Liang had speared, and flew over the peak of the north hill to escape to Black Dragon Lake. All these things happened at once, as fast as lightning. Before Gao Liang could decide what to do, the Dragon King roared, "You've ruined my grand scheme, damn you! Don't think you can get away."

With a start Gao Liang took to his heels, pursued by what sounded like a racing tide. When he speeded up, so did the water; when he slowed down, it slowed down too. Now *Xi Zhi Men* came in sight, and he could distinctly see Liu Bowen above it. In his relief he forgot himself and looked round, and the water swept him away.

Since then there has been water in Beijing's wells, but most of it is brackish. What of the sweet water? It was carried off by Dragon Boy to Jade Spring Hill. And the Dragon King? That's another story. Later, over the place where Gao Liang drowned, men built the Gao Liang Qiao.① People seeing this stone bridge may pass on this story.

---

① 译者注：A stream flows from the Jade Spring past Kunming Lake to the canal, formerly known as Gaoliang Stream, which runs southeast past the Zoo and the back of the Exhibition Hall, then east to Gao Liang Qiao. For thousands of years this was Beijing's main waterway, and before the Yongding River was diverted here, it was Beijing's main source of water.

卖蝈蝈笼子

咱们都知道北京的天安门吧，进了天安门，过了端门，一直往北就是紫禁城的正门午门啦。紫禁城是一座砖城，里面在明、清两朝时候，是皇帝老儿办公和住家的地方，现在是故宫博物院。紫禁城有四个门，就是南面的午门，北面的神武门和东面的东华门，西面的西华门。四个门，不用谈它了，单说紫禁城的角楼吧。紫禁城的四个城角上，每一个角上有一座九梁十八柱七十二条脊的角楼，建造的可好看啦，可美丽啦，谁走过这里的时候，谁都要夸赞一句："这四座角楼怎么盖的？画都画不上来啊！"这四座角楼怎么盖的呢？北京有这么一个传说——

北京人都这么说：明朝的燕王（朱棣）在南京做了永乐皇帝以后，因为北京是他做王爷时候的老地方，所以想要迁都到北京来，于是就派了亲信大臣来修盖北京的皇宫。朱棣告诉这个亲信大臣：要在皇宫外墙——紫禁城的四个犄角上，盖四座样子特别美丽的角楼，要盖成九梁十八柱七十二条脊的角楼，并且说："你就做这个管工大臣吧，修盖不好是要杀头的！"管工大臣领了皇帝的谕旨，心里烦的不得了，他想不出怎样修盖这样怪角楼的法子，他只是想：皇帝既然说出这样话来，就得给皇帝盖成了，皇帝的话就是"金口玉言"的旨意嘛，哪个敢驳回！自已虽然想不出什么好法子，工头们是一定能给修盖成的，等到了北京再说吧。管工大臣到了北京以后，刚打下了公馆，就把八十一家大包工木厂（建筑厂）的工头、木匠师傅们都叫了来，跟他们说了皇帝的旨意，叫他们一定要修盖成这四座奇怪样子的角楼来，并且给了三个月的限期，还说："盖不成，皇帝自然要杀我的头，可是在没杀我的头之前，我就先把你们的头都杀了，你们当心你们的脑袋！"工头跟木匠师傅一听，心想：好，反正我们死你也活不了！可是哪敢说个不字。工头跟木匠师傅们，对这样工程，也没准把握，只好常常在一块儿琢磨法子，也有时候，各自盘算各自的主意。都说："这种没样子的奇怪的工程，怎么下手呢？梁怎么上？柱子怎么立？升斗（斗拱）怎么安呢？"有的说："这真没法子下手啊！"只好大家想主意吧。

三个月的期限是很短的，一转眼就是一个月，一个月过去了，工头、木匠师傅们，还没想出一点头绪、一点办法来，做了许多样型，都不合适。这时候，又赶上六七月的三伏天气，热的人都喘不上气来啦，加上心里的烦闷，工头、木匠师傅们，真是坐也不合适，躺也不舒服。有这么一位木匠师傅，实在呆也呆不住了，就上大街闲遛去啦，遛遛达达的走着走着，听见老远蝈、蝈、蝈传来一片蝈蝈的吵叫声音，又听见一声吆喝："买蝈蝈儿，听叫儿去，睡不着解闷儿去！"等到走近啦，看见一年老头儿挑着大大小小许多秫秸编的蝈蝈笼子，木匠师傅看见其中有一个细秫秸棍插的蝈蝈笼子，细巧得跟画里的一座楼阁一样，里头装着几个蝈蝈，他想：反正是烦心的事，该死活不了，买这个好看的笼子，看着也有个趣儿。木匠师傅提了这个蝈蝈笼子，回到了"锅伙儿"（工地宿舍），大伙一看就吵嚷起来啦："大伙儿都心里怪烦的，你怎么买一笼子蝈蝈来，成心吵人是怎么着？"木匠师傅笑着说："大家睡不着解个闷儿吧，你们瞧……"他的意思是：你们瞧这个笼子多么好看，多么奇巧，可是他还没说出嘴来，就觉得笼子有点特别来啦，他急忙摆着手说："你们先别吵吵嚷嚷的，等我数数再说。"他把蝈蝈笼子的梁啊，柱啊，脊啊，细细地数了一遍又一遍，大伙被他这一数，也吸引得留了神，静静地直着眼睛地看着，一点儿声音也没有啦。木匠师傅数完了蝈蝈笼子，蹦起来一拍大腿说："这不是九梁十八柱七十二条脊是什么！"大伙听了，都高起兴来啦，这个接过笼子数数，那个也接过笼子数数，都说："这个真是九梁十八柱七十二条脊的楼阁啊！"大伙从这个笼子上面，琢磨出紫禁城角楼的样子来啦，烫出纸浆做的样型来①，修盖成了到现在还存在的故宫角楼。后来，人们就传说起来，说："这个卖蝈蝈笼子的老头，准许是鲁班爷！"这么些年了，谁走到这里，谁看见这四座角楼，谁都会想起这个卖蝈蝈笼子的故事来。

---

① 原文注：明、清两朝，凡是要修建"皇家"宫殿苑囿，都先用纸浆做出立体样型来，和真的宫殿样子、比例数都一样，叫作"烫样"。明、清两朝管烫样的工人姓雷，辈辈相传，人叫他家"样子雷"。样子雷家存的烫样，在一九三一年已然卖给了北京图书馆。北京的故宫——紫禁城，是明朝永乐四年（公元一四零六年）修建的。城四周共六里另八丈。

The Cricket Cage Pedlar

Everyone knows *Tian An Men* in Beijing. Going into *Tian An Men* through *Duan Men*, you go straight north to *Wu Men*, the Meridian Gate, the main entrance to the Forbidden City. The Forbidden City, with its brick walls behind which the Ming and Qing emperors lived and ruled, is now the Palace Museum. It has four gates north, south, east and west. But never mind the gates, let me just describe the watch-towers at the corners of the wall. Each of these four watch-towers in the Forbidden City has nine beams, eighteen pillars and seventy-two roof-ridges. Everyone who passes these magnificent towers exclaims, "However were those watch-towers built? Whoever can have designed them?" Well, there is a Beijing legend to answer these questions.

Beijing people say that after Prince Yan of Ming was enthroned① as Emperor Yongle in Nanjing, because he had lived in Beijing as a prince he decided to move the capital there and to send a trusted minister to repair his Beijing palace. He told this minister: On the outer wall of the palace, at the four corners of the Forbidden City, he wanted four magnificent watch-towers built. He warned him, "You're in charge of the construction. If you bungle it—off with your head!"

This imperial edict made the minister frantic. He had no idea how to build such watch-towers. He thought: Since these are the Emperor's orders, I'll have to build them for him. His words are our golden rules—there's no disputing them! I don't know how to set about this, but once I get to Beijing the builders there are bound to find a way.

As soon as this minister reached Beijing and had settled down in his hostel, he summoned all the overseers and master carpenters of eighty-one big contractors. He told them the Emperor's orders, and gave them three months in which to complete these four extraordinary watch-towers. "If you

---

① 原文注：In 1402.

fail, of course the Emperor will cut off my head," he said. "But before that I'll behead the lot of you. So you'd better look out!"

The overseers and carpenters thought: Fine. Anyway, if we die so will you! But not one of them dared refuse. Not feeling sure that they could do this job, they kept getting together to work out a plan or tried to figure out something on their own. They complained, "There's no model for this extraordinary project, so how can we set about it? Where should the beams and pillars go? Where should the arches be put?" Some declared, "There's really no way we can start work." So they just had to rack their brains.

The time limit—three months—was very short. A month flashed past, and still the builders had not a clue as to how to tackle this work. They made many models, but none of them would do. By now it was the hottest time of summer, the weather was stifling, and in their desperation they felt on tenterhooks.

One carpenter, too restless to stay in, went out to stroll through the town. In the distance he heard the chirruping of crickets and a pedlar's cry: "Buy my crickets! They will cheer you up when you can't sleep!" Going closer he saw an old man with two crates of cricket cages, large and small, all so skilfully made of millet stalks that they looked like towers and pavilions in a painting, and there were crickets in each. The carpenter thought: It's no use worrying; if we're done for we're done for. I may as well buy a pretty cage for fun. He asked the price and bought an ingeniously made, very dainty cage, which he carried back to the builders' living quarters.

At sight of it his mates bawled, "Here we are all worried stiff, yet you bring in that rowdy cricket—what's the idea?"

The carpenter said, "To cheer you up when you can't sleep. Just look...." He meant to go on, "See how cleverly the cage is made!" But just then he was struck by something special about it. He held up one hand, saying, "Don't make such a racket. Wait till I've done some counting...." Then he carefully counted and recounted the beams, pillars and arches of the cricket cage, while the others watched intently in silence with bated breath.

After finishing counting, the carpenter sprang up and slapped his thigh.

"See there—nine beams, eighteen pillars and seventy-two roof-ridges!" he cried.

That put fresh heart in them all. One by one they took the cage to count for themselves. "Yes, it really is a watch-tower with nine beams, eighteen pillars and seventy-two roof-ridges!" they said. From this cage they figured out the design of the watch-towers for the Forbidden City, made a papier-mâché model, and built the four towers still to be seen today.

Later, people said, "That old man selling cricket cages must have been a real Lu Ban!"① Ever since, whoever sees these four corner towers in the Forbidden City is bound to remember this story of the cricket cage pedlar.

① 译者注：A legendary builder and craftsman, regarded as the patron saint of craftsmen.

铸钟娘娘

在一九二四年以前,北京跟北京附近的人,每天到了晚上七点钟的时候,就都听见了连续不断:邪!邪!邪!的钟声①,是一种很好听的声音。这时候,尤其是冬天很冷的时候,妈妈们就会跟孩子说:"睡觉吧,钟楼打钟啦,铸钟娘娘要鞋啦,睡觉吧,别吵了铸钟娘娘。""什么是铸钟娘娘要鞋呀?"妈妈们就说出下面一个故事来。

原来,早年间没有钟表的时候,各省各县都有一个鼓楼,到了定更(下午七点钟)天,就开始打鼓,叫作"交更",老百姓听见鼓楼的鼓声,就知道天到什么时候啦。北京是京城啊,鼓楼当然要比省城、县城的鼓楼,高得多,大得多了,净有这么大的鼓楼多么孤单啊,得配个大的钟楼。皇帝就下了一道"圣旨",派管工程的工部大官,修一座高大的钟楼,铸一口两万斤重的大钟。工部大官接了这道"圣旨",马上把全国各省有名的铸钟匠人,召集到北京来,商量怎样铸这口大钟。有名的铸钟匠人都到齐啦,大家就商量起来啦,工部大官就派一个更有名的匠人老邓头,做铸钟的工匠头,带领大家铸钟。先在鼓楼西面开了一个大的铸钟厂,大家就住在厂里铸钟。老邓头呢,他是有家眷的,他有一个妻子,他有一个读书识字、心思灵巧、长得美丽的大闺女,一家子过着舒舒服服的日子。他们就住在铸钟厂外面不远的一个小胡同里。老邓头天天早晨起来上铸钟厂,晚上回家和妻子、闺女说说笑笑,倒也不觉得有什么别扭的事。老邓头天天回家,闺女总是问:"爹,钟铸成了吗?"老邓头也总是笑着说:"快啦,快啦,快铸成啦。"一天两天过去了,十天二十天过去了,钟真铸成啦,是一口很大的大铁钟,老邓头报告了工部大官,工部大官赶忙奏明了皇帝,请皇帝听听钟声,他以为皇帝听了这个大钟的声音,一定要奖赏他哩。大钟架起来了,皇帝看钟、听钟来啦,没想到皇帝刚一看见这口钟,就好大的不乐意,

---

① 原文注:北京的钟楼,高有九丈多,完全砖石结构,建于元朝至元九年(公元一二七二年)。

说:“怎么不铸个铜钟? 这黑湫湫的多么难看!”等到敲起钟来,皇帝更恼怒啦,发火地说:“这是什么声音? 叭喇叭喇的,不用说全城人听不见,就是我的皇宫里也听不见啊!”当时责罚了工部大官,还说:“给你三个月的限期,铸一口两万斤重的铜钟,平常时候,要四郊都听得见,顺风的时候,要四十里地以外,也听到我这口钟声。铸不成,铸不好,是要杀你头的!”皇帝说完了,甩着袖子,怒气冲冲的就回皇宫去啦。

工部大官早吓傻啦,等皇帝走了以后,他向老邓头们发起威风来啦:“你们是成心要我的好看! 给你们两个月限期,铸成皇帝说的这样的钟,铸不成,铸不好,先杀你这个工头的头! 别的工匠,一个也轻饶不了!”说完了,工部大官也坐上轿子走啦。

老邓头和他的伙伴们,生气极啦。有的说:“他没说叫我们铸铜钟啊!”有的说:“铸铜钟给我们铁料!”大伙一生气,把铁钟摘下来,扔在地上躺着就不管啦,大家从头商量铸铜钟。老邓头气昂昂地回了家,闺女一看见她爹,就问:“钟不是铸成了吗? 爹为什么生气呢?”老邓头说:“成什么!”他把刚才的事说了一遍,闺女也生气啦,只得安慰她爹:“慢慢地想法子铸新钟吧。”老邓头还是天天早晨上铸钟厂,晚上回家,起初一个多月,还不怎么样,过了一个半月,老邓头回家的时候,气色就不同啦,总是愁眉不展的咳声叹气。老婆儿问他,他也不说什么,闺女问他,他只说一句:“没什么。”灵巧的邓姑娘,慢慢地知道了她爹为什么发愁啦,原来这口铜钟怎么也铸不成,不是铜汁子凝结不上,就是铜汁子凝结以后,又不象钟的样子啦,化了又铸,铸了又化,不知道铸了多少回啦,总是铸不成。老邓头是早就吃不下饭去了,伙伴们也是垂头丧气、愁眉苦脸的。大伙说:“这可真没主意啦,就等着到了俩月领刑吧!”邓姑娘知道了这回事,也是着急的了不得,天天替她爹发愁,老邓头回家的时候,她就安慰爹几句,老邓头不在家的时候,她就和妈妈一起掉眼泪,日子一天天近了,可把灵巧的、美丽的邓姑娘急坏啦。

这一天,是铸新钟限期的末一天啦。前一天,老邓头就没有回家,可把邓姑娘母女急坏啦,愁坏啦。一天早晨起来,邓姑娘就跟妈妈说,要去铸钟厂去看看爹爹,老邓婆说:“你一个姑娘人家的,怎么能进铸钟厂呢?”

邓姑娘一定要去，老邓婆也就依着女儿的心思啦，说："你看看就回来，回来告诉我，我也好放心。"邓姑娘换了衣裳，换了新绣花鞋，就去铸钟厂看爹爹去啦。她到了铸钟厂，太阳是刚出来，一进铸钟厂，就看见爹爹跟他的伙伴们，围着化铜锅乱转，满头大汗，再叫太阳光这么一照，个个的脸上，都一道子青，一道子紫，活活象一群小鬼。邓姑娘喊了一声"爹，我来啦"。老邓头回头看见了闺女，又伤心又着急地说："你，你干什么来啦？""爹没回家，妈妈叫我来看看爹，问问爹铸的钟怎么样啦！"老邓头还没答话，旁边一个工匠就说啦："怎么样！铜汁子怎么也不对头，就剩今天一天啦，太阳一落，我们就都没命啦！大侄女快回家吧。"邓姑娘听了这话，又看看他爹跟他爹的伙伴们，心里难过极啦，她想：爹爹跟这些这么好的叔叔伯伯们，都要为一口钟丧了命，我还活个什么劲儿！不如死在他们头里吧！邓姑娘想到这里，咬一咬牙，狠一狠心，往后一撤步，使足了力气，往化铜锅那边一跑，临近了一长腰，只听哗的一声，铜汁乱溅，邓姑娘掉在化铜锅里啦。咱们翻回来再说，在邓姑娘往前跑的时候，大伙工匠一看情形不对，异口同声地喊了一句："不好！快揪住她！"老邓头先是呆呆的发怔，大家一喊，他才着了急，三步两步，往前就追，等到老邓头手到了，邓姑娘的身子已然进了化铜锅啦，老邓头一把没揪住，只是揪下邓姑娘一只绣花鞋来，在老邓头拿着闺女的绣花鞋大哭的时候，邓姑娘早在化铜锅里化做一缕青烟啦。老邓头自然是哭闺女哭个没完没了，就是大伙工匠也都掉下眼泪来。正在大家伤心的时候，忽然一个年轻的工匠叫起来："你们先别哭啦，看看铜汁怎么变了样啦！"老邓头和他的伙伴们，一齐来看铜汁，果然铜汁放出特别的光彩来，很象能铸成钟的样子，大家擦干了眼泪，马上动手铸钟，就在太阳刚往西转的时候，八寸厚的新铜钟就铸成啦。老邓头和他的伙伴们到底把钟铸成了，交了"皇差"。

这口新钟挂在钟楼上了，每天一到定更，就打紧十八、慢十八、不紧不慢又十八，两番一百零八下钟声，钟声的后音是邪！邪！邪！老妈妈们听了钟声，就伤心地说："铸钟娘娘又要她那只绣花鞋啦。"铸钟厂取消啦，到现在还留下一个"铸钟厂"的地名。"铸钟厂"里有一座"铸钟娘娘庙"，不知道是什么人修的，有人说，是当初那个皇帝修的，有人说，是老邓头的伙伴、邓姑娘的叔叔伯伯们修的，不用管是谁修的这座铸钟娘娘庙吧，铸钟娘娘的故事，是流传下来了。那口先铸的大铁钟呢？大铁钟啊，它一直躺在“铸钟厂”里，不知道躺了几百年，到一九二五年，才把它挪在鼓楼后面，直直地立在那里，谁看见这口大铁钟，谁也联想到铸钟娘娘的故事来。

The Bell Goddess

Before 1924, the people of Beijing and its northern suburbs every evening at seven o'clock would hear the continuous ding-dong of a bell—*xie*! *xie*! *xie*! —a most pleasing sound. Then, especially in the cold winter, mothers would tell their children, "Time for bed. They're striking the bell in the Bell Tower,① and the Bell Goddess wants her slipper.② Go to sleep now. Don't disturb the Bell Goddess." If children asked why the Bell Goddess wanted her slipper, their mothers would tell them this story.

Long ago, before the invention of clocks and watches, all provincial and county towns had drum towers. At seven in the evening, drums were sounded to let the citizens know the time. As Beijing was the capital, of course its drum tower had to be much higher and bigger than those in provincial and county towns, and a big bell tower had to be built as well to keep it company. So the Emperor issued an imperial edict and ordered the Minister of Works to build a great bell tower and cast a bell weighing ten tons.

The Minister of Works lost no time in summoning all the best foundrymen from the provinces to Beijing, to discuss how to cast this great bell. When these skilled craftsmen were assembled, they talked the matter over and the Minister of Works put the best-known of them, Master Deng, in charge of all the rest. First they set up a large foundry west of the Bell Tower, and the workmen moved in to live there.

Master Deng was a family man with a wife and a lovely daughter, an intelligent girl who could read and write, and they were very comfortably off. They lived in an alley not far from the foundry, and when he went home in the evening they would laugh and chat together without a care in

---

① 译者注：The Bell Tower in Beijing, over ninety feet high and built entirely of brick, dates from 1272 in the Yuan Dynasty.

② 译者注：The word for slipper is pronounced *xie*.

the world.

Each time Master Deng came home, his daughter would ask, "Dad, has the bell been cast yet?"

"It soon will be," he told her, smiling. "Very soon."

Time slipped by, and when twenty days had passed the bell was finished—a big cast-iron bell. Master Deng reported this to the Minister of Works, who immediately informed the Emperor, requesting him to inspect it. He was sure that after hearing the big bell the Emperor would reward him. The bell was set up and the Emperor arrived, but at sight of it his face darkened.

"Why not cast a bronze bell?" he demanded. "Instead of this ugly black thing!"

When the bell was struck, the Emperor flew into a rage. "What sound is that?" he roared. "Those cracked notes won't even carry to my palace, let alone all over the city!" He penalized the Minister and warned him, "I give you three months, no more, to cast a ten-ton bronze bell. In fine weather its sound must carry to all four suburbs, and on windy days to forty *li* away. If you fail to make it, or botch it, I'll cut off your head!" Then, with a swish of his sleeves, he stormed back to the palace.

The Minister of Works was frightened out of his wits. After the Emperor had left he bellowed at Master Deng, "Why lose face for me like this! I give you two months, no more, to cast the bell the Emperor wants. If you fail, or botch it, you'll be the first to lose your head. I won't spare one of the other workmen either!" This said, he got into his sedan-chair and left.

Master Deng and his mates were livid.

"He never told us he wanted a bronze bell!" one pointed out.

"He gave us iron not bronze!" another said.

They angrily took down the iron bell and left it lying on the ground, then discussed how to cast a bronze one. Master Deng went home fuming. At sight of him his daughter asked, "Haven't you finished the bell, dad? Why are you angry?"

"Finished it?" Her father told her what had happened, making the girl angry too.

She could only say consolingly, "Well, you can think out a way to cast a bronze one."

Master Deng went on going to the foundry every morning and coming home in the evening. For the first six weeks or so all seemed to be well, but then a change came over him and he kept frowning and sighing. Questioned by his wife, he said nothing. Questioned by his daughter, he simply said, "It's all right." It dawned on the clever girl that her father was anxious because they had not succeeded in casting the bronze bell. Either molten bronze would not set, or it set in the wrong shape. For some time Master Deng had been off his food. His worried mates pulled long faces.

"We're really stumped," they said. "When the two months are up we'll be executed!"

When Deng's daughter knew this she was frantic too. Every single day she worried over her father, trying to comfort him when he came home and weeping with her mother when he was out. Soon the time would run out. The intelligent, lovely girl was at her wit's end.

Finally the deadline for casting the bell was reached. The day before, Master Deng had not gone home, making his wife and daughter fearfully anxious. So when she got up that morning, the girl told her mother she meant to go to the foundry.

"How can a girl like you go into the foundry?" her mother objected. When her daughter insisted she agreed, "All right then. But come straight home to set my mind at rest."

The girl changed into clean clothes and new embroidered slippers, then went to the foundry. The sun had just come out as she went in and found her dad and his mates milling round the great smelting cauldron, covered with sweat. In the sunshine their faces streaked with grime made them seem a horde of demons.

"It's me, dad!" she called.

Master Deng turned, and at sight of her his heart ached. He asked anxiously, "What are you doing here?"

"Because you didn't come home, mum told me to come and ask how you're getting on with the bell."

Before Deng could answer, one of the workmen put in, "The bell, eh! This bronze won't come right and today is the last day left. At sunset we'll all be dead men. Better hurry home, lass."

Hearing this, and looking at her dad and his mates, her heart bled for them. She thought: If dad and all these good uncles are to lose their lives because of a bell, I don't want to go on living. I'd rather die first! She gritted her teeth and braced herself to dash over to the great cauldron. Splash! She vaulted into it, spattering molten bronze in all directions.

When she darted forward the workmen had yelled, "Look out! Stop her!"

At first Deng had been stupefied. At this cry he charged after her, but too late to stop her. All he managed to catch hold of was one embroidered slipper. He held it, choking with sobs, for by now his daughter had become a wisp of blue smoke in the cauldron. Her father broke down, and the workmen all shed tears too, till suddenly one youngster shouted:

"Stop crying—look! The molten bronze has changed!"

The others crowded round to look and, sure enough, the molten bronze was giving off an extraordinary radiance. Sure now that they could cast it into a bell, they dried their eyes and set to work, and just as the sun was sinking in the west the new bronze bell, eight inches thick, was cast. So at last Master Deng and his mates had finished the task given them by the Emperor.

This new bronze bell was hung in the Bell Tower. Every evening at seven o'clock it is given eighteen swift strokes, then eighteen slow ones, then eighteen neither swift nor slow, and this sequence is repeated, making a hundred and eight strokes in all, each tailing off: *xie*! *xie*! *xie*!

Mothers hearing that sound say sadly, "The Bell Goddess is asking for her slipper again."

The foundry was dismantled, but that place is still called The Foundry, and there someone built a Temple of the Bell Goddess. Some say it was the Emperor who built it, others that it was Master Deng's mates, his daughter's uncles. But no matter who built that temple, the story of the Bell Goddess has been handed down. And what about the big iron bell? That was left lying in The Foundry for hundreds of years, but in 1925 it was moved to the back of the Bell Tower and set up straight. All who see it remember the story of the Bell Goddess.

第三编

戴乃迭散文、寓言式杂文英译

一

朱自清散文四篇[①]

匆　匆

燕子去了,有再来的时候;杨柳枯了,有再青的时候;桃花谢了,有再开的时候。但是,聪明的,你告诉我,我们的日子为什么一去不复返呢?——是有人偷了他们罢:那是谁?又藏在何处呢?是他们自己逃走了罢——如今又到了哪里呢?

我不知道他们给了我多少日子;但我的手确乎是渐渐空虚了。在默默里算着,八千多日子已经从我手中溜去;像针尖上一滴水滴在大海里,我的日子滴在时间的流里,没有声音,也没有影子。我不禁头涔涔而泪潸潸了。

去的尽管去了,来的尽管来着;去来的中间,又怎样地匆匆呢?早上我起来的时候,小屋里射进两三方斜斜的太阳。太阳他有脚啊,轻轻悄悄地挪移了;我也茫茫然跟着旋转。于是——洗手的时候,日子从水盆里过去;吃饭的时候,日子从饭碗里过去;默默时,便从凝然的双眼前过去。我觉察他去的匆匆了,伸出手遮挽时,他又从遮挽着的手边过去,天黑时,我躺在床上,他便伶伶俐俐地从我身上跨过,从我脚边飞去了。等我睁开眼和太阳再见,这算又溜走了一日。我掩着面叹息。但是新来的日子的影

---

① 中文选自:朱自清.朱自清诗文选集.北京:人民文学出版社,1955;英译文选自:Zhu, Z. Q. Prose Writings. Gladys Yang (trans.). *Chinese Literature*, 1958(1): 62-75.

儿又开始在叹息里闪过了。

在逃去如飞的日子里,在千门万户的世界里的我能做些什么呢? 只有徘徊罢了,只有匆匆罢了;在八千多日的匆匆里,除徘徊外,又剩些什么呢? 过去的日子如轻烟,被微风吹散了,如薄雾,被初阳蒸融了;我留着些什么痕迹呢? 我何曾留着像游丝样的痕迹呢? 我赤裸裸来到这世界,转眼间也将赤裸裸的回去罢? 但不能平的,为什么偏要白白走这一遭啊?

你聪明的,告诉我,我们的日子为什么一去不复返呢?

Fleeting Time

Swallows fly away, yet return; willows wither, yet burgeon again; peach-blossom fades, yet blooms afresh. But tell me, you who are wise, why do our days depart never to return? Does someone steal them—if so, who? And where are they being hidden? Or have they fled of their own accord—and if so, where are they now?

I do not know how many days have been granted me, but my hand is growing emptier all the time. In silence I compute that more than eight thousand days have already slipped through my fingers. Like a drop of water on the point of a needle which drips into the ocean, my days have dripped noiselessly into the stream of time, leaving not a trace behind.

The past has gone whither it listed, and the future is coming as it wills; but why is this junction of past and future so fleeting? When I get up in the morning, two or three rays of sunlight slant into my chamber. The sun has feet which pad lightly, stealthily on; and I follow, revolving bemusedly in its wake. And so—when I wash my hands, my time slips out of the basin; when I eat, it slips away through my bowl; when I am silent, it slips past my abstracted eyes. Conscious that it is fleeting away, I stretch out my hands to catch it, but it streams through my outstretched fingers; and at night when I lie in bed, it glides nimbly over my body or flies from beside my feet. When I open my eyes to see the sun again, another day has slipped past. I sigh and cover my face. But the shadow of the new-come day begins to flutter off in my sigh.

What can I do in these days which escape so fast in this world with its teeming millions? I can only wander, only hasten away. What have I achieved, apart from wandering, in the eight thousand days which have flitted by? My past has been scattered like smoke by the light breeze, or dispersed like mist by the morning sun. And what traces are left me? What vestiges? Naked I came into the world, and naked no doubt I shall go from it very soon. What makes me indignant, though, is the question: Why should

I have to make this aimless trip?

Answer me, you who are wise: Why do our days depart never to return?

温州的踪迹

一 “月朦胧，鸟朦胧，帘卷海棠红”

这是一张尺多宽的小小的横幅，马孟容君画的。上方的左角，斜着一卷绿色的帘子，稀疏而长；当纸的直处三分之一，横处三分之二。帘子中央，着一黄色的，茶壶嘴似的钩儿——就是所谓软金钩么？“钩弯”垂着双穗，石青色；丝缕微乱，若小曳于轻风中。纸右一圆月，淡淡的青光遍满纸上；月的纯净，柔软与平和，如一张睡美人的脸。从帘的上端向右斜伸而下，是一枝交缠的海棠花。花叶扶疏，上下错落着，共有五丛；或散或密，都玲珑有致。叶嫩绿色，仿佛掐得出水似的；在月光中掩映着，微微有浅深之别。花正盛开，红艳欲流；黄色的雄蕊历历的，闪闪的。衬托在丛绿之间，格外觉着妖娆了。枝欹斜而腾挪，如少女的一只臂膊。枝上歇着一对黑色的八哥，背着月光，向着帘里。一只歇得高些，小小的眼儿半睁半闭的，似乎在入梦之前，还有所留恋似的。那低些的一只别过脸来对着这一只，已缩着颈儿睡了。帘下是空空的，不着一些痕迹。

试想在圆月朦胧之夜，海棠是这样的妩媚而嫣润；枝头的好鸟为什么却双栖而各梦呢？在这夜深人静的当儿，那高踞着的一只八哥儿，又为何尽撑着眼皮儿不肯睡去呢？他到底等什么来着？舍不得那淡淡的月儿么？舍不得那疏疏的帘儿么？不，不，不，您得到帘下去找，您得向帘中去找——您该找着那卷帘人了？他的情韵风怀，原是这样这样的哟！朦胧的岂独月呢；岂独鸟呢？但是，咫尺天涯，教我如何耐得？我拼着千呼万唤；你能够出来么？

这页画布局那样经济，设色那样柔活，故精彩足以动人。虽是区区尺幅，而情韵之厚，已足沦肌浃髓而有余。我看了这画。瞿然而惊；留恋之怀，不能自已。故将所感受的印象细细写出，以志这一段因缘。但我于中西的画都是门外汉，所说的话不免为内行所笑。——那也只好由他了。

二　绿

我第二次到仙岩的时候,我惊诧于梅雨潭的绿了。

梅雨潭是一个瀑布潭。仙岩有三个瀑布,梅雨瀑最低。走到山边,便听见哗哗哗哗的声音;抬起头,镶在两条湿湿的黑边儿里的,一带白而发亮的水便呈现于眼前了。我们先到梅雨亭。梅雨亭正对着那条瀑布;坐在亭边,不必仰头,便可见它的全体了。亭下深深的便是梅雨潭。这个亭踞在突出的一角的岩石上,上下都空空儿的;仿佛一只苍鹰展着翼翅浮在天宇中一般。三面都是山,像半个环儿拥着;人如在井底了。这是一个秋季的薄阴的天气。微微的云在我们顶上流着;岩面与草丛都从润湿中透出几分油油的绿意。而瀑布也似乎分外的响了。那瀑布从上面冲下,仿佛已被扯成大小的几绺;不复是一幅整齐而平滑的布。岩上有许多棱角;瀑流经过时,作急剧的撞击,便飞花碎玉般乱溅着了。那溅着的水花,晶莹而多芒;远望去,像一朵朵小小的白梅,微雨似的纷纷落着。据说,这就是梅雨潭之所以得名了。但我觉得像杨花,格外确切些。轻风起来时,点点随风飘散,那更是杨花了。——这时偶然有几点送入我们温暖的怀里,便倏的钻了进去,再也寻它不着。

梅雨潭闪闪的绿色招引着我们;我们开始追捉她那离合的神光了。揪着草,攀着乱石,小心探身下去,又鞠躬过了一个石穹门,便到了汪汪一碧的潭边了。瀑布在襟袖之间;但我的心中已没有瀑布了。我的心随潭水的绿而摇荡。那醉人的绿呀！仿佛一张极大极大的荷叶铺着,满是奇异的绿呀。我想张开两臂抱住她;但这是怎样一个妄想呀。——站在水边,望到那面,居然觉着有些远呢！这平铺着,厚积着的绿,着实可爱。她松松的皱缬着,像少妇拖着的裙幅;她轻轻的摆弄着,像跳动的初恋的处女的心;她滑滑的明亮着,像涂了"明油"一般,有鸡蛋清那样软,那样嫩,令人想着所曾触过的最嫩的皮肤;她又不杂些儿尘滓,宛然一块温润的碧玉,只清清的一色——但你却看不透她！我曾见过北京十刹海拂地的绿杨,脱不了鹅黄的底子,似乎太淡了。我又曾见过杭州虎跑寺近旁高峻而深密的"绿壁",丛叠着无穷的碧草与绿叶的,那又似乎太浓了。其余呢,西湖的波太明了，秦淮河的也太暗了。可爱的，我将什么来比拟你呢？我怎么比拟得出呢？大约潭是很深的，故能蕴蓄着这样奇异的绿；仿佛蔚蓝的天融了一块在里面似的，这才这般的鲜润呀。——那醉人的绿呀！我若能裁你以为带，我将赠给那轻盈的舞女；她必能临风飘举了。我若能挹你以为眼，我将赠给那善歌的盲妹；她必明眸善睐了。我舍不得你；我怎舍得你呢？我用手拍着你，抚摩着你，如同一个十二三岁的小姑娘。我又掬你入口，便是吻着她了。我送你一个名字，我从此叫你"女儿绿"，好么？

我第二次到仙岩的时候，我不禁惊诧于梅雨潭的绿了。

三　白水漈

几个朋友伴我游白水漈。

这也是个瀑布；但是太薄了，又太细了。有时闪着些须的白光；等你定睛看去，却又没有——只剩一片飞烟而已。从前有所谓"雾縠"，大概就是这样了。所以如此，全由于岩石中间突然空了一段；水到那里，无可凭依，凌虚飞下，便扯得又薄又细了。当那空处，最是奇迹。白光嬗为飞烟，已是影子，有时却连影子也不见。有时微风过来，用纤手挽着那影子，它便袅袅的成了一个软弧；但她的手才松，它又像橡皮带儿似的，立刻伏伏帖帖的缩回来了。我所以猜疑，或者另有双不可知的巧手，要将这些影子织成一个幻网。——微风想夺了她的，她怎么肯呢？

幻网里也许织着诱惑；我的依恋便是个老大的证据。

Memories of Wenchow

I "A MISTY MOON, A DROWSY BIRD, A ROLLED-UP CURTAIN AND RED CRAB-APPLE BLOSSOM"

This is the legend on a tiny horizontal scroll, just over a foot wide, by Ma Meng-jung. Slanting across the top left-hand corner is a long, flimsy green curtain, one-third of the length and two-thirds of the width of the paper, caught in the middle by a yellow hook shaped like a teapot spout. Hanging from the curve of the hook are two slate-grey tassels, their strands ruffled as if by a breeze. To the right is a full moon, whose pale blue light diffuses the whole scroll, as pure, tender and tranquil as the face of a sleeping beauty. Stretching down to the right from the top of the curtain is a branch of crab-apple. It is studded above and below with flowers and leaves—five clusters altogether—some scattered, some close, but all quite exquisite. The tender green of the leaves appears moist and dewy, and under the soft moonlight slight differences in shade are visible. The blossoms in full bloom blush with loveliness, their yellow stamens flashing in vivid detail, shown off to great advantage by the greenery. The pliant, out-thrust branch is like a girl's arm. On it perch two black birds with their back to the moon, facing the curtain. The slightly higher one has half closed its tiny eyes as if about to start dreaming, and there is something wistful in its air. The lower one has turned towards its mate, but has tucked in its head already and is asleep. Below the curtain is a blank—there is nothing there.

On such a night as this, with a misty full moon and such soft, pretty crab-apple blossoms, why should these good birds on the bough lean together dreaming different dreams? And why, so late at night when all is still, is the higher of the two straining to keep its eyes open, unwilling to fall asleep?

What is it waiting for? Is it reluctant to lose sight of the pale moonlight? Or of the flimsy curtain? No, decidedly no! You must look under the curtain, you must look inside the curtain—you must look for the one who has rolled up the curtain! So this is the bird's secret. It is not the moon alone which is enchanted, nor yet the bird alone. But how can I bear to see the person behind the curtain so near and yet so far? If I shout at the top of my voice, will you come out?

This picture is constructed with such economy of line and its colours are so tender that its loveliness is enough to move any spectator. And though it is such a small scroll, the depth of feeling conveyed is more than enough to penetrate to your marrow. This painting made me catch my breath in amazement, and stirred a longing I could not overcome. That is why I have recorded my impressions in detail here. However, as I know nothing of either Chinese or Western painting, connoisseurs are bound to laugh at my remarks. Well, let them!

II GREEN

The second time I visited the Hsienyen Mountain I was staggered by the green of Plum Rain Pool.

Plum Rain Pool is at the foot of a waterfall, the lowest of the three waterfalls on Hsienyen. If you come near to the mountain, you hear the gurgle and plash, and looking up see a belt of sparkling white water edged by two moist black borders. First we reached Plum Rain Pavilion. This stands opposite the waterfall, and seated beside it you need not raise your head to see the whole cascade. At the foot of the pavilion is the deep Plum Rain Pool. The pavilion stands on a projecting rock with nothing above or below it, like an eagle poised in the sky with outstretched wings. Mountains on three sides form a semi-circle round it, making you feel as if at the bottom of a well. It was a hazy autumn day when we went there. Fleecy clouds floated overhead, and rich green oozed from the moisture on the face of the rock and on the clumps of grass. The waterfall seemed unusually clamorous too. It plunged down like a smooth length of whole material; then it was irrevocably torn into silken tatters large and small. And as it charged past the sharp-edged rock, foam like chips of jade spattered wildly. This spatter of brilliant, scintillating foam looked from a distance like a shower of minute white plum petals fluttering slowly down. They say this is the origin of the name Plum Rain Pool. But I think it would be more accurate to compare it to willow seeds. For when a breeze springs up and the specks scatter with the wind, they look even more like willowdown.— Suddenly a few drops sprayed against our warm breasts, piercing our clothes at once and disappearing for ever.

The flashing green of Plum Rain Pool was beckoning to us, and we set out to seize its elusive splendour. Clutching the grass and grasping jagged rocks, we cautiously made our way down, till dipping our heads to pass through a low stone gate we came to the edge of the broad, deep, emerald pool. The waterfall was so close I could have touched it, but already I was oblivious to it. My heart was dancing with the green of the pool. That intoxicating hue was spread out like a huge lotus leaf, the whole of it a quite fantastic green. I wanted to throw out my arms and embrace it—but this was a wild impulse. When I stood at the water's edge and looked over the pool, it still seemed a fair expanse. This smooth-spread, compact green is utterly charming. It undulates and ripples like the folds of a young wife's skirt; it palpitates like a maiden's heart when first she falls in love; it glimmers as if coated with oil, soft and light as the white of an egg, reminding you of the silkiest skin you ever touched. It is unmixed, too, with any dust or dregs, remaining one whole sheet of enchanting turquoise, a single, translucent colour—yet one you cannot see through! I have noticed how the green willows sweeping the ground at Shihchahai Park in Peking seem too pale and gosling-yellow, and how the high, dense "greenwall" near Hupao Temple at Hangchow seems too solid with its endless green grass and foliage. For the rest, the waves of the West Lake are too bright, while those of the Chinhuai River are too dark. Then what can I compare you to, my darling? What comparison can there be? This pool must be very deep to produce this remarkable green, as if a fragment of the deep blue sky had melted here to make this exquisite colour. You intoxicating green! If I could make a girdle out of you, I would give it to that graceful dancing girl so that she could whirl and flutter with the wind. If I could make a pair of eyes out of you, I would give them to that blind girl who loves to sing, so that she could have bright eyes and perfect eyesight. I cannot bear to leave you—how can I leave you? I stroke and caress you as if you were a girl of twelve or thirteen. I carry you to my lips, as if I were kissing her. Would you like me to give you a name? What about Girl Green?

The second time I visited Hsienyen I was staggered by the green of Plum Rain Pool.

III THE WHITE CASCADE

A few friends took me to see the White Cascade.

This is another waterfall, but how thin and tenuous! Sometimes it sheds a white radiance, yet when you look closely this disappears—only drifting mist remains. I imagine the "misty garment" of old legend was like this. The reason for this phenomenon is a sudden chasm in the rock; when the water reaches this point it finds no support and takes a leap into the void, attenuating in this thin, tenuous manner. It is at its most miraculous as it falls. The white light is transformed into drifting smoke, and that into a shadow, while at moments even the shadow vanishes. At times a light breeze rises and bears up the shadow in its slender fingers, bending it into a soft arc; but the moment its grip relaxes the arc contracts again like an elastic. So I wonder if a pair of secret and skilful hands are not weaving these shadows into a magic web—and not allowing the breeze to snatch them away.

In that magic web may be woven enchantment—my captivation is firm proof of this.

房东太太

歇卜士太太(Mrs. Hibbs)没有来过中国，也并不怎样喜欢中国，可是我们看，她有中国那老味儿。她说人家笑她母女是维多利亚时代的人，那是老古板的意思；但她承认她们是的，她不在乎这个。

真的，圣诞节下午到了她那间黯淡的饭厅里，那家具，那人物，那谈话，都是古气盎然，不像在现代。这时候她还住在伦敦北郊芬乞来路(Finchley Road)。那是一条阔人家的路；可是她的房子已经抵押满期，经理人已经在她门口路边上立了一座木牌，标价招买，不过半年多还没人过问罢了。那座木牌，和篮球架子差不多大，只是低些；一走到门前，准看见。晚餐桌上，听见厨房里尖叫了一声，她忙去看了，回来说，火鸡烤枯了一点，可惜，二十二磅重，还是卖了几件家具买的呢。她可惜的是火鸡，倒不是家具；但我们一点没吃着那烤枯了的地方。

她爱说话，也会说话，一开口滔滔不绝；押房子，卖家具等等，都会告诉你。但是只高高兴兴地告诉你，至少也平平淡淡地告诉你，决不垂头丧气，决不唉声叹气。她说话是个趣味，我们听话也是个趣味(在她的话里，她死了的丈夫和儿子都是活的，她的一些住客也是活的)；所以后来虽然听了四个多月，倒并不觉得厌倦。有一回早餐时候，她说有一首诗，忘记是谁的，可以作她的墓铭，诗云：

这儿一个可怜的女人，
她在世永没有住过嘴。
上帝说她会复活，
我们希望她永不会。

其实我们倒是希望她会的。

道地的贤妻良母，她是；这里可以看见中国那老味儿。她原是个阔小姐，从小送到比利时受教育，学法文、学钢琴。钢琴大约还熟，法文可生疏了。她说街上如有法国人向她问话，她想起答话的时候，那人怕已经拐了弯儿了。结婚时得着她姑母一大笔遗产；靠着这笔遗产，她支持了这个家庭二十多年。歇卜士先生在剑桥大学毕业，一心想作诗人，成天住在云里雾里。他二十年只在家里待着，偶然教几个学生。他的诗送到剑桥的刊物上去，原稿却寄回了，附着一封客气的信。他又自己花钱印了一小本诗集，封面上注明，希望出版家采纳印行，但是并没有什么回响。太太常劝先生删诗行，譬如说，四行中可以删去三行罢；但是他不肯割爱，于是乎只好敝帚自珍了。

歇卜士先生却会说好几国话。大战后太太带了先生小姐，还有一个朋友去逛意大利；住旅馆雇船等等，全交给诗人的先生办，因为他会说意大利话。幸而没出错儿。临上火车，到了站台上，他却不见了。眼见车就要开了，太太这一急非同小可，又不会说给别人，只好教小姐去张看，却不许她远走。好容易先生钻出来了，从从容容的，原来他上"更衣室"来着。

太太最伤心她的儿子。他也是大学生，长的一表人才。大战时去从军；训练的时候偶然回家，非常爱惜那庄严的制服，从不教它有一个褶儿。大战快完的时候，却来了恶消息，他尽了他的职务了。太太最伤心的是这个时候的这种消息，她在举世庆祝休战声中，迷迷糊糊过了好些日子。后来逛意大利，便是解闷儿去的。她那时甚至于该领的恤金，无心也不忍去领——等到限期已过，即使要领，可也不成了。

小姐现在是她唯一的亲人；她就为这个女孩子活着。早晨一块儿拾掇拾掇屋子，吃完了早饭，一块儿上街散步，回来便坐在饭厅里，说说话，看看通俗小说，就过了一天。晚上睡在一屋里。一星期也同出去看一两回电影。小姐大约有二十四五了，高个儿，总在五英尺十寸左右；蟹壳脸，露牙齿，脸上倒是和和气气的。爱笑，说话也天真得像个十二三岁小姑娘。先生死后，他的学生爱利斯（Ellis）很爱歇卜士太太，几次想和她结婚，她不肯。爱利斯是个传记家，有点小名气。那回诗人德拉梅在伦敦大学院讲文学的创造，曾经提到他的书。他很高兴，在歇卜士太太晚餐桌上特意说起这个。但是太太说他的书干燥无味，他送来，她们只翻了三五页就搁在一边儿了。她说最恨猫怕狗，连书上印的狗都怕，爱利斯却养着一大堆。她女儿最爱电影，爱利斯却瞧不起电影。她的不嫁，怎么穷也不嫁，一半为了女儿。

这房子招徕住客,远在歇卜士先生在世时候。那时只收一个人,每日供早晚两餐,连宿费每星期五镑钱,合八九十元,够贵的。广告登出了,第一个来的是日本人,他们答应下了。第二天又来了个西班牙人,却只好谢绝了。从此住这所房的总是日本人多;先生死了,住客多了,后来竟有“日本房”的名字。这些日本人有一两个在外边有女人,有一个还让女人骗了,他们都回来在饭桌上报告,太太也同情的听着。有一回,一个人忽然在饭桌上谈论自由恋爱,而且似乎是冲着小姐说的。这一来太太可动了气。饭后就告诉那个人,请他另外找房住。这个人走了,可是日本人有个俱乐部,他大约在俱乐部里报告了些什么,以后日本人来住的便越过越少了。房间老是空着,太太的积蓄早完了;还只能在房子上打主意,这才抵押了出去。那时自然盼望赎回来,可是日子一天一天过去,情形并不见好。房子终于标卖,而且圣诞节后不久,便卖给一个犹太人了。她想着年头不景气,房子且没人要呢,那知犹太人到底有钱,竟要了去,经理人限期让房。快到期了,她直说来不及。经理人又向法院告诉,法院出传票教她去。她去了,女儿搀扶着;她从来没上过堂,法官说欠钱不让房,是要坐牢的。她又气又怕,几乎昏倒在堂上;结果只得答应了加紧找房。这种种也都是为了女儿,她可一点儿不悔。

她家里先后也住过一个意大利人,一个西班牙人,都和小姐做过爱;那西班牙人并且和小姐定过婚,后来不知怎样解了约。小姐倒还惦着他,说是“身架真好看!”太太却说,“那是个坏家伙!”后来似乎还有个“坏家伙”,那是太太搬到金树台的房子里才来住的。他是英国人,叫凯德,四十多了。先是作公司兜售员,沿门兜售电气扫除器为生。有一天撞到太太旧宅里去了,他要表演扫除器给太太看,太太拦住他,说不必,她没有钱;她正要卖一批家具,老卖不出去,烦着呢。凯德说可以介绍一家公司来买;那一晚太太很高兴,想着他定是个大学毕业生。没两天,果然介绍了一家公司,将家具买去了。他本来住在他姊姊家,却搬到太太家来了。他没有薪水,全靠兜售的佣金;而电气扫除器那东西价钱很大,不容易脱手。所以便干搁起来了。这个人只是个买卖人,不是大学毕业生。大约穷了不止一天,他有个太太,在法国给人家看孩子,没钱,接不回来;住在姊姊家,也因为穷,让人家给请出来了。搬到金树台来,起初整付了一回房饭钱,后来便零碎的半欠半付,后来索性付不出了。不但不付钱,有时连午饭也要叨光。如是者两个多月,太太只得将他赶了出去。回国后接着太太的信,才知道小姐却有点喜欢凯德这个"坏蛋",大约还跟他来往着。太太最提心这件事,小姐是她的命,她的命决不能交在一个"坏蛋"手里。

小姐在芬乞来路时,教着一个日本太太英文。那时这位日本太太似乎非常关心歇卜士家住着的日本先生们,老是问这个问那个的;见了他们,也很亲热似的。歇卜士太太瞧着不大顺眼,她想着这女人有点儿轻狂。凯德的外甥女有一回来了,一个摩登少女。她照例将手绢掖在袜带子上,拿出来用时,让太太看在眼里。后来背地里议论道,"这多不雅相!"太太在小事情上是很敏锐的。有一晚那爱尔兰女仆端菜到饭厅,没有戴白帽檐儿。太太很不高兴,告诉我们,这个侮辱了主人,也侮辱了客人。但那女仆是个"社会主义"的贪婪的人,也许匆忙中没想起戴帽檐儿;压根儿她怕就觉得戴不戴都是无所谓的。记得那回这女仆带了男朋友到金树台来,是个失业的工人。当时刚搬了家,好些零碎事正得一个人。太太便让这工人帮帮忙,每天给点钱。这原是一举两得,各相情愿的。不料女仆却当面说太太揩了穷小子的油。太太听说,简直有点莫名其妙。

太太不上教堂去,可是迷信。她虽是新教徒,可是有一回丢了东西,却照人家传给的法子,在家点上一支蜡,一条腿跪着,口诵安东尼圣名,说是这么着东西就出来了。拜圣者是旧教的花样,她却不管。每回作梦,早餐时总翻翻占梦书。她有三本占梦书;有时她笑自己,三本书说的都不一样,甚至还相反呢。喝碗茶,碗里的茶叶,她也爱看;看像什么字头,便知是姓什么的来了。她并不盼望访客,她是在盼望住客啊。到金树台时,前任房东太太介绍一位英国住客继续住下。但这位半老的住客却嫌客人太少,女客更少,又嫌饭桌上没有笑,没有笑话,只看歇卜士太太的独角戏,老母亲似的唠唠叨叨,总是那一套。他终于托故走了,搬到别处去了。我们不久也离开英国,房子于是乎空空的。去年接到歇卜士太太来信,她和女儿已经作了人家管家老妈了;"维多利亚时代"的上流妇人,这世界已经不是她的了。

My Landlady

Mrs. Hibbs has never been to China and is not particularly fond of China either, yet she struck us as having many old Chinese ways. People laughed at her and her daughter for being so Victorian and old-fashioned, she said. She admitted they were, but it did not worry her.

It was true. That Christmas afternoon in her sombre dining-room, furniture, people and conversation alike seemed out of date, belonging to some earlier age. She was still living in Finchley Road in north London at the time. That was a superior residential district, but the mortgage on her house had been foreclosed, and the agent had already posted up a wooden sales placard beside her gate, though for over six months no one had made any inquiries. The placard was about the size of a basketball stand, but rather lower, so that you could not miss it when you passed the gate. At dinner we heard a scream from the kitchen and she hurried out to investigate, coming back to announce that the turkey had been burned—such a pity with that twenty-two-pound bird which she had sold some furniture to buy. She was sorry about the bird, not about the furniture, but none of us ate any of the overdone parts.

She loved to talk and had such a ready tongue that she could go on for hours once she started. The mortgage on the house, the sale of furniture—she told you everything. But she spoke quite cheerfully, or at least matter-of-factly, never in a complaining or dispirited way. She enjoyed speaking and we enjoyed listening, for her dead husband and son lived in her talk, as well as all her old lodgers; so though I listened to her for over four months, I never found her boring. At breakfast once she quoted a poem, she could not remember by whom, which she declared would make a good epitaph for her

Here lies a poor, dead woman,
Who talked her whole life long;
The Lord says she will live again,

We only hope He's wrong!

As a matter of fact we hoped she would.

A genuinely virtuous wife and devoted mother she was—the traditional Chinese qualities again. She had been a well-to-do girl, sent to Belgium to learn French and the piano. She could probably still play the piano, but she had forgotten her French. If a Frenchman stopped her in the street to ask her a question, she said, he would probably be round the corner before she thought of the answer. At the time of her marriage she inherited a considerable legacy from an aunt, and on that she maintained the family for over twenty years. Mr. Hibbs was a Cambridge graduate whose one ambition was to become a poet, and who lived with his head in the clouds. He stayed at home for twenty years, occasionally tutoring a few private students. When he sent his poems to a Cambridge magazine, the manuscripts were returned with a polite note. Then he printed a small volume at his own expense, stating on the cover that he hoped some publishers would make use of them, but no response was ever received. His wife often urged him to cut certain lines, sometimes as many as three out of four; but he could not bring himself to do it, and so he had to keep his treasures to himself.

Mr. Hibbs was quite a linguist. After the Great War Mrs. Hibbs took him, their daughter and a friend for a tour of Italy, and his was the entire responsibility for booking rooms in hotels, hiring boats and so on, as he could speak Italian. And luckily all went well. But as they were on the platform waiting for the train back, he disappeared. Since the train was due to start at any moment, Mrs. Hibbs was quite frantic; but unable to communicate with anyone, all she could do was tell her daughter to go and look for him, but not to go far. At last he popped up, cool as a cucumber—he had been in the cloakroom all the time!

She grieved most for her son. He was a university graduate too, and a fine, handsome young fellow. When war broke out he joined up, and during his training he came home occasionally, very careful of his impressive uniform and unwilling to allow a single crease in it. The war was nearly over when the bad news came that he had fallen in action. What upset her most was such news coming at such a time, and as the whole world celebrated the armistice she went about in a daze. The tour of Italy was to cheer them all up. She had not even the heart to collect her allowance from the War Office, leaving it until it was too late.

Now Miss Hibbs was the only one of the family left her, and Mrs. Hibbs lived for her daughter. In the mornings they tidied the rooms together, went out for a walk together after breakfast, and sat in the dining-room when they came back, chatting or reading popular novels—and so the day went on. At night they shared one bedroom, and each week they went to one or two films together. Miss Hibbs must have been twenty-four or five. She was tall—a good five foot ten—with a face like a crab and prominent teeth, but an amiable expression. She often laughed, and talked as naively as a girl of twelve. After Mr. Hibbs died, his student Ellis took a great fancy to Mrs. Hibbs and asked her several times to marry him, but she always refused. Ellis was a biographer with some slight reputation. When Walter de la Mare gave a talk on literature at London University and mentioned his works he was delighted, and this fact was aired at Mrs. Hibbs' dinner table. But she found his books dry and uninteresting: each time he gave her one she laid it aside after turning a few pages. She was so terrified of dogs and cats that even a picture of a dog could scare her, but Ellis kept a whole menagerie. And whereas her daughter was a regular film-fan, Ellis looked down on the cinema. She would not marry, no matter how poor she was, largely because of her daughter.

They had started taking lodgers in Mr. Hibbs' time, beginning with one. Their charges were high—five pounds a week for lodging, breakfast and dinner. The first to show up after their advertisement appeared was a Japanese, whom they accepted. The next day a Spaniard arrived, but they had to turn him away. After that the majority of lodgers were Japanese, and following Mr. Hibbs' death she took in more, till they became known as "the Japanese house." One or two of these Japanese had mistresses, in fact one was swindled by his mistress, and all this they reported at the dinner table while Mrs. Hibbs listened sympathetically. But when once at table someone talked of free love, apparently aiming his remarks at Miss Hibbs, Mrs. Hibbs was angry. After the meal the offender was asked to look for other lodgings. He left, but the Japanese had a club and he must have said something there, for gradually fewer and fewer Japanese came. As her rooms were usually empty and all her money was gone, the only thing she could do was mortgage the house. Of course she hoped at the time to pay it off later, but day after day slipped by, and things did not improve. Finally the notice for sale went up, and not long after Christmas it was sold to a Jew. She had imagined that since times were hard no one would want the house, but apparently the Jew had money, and as soon as he bought it the agent told her she must be out by a certain date. When the time was nearly up she refused to move. The agent sued her and she received a summons. Supported by her daughter she went to court—her first experience of such a place—and the judge pointed out that her failure to vacate the house was a prison matter. Between indignation and terror she nearly fainted; but she had to promise to look harder for new lodgings. All this was for her daughter too, yet she never once complained.

At different times she also had an Italian and a Spaniard as lodgers, both of whom made love to her daughter; in fact the Spaniard promised to marry her, though later he broke his word. Miss Hibbs kept a soft place in her heart for him though—"He was such a handsome man!" But her mother said: "He was a ne'er-do-well."Later, it seems, another ne'er-do-well made his appearance, after they had moved to Laburnum Terrace. This was an Englishman in his forties named Cayte, a travelling salesman who sold vacuum cleaners. One day he made his way into Mrs. Hibbs' old house and tried to demonstrate his cleaner to her, but she stopped him by explaining that she had no money: she was trying to sell some furniture, and was worried because she could find no customer. Cayte promised to introduce her to a firm, and that evening Mrs. Hibbs was very pleased, sure that he must be a university graduate. In a day or two, sure enough, he introduced her to a firm which bought her furniture. He had been living with his sister, but now he moved into Mrs. Hibbs' house. He had no salary but lived on commissions; however, vacuum cleaners were so expensive that it was hard to sell them, so he stopped making the rounds. He was only a salesman, not a university graduate, and evidently he had been hard up for some time, for he had a wife who was working as a governess in France yet he could not afford to fetch her home. Indeed because he was so poor his sister asked him to leave. After moving to Laburnum Terrace he paid in full the first week for his board and lodging; after that he paid a little off and on, and then stopped paying at all. Not only that, he sometimes cadged lunch from them; and when this had gone on for more than two months Mrs. Hibbs had to ask him to leave. After my return to China I had a letter from her which reported that Miss Hibbs had taken rather a fancy to this "ne'er-do-well" and was probably still seeing him. This was what Mrs. Hibbs dreaded most, for her daughter was everything to her, and how could she hand her over to such a man?

While at Finchley Road, Miss Hibbs gave English lessons to a Japanese lady who apparently showed great concern for all the Japanese gentlemen living there, for she kept asking questions about them and was very intimate with them. Mrs. Hibbs thought poorly of her because of this, considering her a woman of light character. Once they had a visit from Cayte's niece, a modern miss who kept her handkerchief tucked in her garter as was then the custom, and allowed Mrs. Hibbs to see her taking it out. Later this was criticized as "most unladylike." My landlady was fastidious about trifles. One evening when the Irish maid did not put on her cap to bring in the dinner, Mrs. Hibbs was very put out and told us this was an insult to her as mistress and to us as guests. But the maid was a silly girl who may simply have forgotten her cap, or considered it quite unimportant. Another time, I remember, this maid brought her young man, then unemployed, to Laburnum Terrace. They had just finished moving and many odd jobs needed doing, so Mrs. Hibbs asked him to help and gave him a little money every day. This was killing two birds with one stone, and suited both sides. But the maid accused her of taking advantage of the poor—Mrs. Hibbs was quite dumbfounded.

No churchgoer, Mrs. Hibbs was still superstitious. Although she was a Protestant, once when she lost something she followed a friend's advice and lit a candle, knelt on one knee before it and invoked Saint Anthony's name, believing that this would bring her property back. Kneeling to saints is a Catholic practice, but that made no difference to her. And after any dream she would go through her books on dreams at the breakfast table. She had three of these books, and sometimes she laughed at herself because they gave different or contradictory interpretations. She liked to study the tea-leaves in her cup as well, to see what letter they made, for that showed what visitors to expect. Actually she was not hoping for visitors, but only for new lodgers. When she went to Laburnum Terrace, the former landlady introduced her to an English paying guest. But she had too few lodgers, especially too few women lodgers, to suit this middle-aged man, who liked laughter and jokes at table. All you could hear was Mrs. Hibbs' monologue, for she chattered away like an old matriarch, always on the same themes. So he made some excuse to leave, and found different lodgings. Not long after that we left England too, and her rooms fell vacant. In the letter I had from her last year, Mrs. Hibbs told me that she and her daughter had taken posts as housekeepers. This world is no longer a place for Victorian ladies like these.

荷塘月色

这几天心里颇不宁静。今晚在院子里坐着乘凉，忽然想起日日走过的荷塘，在这满月的光里，总该另有一番样子吧。月亮渐渐地升高了，墙外马路上孩子们的欢笑，已经听不见了；妻在屋里拍着闰儿，迷迷糊糊地哼着眠歌。我悄悄地披了大衫，带上门出去。

沿着荷塘，是一条曲折的小煤屑路。这是一条幽僻的路；白天也少人走，夜晚更加寂寞。荷塘四周，长着许多树，蓊蓊郁郁的。路的一旁，是些杨柳，和一些不知道名字的树。没有月光的晚上，这路上阴森森的，有些怕人。今晚却很好，虽然月光也还是淡淡的。

路上只我一个人，背着手踱着。这一片天地好像是我的；我也像超出了平常的自己，到了另一个世界里。我爱热闹，也爱冷静；爱群居，也爱独处。像今晚上，一个人在这苍茫的月下，什么都可以想，什么都可以不想，便觉是个自由的人。白天里一定要做的事，一定要说的话，现在都可不理。这是独处的妙处，我且受用这无边的荷香月色好了。

曲曲折折的荷塘上面，弥望的是田田的叶子。叶子出水很高，像亭亭的舞女的裙。层层的叶子中间，零星地点缀着些白花，有袅娜地开着的，有羞涩地打着朵儿的；正如一粒粒的明珠，又如碧天里的星星，又如刚出浴的美人。微风过处，送来缕缕清香，仿佛远处高楼上渺茫的歌声似的。这时候叶子与花也有一丝的颤动，像闪电般，霎时传过荷塘的那边去了。叶子本是肩并肩密密地挨着，这便宛然有了一道凝碧的波痕。叶子底下是脉脉的流水，遮住了，不能见一些颜色；而叶子却更见风致了。

月光如流水一般，静静地泻在这一片叶子和花上。薄薄的青雾浮起在荷塘里。叶子和花仿佛在牛乳中洗过一样；又像笼着轻纱的梦。虽然是满月，天上却有一层淡淡的云，所以不能朗照；但我以为这恰是到了好处——酣眠固不可少，小睡也别有风味的。月光是隔了树照过来的，高处丛生的灌木，落下参差的斑驳的黑影，峭楞楞如鬼一般；弯弯的杨柳的稀疏的倩影，却又像是画在荷叶上。塘中的月色并不均匀；但光与影有着和谐的旋律，如梵婀玲上奏着的名曲。

荷塘的四面，远远近近，高高低低都是树，而杨柳最多。这些树将一片荷塘重重围住；只在小路一旁，漏着几段空隙，像是特为月光留下的。树色一例是阴阴的，乍看像一团烟雾；但杨柳的丰姿，便在烟雾里也辨得出。树梢上隐隐约约的是一带远山，只有些大意罢了。树缝里也漏着一两点路灯光，没精打采的，是渴睡人的眼。这时候最热闹的，要数树上的蝉声与水里的蛙声；但热闹是他们的，我什么也没有。

忽然想起采莲的事情来了。采莲是江南的旧俗，似乎很早就有，而六朝时为盛；从诗歌里可以约略知道。采莲的是少年的女子，她们是荡着小船，唱着艳歌去的。采莲人不用说很多，还有看采莲的人。那是一个热闹的季节，也是一个风流的季节。梁元帝《采莲赋》里说得好：

> 于是妖童媛女，荡舟心许；鷁首徐回，兼传羽杯；櫂将移而藻挂，船欲动而萍开。尔其纤腰束素，迁延顾步；夏始春余，叶嫩花初，恐沾裳而浅笑，畏倾船而敛裾。

可见当时嬉游的光景了。这真是有趣的事，可惜我们现在早已无福消受了。

于是又记起，《西洲曲》里的句子：

> 采莲南塘秋，莲花过人头；低头弄莲子，莲子清如水。

今晚若有采莲人，这儿的莲花也算得“过人头”了；只不见一些流水的影子。这令我到底惦着江南了。——这样想着，猛一抬头，不觉已是自己的门前；轻轻地推门进去，什么声息也没有，妻已睡熟好久了。

The Lotus Pool by Moonlight

The last few days have found me very restless. This evening as I sat in the yard to enjoy the cool, it struck me how different the lotus pool I pass every day must look under a full moon. The moon was sailing higher and higher up the heavens, the sound of childish laughter had died away from the lane beyond our wall, and my wife was in the house patting Jun-erh and humming a lullaby to him. I quietly slipped on a long gown, and walked out leaving the door on the latch.

A cinder-path winds along by the side of the pool. It is off the beaten track and few pass this way even by day, so at night it is still more quiet. Trees grow thick and bosky all around the pool, with willows and other trees I cannot name by the path. On nights when there is no moon the track is almost terrifyingly dark, but tonight it was quite clear, though the moonlight was pale.

Strolling alone down the path, hands behind my back, I felt as if the whole earth and sky were mine and I had stepped outside my usual self into another world. I like both excitement and stillness, enjoy both a crowd and solitude. Take tonight, for instance. Alone under the full moon, I could think of whatever I pleased or of nothing at all, and that gave me a sense of freedom. All daytime duties could be disregarded. That was the advantage of solitude: I could savour to the full that expanse of fragrant lotus and the moonlight.

As far as eye could see, the pool with its winding margin was covered with trim leaves, which rose high out of the water like the flared skirts of dancing girls. And starring these tiers of leaves were white lotus flowers, alluringly open or bashfully in bud, like glimmering pearls, stars in an azure sky, or beauties fresh from the bath. The breeze carried past gusts of fragrance, like the strains of a song faintly heard from a far-off tower. And leaves and blossoms trembled slightly, while in a flash the scent was carried away. As the closely serried leaves bent, a tide of opaque emerald could be glimpsed. That was the softly running water beneath, hidden from sight, its colour invisible, though the leaves looked more graceful than ever.

Moonlight cascaded like water over the lotus leaves and flowers, and a light blue mist floating up from the pool made them seem washed in milk or caught in a gauzy dream. Though the moon was full, a film of pale clouds in the sky would not allow its rays to shine through brightly; but I felt this was all to the good—though refreshing sleep is indispensable, short naps have a charm all their own. As the moon shone from behind them, the dense trees on the hills threw checkered shadows, dark forms loomed like devils, and the sparse, graceful shadows of willows seemed painted on the lotus leaves. The moonlight on the pool was not uniform, but light and shadow made up a harmonious rhythm like a beautiful tune played on a violin.

Far and near, high and low around the pool were trees, most of them willows. These trees had the pool entirely hemmed in, the only small clearings left being those by the path, apparently intended for the moon. All the trees were sombre as dense smoke, but among them you could make out the luxuriant willows, while faintly above the tree-tops loomed distant hills—their general outline only. And between the trees appeared one or two street lamps, listless as the eyes of someone drowsy. The liveliest sounds at this hour were the cicadas chirruping on the trees and the frogs croaking in the pool; but this animation was theirs alone, I had no part in it.

Then lotus-gathering flashed into my mind. This was an old custom south of the Yangtse, which apparently originated very early and was most popular in the period of the Six Kingdoms,① as we see from the songs of the time. The lotus were picked by girls in small boats, who sang haunting songs as they paddled. They turned out in force, we may be sure, and there were spectators too, for that was a cheerful festival and a romantic one. We have a good account of it in a poem by Emperor Yuan of the Liang dynasty called *Lotus Gatherers*:

---

① 译者注：222—587 A.D.

Deft boys and pretty girls
Reach an understanding while boating;
Their prows veer slowly,
But the winecups pass quickly;
Their oars are entangled,
As they cut through the duckweed,
And girls with slender waists
Turn to gaze behind them.
Now spring and summer meet,
Leaves are tender, flowers fresh;
With smiles they protect their silks,
Drawing in their skirts, afraid lest the boat upset.

There we have a picture of these merry excursions. This must have been a delightful event, and it is a great pity we cannot enjoy it today.

I also remember some lines from the poem *West Islet*:

When they gather lotus at Nantang in autumn
The lotus blooms are higher than their heads;
They stoop to pick lotus seeds,
Seeds as translucent as water.

If any girls were here now to pick the lotus, the flowers would reach above their heads too—ah, rippling shadows alone are not enough! I was feeling quite homesick for the south, when I suddenly looked up to discover I had reached my own door. Pushing it softly open and tiptoeing in, I found all quiet inside, and my wife fast asleep.

二

李广田散文三篇[①]

悲哀的玩具

依然不记得年龄,只知道是小时候罢了。

我不曾离开过我的乡村——除却到外祖家去——而对于自己的乡村又是这样的生疏,甚至有着几分恐怖。虽说只是一个村子吧,却有着三四里长的大街,漫说从我家所在的村西端到街东首去玩,那最热闹的街的中段,也不曾有过我的足迹,那时候我的世界是那样狭小而又那样广漠呀。

父亲在野外忙,母亲在家里忙,剩下的只有老祖母,她给我说故事,唱村歌,有时听着她的纺车声嗡嗡地响着,我便独自坐在一旁发呆。这样的,便是我的家了。

我也常到外面去玩,但总是自己个。街上的孩子们都不和我一块游戏,即使为了凑人数而偶尔参加进去,不幸,我却每是作了某方面失败的原因,于是自己也觉得无趣了。起初是怕他们欺侮我,也许,欺侮了无能的孩子便不英雄吧,他们并不曾对我有什么欺侮,只是远离着我,然而这远离,就已经是向我欺侮了。时常,一个人踽踽地沿着墙角走回家去,"他们不和俺玩",这样说着一头扑在了祖母的怀里,祖母摸着我的头顶,说:

---

① 《悲哀的玩具》《野店》选自:蔡清富. 李广田散文选集. 天津:百花文艺出版社,1981/1982;《花鸟舅爷》选自:李广田. 银狐集. 广州:花城出版社,1982;英译文选自:Li, G. T. *A Pitiful Plaything and Other Essays*. Gladys Yang (trans.). Beijing: Chinese Literature Press, 1982.

“好孩子,自己玩吧。”

虽然还是小孩子,寂寞的滋味是知道得很多了。到了成年的现在,也还是苦于寂寞,然而这寂寞已不是那寂寞,现在想起那孩子时代的寂寞,也觉得是颇可怀念的了。

父亲老是那么阴沉,那么严峻,仿佛历来就不曾看见过他有笑脸。母亲虽然是爱我——我心里如是想——但她从未曾背着父亲给我买过糖果,只说:“见人家买糖果就得走开。”虽然幼小,也颇知道母亲的用心了,见人家大人孩子围着敲糖锣的担子时,我便咽着唾沫,幽手幽脚地走开;后来,只要听到外面有糖锣声,便不再出门去了。

实际上说来,那时候也就只有祖母一个人是爱我的,她尽可能地安慰我,如用破纸糊了小风筝,用草叶作了小笛,用秫秸扎了车马之类,都很喜欢。某日,我刚从外边回家,她老远地用手招我,低声说:“来。”

我跑去了,“什么呢,奶奶?”我急喘地问。

“玩艺儿,孩子。”

说着,从针线筐里取出一包棉花,伸开看时,里面却是包着一只小麻雀。我简直喜得雀跃了。

“哪来的麻雀呀,奶奶?”

“拾的,从檐下。八成是它妈妈从窝里带出来的。”

“怎么带到地下来?”

“傻孩子!大麻雀在窝里抱它,要到外面去给它打食,不料出窝时飞得太猛了,就把它带了出来,几乎把它摔死哩。”

我半信半疑地,心里有点黯然了,原来是只不幸的小麻雀呀,然而我有了好玩具了。立刻从床下取出了小竹筐,里面铺了棉花,上面蒙了布片,这就是我的鸟笼了。饿了便喂它,我吻它那黄嘴角;不饿也喂它,它却不开口了。携了竹筐在院里走来走去,母亲见了说,“你可有了好玩物了!”

这时,我心里暗暗地想道:那些野孩子,要远离就远离了吧,今后我就不再出门了,反正家里有祖母,又有了这玩物,要它长大起来能飞的时候就更好了。

晌午，父亲从野外归来，照例，一见他就觉得不快，但，我又怎晓得养麻雀是不应当呢！

“什么？”父亲厉声问。

“麻——雀——。”我的头垂下了。

“拿过来！”话犹未了，小竹筐已被攫去了；不等我抬起头来，只听忽地一声，小竹筐已经飞上了屋顶。

我自然是哭了，哭也不敢高声，高声了不是就要挨打吗？当这些场合，母亲永远是站在父亲一边，有时还说“狠打！很打！”似乎又痛又恨的样子。有时候母亲也曾为了我而遭父亲的拳脚，这样的心，在作为小孩子的我就不大懂得了。最后，还是倒在祖母怀里去啜泣。这时，父亲好象已经息怒，只远远地说：“小孩子家，糟践信门，还不给我下地去拾草去！”接着是一声叹气。

祖母低声骂着，说：“你爹不是好东西，上不痛老的，下不痛小的，只知道省吃俭用敲坷垃！不要哭了，好孩子，到明天奶奶爬树给你摸只小野鹊吧。”说着，给我擦眼泪。

哭一阵，什么也忘了，反正，这类事是层出不穷的。究竟那只小麻雀的下落怎样，已经不记得了。似乎到了今日才又关心到了二十年前的那只小麻雀，那只不幸的小麻雀，我觉得它是更可哀的了，离开了父母的爱，离开了兄弟姊妹，离开了温暖的巢穴被老祖母捡到了我的小竹筐里，不料又被父亲抛到那荒凉的屋顶上去，寂寞的小鸟，没有爱的小鸟，遭了厄运的小鸟！

在当时，确是恨父亲的，现在却是不然：反觉得他是可悯的。正当我想起：一个头发已经斑白的农夫，还是在披星戴月地忙碌，为饥寒所逼迫，为风日所摧损，前面也只剩着短短的岁月了，便不由地悲伤起来。而且，他生自土中，长自土中，从年少就用了他的污汗去灌溉那些砂土，想从那些砂土里去取得一家老幼之所需，父亲有着那样的脾气，也是无足怪的了。听说，现在他更衰老了些，而且也时常念想到他久客他乡的儿子。

A Pitiful Plaything

I can't remember in which year this happened, but know it was in my childhood.

I'd never left our village—except to visit my mother's old home—and I was unfamiliar, even rather afraid of our own village. Though it was only a village, the main street was three or four *li* long. We lived at the west end. I never ventured to loiter in the middle, the liveliest part of the street, let alone go all the way to the east end to play. My world at that time was both so restricted and so vast.

Father busied himself in the fields, Mother in the house. That left only Granny to tell me stories and sing me folk-songs. Sometimes I sat woodenly all by myself on one side, listening to the whirr of her spinning-wheel. That was the home I had.

I often went outside to play too, but always on my own. The children in the street wouldn't let me join in their games, unless by any chance they needed someone to make up the right number. Unfortunately I was always the cause of my side losing, so I soon lost interest in their games myself. To start with I was afraid they would bully me, but they never did, perhaps thinking it unsporting to bully a helpless child. They simply ostracized me, which was already humiliating enough. Often I would sneak home alone, skirting the walls. "They won't play with me," I'd say, running into Granny's arms. Stroking my head she would answer, "Play by yourself, there's a good boy."

Though I was only a child, I knew what it was to be lonely. Now that I am a man, I still suffer from loneliness, but it isn't the same; and I look back nostalgically on the loneliness of my childhood.

Father was always grim and stern. I don't believe I ever saw him smile. Mother, though she loved me—or so I thought—never bought me any sweets behind his back. She told me, "When you see people buying sweets, scram." Small as I was, I knew quite well what she meant; so whenever I saw grown-ups or other children crowd round the sweet pedlar at the sound of his gong, which set my mouth watering, I slipped away. Later on, if I heard the sweet pedlar's gong outside I stayed indoors.

The fact is, the only one who loved me in those days was Granny. She did her best to comfort me, making me little kites of waste paper, little whistles of grass or carts and horses of millet stalks, all of which delighted me. One day, the moment she saw me coming home, she beckoned me, calling softly, "Come here."

I ran over. "What is it, Granny?" I asked eagerly.

"A plaything for you, child."

With that, from her sewing-basket she took out a wad of cotton-wool and opened it to disclose a fledgling sparrow. I jumped for joy.

"Where's this sparrow from, Granny?"

"Picked it up under the eaves. Most likely its mother carried it out from its nest."

"Why should she carry it down?"

"Little silly! Its mother'd been holding it in the nest. She must have flown off so fast to find food for it that she carried it with her. The fall could have killed it!"

I only half believed her, and felt rather upset. Poor little fledgling! But now I had a fine plaything. I promptly pulled out a small bamboo crate from under the bed, spread cotton-wool on the bottom and put rags on top to make a cage for it. When it was hungry I fed it, kissing its yellow beak. I offered it food when it wasn't hungry too, but it wouldn't open its beak. I carried that bamboo crate back and forth in our yard, and Mother seeing this said, "Now you've a fine plaything!"

I was thinking to myself: Let those rough children keep away from me. I shan't go out any more. At home I've Granny and this pet. It'll be even better when it's big enough to fly.

At noon Father came back from the fields. As usual, the sight of him depressed me; but how could I know it was wrong to keep a sparrow?

"What's that?" he demanded sternly.

"A... sparrow." I hung my head.

"Bring it here!" He snatched the little bamboo crate, and before I looked up I heard a thud—the crate had been flung on the roof.

Naturally I cried, but I didn't dare sob loudly, not wanting to be beaten. At such times Mother always took Father's side, sometimes saying, "Give him a good beating!" as if both angry with me yet sorry for me. There were times when, because of me, Father slapped or kicked her too. As a child I couldn't understand her psychology. Finally I climbed on to Granny's lap to weep disconsolately. By now Father seemed less angry. He just growled, "Useless brat. Why don't you go out and pick some grass for me!" Then he sighed.

Granny swore under her breath, "Your dad's heartless, with no feeling for old or young. All he can do is skimp and scrape to scratch a living from the soil. Don't cry, there's a good boy. Tomorrow Granny will climb a tree to catch a little magpie for you." She wiped away my tears.

After crying I forgot the whole incident, because things like this kept happening all the time. And I can no longer remember what became of that fledgling sparrow. It seems that only now, after twenty years, I feel any concern for that unfortunate fledgling. Poor thing, deprived of its parents' love, its brothers and sisters, its warm nest, then picked up by Granny and put in my little crate, only to be thrown on the cold, bare roof by my father. What a wretched fate for a lonely, unloved fledgling!

At the time I really hated Father; but now, instead, I pity him. My heart aches at the thought of that grizzled peasant working away by starlight, threatened by cold and hunger and exposed to the elements, without much hope of living many years longer. Besides, born and bred on the land, from boyhood he had watered it with his sweat, hoping the sandy soil would produce enough to support his family. No wonder he had such a temper. I hear his health is failing now and he often thinks of his son so long away from home.

野　店

太阳下山了，又是一日之程，步行人，也觉得有点疲劳了。

你走进一个荒僻的小村落——这村落对你很生疏，然而又好象很熟悉，因为你走过许多这样的小村落了。看看有些人家的大门已经闭起，有些也许还在半掩，有几个人正迈着沉重的脚步回家，后面跟随着狗或牛羊，有的女人正站在门口张望，或用了柔缓的声音在招呼谁来晚餐，也许，又听到几处闭门声响了，“如果能到哪家门里去息下呀”，这时候你会这样想吧。但走不多远，你便会发现一座小店待在路旁，或十字路口，虽然明早还须赶路，而当晚你总能作得好梦了。“荒村雨露眠宜早，野店风霜起要迟”，这样的对联，会发现在一座宽大而破陋的店门上，有意无意地，总会叫旅人感到心暖吧。在这儿你会受到殷勤的招待，你会遇到一对很朴野、很温良的店主夫妇，他们的颜色和语气，会使你发生回到了老家的感觉。但有时，你也会遇着一个刁狡的村少，他会告诉你到前面的村镇还有多远，而实在并不那么远；他也会向你讨多少脚驴钱，而实在也并不值那么多。然而，他的刁狡，你也许并未看出刁狡得讨厌，他们也只是有点拙笨罢了。什么又不是拙笨的呢。一个青生铁的洗脸盆，象一口锅，那会是用过几世的了；一把黑泥的宜兴茶壶，尽够一个人喝半天，也许有人会说是非常古雅呢。饭菜呢，则只在分量上打算：“总得够吃，千里有缘的，无论如何，总不能亏心哪。”店主人会对了每个客人这样说。

在这样地方，你是很少感到寂寞的。因为既已疲劳了，你需要休息，不然，也总有些伙伴谈天儿。“四海之内皆兄弟呀。”你会听到有人这样大声笑着，喊：“啊，你不是从山北的下洼来的吗？那也就算是邻舍人了。”常听到这样的招呼。从山里来卖山果的，渡了河来卖鱼的，推车的、挑担子的、卖皮鞭的、卖泥人的、拿破绳子换洋火的……也许还有一个老学究先生，现在却做着走方郎中了，这些人，都会偶然地成为一家了。他们总能说慷慨义气话，总是那样亲切而温厚地相照应，他们都很重视这些机缘，总以为这也有神的意思，说不定是为了将来的什么大患难，或什么大前程,而才先有了这样一夕呢。如果是在冬天,便会有大方的店主抱了松枝或干柴来给煨火,这只算主人的款待,并不另取火钱。在和平与温暖中,于是一伙陌路人都来烘火而话家常了。

直到现在,虽然交通是比较便利了,但象这样的僻野地方,依然少有人知道所谓报纸新闻之类的东西。但这些地方也并非完全无新闻,那就专靠这些挑担推车的人们了。他们走过了多少地方,他们同许多异地人相遇,一到了这样场合,便都争先恐后地倾吐他们听见所闻的一切。某个村子里出了什么人命盗案了,或是某个县城里正在哄传着一件什么阴谋的谣言,以及各地的货物行情等,他们都很熟悉。这类新闻,一经在这小店里谈论之后,一到天明,也就会传遍了全村,也许又有许多街头人在那里议论纷纭,借题发挥起来呢。说是新闻,其实也并不全新,也许已是多少年前的故事了,传说过多少次,忘了,又提起来了,鬼怪的,狐仙的,吊颈女人的,马贩子的艳遇,尼姑的犯规……都重在这里开演了。有的人要唱一支山歌,唱一阵南腔北调了。他们有时也谈些国家大事,譬如战争灾异之类,然而这也只是些故事,象讲《封神演义》那样子讲讲罢了。火熄了,店主东早已去了,有些人也已经打了合铺,睡了,也许还有两个人正谈得很密切。譬如有两个比较年轻的人,这时候他们之中的一个也许会告诉,说是因为在故乡曾犯了什么不可饶恕的大罪过,他逃出来了,逃了这么远,几百里、几千里还不知道,而且也逃出了这许多年了。“我呢……”另一个也许说,“——我是为了要追寻一个潜逃了的老婆,为了她,我便作了这小小生意了。”他们也许会谈了很久,谈了整夜,而且竟订下了很好的交情。“鸡声茅店月,人迹板桥霜”,窗上发白,街上已经有人在走动着了,水筒的声音,辘轳的声音,仿佛是很远,很远,已经又到了赶路的时候了。

呼唤声、呵欠声、马蹄声……这时候忙乱的又是店主人。他又要向每个客人打招呼,问每个客人:盘费可还足吗?不曾丢掉了什么东西吗?如不是急于赶路,真应当用了早餐再走呢,等等。于是一伙路人,又各自拾起了各人的路,各向不同的方向跋涉去了。“几时再见呢?”“谁知道?一切都没准呢!”有人这样说。也许还有人多谈几句,也许还听到几声叹息,也许说:“我们这些浪荡货,一夕相聚又散了。散了,永不再见了,话谈得真投心,真投心呢!”

真是的,在这些场合中,纵然一个老江湖,也不能不有些惘然之情吧。更有趣的是在这样野店的土墙上,偶尔你也会读到用小刀或瓦砾写下来的句子,如某县某村某人在此一宿之类。有时,也会读到些诗样的韵语,虽然都鄙俚不堪,而这些陌路人在一个偶然的机会里,陌路的相遇又相知,他们一时高兴了,忘情一切了,或是想起一切了,便会毫不计较地把真情流露了出来,于是你就会感到一种特别的人间味。就如古人所歌咏的:

君乘车,我戴笠,
他日相逢下车揖;
君担簦,我跨马,
他日相逢为君下。

——这样的歌子,大概也是在这样的情形下产生的吧。

A Country Inn

The sun is setting. After another day on the road wayfarers are weary.

When you enter a small out-of-the-way village, it may be quite strange to you yet seem familiar, because you have passed so many little villages like this before. You will find a number of gates already closed, some others perhaps still ajar, a few men plodding home followed by a dog or cattle, some women standing in their doorways looking out, maybe softly calling their menfolk back to supper. You will hear doors slam shut. It will occur to you, "How I wish I could go into one of those houses to rest."

Before long, however, you reach a small inn by the highway or at a crossroad. Though you have to make an early start tomorrow, tonight you will be able to have sweet dreams. On the battered gates of some inns you may read such couplets as:

Rain in the lonely village, early to rest;
In wind and frost lying in is best.

These, whether intentionally or not, warm the hearts of travellers. Here you will be well looked after by the simple, warm-hearted inn-keeper and his wife, who will make you feel at home. Occasionally, though, you will meet a crafty young fellow who will tell you that the next village is much further away than it actually is, and who will overcharge you for a ride on his donkey. But you may not feel this excessive—such people are simply rather crude. Everything there is crude. The iron wash basin resembling a cauldron has been in use for several generations; the black earthenware teapot holds enough to drink for half a day, and some people may consider it a fine antique. As for food, the size of the helpings is all that counts. "You must fill up for a long journey," the inn-keeper will tell his guests. "No matter what, we can't stint you."

You seldom feel lonely in such places. Because either you are so tired that you want to rest, or there are other lodgers to chat with you. "Within the Four Seas all men are brothers," they chortle, then ask, "Hey, aren't you from the foot of the north mountain? That makes us as good as neighbours." A greeting like this is common. Fruit sellers from the hills, fish pedlars from across the river, men pushing barrows or carrying loads on poles, pedlars of whips or clay figures, men exchanging old ropes for matches, maybe even former teachers who have become itinerant doctors, thrown together by chance, talk cordially and frankly. They make the most of these opportunities, considering them predestined, for who knows if they may not lead to some disaster or some splendid stroke of luck. If it is winter, a generous inn-keeper will make a gratis fire of pine branches or kindling—this is his treat. In that peaceful warmth, complete strangers toast themselves before the fire and tell yarns.

Even now, though communications have improved, in out-of-the-way parts like these there are still very few people who know the so-called news in the press. But such places are not completely cut off from the news, for which they rely on these pedlars, who in their wide travels meet people from all parts of the country. So on such occasions they compete to pass on everything they have seen and heard. They know what murders and robberies there have been in different villages, what rumoured conspiracies there now are in different county towns, and the state of the market in different localities. As soon as they leave the little inn the next morning, the news they have relayed spreads throughout the village, to be discussed and embroidered on by people in the street. These items of news may not be entirely new; some of them may be old tales which have often been spread then forgotten, and are now resuscitated. Stories of ghosts, fox-fairies, women who hanged themselves, the romances of horse-dealers, the misdeeds of nuns... all are enacted again here. Some men also sing folk-songs or discordant opera arias. They may discuss affairs of state and the ravages of the war, but only much as they would relate *The Canonization of the Gods*.① By the time the fire dies down, the inn-keeper has long since gone to bed and some of the travellers have turned in as well; but one or two of

---

① 译者注：A popular Ming-dynasty novel.

them may still be deep in conversation. For instance, one young fellow may confide to another that he fled his home after committing a capital crime and for several years has been a fugitive. He has no idea how far he has come, how many hundreds or thousands of *li*. "Well, I took to peddling," the other may respond, "because I wanted to find my runaway wife." They may talk for hours, perhaps all through the night, and become firm friends.

A thatched inn in the moonlight, a cock crows;
The frosted wooden bridge men's footprints shows.

Now the window is growing white, distant footsteps can be heard in the street, as well as the clank of buckets and the creak of the pulley by the well. Time to take to the road again.

Calls, yawns, the sound of horses pawing the ground... the inn-keeper has to bestir himself once more. He bids each guest good day and asks if he has enough money for his journey. Has he lost anything? If he isn't pressed for time, why not have breakfast here before setting out? The travellers then choose their different ways, to different destinations. "When shall we meet again?" "Who knows? There's no telling!" Some chat a little longer, or say with a sigh, "We wayfaring folk spend one night together then part, never to meet again. We hit it off so well, I really enjoyed our talk!"

Yes, these itinerant pedlars cannot but look back wistfully on these encounters. And more intriguing are the short inscriptions cut with a knife or scratched with a shard on the walls of these country inns. You may read that so-and-so of such-and-such a village spent a night here. There are even doggerel verses in which strangers finding each other so congenial, oblivious to everything, recall the past and pour out their true feelings. That gives you a strong sense of affinity. It is reminiscent of the old verse:

Thou ridest a carriage, I wear a bamboo hat;
If we meet again, thou wilt dismount to greet me.
Thou bearest a load, I ride a horse;
If we meet again I shall dismount to greet thee.

Perhaps verses of this kind were written after such encounters.

花鸟舅爷

夏天。

我从洛口铁桥搭上了下行的双桅船。时候是上午十点左右。天晴着。河风吹得很凉爽。故虽有炎热的太阳炙晒,仍觉得十分快适。这是一段颇可喜爱的水程。船在急流中颠簸前进,夹岸两堤官柳,以及看来好象紧贴着堤柳的天边白云,都电掣般向后闪去。船上人都欣喜于遇着了一次顺风。而我所更喜欢的则是正午前后便可以下船登岸了。

“到苗家渡可还远着吗?”

“不远不远,面前那座林子就是了。”

划船人指着二里开外的一丛绿树答我。时候还不到十二点。我是等船到苗家渡就登岸的。目的地是住在马家道口的舅爷家。从苗家渡到马家道口不过三里。这三里路是在堤柳的浓荫下面走过的。计算时间,我早该到达舅爷的家了,但依然看不见我记忆中的舅家的标识。我心里焦急起来了。

沿堤一带居民,都靠了堤身建造房屋。这不但有占居官地的便利,且可利用了堤身作为房屋的后墙。故从河堤的前面看来,则沿堤均如建造了一排土楼,自然,也很容易辨识出是谁家的门户。但从堤后看来,则仅仅是高出堤面一尺的茅檐,而家家茅檐又大多数无甚区别。走在堤后的人想取了捷径以直达所要去的人家,象我这样久不归乡的人,就是一件难事了。并不是不能转到堤前去认出舅爷的家,只是愈找不到舅爷家的标识就愈想找个究竟。“莫非是走错了路吗?”这样想。心里焦急着,仍不能从那些茅檐上认出舅爷的家。

舅爷的家是有着标识的。在过去,从外边回到故乡时,我每每先从那些标识上认出舅爷的家,又每每先看了舅爷,再由舅爷伴送着回到自己家里去。

从自己最初的记忆起,舅爷家就过着非常贫苦日子。然而就在这贫苦日月中,舅爷却永是一个快乐人。舅爷的年轻时代,我知道得不详细。

据说他曾一度作过鞋匠，但究竟为了什么而不能以此为业呢，我不得而知。生有一副病弱的身体，有时又不能不靠了身体去换取一点生活之资。自家原有几亩薄田，也多半坍塌到河里去了，未曾坍塌的，也以任其荒芜的时候居多。自然，象舅爷这样人，是不能靠自己耕种来过活的了。这一半固由于他有一个懒散性子，一半也由于那条称作这个国家的“败家子”的河流的教训(这条不能正正经经流到海里去的河水，使这一带居民都信任了他们的不可挽回的命运)。水缸里，有从河上取了来沉淀着待用的饮料。河堤空地上，也有随时种植的家常蔬果。河堤两旁的树上，又有随时取用不竭的燃料。只要于高兴卖力气时出去做几日短工，就可以赚得来暂时需用的口粮了。就在这种情形中，象其他居民相仿，舅爷打发了自己的日子，并尽可能地维持了一家四口。我已经说过，我这位舅爷是一个在贫苦中有快乐的人，而他的乐趣却不仅在于他能够对付得他的贫苦。

象舅爷这样人，在生活中，照例是不缺少闲散的。在闲散中，他才有他自己享受的生活。他会以几个小钱的胜负去抹把纸牌。会用极粗俗的腔调唱几支山歌。又会坐在自家门槛上吹弄着什么唢呐。而他在日常生活中最感兴趣，最肯花费自己精神时间的，就是种种花、养养鸟这一类玩意了。他喜欢一切花、一切鸟，不但是自家的，就连人家的，以及飞在空中的，开在道旁的，他都喜欢。一只不知名的小鸟，叫着，从空中飞过了，不见了，他会仰面朝天，呆望了许久。他也会一个人徘徊在荒道上，墓田上，寻找着什么野生的花草。舅爷的自己家里当然是养着许多花鸟的。虽然花草中也没有什么值得珍惜的东西，但借了那些红红绿绿的颜色，又仗了他的细心和闲暇，把许多花草都安排在一种近于天然艺术的图案里，虽然是破屋烂墙的人家，但是也装点得极其好看。故从河堤前面走过的人，都很容易指点出这有着小小花园的人家。至于鸟呢，当然，也不过什么碧玉黄雀之流，甚至连麻雀也养在里边。然而它们都生活得极其舒适，仿佛很乐意活在这个主人的笼中似的，叫着，跳着，高高地被挂在檐前，挂在树上，使主人喜欢，使过路人欣羡。从自己用极困难方法得来的粮米中，省俭出一部分米粒来饲养了这些鸟族的舅爷，他的快乐恐怕是我们所不能想象的了。

舅爷的庭前原有着几株榆树，满树上都载着鸟窠。这几棵榆树的年龄恐怕比舅爷的年龄还要大些，舅爷也已是五十过后的人了。在一般贫苦人家，这样的木材是早应当伐下来换钱的，但这几株榆树却依然保有着它们的幸运。我想，这虽然也有什么风水迷信之说，但最大的原因，恐怕还是为了榆树上的那些鸟窠吧。仿佛那些喜鹊都认定了这是一个可以久居的地方，巢窠是与日俱增着，而且这也是多少年来的事情了。依照外祖母的，以及其他人的意见，这几株树也是应当伐了出卖的，当然，阻止了这事的仍是舅爷。他喜欢那些喜鹊，他爱护它们，他好象把它们当作一家人似的，在一处生活过来了这些年。"假如把榆树伐倒，岂不是拆毁了人家的家吗？"他这样说。于是，这几棵树，连同这些鸟窠，就一直保留了下来。而且，多少年来，这几株树上永有红色的牵牛花攀缘，花发时节，是满树红花，故远远望去，这就是一个很显然的标识了。走在河堤后面的人，也很容易指点着说，"这就是某某人的家了。"我所寻找的就是这个标识，然而这个标识却永不曾找到。

等我越到河堤前面，并向人探询之后，才知道已走过马家道口有里余之遥了。再等我转了回来，到得舅爷家时，已是时近下午一点的样子。连喊了几声外祖母，都没有回答。出来迎接我的却是我的舅母。问舅爷可曾在家吗，说是已经被人家雇去作短工去了。表弟呢，说是也去同舅爷作着同样的事情（这个表弟也不过十岁左右的孩子，怎能做得了什么工作呢，我当时这么想）。看了舅母脚上的白鞋，头上的白头绳，我就不再问外祖母了。庭前那棵榆树，连同那些鸟窠，以及牵牛花的下落，也就可以知道了。舅母告诉我外祖母过世时的情形，说一切都靠了街坊戚友们的帮助，人家都知道舅爷是一个非常孝顺的人，平日虽然困苦，却总能使外祖母不受艰窘，故人家皆乐意输米输面。一口上好棺木，是用庭前那几棵大树换来的，并说到外祖母临危的时候很想念我，盼我在外边能早早发迹。舅母一边说着，一边落泪，还要张罗着给我预备午餐。我怎能再用得下午餐呢，说一些安慰舅母的话，就自己告辞了。

到家的次日，舅爷竟为了跑来看我而不去做工了。人是老了许多，但还是那快活样子，大声说话，大声喧笑，话说不尽，仿佛懂得天地间一切事情。说话间又谈到外祖母，谈到外祖母的病状，并说，“过世了。也倒罢了，养了我这样儿子，活了一世还不是受罪一世吗？”说着也变得黯然起来。又说，假如我将来能回到故乡来做些事业，很愿意把表弟托给我照顾。“希望你表弟不再象我就好了。”最后又这么说。

“舅爷也实在衰老得可怜了呢，头发都变得白参参的了。”

舅爷去后，我向母亲这样说。

“白了头发呀，却还是那么孩子气。”母亲带一点笑意说，“一辈子花啦鸟啦的，就是知道调皮着玩儿。你还不知道呢，人家竟能在那一头白参参的发辫上扎了鲜红的头绳，又戴了各色的野花，在外祖母的病床前跳来跳去，唱山歌儿使外祖母喜欢。人倒是一个有心肠人，可惜命穷，也就无可如何罢了。”

Flower-and-Bird Uncle

Summer.

By the iron bridge at Lekou I boarded a two-masted boat heading downstream at about ten in the morning. It was a fine day. As the wind on the river was pleasantly cool, in spite of the blazing sun overhead I felt in the highest of spirits. This was a most delightful stretch of the river. The boat pitched forward through the waves between two dikes planted by the authorities with willows. These flashed fast as lightning behind us, together with the white clouds at the horizon which seemed nestling above the trees. Travellers by boat all enjoy sailing with the wind. What I enjoyed more was the prospect of going ashore at noon.

"How much further is it to Miao Family Ferry?"

"Not far now. That's it, that wood in front."

An oarsman indicated a green coppice a couple of *li* ahead. It was not yet twelve. When we reached Miao Family Ferry I went ashore. My destination was my maternal uncle's home in Ma Family Creek, only three *li* away. The road lay over the dike in the deep shade of willows. After walking for a time I reckoned I should have reached Uncle's house long before this, but having seen none of the familiar landmarks I started feeling uneasy.

The countryfolk living by the dike all built their houses against it. That way they were able to occupy public land and use the dike for their back wall. So seen from the front, the dike had a row of adobe houses skirting it, and it was naturally easy to make out to which family each belonged. But from the back nothing could be seen except thatched eaves a foot above the dike, and those of different households were for the most part indistinguishable. This made it hard for someone like me walking behind the dike to find a short cut to his destination, if he had been away for a long time. I could have gone round to the front to locate Uncle's home, but I wanted to discover why I had seen none of the old landmarks. "Can I have come the wrong way?" I wondered. It worried me, being unable to recognize his house among all those thatched roofs.

Uncle's house had distinguishing features. In the past, going back to my village from outside, I had always been able to locate it from them and to find my uncle in the yard. He would then take me home.

As far back as I can remember, Uncle's family was very poor. But living in poverty he was always happy. I knew little about his young days. I heard that he had once been a shoemaker, but have no idea why he abandoned this trade. He had a poor constitution, yet sometimes had to do some manual labour to make enough to live on. Their family had once owned several small fields, most of which had now been washed away by the river, and the land remaining was generally left untilled. Of course, a man like Uncle could not make a living by farming. Partly because of his indolence, partly because that river, known as our country's "black sheep", was unable to flow out to sea by the right channel and taught the peasants in its vicinity to resign themselves to their fate. The different families filled their vats with muddy river water, left to settle before being drunk. They grew vegetables and fruit on the waste land on the dike, while the trees on either side of it provided unlimited fuel. Anyone willing to go out and work as a casual labourer for a few days could earn food to tide the family over a lean spell. This being the case, Uncle spent his time like his neighbours, and contrived to support his family of four. As I said, living in poverty he was happy, but his happiness did not stem solely from this ability to cope with poverty.

A man living like Uncle had plenty of spare time in which to enjoy himself. He might play cards for small stakes, sing some crude folk-songs, or sit on his doorstep trumpeting on his *suona*. But his main interests, on which he was most willing to expend money, time and energy, were gardening and keeping birds. He loved flowers and birds of every kind, whether his own or those belonging to others, birds flying through the air or roadside flowers—he loved them all. If a nameless little bird flew over, singing, then vanished from sight, he would search the sky for a long time, watching for it. He also roamed alone over rough tracks and through graveyards in search of wild flowers.

Naturally Uncle had many flowers and birds in his home. Though none of his flowers were rare ones, he devoted much care and leisure to setting them out in an artistic, very natural design with vividly contrasting colours, so that his house though tumbledown was most attractive. People passing along the front of the dike could easily pick out the family with the small garden.

As for birds, of course these were only little song-birds, or even sparrows. But they were so cosseted, they seemed to enjoy living in their master's cages hung high in front of the eaves or on the trees, where they sang and hopped to his great delight and the envy of passers-by. When from his grain, so hard to come by, he saved some for these birds, his happiness was greater than we could imagine.

There were some elms in front of Uncle's house, their boughs filled with nests. These trees were probably older than he, and he was over fifty. Most poor families would long ago have felled them to raise money, but the luck of these elms held. Due partly, I suppose, to geomantic superstitions, but more likely to all the nests on their boughs. As the magpies seemed to realize that here was a permanent residence, their nests had been steadily increasing for years. In the view of Grandma and other people, these trees should be cut down and sold. Of course it was Uncle who prevented this. After living together so long he loved those magpies and protected them as if they were a part of the family. "If those trees were felled, wouldn't that destroy their homes?" he protested. So the trees with their nests remained. And year after year the green vines of convolvulus covered the elms and, when their flowers opened, the trees were a mass of crimson. That made a distinctive landmark seen from the distance. People walking behind the dike could easily pick it out and identify the place. This was the landmark I now sought in vain.

By the time I went to the front of the dike to ask my way, I found I was over a *li* past Ma Family Creek. By the time I retraced my steps to Uncle's house, it was nearly one in the afternoon. I called Grandma several times, but received no answer. It was Aunt who came out to meet me. Asked if Uncle was in, she said he had been hired out, and my younger cousin too. (As he was only a boy of about ten, I wondered what work he could do!) Seeing Aunt's white socks and the white ribbon① in her hair, I refrained from asking about Grandma. And I understood what had become of the elms in the courtyard, the nests and convolvulus.

Aunt told me that their neighbours and friends had helped with all Grandma's funeral preparations. Knowing that Uncle had been a most dutiful son, who even when hard up never let his mother feel the pinch, they gladly brought over gifts of flour and rice. The big trees in the courtyard had paid for a good coffin. Aunt told me too that Grandma had thought of me on her death-bed, and hoped I would soon make my way in the world. She told me this with tears, then said she must get me a meal. Of course I couldn't allow this. After trying to comfort her I said goodbye.

The next day Uncle took time off to come to my home to see me. Though considerably aged he was still his old cheerful self, talking loudly and roaring with laughter. He talked on and on as if he understood everything under the sun. He spoke of Grandma and of her illness. "She's gone, well, so be it," he sighed. "Her whole life was hard, wasn't it, with a son like me?" His face clouded as he said this. He added that if I could go home and find a job there, he would like to entrust my younger cousin to me. "I just hope he won't turn out like me!" were his final words.

After he took his leave I remarked to Mother, "It's really pathetic the way Uncle has aged—his hair is growing grizzled."

"His hair may be white but he's still a child at heart," she answered whimsically. "He's played around all his life with flowers and birds. Know what he did? Tied a bright red ribbon on his grizzled hair and wore flowers of different colours to skip about in front of Grandma's sick bed and try to cheer her up by singing folk-songs. He's a warm-hearted fellow. Too bad he's fated to be poor, so there's nothing he can do about it."

---

① 译者注：White was worn as mourning.

三

鲁迅、冯雪峰、张天翼寓言六则[①]

古　城

鲁　迅

你以为那边是一片平地么？不是的。其实是一座沙山，沙山里面是一座古城。这古城里，一直从前住着三个人。

古城不很大，却很高。只有一个门，门是一个闸。

青铅色的浓雾，卷着黄沙，波涛一般的走。

少年说："沙来了，活不成了。孩子快逃罢。"

老头子说："胡说，没有的事。"

这样的过了三年和十二个月另八天。

少年说："沙积高了，活不成了。孩子快逃罢。"

老头子说："胡说，没有的事。"

少年想开闸，可是重了。因为上面积了许多沙了。

少年拼了死命，终于举起闸，用手脚都支着，但总不到二尺高。

少年挤那孩子出去说："快走罢！"

---

① 中文分别选自如下作品：《鲁迅研究》编辑部．鲁迅研究 1．上海：上海文艺出版社，1980：16-17；鲁迅．野草．北京：人民文学出版社，1973：45-46；张天翼．张天翼寓言．安徽：安徽少年儿童出版社，1986：80-81；冯雪峰．雪峰寓言．北京：人民文学出版社，1980：4；英译文选自：Lu，X.，Feng，X. F. & Zhang，T. Y. Fables. Gladys Yang（trans.）．*Chinese Literature*，1984（Winter）：168-171.

老头子拖那孩子回来说:“没有的事!”

少年说:“快走罢! 这不是理论,已经是事实了!”

青铅色的浓雾,卷着黄沙,波涛一般的走。

以后的事,我可不知道了。

你要知道,可以掘开沙山,看看古城。闸门下许有一个死尸。闸门里是两个还是一个?

An Old Castle

Lu Xun

Do you think that is flat ground over there? No, it isn't. It is, in fact, a sand dune, under which is an old castle. Three people once lived in it.

The castle was not large but it was very high. There was only one gate, which was like a sluice gate.

Yellow sand in the heavy, dark grey mist was blown forward in waves.

"The sand is coming. We can't survive. Run for your life, child." said the young man.

"Nonsense. It's nothing," the old man retorted.

So they stayed, and three years, twelve months and eight days elapsed.

"The sand has piled up high. We can't survive. Run for your life, child," said the young man.

"Nonsense. It's nothing," the old man retorted.

The young man wanted to lift the gate. But it was heavy, weighted down with sand.

The young man tried again, desperately. At last, he lifted the gate. Although holding the gate with his hands and feet, he could not lift it higher than two feet.

He pushed the child out, saying, "Run away quickly!"

But the old man dragged the child back, arguing, "It's nothing serious!"

"Be quick! This isn't a theoretical problem. It's a fact!" urged the young man.

Yellow sand in the heavy, dark grey mist was blown forward in waves.

I do not know what happened then.

If you want to know, you can excavate the sand dune and examine the old castle. Perhaps there is a corpse under the gate. Or one or two inside?

立　论

鲁　迅

我梦见自己正在小学校的讲堂上预备作文,向老师请教立论的方法。

“难!”老师从眼镜圈外斜射出眼光来,看着我,说。“我告诉你一件事——

“一家人家生了一个男孩,合家高兴透顶了。满月的时候,抱出来给客人看,——大概自然是想得一点好兆头。

“一个说:‘这孩子将来要发财的。’他于是得到一番感谢。

“一个说:‘这孩子将来要做官的。’他于是收回几句恭维。

“一个说:‘这孩子将来是要死的。’他于是得到一顿大家合力的痛打。

“说要死的必然,说富贵的许谎。但说谎的得好报,说必然的遭打。你……”

“我愿意既不谎人,也不遭打。那么,老师,我得怎么说呢?”

“那么,你得说:‘啊呀!这孩子呵!您瞧!多么……。阿唷!哈哈!Hehe!he, hehehehe!’”

On Expressing an Opinion

Lu Xun

I dreamed I was in the classroom of a primary school preparing to write an essay, and asked the teacher how to express an opinion.

"That's hard!" Glancing sideways at me over his glasses, he said, "Let me tell you a story —

"When a son is born to a family, the whole household is delighted. When he is one month old they carry him out to display him to the guests—usually expecting some compliments, of course.

"One says, 'This child will be rich.' Then he is heartily thanked.

"One says, 'This child will be an official.' Then some compliments are paid him in return.

"One says, 'This child will die.' Then he is severely beaten by the whole family.

"That the child will die is inevitable, while to say that he will be rich or a high official may be a lie. Yet the lie is rewarded, whereas the statement of the inevitable gains a beating. You...."

"I don't want to tell lies, sir, neither do I want to be beaten. So what should I say?"

"In that case, say, 'Aha! Just look at this child! My word.... Oh, my! Oho! Hehe! He, hehehehehe!'"

一条好蛇

张天翼

一条心地很好的蛇抓到一只麻雀,想要把她一口吞掉,于心又不忍。于是把她盘得紧紧的,谆谆善诱地,劝她服从命运,还劝她拿出牺牲精神来献身于他。讲完之后,才客客气气要动手吞吃,并且说:“你看,我不象别的蛇那样不讲理:我和他们是毫无共同之点的。”

A Kind Snake

Zhang Tianyi

A kind snake caught a sparrow. He wanted to devour her in one go, but could not bear to do it so cruelly. So he coiled around her tightly, repeatedly trying to persuade her to resign herself to her fate and sacrifice herself to him. Then he swallowed her, saying modestly, “Look, I’m not as rude as other snakes. I’m quite different from them.”

雪地上的鸟

冯雪峰

有一只鸟,在雪地上散步。他一脚一脚地把脚印印在雪地上,一面不停口地自己称赞说:"好文章! 好文章!"但他的尾巴,又当作一把勤快的扫帚,连忙把好文章扫得不留痕迹了。总之,他是一面写,一面自己拍案叫绝,一面又马上抹得干干净净,不让别人看见一个字。

A Bird in the Snow

Feng Xuefeng

A bird strutted on the snowy ground leaving his tracks. He kept praising himself at the same time, "A good article! A good article!" But, his tail, like a broom, erased the article leaving no traces. In his work, he wrote and bragged while immediately erasing it, so that nobody could see a word.

三个打碎了瓦器的人

冯雪峰

有三个人，各推着一车瓦器，例如茶瓶呀，汤罐呀，瓦锅呀之类，一同去爬过一条山岭。

那条山岭，又高又陡，全都是羊肠鸟道，一面是高不可攀的岩壁，一面是深不可测的沟壑，的的确确是非常的险恶。显然因为这种困难的条件，他们中的一个，刚刚上了一段岭，就把一车瓦器打碎了，一个完整的也不剩。

第二个人是比较地运气一点，他刚好推到了半岭，碰了一下岩石，这才也把一车瓦器打翻了，但同样没有剩下一个好的。

第三个人是推到了岭头，叫了一声："喔呀，终于到了！"同时喘了一口气，把手也松了一下，不料就此翻了车，全部瓦器都倒在地下了，仔细看看也没有留下一个不破的。

这样，不可讳言，三个人都把瓦器打碎了，但他们倒也都不悲哀，相互微笑着点点头，立刻都想到，姑且比较一下得失罢。三个人一起坐在岭头，这样谈起来了：

"说到爬岭的本领，自然是我顶差，但我省下了顶多的力气呀，这是我的便宜！"第一个人说。

"我没有话说，因为我恰好花了一半的力气，却也爬上了一半岭，我没有吃亏什么！"第二个人说。

"可是只有我是爬完了岭的，这是我的光荣！"第三个人说。

最后他们共同达到了一个结论，说："我们各人都有不同的优点，虽然打碎了瓦器是一模一样的。"说后就都快快乐乐地推着空车回去了。

The Three Men Who Smashed Their Earthenware

Feng Xuefeng

Three men were pushing three barrows of earthenware pitchers, bowls and pots up a mountain ridge.

The mountain ridge was steep and high, and the path was no better than a goat track, with a high cliff towering on one side and a sheer drop into the valley on the other. No doubt about it, it was very dangerous. Because of these difficulties, they had only gone a short way when one of them smashed his entire cartload, leaving not a piece intact.

The second man was little luckier: He had pushed his barrow halfway up, when he bumped against a rock and spilled his whole load. But again not a single piece was left whole.

The third man pushed his barrow right up to the summit, where he exclaimed, "Hooray! I've made it!" At the same time he heaved a sigh of relief and relaxed his hold. Then his cart turned over, all the crockery fell out, and a careful inspection showed every piece was broken.

Thus, there was no denying that all three of them had broken their rockery; but, undeterred, nodding and smiling to each other, they at once decided to compare their achievements. Sitting down on the mountain top, they started a discussion.

"Clearly, I'm the worst climber," said the first. "But I've saved the most energy, that's where I come off best."

"I've nothing to complain of," said the second. "I had to exert myself half the way, but I succeeded in bringing my barrow halfway up. I don't lose out."

"But I'm the only one to have brought my barrow right to the top. That's my glory!" said the third.

Finally they reached the following conclusion, "We each have our good points, although the smashing of the crockery was the same in each case." This said, they cheerfully pushed their empty barrows home again.

井水与河水

冯雪峰

井水不干涉河水的时代已经过去了。有一口井，离河边不远，那井里的水就在批评着河水说："浑身泥浊，一意嚣张，整天哗啦哗啦，滔滔不绝；难道这是人生么？必须像我似地深刻、永恒，一尘不染，终日从小窗孔里瞧着蔚蓝的天空，探究着宇宙的秘密，这才配得上称人生呢。"

河水不干涉井水的时代也已经过去了。那浑身泥浊的河水，只是涨，涨，涨；终至澎湃汹涌，冲出了堤岸，泛滥四野，把井圈都冲走了；井水也就淹死在洪水里，连同他的深刻和永恒的人生。

The Well and the River

Feng Xuefeng

Gone are the days when the well would not meddle with the river. A well not far from the river set about criticizing the river.

"Full of mud and completely uncontrolled, babbling all day long and running on and on—what kind of life is that? You need to be deep and enduring like me, unsoiled by a speck of dust. All day I gaze through a small window at the azure sky, exploring the secrets of the universe—that is the only proper existence."

Gone too are the days when the river would not meddle with the well. The muddy river rose higher and higher until it burst its banks with a roar and overflowed the surrounding country, washing away the wooden frame of the well too. So the well was drowned in the flood, along with its deep and enduring existence.

第四编

戴乃迭乡土文学英译

一

多收了三五斗[①]

叶圣陶

万盛米行的河埠头,横七竖八停泊着乡村里出来的敞口船。船里装载的是新米,把船身压得很低。齐船舷的菜叶和垃圾给白腻的泡沫包围着,一漾一漾地,填没了这船和那船之间的空隙。

河埠上去是仅容两三个人并排走的街道。万盛米行就在街道的那一边。朝晨的太阳光从破了的明瓦天棚斜射下来,光柱子落在柜台外面晃动着的几顶旧毡帽上。

那些戴旧毡帽的大清早摇船出来,到了埠头,气也不透一口,便来到柜台前面占卜他们的命运。

"糙米五块,谷三块,"米行里的先生有气没力地回答他们。

"什么!"旧毡帽朋友几乎不相信自己的耳朵。美满的希望突然一沉,一会儿大家都呆了。

"在六月里,你们不是卖十三块么?"

"十五块也卖过,不要说十三块。"

"哪里有跌得这样厉害的!"

"现在是什么时候,你们不知道么?各处的米像潮水一般涌来,过几天还要跌呢!"

刚才出力摇船犹如赛龙船似的一股劲儿,现在在每个人的身体里松

① 中文选自:叶圣陶. 叶圣陶文集(第二卷). 北京:人民文学出版社,1958:360-369;英译文选自:Ye, S. T. A Year of Good Harvest. Gladys Yang (trans.). *Chinese Literature*, 1960(4): 37-45.

懈下来了。今年天照应，雨水调匀，小虫子也不来作梗，一亩田多收这么三五斗，谁都以为该得透一透气了。哪里知道临到最后的占卜，却得到比往年更坏的课兆！

“还是不要粜的好，我们摇回去放在家里吧！”从简单的心里喷出了这样的愤激的话。

“嗤，”先生冷笑着，“你们不粜，人家就饿死了么？各处地方多的是洋米，洋面，头几批还没吃完，外洋大轮船又有几批运来了。”

洋米，洋面，外洋大轮船，那是遥远的事情，仿佛可以不管。而不粜那已经送到河埠头来的米，却只能作为一句愤激的话说说罢了。怎么能够不粜呢？田主方面的租是要缴的，为了雇帮工，买肥料，吃饱肚皮，借下的债是要还的。

“我们摇到范墓去粜吧，”在范墓，或许有比较好的命运等候着他们，有人这么想。

但是，先生又来了一个“嗤”，捻着稀微的短髭说道：“不要说范墓，就是摇到城里去也一样。我们同行公议，这两天的价钱是糙米五块，谷三块。”

“到范墓去粜没有好处，”同伴间也提出了驳议。“这里到范墓要过两个局子，知道他们捐我们多少钱！就说依他们捐，哪里来的现洋钱？”

“先生，能不能抬高一点？”差不多是哀求的声气。

“抬高一点，说说倒是很容易的一句话。我们这米行是拿本钱来开的，你们要知道。抬高一点，就是说替你们白当差，这样的傻事谁肯干？”

“这个价钱实在太低了，我们做梦也没想到。去年的粜价是七块半，今年的米价又卖到十三块，不，你先生说的，十五块也卖过；我们想，今年总该比七块半多一点吧。哪里知道只有五块！”

“先生，就是去年的老价钱，七块半吧。”

“先生，种田人可怜，你们行行好心，少赚一点吧。”

另一位先生听得厌烦，把嘴里的香烟屁股扔到街心，睁大了眼睛说：“你们嫌价钱低，不要粜好了。是你们自己来的，并没有请你们来。只管多啰嗦做什么！我们有的是洋钱，不买你们的，有别人的好买。你们看，船埠头又有两只船停在那里了。”

三四顶旧毡帽从石级下升上来,旧毡帽下面是表现着希望的酱赤的脸。他们随即加入先到的一群。斜伸下来的光柱子落在他们的破布袄的肩背上。

“听听看,今年什么价钱。”

“比去年都不如,只有五块钱!”伴着一副懊丧到无可奈何的神色。

“什么!”希望犹如肥皂泡,一会儿又迸裂了三四个。

希望的肥皂泡虽然迸裂了,载在敞口船里的米可总得粜出;而且命里注定,只有卖给这一家万盛米行。米行里有的是洋钱,而破布袄的空口袋里正需要洋钱。

在米质好和坏的辩论之中,在斛子浅和满的争持之下,结果船埠头的敞口船真个敞口朝天了;船身浮起了好些,填没了这船那船之间的空隙的菜叶和垃圾就看不见了。旧毡帽朋友把自己种出来的米送进了万盛米行的廒间,换到手的是或多或少的一叠钞票。

“先生,给现洋钱,袁世凯,不行么?”白白的米换不到白白的现洋钱,好像又被他们打了个折扣,怪不舒服。

“乡下曲辫子!”夹着一支水笔的手按在算盘珠上,鄙夷不屑的眼光从眼镜上边射出来,“一块钱钞票就作一块钱用,谁好少作你们一个铜板。我们这里没有现洋钱,只有钞票”。

“那末,换中国银行的吧。”从花纹上辨认,知道手里的钞票不是中国银行的。

“吓!”声音很严厉,左手的食指强硬地指着,“这是中央银行的,你们不要,可是要想吃官司?”

不要这钞票就得吃官司,这个道理弄不明白。但是谁也不想弄明白;大家看了看钞票上的人像,又彼此交换了将信将疑的一眼,便把钞票塞进破布袄的空口袋或者缠着裤腰的空褡裢。

一批人咕噜着离开了万盛米行,另一批人又从船埠头跨上来。同样地,在柜台前迸裂了希望的肥皂泡,赶走了入秋以来望着沉重的稻穗所感到的快乐。同样地,把万分舍不得的白白的米送进万盛的廒间,换到了并非白白的现洋钱的钞票。

街道上见得热闹起来了。

旧毡帽朋友今天上镇来，原来有很多的计划的。洋肥皂用完了，须得买十块八块回去。洋火也要带几匣。洋油向挑着担子到村里去的小贩买，十个铜板只有这么一小瓢，太吃亏了；如果几家人家合买一听分来用，就便宜得多。陈列在橱窗里的花花绿绿的洋布听说只要八分半一尺，女人早已眼红了好久，今天粜米就嚷着要一同出来，自己几尺，阿大几尺，阿二几尺，都有了预算。有些女人的预算里还有一面蛋圆的洋镜，一方雪白的毛巾，或者一顶结得很好看的绒线的小团帽。难得今年天照应，一亩田多收这么三五斗，让一向捏得紧紧的手稍微放松一点，谁说不应该？缴租，还债，解会钱，大概能够对付过去吧；对付过去之外，大概还有多余吧。在这样的心境之下，有些人甚至想买一个热水瓶。这东西实在怪，不用生火、热水冲下去，等会儿倒出来照旧是烫的；比起稻柴做成的茶壶窠来，真是一个在天上，一个在地下。

他们咕噜着离开万盛米行的时候，犹如走出一个一向于己不利的赌场——这回又输了！输多少呢？他们不知道。总之，袋里的一叠钞票没有半张或者一角是自己的了。还要添补上不知在哪里的多少张钞票给人家，人家才会满意，这要等人家说了才知道。

输是输定了，马上开船回去未必就会好多少；镇上走一转，买点东西回去，也不过在输账上加上一笔，况且有些东西实在等着要用。于是街道上见得热闹起来了。

他们三个一群，五个一簇，拖着短短的身影，在狭窄的街道上走。嘴里还是咕噜着，复算刚才得到的代价，咒骂那黑良心的米行。女人臂弯里钩着篮子，或者一只手牵着小孩，眼光只是向两旁的店家直溜。小孩给赛璐珞的洋囝囝，老虎，狗，以及红红绿绿的洋铁铜鼓，洋铁喇叭勾引住了，赖在那里不肯走开。

“小弟弟，好玩呢，洋铜鼓，洋喇叭，买一个去，”故意作一种引诱的声调。接着是——冬，冬，冬，——叭，叭，叭。

当，当，当，——“洋瓷面盆刮刮叫，四角一只真公道，乡亲，带一只去吧。”

“喂，乡亲，这里有各色花洋布，特别大减价，八分五一尺，足尺加三，要不要剪些回去?”

万源祥大利老福兴几家的店伙特别卖力，不惜工本叫着“乡亲”，同时拉拉扯扯地牵住“乡亲”的布袄；他们知道惟有今天，“乡亲”的口袋是充实的，这是不容放过的好机会。

在节约预算的踌躇之后，“乡亲”把刚到手的钞票一张两张地交到店伙手里。洋火，洋肥皂之类必需用，不能不买，只好少买一点。整听的洋油价钱太“咬手”，不买吧，还是十个铜板一小瓢向小贩零沽。衣料呢，预备剪两件的就剪了一件，预备娘儿子俩一同剪的就单剪了儿子的。蛋圆的洋镜拿到了手里又放进了橱窗。绒线的帽子套在小孩头上试戴，刚刚合式，给爷老子一句“不要买吧”，便又脱了下来。想买热水瓶的简直不敢问一声价。说不定要一块块半吧。如果不管三七二十一买回去，别的不说，几个白头发的老太公老太婆就要一阵阵地骂:“这样的年时，你们贪安逸，花了一块块半买这些东西来用，永世不得翻身是应该的！你们看，我们这么一把年纪，谁用过这些东西来！”这啰嗦也就够受了。有几个女人拗不过孩子的欲望，便给他们买了最便宜的小洋囝囝。小洋囝囝的腿臂可以转动，要他坐就坐，要他站就站，要他举手就举手；这不但使拿不到手的别的孩子眼睛里几乎冒火，就是大人看了也觉得怪有兴趣。

“乡亲”还沽了一点酒，向熟肉店里买了一点肉，回到停泊在万盛米行船埠头的自家的船上，又从船梢头拿出咸菜和豆腐汤之类的碗碟来，便坐在船头开始喝酒。女人在船梢头煮饭。一会儿，这条船也冒烟，那条船也冒烟，个个人淌着眼泪。小孩在敞口朝天的空舱里跌交打滚，又捞起浮在河面的脏东西来玩，惟有他们有说不出的快乐。

酒到了肚里，话就多起来。相识的，不相识的，落在同一的命运里，又在同一的河面上喝酒，你端起酒碗来说几句，我放下筷子来接几声，中听的，喊声“对”，不中听，骂一顿:大家觉得正需要这样的发泄。

“五块钱一担，真是碰见了鬼！”

“去年是水灾，收成不好，亏本。今年算是好年时，收成好，还是亏本!”

“今年亏本比去年都厉害；去年还粜七块半呢。”

“又得把自已吃的米粜出去了。唉,种田人吃不到自已种出来的米!”

“为什么要粜出去呢,你这死鬼!我一定要留在家里,给老婆吃,给儿子吃。我不缴租,宁可跑去吃官司,让他们关起来!”

“也只好不缴租呀。缴租立刻借新债。借了四分钱五分钱的债去缴租,贪图些什么,难道贪图明年背着更重的债!”

“田真个种不得了!”

“退了租逃荒去吧。我看逃荒的倒是满写意的。”

“逃荒去,债也赖了,会钱也不用解了,好打算,我们一块儿去!”

“谁出来当头脑?他们逃荒的有几个头脑,男男女女,老老小小,都听头脑的话。”

“我看,到上海去做工也不坏。我们村里的小王,不是么?在上海什么厂里做工,听说一个月工钱有十五块。十五块,照今天的价钱,就是三担米呢!”

“你翻什么隔年旧历本!上海东洋人打仗,好多的厂关了门,小王在那里做叫化子了,你还不知道?”

路路断绝。一时大家沉默了。酱赤的脸受着太阳光又加上酒力,个个难看不过,好像就会有殷红的血从皮肤里迸出来似的。

“我们年年种田,到底替谁种的?”一个人呷了一口酒,幽幽地提出疑问。

就有另一个人指着万盛的半新不旧的金字招牌说:“近在眼前,就是替他们种的。我们吃辛吃苦,赔重利钱借债,种了出来,他们嘴唇皮一动,说‘五块钱一担!’就把我们的油水一古脑儿吞了去!”

“要是让我们自己定价钱,那就好了。凭良心说,八块钱一担,我也不想多要。”

“你这囚犯,在那里做什么梦!你不听见么?他们米行是拿本钱来开的,不肯替我们白当差。”

“那么,我们的田也是拿本钱来种的,为什么要替他们白当差!为什么要替田主白当差!”

“我刚才在廒间里这么想:现在让你们沾便宜,米放在这里;往后没得吃，就来吃你们的！”故意把声音压得很低，网着红丝的眼睛向岸上斜溜。

“真个没得吃的时候，什么地方有米，拿点来吃是不犯王法的！”理直气壮的声口。

“今年春天，丰桥地方不是闹过抢米么？”

“保卫团开了枪，打死两个人。”

“今天在这里的，说不定也会吃枪，谁知道！”

散乱的谈话当然没有什么议决案。酒喝干了，饭吃过了，大家开船回自己的乡村。船埠头便冷清清地荡漾着暗绿色的脏水。

第二天又有一批敞口船来到这里停泊。镇上便表演着同样的故事。这种故事也正在各处市镇上表演着，真是平常而又平常的。

“谷贱伤农”的古语成为都市间报上的时行标题。

地主感觉收租棘手，便开会，发通电，大意说：今年收成特丰，粮食过剩，粮价低落，农民不堪其苦，应请共筹救济的方案。

金融界本来在那里要做买卖，便提出了救济的方案：(一)由各大银行钱庄筹集资本，向各地收买粮米，指定适当地点屯积，到来年青黄不接的当儿陆续售出，使米价保持平衡；(二)提倡粮米抵押，使米商不至群相采购，造成无期的屯积；(三)由金融界负责募款，购屯粮米，到出售后结算，依盈亏的比例分别发还。

工业界是不声不响。米价低落，工人的“米贴”之类可以免除，在他们是有利的。

社会科学家在各种杂志上发表论文，从统计，从学理，指出粮食过剩之说简直是笑话；“谷贱伤农”也未必然，谷即使不贱，在帝国主义和封建势力双重压迫之下，农也得伤。

这些都是都市里的事情，在“乡亲”是一点也不知道。他们有的粜了自己吃的米，卖了可怜的耕牛，或者借了四分钱五分钱的债缴租；有的挺身而出，被关在拘押所里，两角三角地，忍痛缴纳自己的饭钱，有的沉溺在赌博里，希望骨牌骰子有灵，一场赢它十块八块；有的求人去说好话，向田主退租，准备做一个干干净净的穷光蛋；有的溜之大吉，悄悄地爬上开往上海的四等车。

A Year of Good Harvest

Ye Shengtao①

In front of Wan Sheng Rice Shop was a wharf, and moored at all angles to this wharf were the open boats in which the villagers had come to sell their rice. These boats, loaded with new rice, were riding low in the water. The space between them was filled with cabbage leaves and refuse, round which swirled greasy bubbles of white scum.

From the wharf climbed narrow steps, up which no more than three men could walk abreast. The rice shop stood at the top of these steps. The morning sun, slanting down through gaps in the title of the roof, shed broad beams of light on the tattered felt hats bobbing up to the counter.

The owners of the felt hats had risen at dawn to row here. And once at the wharf, not waiting to catch their breath, they rushed up to this counter to see what fate had to offer.

"Polished rice, five dollars. Paddy, three," was the manager's laconic answer to their question.

"What!" The peasants in the old felt hats could hardly believe their ears. Their hopes were dashed to the ground. They were dumbfounded.

"In June you paid thirteen dollars, didn't you?"

"We paid as much as fifteen, let alone thirteen."

"How could the price drop so sharply?"

---

① 译者注：Ye Shengtao, well-known novelist, is Vice-Minister of Education of the People's Republic of China. This story was written in the early thirties.

"What else do you expect in times like these? Rice is flooding the market. A few more days and the price will fall even lower."

Coming here, the men had plied their oars as if rowing in the dragon-boat race, but now all the energy drained out of them. This year Heaven had been kind, rain had fallen in due season, there had been no plague of pests and each *mou* had yielded a few pecks more than usual. This time, they had thought they could have a breathing space. To end up even worse off than the previous year was the last thing they had expected.

"Let's not sell. Row it home and keep it!" cried one simple soul indignantly.

The manager uttered a sarcastic laugh. "Do you think folk are going to starve because you won't sell? The whole country's full of foreign rice and flour. Before the first lot's finished, foreign steamboats are shipping in a second."

Foreign rice, foreign flour and foreign steamboats were too remote to worry them. But not to sell the rice in their boats was unthinkable. That was simply angry talk. They had to sell. The landlord would be coming for his rent, and old debts must be cleared—they had run into debt to pay day-labourers and buy fertilizer and food.

"Why don't we try Fanmu?" It occurred to one of them that they might find a better price there.

But the manager snorted with laughter again and tweaked his sparse beard as he said: "Even if you go to the city, you'll find our rice guild has reached a common agreement. The price everywhere these days is five dollars for polished rice, three for paddy."

"It's no good going to Fanmu," put in one of the peasants. "You have to pass two toll-houses, and there's no knowing how much they'd charge by way of tax. Who's got so much money to spare?"

"Won't you raise that price a little, sir?" another pleaded.

"That's easy to ask. We've sunk capital into this business, I'd have you know. To raise the price would mean giving you something for nothing. Do you take me for a fool?"

"But this price is too low, honestly it is. Who ever dreamed of such a thing? Last year we sold at seven dollars fifty. This summer rice went up to thirteen, no, fifteen, sir, as you said yourself just now. We were sure this year we'd get at least more than seven dollars fifty. Only five dollars—no!"

"Give us last year's price, sir! Seven fifty."

"Have a heart, sir. Be content with a smaller profit."

Another merchant, losing patience, hurled the stub of his cigarette into the street. "So you think the price too low!" He glared round at them. "You came of your own free will. You weren't asked to come. What's all this fuss about? We have silver dollars. If you don't sell, others will. Look, more boats have just stopped at the wharf."

Three or four more old felt hats were mounting the stone steps, the ruddy faces beneath them bright with hope. The sunlight slanted on the shoulders of their tattered cloth jackets as they joined the group.

"Wait till you hear this year's price!"

"It's even worse than last year—a paltry five dollars!" Utter despair was on the speaker's face.

"What!" Hope vanished like a pricked bubble.

But though hope vanished, they had no choice but to sell the rice in their boats. And fate compelled them to sell to Wan Sheng Rice Shop. For the rice shop had silver dollars, and silver dollars were precisely what the empty pockets of those tattered cloth jackets lacked.

As they haggled over the grading of the rice and whether the measure was full enough or not, the rice boats were slowly emptied of their loads. They rode higher in the water, and the cabbage leaves and refuse between them disappeared. The peasants in the old felt hats carried the rice they had grown into Wan Sheng's godown in exchange for varying numbers of notes.

"Give me silver dollars, sir!" White rice should at least be exchanged for white silver dollars. If not, the bargain seemed an even worse one.

"Ignorant clods!" A hand holding a fountain-pen rested on the abacus, while scornful eyes looked at them from over spectacles. "A dollar note is as good as a silver dollar. You're not being cheated of a single cent. We don't have silver dollars here, only notes."

"Let me have notes of the Bank of China then." Judging by the design, the notes in this speaker's hand were from some other bank.

"Pah! These *are* from the Central Bank of China." The accountant levelled the forefinger of his left hand. "If you refuse them, we can take you to court."

Why should refusing bank-notes be a crime? None of them understood that. After checking the figures on the notes and exchanging half-convinced, half-sceptical glances, they tucked the money into the empty pockets of their shabby jackets or the empty wallets at their belts.

Cursing under their breath, they left Wan Sheng Rice Shop as another group mounted the steps from the wharf. More bubbles of hope were pricked, destroying all the joy the peasants had taken since early autumn in their heavy ears of paddy. They carried their precious white rice into Wan Sheng's godown in exchange not for white silver dollars but paper notes.

The streets began to hum.

The owners of the old felt hats had come to the market today intending to buy many different imported products. They had run out of soap and must take back another ten bars or so, as well as a few packages of matches. Paraffin bought from the pedlars who came to the villages cost ten coppers for a small ladle, if several households combined to buy a tin they would get much better value. Moreover it was said that the gay foreign prints displayed in the shop windows were only eighty-five cents a foot, and for months now the womenfolk had been dreaming of buying some. That was why they had insisted on coming today when the rice was to be sold, having worked out exactly how many feet they needed for themselves, how many for Big Treasure and Small Treasure. Some of the women's plans included one of those oval foreign mirrors, a snowy white square towel or a pretty knitted cap for baby. Surely this year, when Heaven had been kind and each *mou* had yielded an extra three or four pecks, they were entitled to loosen the purse-strings usually held so tightly. For there ought to be something left over even after paying the rent, their debts and the guild. With this in mind, a few of them had even toyed with the idea of buying a thermos flask. Now that was an extraordinary thing! Without a fire, the hot water you'd poured in stayed just as hot hours later when you poured it out. The difference between heaven and earth could hardly be greater than between a thermos flask and the straw-lined box in which they kept the teapot warm.

Cursing beneath their breath, they left Wan Sheng Rice Shop like gamblers who have lost—lost yet again! The extent of their losses was still not clear to them. At all events, of the wad of notes in their pockets not half a note or ten cents was truly their own. In fact, they would have to raise a good many more notes somewhere to discharge their obligations—they had no idea how they were going to satisfy their creditors.

It was clear anyway that they had lost, and rowing straight home would not save the situation. If they strolled round the town and made a few purchases that would merely put them a little further in the red. Besides, there were some things they simply had to buy. So the streets began to hum.

In threes and fours, casting short shadows behind them, they walked the narrow streets. The men muttered over the price they had just been given and damned all black-hearted rice merchants. The women, a basket on one arm a baby on the other, let their eyes dart from shop to shop on both sides of the street. As for the children, they were fascinated by the celluloid dolls, tigers and dogs from abroad, as well as the red and green tin drums and tin trumpets—also made abroad. It was almost impossible to drag them away.

"Look, sonny, at this fine foreign drum, this foreign trumpet! Want one?" Tempting voices were followed by a rub-a-dub-dub, a toot-toot-toot!

Dong-dong-dong! "Highest quality face-basins of foreign enamel! At forty cents a piece they're going dirt cheap. Buy a basin, friends!"

"Walk up, friends! Here's a splendid variety of foreign prints selling at cut prices. Eighty-five cents a foot! Let me measure a few feet for you!"

The assistants in the chief shops were going all out, shouting to the villagers at the top of their voices, pulling at their cotton sleeves. For this was the only day in the year when the peasants' pockets were lined. This was a chance not to be missed.

After some deliberation spent in cutting down their budgets, the villagers handed one note and then another to the shop assistants. Soap, matches and the like were necessities, but they bought a little less than originally planned. The price of a tin of foreign paraffin was so shocking that they refrained from buying; they would have to go on purchasing a ladleful at a time from the pedlar. As for cloth, those who had decided to make two suits bought cloth for one; those who had planned new jackets for mother and son, bought enough for the son only. The oval foreign mirror, after being lovingly handled, was replaced on the counter. The knitted cap proved a perfect fit for baby; but his father's sharp veto made mother put it hastily down again. Those who had wanted a thermos flask dared not even ask the price. It might be as much as a dollar or a dollar fifty. If one threw caution to the winds and bought one, white-haired grandad and granny would be bound to scold: "Hard times like these—yet all you can think of is comfort! Throwing away a dollar fifty on a falderal like that! No wonder you've never amounted to anything. We've managed all these years without a thermos." No, life would not be worth living. Some mothers couldn't resist the longing in their children's eyes and bought the cheapest and smallest celluloid doll: you could move its arms and legs, make it sit down, stand up or raise its arms. Naturally, the children without one were green with envy, while even the grown-ups were much impressed.

Finally, having bought a little wine and some pork from the butchers, the villagers went back to their own boats moored by the Wan Sheng wharf. From the stern they brought out dishes of pickled vegetables and beancurd; then the men sat down in the bow to drink while the women started cooking in the stern. Presently smoke was rising from most of the boats, and tears were flowing from the peasants' eyes. The children alone, tumbling and rolling in the empty holds or playing with grimy treasures rescued from the water, were happier than words can tell.

Wine loosened the peasants' tongues. Neighbours or strangers, the same fate had befallen them all, and they drank together on the river. Raising his wine bowl one would voice his views, while another, putting down his chopsticks, would chime in with approbation or an oath according to the sentiments expressed. They needed this outlet for their feelings.

"Five dollars a bushel, devil take it!"

"Last year a flood, a poor crop—we lost out. This time a good year, a big crop—but we lose out again."

"We are worse off this year than last. Last year we still got seven dollars fifty."

"We've had to sell the rice we need ourselves. Heaven! The men who grow the grain can't eat it!"

"Why did you have to sell it, you old devil? I'd have kept some for the wife and sonny. I wouldn't pay the rent, but let them have the law of me and lock me up."

"We can't pay the rent whether we want to or not. To pay the rent we'd have to run up fresh debts. If we borrow more money at forty or fifty per cent interest, what's to become of us? Next year we'd be crushed by debt."

"There's no living to be made on the land any more."

"Give up the land, I say, and take the road. Tramps have a better time of it than we do."

"Famine refugees needn't pay their debts or guild money. A good idea. I'm for the road."

"Who'll be the leaders? Refugees always have a few leaders whom all the others—men and women, old and young—must obey."

"Seems to me it wouldn't be a bad idea to go to Shanghai to find work. Young Wang of our village went, didn't he? He works in a Shanghai factory and gets fifteen dollars a month. Fifteen dollars—that's worth three bushels of rice today."

"You're behind the times, you fool! In Shanghai the Japs are fighting. Most of the factories have closed down. Young Wang's a beggar now, didn't you know?"

Every road was closed. They were silent for a moment. Their bronzed faces flushed with sun and wine were ugly, as if dark blood were oozing through their skin.

"Who are we sweating for every year anyway?" asked one man hoarsely after a swig of wine.

"It's staring you in the face. We're sweating for them!" Someone pointed to the tarnished gilt signboard of Wan Sheng Rice Shop. "We nearly kill ourselves growing the rice and running into debt at wicked rates of interest. And without moving a muscle they say: 'Five dollars a bushel!' They might as well tear out our hearts and have done with it."

"If only we could fix the price ourselves! We'd be fair. I wouldn't ask more than eight dollars a bushel."

"Are you crazy? Didn't you hear? The rice merchants sink capital into the business—they can't let us have something for nothing."

"Well, we sink capital into the land. Why should we give them something for nothing? Why should we give the landlord something for nothing?"

"In the godown just now I was thinking: You're sitting pretty today with all this rice stored here. But if a time comes when we've nothing to eat, we'll be back to help ourselves." The speaker kept his voice down, his bloodshot eyes flickering towards the shore.

"If men are starving, it's no crime to take a little rice from those who have plenty." This was said in righteous tones.

"This spring, didn't they break into the Fengchiao rice shops?"

"The militia opened fire and two men were killed."

"There may be shooting here this year, for all we know."

Nothing came, naturally, of this wild talk. When the wine was drunk and the food eaten, they rowed back to their respective villages. The wharf was left silent and deserted, lapped by dark, dirty green water.

The next day another batch of boats rowed up to moor here and the same scene was re-enacted in the town. This scene was being enacted in towns all over the country. In fact, it was only too common.

"When grain is cheap the peasants suffer." This old saying made the headlines in the papers in town.

The landlords, finding it hard to collect their rent, held meetings and dispatched telegrams. The gist of these was: This year there was a bumper harvest. A glut in grain has caused a drop in prices and the peasants are destitute. Public assistance should be given.

The financiers, anxious to do business, drafted a plan for relief: 1. Funds should be raised by the large banks and money-changers for the purchase of rice from all parts of the country, and appropriate places appointed for its storage. The rice was to be sold the next spring when there was a shortage of food. This would keep the rice price stable. 2. The rice should be mortgaged as security for loans to prevent the rice merchants from buying up the whole crop and hoarding it. 3. The financiers should be responsible for collecting the fund to buy grain to be stored. The funds should be paid back after the sale of grain with interest calculated according to the profit made or losses incurred.

The industrialists said nothing. The drop in the price of rice was to their advantage since it freed them from the necessity of giving their workers a "rice subsidy."

The social scientists published their views in different journals. They marshalled statistics and theories to prove that it was ridiculous to talk of a glut in grain, and not necessarily true that "when grain is cheap the peasants suffer." Even if grain were not cheap, the peasants would suffer anyway under the double oppression of imperialism and feudalism.

Since all this happened in the towns, the villagers remained totally ignorant of it. Some of them sold rice they needed for themselves, or their gaunt, half-starved buffalo. Some borrowed money at forty to fifty per cent interest to pay the rent. Some stubbornly refused to pay and were arrested. In bitterness of spirit some paid a few cents today, a few more tomorrow, depriving themselves of food. Some took to gambling, hoping for a run of luck enabling them to win nine or ten dollars. Some begged friends to put in a good word for them to the landlord, so that they might stop renting his land, for they would be better off without. Some left home to seek their fortune, buying a fourth-class ticket on the train to Shanghai.

二

边城(1—5节)①

沈从文

一

由四川过湖南去，靠东有一条官路。这官路将近湘西边境，到了一个地方名叫“茶峒”的小山城时，有一小溪，溪边有座白色小塔，塔下住了一户单独的人家。这人家只一个老人，一个女孩子，一只黄狗。

小溪流下去，绕山岨流，约三里便汇入茶峒大河，人若过溪越小山走去，只一里路就到了茶峒城边。溪流如弓背，山路如弓弦，故远近有了小小差异。小溪宽约二十丈，河床是大片石头作成。静静的河水即或深到一篙不能落底，却依然清澈透明，河中游鱼来去都可以计数。小溪既为川、湘来往孔道，水常有涨落，限于财力不能搭桥，就安排了一只方头渡船。这渡船一次连人带马，约可以载二十位搭客过河，人数多时必反复来去。渡船头竖了一根小小竹竿，挂着一个可以活动的铁环；溪岸两端水面横牵了一段竹缆，有人过渡时，把铁环挂在竹缆上，船上人就引手攀缘那条缆索，慢慢的牵船过对岸去。船将拢岸时，管理这渡船的，一面口中嚷着“慢点慢点”，自己霍的跃上了岸，拉着铁环，于是人货牛马全上了岸，翻过小山不见了。渡头属公家所有，过渡人本不必出钱；有人心中不安，抓

---

① 中文选自：沈从文．沈从文小说选集．北京：人民文学出版社，1957:226-247；英译文选自：Shen, C. W. *The Border Town* (part 1). Gladys Yang (trans.). *Chinese Literature*, 1962(10).

了一把钱掷到船板上时，管渡船的必为一一拾起，依然塞到那人手心里去，俨然吵嘴时的认真神气："我有了口粮，三斗米，七百钱，够了！谁要你这个?!"

但是，凡事求个心安理得，出气力不受酬谁好意思，不管如何还是有人要把钱的。管船人却情不过，也为了心安起见，便把这些钱托人到茶峒去买茶叶和草烟，将茶峒出产的上等草烟，一扎一扎挂在自己腰带边，过渡的谁需要这东西必慷慨奉赠。有时从神气上估计那远路人对于身边草烟引起了相当的注意时，这弄渡船的便把一小束草烟扎到那人包袱上去，一面说："大哥，不吸这个吗？这好的，这妙的，看样子不成材，巴掌大叶子，味道蛮好，送人也很合式!"茶叶则在六月里放进大缸里去，用开水泡好，给过路人随意解渴。

管理这渡船的，就是住在塔下的那个老人。活了七十年，从二十岁起便守在这小溪边，五十年来不知把船来去渡了若干人。年纪虽那么老了，骨头硬硬的，本来应当休息了，但天不许他休息，他仿佛便不能够同这一份生活离开。他从不思索自己职务对于本人的意义，只是静静的很忠实的在那里活下去。代替了天，使他在日头升起时，感到生活的力量；当日头落下时，又不至于思量和日头同时死去的，是那个近在他身旁的女孩子。他唯一的伙伴是一只渡船和一只黄狗，唯一的亲人便只那个女孩子。

女孩子的母亲，老船夫的独生女，十七年前同一个茶峒屯防军人唱歌相熟后，很秘密的背着那忠厚爸爸发生了暧昧关系。有了小孩子后，结婚不成，这屯戍兵士便想约了她一同向下游逃去。但从逃走的行为上看来，一个违悖了军人的责任，一个却必得离开孤独的父亲。经过一番考虑后，屯戍兵见她无远走勇气，自己也不便毁去作军人的名誉，就心想一同去生既无法聚首，一同去死应当无人可以阻拦，……在一场偶然来到的疾病中就死了。女的却关心腹中的一块肉，不忍心，拿不出主张。事情业已为作渡船夫的父亲知道，父亲却不加上一个有分量的字眼儿，只作为并不听到过这事情一样，仍然把日子很平静的过下去。女儿一面怀了羞惭，一面却怀了怜悯，依旧守在父亲身边。等待腹中小孩生下后，却到溪边故意吃了许多冷水死去了。在一种近乎奇迹中这遗孤居然已长大成人，一转眼间便十五岁了。为了住处两山多竹篁,翠色逼人而来,老船夫随便给这个可怜的孤雏,拾取了一个近身的名字,叫作"翠翠"。

翠翠在风日里长养着,把皮肤变得黑黑的,触目为青山绿水,一对眸子清明如水晶,自然既长养她且教育她。为人天真活泼,处处俨然如一只小兽物。人又那么乖,和山头黄麂一样,从不想到残忍事情,从不发愁,从不动气。平时在渡船上遇陌生人对她有所注意时,便把光光的眼睛瞅着那陌生人,作成随时都可举步逃入深山的神气,但明白了面前的人无机心后,就又从从容容的来完成任务了。

老船夫不论晴雨,必守在船头,有人过渡时,便略弯着腰,两手缘引了竹缆,把船横渡过小溪。有时疲倦了,躺在临溪大石上睡着了,人在隔岸招手喊过渡,翠翠不让祖父起身,就跳下船去,很敏捷的替祖父把路人渡过溪,一切溜刷在行,从不误事。有时又和祖父、黄狗一同在船上,过渡时与祖父一同动手牵缆索。船将近岸边,祖父正向客人招呼"慢点,慢点"时,那只黄狗便口衔绳子,最先一跃而上,且俨然懂得如何方称尽职似的,把船绳紧衔着拖船拢岸。茶峒附近村子里人不仅认识弄渡船的祖孙二人,也对于这只狗充满好感。

风日清和的天气,无人过渡,镇日长闲,祖父同翠翠便坐在门前大岩石上晒太阳;或把一段木头从高处向水中抛去,嗾使身边黄狗自岩石高处跃下,把木头衔回来;或翠翠与黄狗皆张着耳朵,听祖父说些城中多年以前的战争故事;或祖父同翠翠两人,各把小竹作成的竖笛,逗在嘴边吹着迎亲送女的曲子,过渡人来了,老船夫放下了竹管,独自跟到船边去横溪渡人。在岩上的一个,见船开动时,于是锐声喊着:

"爷爷,爷爷,你听我吹,你唱!"

爷爷到溪中央于是便很快乐的唱起来,哑哑的声音同竹管声,振荡在寂静空气里,溪中仿佛也热闹了些。实则歌声的来复,反而使一切更加寂静。

有时过渡的是从川东过茶峒的小牛,是羊群,是新娘子的花轿,翠翠必争着作渡船夫,站在船头,懒懒的攀引缆索,让船缓缓的过去。牛、羊、花轿上岸后,翠翠必跟着走,送队伍上山,站到小山头,目送这些东西走去很远了，方回转船上，把船牵靠近家的岸边；且独自低低的学小羊叫着，学母牛叫着，或采一把野花缚在头上，独自装扮新娘子。

茶峒山城只隔渡头一里路，买油买盐时，逢年过节祖父得喝一杯酒时，祖父不上城，黄狗就伴同翠翠入城里去备办节货。到了卖杂货的铺子里，有大把的粉条，大缸的白糖，有炮仗，有红蜡烛，莫不给翠翠一种很深的印象，回到祖父身边，总把这些东西说个半天。那里河边还有许多上行船，百十船夫忙着起卸百货，这种船只比起渡船来全大得多，有趣味得多，翠翠也不容易忘记。

二

茶峒地方凭水依山筑城，近山一面，城墙俨然如一条长蛇，缘山爬去。临水一面则在城外河边留出余地设码头，湾泊小小篷船。船下行时运桐油、青盐、染色的五倍子。上行则运棉花、棉纱，以及布匹、杂货同海味。贯串各个码头有一条河街，人家房子多一半着陆，一半在水，因为余地有限，那些房子莫不设有吊脚楼。河中涨了春水，到水脚逐渐进街后，河街上人家，便各用长长的梯子，一端搭在自家屋檐口，一端搭在城墙上，人人争骂着嚷着，带了包袱、铺盖、米缸，从梯子上进城里去，等待水退时，方又从城门口出城。某一年水若来得特别猛一些，沿河吊脚楼，必有一处两处为大水冲去，大家皆在城上头呆望，受损失的也同样呆望着，对于所受的损失仿佛无话可说，与在自然安排下，眼见其他无可挽救的不幸来时相似。涨水时在城上还可望着骤然展宽的河面，流水浩浩荡荡，随同山水从上流浮沉而来的有房子、牛、羊、大树。于是在水势较缓处，税关趸船前面，便常常有人驾了小舢舨，一见河心浮沉而来的是一匹牲畜、一段小木或一只空船，船上有一个妇人或一个小孩哭喊的声音，便急急的把船桨去，在下游一些迎着了那个目的物，把它用长绳系定，再向岸边桨去。这些诚实勇敢的人，也爱利，也仗义，同一般当地人相似。不拘救人救物，却同样在一种愉快冒险行为中，做得十分敏捷勇敢，使人见及不能不为之喝彩。

那条河水便是历史上知名的酉水，新名字叫作白河。白河下游到辰州与沅水汇流后，便略显浑浊，有出山泉水的意思。若溯流而上，则三丈五丈的深潭可清澈见底。深潭中为白日所映照，河底小小白石子、有花纹的玛瑙石子，全看得明明白白。水中游鱼来去，全如浮在空气里，两岸多高山，山中多可以造纸的细竹，长年作深翠颜色，逼人眼目。近水人家多在桃杏花里，春天时只需注意，凡有桃花处必有人家，凡有人家处必可沽酒。夏天则晒晾在日光下耀目的紫花布衣袴，可以作为人家所在的旗帜。秋冬来时，酉水中游如王村、岔衆、保靖、里耶和许多无名山村，人家房屋在悬崖上的、滨水的，无不朗然入目。黄泥的墙，乌黑的瓦，位置却永远那么妥贴，且与四围环境极其调和，使人迎面得到的印象，实在非常愉快。一个对于诗歌、图画稍有兴味的旅客，在这小河中，蜷伏于一只小船上，作三十天的旅行，必不至于感到厌烦。正因为处处若有奇迹可以发现，人的劳动的成果，自然的大胆处与精巧处，无一地无一时不使人神往倾心。

白河的源流，从四川边境而来，从白河上行的小船，春水发时可以直达川属的秀山。但属于湖南境界的，茶峒算是最后一个水码头。这条河水的河面，在茶峒时虽宽约半里，当秋冬之际水落时，河床流水处还不到二十丈，其余只是一滩青石。小船到此后，既无从上行，因此凡是川东的进出口货物，得从这地方落水起岸。出口货物俱由脚夫用桑木扁担压在肩膊上挑抬而来，入口货物也莫不从这地方成束成担的用人力搬去。

这地方城中只驻扎一营由昔年绿营屯丁改编而成的戍兵，及五百家左右的住户。(这些住户中，除了一部分拥有一些山田同油坊，或放账屯油、屯米、屯棉纱的小资本家外，其余多数是当年屯戍来此有军籍的人家。)地方还有个厘金局，办事机关在城外河街下面小庙里，经常挂着一面长长的幡信。局长则长住城中。一营兵士驻扎老参将衙门，除了号兵每天上城吹号玩，使人知道这里还驻有军队以外，其余兵士仿佛并不存在。冬天的白日里，到城里去，便只见各处人家门前各晾晒有衣服同青菜；红薯多带藤悬挂在屋檐下；用棕衣作成的口袋，装满了栗子、榛子和其他硬壳果，也多悬挂在檐口下。屋角隅各处有大小鸡叫着玩着。间或有什么男子，占据在自己屋前门限上锯木，或用斧头劈树，劈好的柴堆到敞坪里去如一座一座宝塔。又或可以见到几个中年妇人，穿了浆洗得极硬的蓝布衣裳，胸前挂有白布扣花围裙，躬着腰在日光下一面说话一面作事。一切总永远那么静寂，所有的人每个日子都在这种不可形容的单纯寂寞里过去。一分安静增加了人对于“人事”的思索力，增加了梦。在这小城中生活的，各人自然也一定各在分定一份日子里，怀了对于人事爱憎必然的期待。但这些人想些什么？谁知道！住在城中较高处，门前一站便可以眺望对河以及河中的景致，船来时，远远的就从对河滩上看着无数纤夫。那些纤夫也有从下游地方，带了细点心、洋糖之类，拢岸时却拿进城中来换钱的。船来时，小孩子的想像，应当在那些拉船人一方面。大人呢，孵一窠小鸡，养两只猪，托下行船夫打副金耳环，带两丈官青布，或一坛好酱油，一个双料的美孚灯罩回来，便占去了大部分作主妇的心了。

这小城里虽那么安静和平，但地方既为川东商业交易接头处，因此城外小小河街，情形却不同了一点。也有商人落脚的客店，坐镇不动的理发馆。此外饭店、杂货铺、油行、盐栈、花衣庄，莫不各有一种地位，装点这条小河街。还有卖船上檀木活车竹缆与锅罐铺子，介绍水手职业吃码头饭的人家。小饭店门前长案上常有煎得焦黄的鲤鱼豆腐，身上装饰了红辣椒丝，卧在浅口钵头里，钵旁大竹筒中插着大把朱红筷子，不拘谁个愿意花点钱，这人就可以傍了门前长案坐下来，抽出一双筷子捏到手上，那边一个眉毛扯得极细、脸上擦了白粉的妇人，就走过来问：“大哥，副爷，要甜酒？要烧酒？”男子火焰高一点的，谐趣的，对内掌柜有点意思的，必故意装成生气似的说：“吃甜酒？又不是小孩子，还问人吃甜酒！”那么，酽冽的烧酒，从大瓮里用木滤子舀出，倒进土碗里，即刻就来到身边案桌上了。这烧酒自然是浓而且香的，能醉倒一个汉子的，所以照例也不会多吃。杂货铺卖美孚油及点美孚油的洋灯与香烛、纸张。油行屯桐油。盐栈堆四川火井出的青盐。花衣庄则有白棉纱、大布、棉花，以及包头的黑绉绸出卖。卖船上用物的，百物罗列，无所不备，且间或有重到百斤的铁锚，搁在门外路旁，等候主顾问价的。专以介绍水手为事业，吃水码头饭的，在河街的家中，终日大门必敞开着，常有穿青羽缎马褂的船主与毛手毛脚的水手进出，地方像茶馆却不卖茶，不是烟馆又可以抽烟。来到这里的，虽说所谈的是船上生意经，然而船只的上下，划船拉纤人大都有一定规矩，不必作数目上的讨论。他们来到这里大多数倒是在“联欢”。以“龙头管事”作中心，谈论点本地时事，两省商务上情形，以及下游的“新事”。邀会的，集款时大多数皆在此地；扒骰子看点数多少轮作会首时，也常常在此举行。真真成为他们生意经的，有两件事：买卖船只，买卖媳妇。

大都市随了商务发达而产生的某种寄食者，因为商人的需要，水手的需要，这小小边城的河街，也居然有那么一群人，聚集在一些有吊脚楼的人家。这种小妇人不是从附近乡下弄来，便是随同川军来湘流落后的妇人，穿了假洋绸的衣服，印花标布的裤子，把眉毛扯得成一条细线，大大的发髻上敷了香味极浓俗的油类，白日里无事，就坐在门口小凳子上做鞋子，在鞋尖上用红绿丝线挑绣双凤，或为情人水手作绣花抱肚，一面看过往行人，消磨长日。或靠在临河窗口上看水手起货，听水手爬桅子唱歌。到了晚间，却轮流的接待商人同水手，切切实实尽一个妓女应尽的义务。

由于边地的风俗淳朴，便是作妓女，也永远那么浑厚，遇不相熟的主顾，做生意时得先交钱，数目弄清楚后，再关门撒野。人既相熟后，钱便在可有可无之间了。妓女多靠四川商人维持生活，但恩情所结，却多在水手方面。感情好的，别离时互相咬着嘴唇咬着颈脖发了誓，约好了“分手后各人不许胡闹”；四十天或五十天，在船上浮着的那一个，同在岸上蹲着的这一个，便各在分上呆着打发这一堆日子，尽把自己的心紧紧缚定远远的一个人。尤其是妇人，情感真挚痴到无可形容，男子过了约定时间不回来，做梦时，就总常常梦船拢了岸，那一个人摇摇荡荡的从船跳板到了岸上，直向身边跑来。或日中有了疑心，则梦里必见那个男子在桅上向另一方面唱歌，却不理会自己。性格弱一点儿的，接着就在梦里投河、吞鸦片烟；性格强一点儿的，便手执菜刀，直向那水手奔去。他们生活虽那么同一般社会疏远，但是眼泪与欢乐，在一种爱憎得失间，揉进了这些人生活里时，也便同另外一片土地另外一些年轻生命相似，全个身心为那点爱憎所浸透，见寒作热，忘了一切。若有多少不同处，不过是这些人更真切一点，也就更近于胡涂一点罢了。短期的包定，长期的嫁娶，一时间的关门，这些关于一个女人身体上的交易，由于民情的淳朴，身当其事的不觉得如何下流可耻，旁观者也就从不用读书人的观念，加以指摘与轻视。这些人既重义轻利，又能守信自约，即便是娼妓，也常常较之讲道理知羞耻的城市中绅士还更可信任。

掌水码头的名叫顺顺，一个前清时便在营伍中混过日子来的人物，辛亥革命时在著名的陆军四十九标做个什长。同样做什长的，有因革命成了伟人名人的，有杀头碎尸的，他却带着少年喜事得来的脚疯痛，回到了家乡，把所积蓄的一点钱，买了一条六桨白木船，租给一个穷船主，代人装货在茶峒与辰州之间来往。气运好，两年之内船不坏事，于是他从所赚的钱上，又讨了一个略有产业的白脸黑发小寡妇。因此一来，数年后，在这条河上，他就有了大小四只船，一个妻子，两个儿子了。

但这个大方洒脱的人，事业虽十分顺手，却因欢喜交朋结友，慷慨而又能济人之急，便不能同贩油商人一样大大发作起来。自己既在粮子里混过日子，明白出门人的甘苦，理解失意人的心情，于是凡因船只失事破产的船家、过路的退伍兵士、游学文墨人，到了这个地方，闻名求助的莫不尽力帮助。一面从水上赚来钱，一面就这样洒脱散去。这人虽然脚上有点小毛病，还能泅水，走路难得其平，为人却那么公正无私。水面上各事原本极其简单，一切都为一个习惯所支配，谁个船碰了头，谁个船妨害了别一人别一只船的利益，照例有习惯方法来解决。惟运用这种习惯规矩排调一切的，必须一个高年硕德的中心人物。某年秋天，那原来执事的人死去了，顺顺作了这样一个代替者。那时他还只五十岁，为人既明事明理，正直和平，又不爱财，因此无人对他年龄怀疑。

到如今，他的儿子大的已十八岁，小的已十六岁。两个年青人都结实如小公牛，能驾船，能泅水，能走长路。凡从小乡城里出身的年青人所能够作的事，他们无一不作，作去无一不精。年纪较长的，性情如他们爸爸一样，豪放豁达，不拘常套小节。年幼的则气质近于那个白脸黑发的母亲，不爱说话，眼眉却秀拔出群，一望即知其为人聪明而又富于感情。

两兄弟既年已长大，必须在各一种生活上来训练他们的人格，作父亲的就轮流派遣两个小孩子各处旅行。向下行船时，多随了自己的船只充当伙计，甘苦与人相共。荡桨时选最重的一把，背纤时拉头纤二纤，吃的是干鱼、辣子、臭酸菜，睡的是硬帮帮的舱板。向上行从旱路走去，则跟了川东客货，过秀山、龙潭、酉阳作生意，不论寒暑雨雪，必穿了草鞋按站赶路。且佩了短刀，遇不得已必须动手，便霍的把刀抽出，站到空阔处去，等候对面的一个，继着就同这个人用肉搏来解决。地方的风气，既为“对付仇敌必须用刀，联结朋友也必须用刀”，到需要刀时，他们也就从不让它失去那点机会。学贸易，学应酬，学习到一个新地方去适应各种生活，且学习用刀保护身体同名誉。教育的目的，似乎在使两个孩子学得做人的勇气与义气。一分教育的结果，弄得两个人皆结实如老虎，却又和气亲人，不骄惰，不浮华，不倚势凌人。故父子三人在茶峒边境上，为人所提及时，人人对这个名姓无不加以一种尊敬。

作父亲的当两个儿子很小时，就明白大儿子一切和自己相似，能成家立业，却稍稍见得溺爱那第二个儿子。由于这点不自觉的私心，他把长子取名天保，次子取名傩送。意思是天保佑的在人事上或不免有些龃龉处，至于傩神所送来的，照当地习气，人便不能稍加轻视了。傩送美丽得很，茶峒船家人拙于赞扬这种美丽，只知道为他取出一个诨名为“岳云”。虽无什么人亲眼看到过岳云，一般的印象，却从戏台上小生穿白盔白甲的岳云，得来一个相近的神气。

三

两省接壤处，十余年来主持地方军事的，知道注重在安辑保守，处置还得法，并无特别变故发生。水陆商务既不至于受战争停顿，也不至于为土匪影响，一切莫不极有秩序，人民也莫不安分乐生。这些人，除了家中死了牛，翻了船，或发生别的死亡大变，为一种不幸所绊倒，觉得十分伤心外，中国其他地方正在如何不幸挣扎中的情形，似乎就还不曾为这边城人民所感到。

边城所在一年中最热闹的日子，是端午、中秋和过年。三个节日过去三五十年前，如何兴奋了这地方人，直到现在，还毫无什么变化，仍旧是那地方居民最有意义的几个日子。

端午日,当地妇女、小孩子,莫不穿了新衣,额角上用雄黄蘸酒画了个王字。任何人家到了这天必可以吃鱼吃肉。大约上午十一点钟左右,全茶峒人就吃了午饭,把饭吃过后,在城里住家的,莫不倒锁了门,全家出城到河边看划船。河街有熟人的,可到河街吊脚楼门口边看,不然就站在税关门口与各个码头上看。河中龙船以长潭某处作起点,税关前作终点,作比赛竞争。因为这一天军官、税官以及当地有身分的人,莫不在税关前看热闹。划船的事各人在数天以前就早有了准备,分组分帮,各自选出了若干身体结实、手脚伶俐的小伙子,在潭中练习进退。船只的形式,与平常木船大不相同,形体一律又长又狭,两头高高翘起,船身绘着朱红颜色长线,平常时节多搁在河边干燥洞穴里,要用它时,才拖下水去。每只船可坐十二个到十八个桨手,一个带头的,一个鼓手,一个锣手。桨手每人持一支短桨,随了鼓声缓促为节拍,把船向前划去。带头的坐在船头上,头上缠裹着红布包头,手上拿两支小令旗,左右挥动,指挥船只的进退。擂鼓打锣的,多坐在船只的中部,船一划动便即刻蓬蓬铛铛把锣鼓很单纯的敲打起来,为划桨水手调理下桨节拍。一船快慢既不得不靠鼓声,故每当两船竞赛到剧烈时,鼓声如雷鸣,加上两岸人呐喊助威,便使人想起小说故事上梁红玉老鹳河时水战擂鼓种种情形。凡是把船划到前面一点的,必可在税关前领赏,一疋红、一块小银牌,不拘缠挂到船上某一个人头上去,都显出这一船合作努力的光荣。好事的军人,当每次某一只船胜利时,必在水边放些表示胜利庆祝的五百响鞭炮。

赛船过后,城中的戍军长官,为了与民同乐,增加这个节日的愉快起见,便派兵士把三十只绿头长颈大雄鸭,颈脖上缚了红布条子,放入河中,尽善于泅水的军民人等,自由下水追赶鸭子。不拘谁把鸭子捉到,谁就成为这鸭子的主人。于是长潭换了新的花样,水面各处是鸭子,同时各处有追赶鸭子的人。

船和船的竞赛,人和鸭子的竞赛,直到天晚方能完事。

掌水码头的龙头大哥顺顺,年青时节便是一个泅水的高手,入水中去追逐鸭子,在任何情形下总不落空。但一到次子傩送年过十岁时,已能入水闭气汆着到鸭子身边,再忽然冒水而出,把鸭子捉到,这作爸爸的便解嘲似的向孩子们说:“好,这种事情有你们来作,我不必再下水和你们争显本领了。”于是当真就不下水与人来竞争捉鸭子。但下水救人呢,当作别论。凡帮助人远离患难,便是入火,人到八十岁,也还是成为这个人一种不可逃避的责任!

天保、傩送两人都是当地泅水划船的好选手。

端午又快来了,初五划船,河街上初一开会,就决定了属于河街的那只船当天入水。天保恰好在那天应当向上行,随了陆路商人过川东、龙潭送节货,故参加的就只傩送。十六个结实如牛犊的小伙子,带了香烛鞭炮,同一个用生牛皮蒙好、绘有朱红太极图的高脚鼓,到了搁船的河上游山洞边,烧了香烛,把船拖入水中后,各人上了船,燃着鞭炮,擂着鼓,这船便如一支没羽箭似的,很迅速的向下游长潭射去。

那时节还是上午,到了午后,对河渔人的龙船也下了水,两只龙船就开始预习种种竞赛的方法。水面上第一次听到了鼓声,许多人从这鼓声中,都感到了节日临近的欢悦。住临河吊脚楼对远方人有所等待的、有所盼望的,也莫不因鼓声想到远人。在这个节日里,必然有许多船只可以赶回,也有许多船只只合在半路过节,这之间,便有些眼目所难见的人事哀乐,在这小山城河街间,让一些人开心,也让一些人皱眉!

蓬蓬鼓声掠水越山到了渡船头那里时,最先注意到的是那只黄狗。那黄狗汪汪的吠着,受了惊似的绕屋乱走;有人过渡时,便随船渡过河东岸去,且跑到那小山头向城里一方面大吠。

翠翠正坐在门外大石上用棕叶编蚱蜢、蜈蚣玩,见黄狗先在太阳下睡着,忽然醒来便发疯似的乱跑,过了河又回来,就问它骂它:

“狗,狗,你做什么!不许这样子!”

可是一会儿那远处声音被她发现了,她于是也绕屋跑着,并且同黄狗一块儿渡过了小溪,站在小山头听了许久,让那点迷人的鼓声,把自己带到一个过去的节日里去。

四

还是两年前的事。五月端阳,渡船头祖父找人作了替身,便带了黄狗同翠翠进城,到大河边去看划船。河边站满了人,四只朱色长船在潭中划着。龙船水刚刚涨过,河中水皆泛着豆绿色,天气又那么明朗,鼓声蓬蓬响着,翠翠抿着嘴一句话不说,心中充满了不可言说的快乐。河边人太多了一点,各人尽张着眼睛望河中,不多久,黄狗还留在身边,祖父却挤得不见了。

翠翠一面注意划船,一面心想:“过不久爷爷总会找来的。”但过了许久,祖父还不来,翠翠便稍稍有点儿着慌了。先是两人同黄狗进城前一天,祖父就问翠翠:“明天城里划船,倘若你一个人去看,人多怕不怕?”翠翠就说:“人多我不怕。但是只是自己一个人可不好玩。”于是祖父想了半天,方想起一个住在城中的老熟人,赶夜里到城里去商量,请那老人来看一天渡船,自己却陪翠翠进城玩一天。且因为那人比渡船老人更孤单,身边无一个亲人,也无一只狗,因此便约好了那人早上过家中来吃饭,喝一杯雄黄酒。第二天那人来了,吃了饭,把职务委托那人以后,翠翠等便进了城。到路上时,祖父想起什么似的,又问翠翠:“翠翠,翠翠,人那么多,好热闹,你一个人敢到河边看龙船吗?”翠翠说:“怎么不敢?可是一个人玩有什么意思。”到了河边后,长潭里的四只红船,把翠翠的注意力完全占去了,身边祖父似乎也可有可无了。祖父心想:“时间还早,到收场时,至少还得三个时刻。溪边的那个朋友,也应当来看看年青人的热闹,回去一趟,换换地位还赶得及。”因此就告翠翠:“人太多了,站在这里看,不要动,我到别处去有点事情,无论如何总赶得回来伴你回家。”翠翠正为两只竞速并进的船迷着,祖父说的话毫不思索就答应了。祖父知道黄狗在翠翠身边,也许比他自己在她身边还稳当,于是便回家看船去了。

祖父到了那渡船处时,见代替他的老朋友,正站在白塔下注意听远处鼓声。

祖父喊叫他,请他把船拉过来,两人渡过小溪仍然站到白塔下去。那人问老船夫为什么又跑回来,祖父就说想替他一会儿,所以把翠翠留在河边,自己赶回来,好让他也过大河边去看看热闹,且说:“看得好,就不必再回来,只须见了翠翠告她一声,翠翠到时自会回家的。小丫头不敢回家,你就伴她走走!”但那替手对于看龙船已无什么兴味,却愿意同老船夫在这溪边大石上各自再喝两杯烧酒。老船夫听说十分高兴，于是把酒葫芦取出，推给城中来的那一个。两人一面谈些端午旧事，一面喝酒，不到一会，那人却在岩石上被烧酒醉倒了。

人既醉倒后，无从入城，祖父为了责任又不便与渡船离开，留在城中河边的翠翠，便不能不着急了。

河中划船的决了最后胜负后，城里军官已派人驾小船在潭中放了一群鸭子，祖父还不见来。翠翠恐怕祖父也正在什么地方等着她，因此带了黄狗向各处人丛中挤着去找寻祖父，结果还是不得祖父的踪迹。后来看看天快要黑了，军人扛了长凳出城看热闹的，都已陆续扛了那凳子回家。潭中的鸭子只剩下三五只，捉鸭人也渐渐的少了。落日向上游翠翠家中那一方落去，黄昏把河面装饰了一层银色薄雾。翠翠望到这个景致，忽然起了一个怕人的想头，她想："假若爷爷死了？"

她记起祖父嘱咐她不要离开原来地方那一句话，便又为自己解释这想头的错误，以为祖父不来，必是进城去或到什么熟人处去，被人拉着喝酒，一时间不能脱身。正因为这也是可能的事，她又不愿在天未断黑以前，同黄狗赶回家去，只好站在那石码头边等候祖父。

再过一会，对河那两只长船已泊到对河小溪里去不见了，看龙船的人也差不多全散了。吊脚楼有娼妓的人家，已上了灯，且有人敲小斑鼓弹月琴唱曲了。另外一些人家，又有猜拳行酒的吵嚷声音。同时停泊在吊脚楼下的一些船只，上面也有人在摆酒炒菜，把青菜萝卜之类，倒进滚热油锅里去时发出吵——的声音。河面已濛濛眬眬，看去好像只有一只白鸭在潭中浮着，也只剩一个人追着这只鸭子。

翠翠还是不离开码头，总相信祖父会来找她，同她一起回家。

吊脚楼上唱曲子声音热闹了一些，只听到下面船上有人说话，一个水手说："金亭，你听你那婊子陪川东庄客喝酒唱曲子，我赌个手指，说这是她的声音！"另一个水手就说："她陪他们喝酒唱曲子，心里可想我。她知道我在船上！"先前那一个又说："身体让别人玩着，心还想着你，你有什么凭据？"另一个说："我有凭据。"于是这水手吹着唿哨，作出一个古怪的记号，一会儿，楼上歌声便停止了。歌声停止后，两个水手哈哈大笑起来。

两人接着便说了些关于那个女人的一切,使用了不少粗鄙字眼,翠翠很不习惯把这种话听下去,但又不能走开。且听水手之一说楼上妇人的爸爸是七年前在棉花坡被人杀死的,一共杀了十七刀,翠翠心中那个古怪的想头:"爷爷死了呢?"便仍然占据到心里有一会儿。

两个水手还正在谈话,潭中那只白鸭却慢慢的向翠翠所在的码头边游过来,翠翠想:"再过来些我就捉住你!"于是静静的等着。但那鸭子将近岸边三丈远近时,却有个人笑着,喊那船上水手。原来水中还有个人,那人已把鸭子捉到手,却慢慢的踹水游近岸边的。船上人听到水面的喊声,在隐约里也喊道:"二老,二老,你真干,你今天得了五只罢?"那水上人说:"这家伙狡猾得很,现在可归我了。""你这时捉鸭子,将来捉女人,一定有同样的本领。"水上那一个不再说什么,手脚并用的拍着水傍了码头。湿淋淋的爬上岸时,翠翠身旁的黄狗,仿佛警告水中人似的,汪汪的叫了几声,表示这里有人,那人方注意到翠翠。码头上已无别的人,那人问:

"是谁人?"

"我是翠翠。"

"翠翠又是谁?"

"是碧溪岨撑渡船的孙女。"

"这里又没有人过渡,你在这儿做什么?"

"我等我爷爷。我等他来好回家去。"

"等他来他可不会来。你爷爷一定到城里军营里喝了酒,醉倒后被人抬回去了!"

"他不会这样子,他答应来找我,他就一定会来的。"

"这里等也不成,到我家里去,到那边点了灯的楼上去,等爷爷来找你好不好?"

翠翠误会了邀他进屋里去那个人的好意,心里记着水手说的妇人丑事,她以为那男子就是要她上有女人唱歌的楼上去,本来从不骂人,这时正因为等候祖父太久了,心中焦急得很,听人要她上去,以为欺侮了她,就轻轻的说:

"你个悖时砍脑壳的!"

话虽轻轻的，那男的却听得出，且从声音上听得出翠翠年纪，便带笑说："怎么，你那么小小的还会骂人！你不愿意上去，要耽在这儿，回头水里大鱼来咬了你，可不要叫喊救命！"

翠翠说："鱼咬了我，也不管你的事。"

那黄狗好像明白翠翠被人欺侮了，又汪汪的吠起来，那男子把手中白鸭举起，向黄狗吓了一下，"老兄，你要怎么！"便走上河街去了。黄狗为了自己被欺侮还想追过去，翠翠便喊："狗，狗，你叫人也看人叫！"翠翠意思仿佛只在告给狗"那轻薄男子还不值得叫"，但男子听去的却是另外一种好意，男的以为是她要狗莫向好人乱叫，放肆的笑着，不见了。

又过了一阵，有人从河街拿了一个废缆做成的火炬一面晃着一面喊叫着翠翠的名字来找寻她，到身边时翠翠却不认识那个人。那人说：老船夫回到家中，不能来接她，故搭了过渡人口信来告翠翠，要她即刻就回去。翠翠听说是祖父派来的，就同那人一起回家，让打火把的在前引路，黄狗时前时后，一同沿了城墙向渡口走去。翠翠一面走一面问那拿火把的人，是谁告他就知道她在河边。那人说这是二老告他的，他是二老家里的伙计，送翠翠回家后还得回转河街。

翠翠说："二老他怎么知道我在河边？"

那人便笑着说："他从河里捉鸭子回来，在码头上见你，他说好意请你上家里坐坐，等候你爷爷，你还骂过他！你那只狗不识吕洞宾，只是叫！"

翠翠带了点儿惊讶轻轻的问："二老是谁？"

那人也带了点儿惊讶说："二老你还不知道？就是我们河街上的傩送二老！就是岳云！他要我送你回去！"

傩送二老在茶峒地方不是一个生疏的名字。

翠翠想起自己先前骂人那句话，心里又吃惊又害羞，再也不说什么，默默的随了那火把走去。

翻过了小山岨，望得见对溪家中火光时，那一方面也看见了翠翠方面的火把，老船夫即刻把船拉过来，一面拉船，一面哑声儿喊问："翠翠，翠翠，是不是你？"翠翠不理会祖父，口中却轻轻的说："不是翠翠，不是翠翠，翠翠早被大河里鲤鱼吃去了。"翠翠上了船，二老派来的人，打着火把走了，祖父牵着船问："翠翠，你怎么不答应我，生我的气了吗？"

翠翠站在船头还是不作声。翠翠对祖父那一点儿埋怨，等到把船拉过了溪，一到了家中，看明白了醉倒的另一个老人后，就完事了。但是另外一件事，属于自己不关祖父的，却使翠翠沉默了一个夜晚。

五

两年日子过去了。

这两年来两个中秋节，恰好无月亮可看，凡在这边城地方，因看月而起整夜男女唱歌的故事，通统不能如期举行，因此两个中秋留给翠翠的印象，极其平淡无奇。两个新年虽照例可以看到军营里和各乡来的狮子龙灯，在小教场迎春，锣鼓喧阗大热闹，到了十五夜晚，城中舞龙耍狮子的镇筸兵士，还各自赤裸着肩膊，往各处去欢迎炮仗烟火。城中军营里，税关局长公馆，河街上一些大字号，莫不预先截老毛竹筒，或镂空棕榈树根株，用洞硝拌和磺炭钢砂，一千槌八百槌把烟火做好。好勇取乐的军士，光赤着个上身，玩着灯打着鼓来了，小鞭炮如落雨的样子，从悬到长竿尖端的空中落到玩灯的光赤赤肩背上，锣鼓催动急促的拍子，大家情绪都为这事情十分兴奋。鞭炮放过一阵后，用长凳脚绑着的大筒烟火，在敞坪一端燃起了引线，先是嗞嗞的流泻白光，慢慢的这白光便吼啸起来，作出如雷如虎惊人的声音，白光向上空冲去，高至二十丈，下落时便洒散着满天花雨。人人把颈脖缩着，又怕又欢喜。玩灯的兵士，却在火花中绕着圈子，俨然毫不在意的样子。翠翠同她的祖父，也看过这样的热闹，留下一个热闹的印象，但这印象不知为什么原因，总不如那个端午所经过的事情甜而美。

翠翠为了不能忘记那件事，上年一个端午又同祖父到城边河街去看了半天船，一切玩得正好时，忽然落了行雨，无人衣衫不被雨湿透。为了避雨，祖孙二人同那只黄狗，走到顺顺吊脚楼上去，挤在一个角隅里。有人扛凳子从身边过去，翠翠认得那人正是去年打了火把送她回家的人，就告给祖父：

"爷爷，那个人去年送我回家，他拿了火把走路时，真像个山上的喽啰！”

祖父当时不作声，等到那人回头又走过面前时，就闪不知一把抓住那个人，笑嘻嘻说：

“嗨嗨，你这个喽啰！要你到我家喝一杯也不成，还怕酒里有毒，把你这个真命天子毒死！”

那人一看是守渡船的，且看到了翠翠，就笑了。“翠翠，你长大了！二老说你在河边大鱼会吃你，我们这里河中的鱼，现在可吞不下你了。”

翠翠一句话不说，只是抿起嘴唇笑着。

这一次虽在这喽啰长年口中听到个“二老”名字，却不曾见及这个人。从祖父和那长年谈话里，翠翠听明白了二老是在下游六百里外沅水中部青浪滩过端午的。但这次不见二老，却认识了大老，且见着了那个一地出名的顺顺。大老把河中的鸭子捉回家里后，因为守渡船的老家伙称赞了那只肥鸭两次，顺顺就要大老把鸭子给翠翠。且知道祖孙二人所过的日子，十分拮据，节日里自己不能包粽子，又送了许多尖角粽子。

那水上名人同祖父谈话时，翠翠虽装作眺望河中景致，耳朵却把每一句话听得清清楚楚。那人向祖父说翠翠长得很美，问过翠翠年纪，又问有不有了人家。祖父则很快乐的夸奖了翠翠不少，且似乎不许别人来关心翠翠的婚事，因此一到这件事便闭口不谈。

回家时，祖父抱了那只白鸭子同别的东西，翠翠打火把引路。两人沿城墙脚走去，一面是城，一面是水。祖父说：“顺顺真是个好人，大方得很。大老也很好。这一家人都好！”翠翠说：“一家人都好，你认识他们一家人吗？”祖父不明白这句话的意思所在，因为今天太高兴一点，便不加检点笑着说：“翠翠，假若大老要你做媳妇，请人来做媒，你答应不答应？”翠翠就说：“爷爷，你疯了！再说我就生你的气！”

祖父话虽不再说了，心中却很显然的还转着这些可笑的不好的念头。翠翠着了恼，把火炬向路两旁乱晃着，向前快快的走去了。

“翠翠，莫闹，我摔到河里去，鸭子会走脱的！”

“谁也不希罕那只鸭子！”

祖父明白翠翠为什么事情不高兴，便唱起摇橹人驶船下滩时催橹的

歌声,声音虽然哑沙沙的,字眼儿却稳稳当当毫不含糊。翠翠一面听着一面向前走去,忽然停住了发问:

“爷爷,你的船是不是正在下青浪滩呢?”

祖父不说什么,还是唱着,两人都记起顺顺家二老的船正在青浪滩过节,但谁也不明白另外一个人的记忆所止处。祖孙二人便沉默的一直走还家中。到了渡口,那另外一个代理看船的,正把船泊在岸边等候他们。几人渡过溪到了家中,剥粽子吃,到后那人要进城去,翠翠赶即为那人点上火把,让他有火把照路。人过了小溪上小山时,翠翠同祖父在船上望着,翠翠说:

“爷爷,看喽啰上山了啊!”

祖父把手攀引着横缆,注目溪面升起的薄雾,仿佛看到了另外一种什么东西,轻轻的吁了一口气。祖父静静的拉船过对岸家边时,要翠翠先上岸去,自己却守在船边,因为过节,明白一定有乡下人从城里看龙船,还得乘黑赶回家乡。

The Border Town (Chapters 1—5)

1

The highway running east from Szechuan to Hunan comes, just west of the border, to Chatung, a small town in the hills. Near by a stream flows past a small pagoda, at the foot of which lives a solitary household: an old man, a girl and a dog.

The stream winds down three *li* or so through the rocks to join the big river at Chatung, and once you cross the water it is only one *li* over the hills to the town. Since the channel curves like a bow, the path through the hills, like a bow-string, is slightly shorter. The stream bed, some twenty feet wide, is made up of boulders. In places the quiet waters are too deep for a pole to reach the bottom, yet so clear that you can count the fish swimming there. The water level fluctuates considerably, and while there is no money to build a bridge a ferry has been provided, a barge which holds about twenty men and horses—more than that and it has to make a second trip. A movable iron hoop is attached to a bamboo post in the bow while a hawser spans the stream. To cross, all you need do is slip the hoop over the hawser and pull yourself slowly to the other side. As the boat nears the bank, the ferryman with a shout of "Steady, now!" leaps ashore holding the hoop; then passengers and horses disembark to disappear over the hills. Since this ferry is public property, no toll is paid. If some well-meaning passenger tosses down a few coins, the ferryman picks them up one by one and thrusts them back into his hand, protesting almost truculently: "I'm paid for this job—three pecks of rice and seven hundred coins! I don't want your money!"

Some insist on paying, however, unable to look on with an easy conscience while hard work goes unrewarded. This upsets the ferryman, who, to ease his own conscience, gets someone to buy tea or tobacco leaves in town and keeps bundles of Chatung's best tobacco hanging from his girdle to offer cheerfully to all and sundry. When he senses a traveller's interest in this tobacco, he sticks a few leaves in his baggage-roll, saying, "Care for a smoke, brother? This is first-rate. Doesn't look much, with leaves as broad as the palm of your hand, but it has a mighty fine flavour. Makes a good present too!" The tea he brews in summer in a large pitcher for any thirsty passer-by.

This ferryman is the old fellow who lives just below the pagoda. Seventy now, he has stayed since the age of twenty beside this stream, ferrying countless passengers in fifty years. It is high time the sturdy old man retired, but evidently fate wills otherwise: no throwing in his hand for him. Without reflecting what this job means, he carries on quietly and faithfully. Fate, in his case, is the girl at his side who makes him feel the lure of life at sunrise and stops him from brooding about death at sunset. His sole companions are the ferry-boat and Brownie, the dog; his sole relation this girl.

The girl's mother, his only daughter, seventeen years ago had a love affair behind her father's back with a soldier at Chatung who serenaded her. He put her in the family way, but could only marry her if they eloped. For him that would have meant deserting his post, for her leaving her father all alone. Her lover knew that she dreaded the thought of eloping and shrank from spoiling his own record as a soldier; there seemed no way for them to live together, but nothing to prevent their dying together... and indeed a severe bout of illness carried him off. His sweetheart hesitated to follow him because of her unborn child. When this came to the knowledge of the ferryman, he uttered not a word of reproach but carried on quietly as if he knew nothing of the matter. Shame and pity kept the girl at her father's side. But as soon as her child was born she killed herself by drinking too much cold stream water. Miraculously the orphan survived: she is now a girl of fifteen. Because their home was among bamboos and hills of a glorious emerald green, the old boatman gave the poor mite the name Emerald.

Wind and sun have tanned the growing girl's skin, her eyes resting on green hills are as clear as crystal. Nature is her mother and teacher, making her innocent, lively and untamed as some small wild creature. She has the gentleness of a fawn and seems not to know the meaning of cruelty, anxiety or anger. Should a stranger on the ferry stare at her, she fixes her brilliant eyes on him as if ready to fly any instant to the mountains; but once she knows no harm is meant, she finishes her task calmly.

Rain or fine, the old man stays at his post. When passengers come he grasps the hawser and, straining forward, hauls the ferry across. Tired out, he lies down to sleep on a rock near by; and if someone hails them from the further shore Emerald will not let her grandfather get up but jumps aboard to take his place as nimbly as you could wish. Sometimes she and Brownie accompany him and she hauls on the hawser with him. As the ferry nears the bank and her grandfather calls, "Steady, now!" the dog bounds ashore with the rope in his mouth to tug the ferry in, proud of the part he is playing. The old man and his grand-daughter are familiar figures to the villagers round Chatung, and Brownie is a favourite with them too.

On a fine day when no one comes by to disturb them, the old man and Emerald may sit sunning themselves on a boulder in front of the door, or throw a stick from the cliff into the water to watch Brownie plunge in to retrieve it. Sometimes Emerald and the dog listen intently to her grandfather's tales of fighting in the town in years long past, or he and his grand-daughter play a wedding tune on their bamboo flutes. The arrival of a traveller makes the old man lay aside his flute and hurry down to ferry the stranger across. Then from the cliff the girl calls:

"I'll play, grandad, and you sing!"

The old man in midstream breaks into cheerful song, his hoarse voice mingling with the strains of the flute to float out into the stillness and bring new life to the stream. Indeed, the echoing music accentuates the stillness.

From east Szechuan sometimes come calves, flocks of sheep or a decorated bridal sedan-chair. Then Emerald insists on taking charge and, standing in the stern, pulls lazily on the hawser while the barge inches slowly across. She follows the calves, sheep or bridal-chair ashore, sees them up the hill and watches them vanish in the distance before turning back to take the boat home again. She imitates the bleating of the lambs, the lowing of the cows, or sticks a flower in her hair to play the part of a bride.

A bare *li* separates Chatung from the ferry. When the old man goes in to buy oil or salt or for New Year or some other festival, he likes to have a drink in town. If he stays at home, Brownie goes in with Emerald to buy what is needed. All she sees in the grocery impresses the girl: the stacks of vermicelli, the huge vats of sugar, the fire-crackers and red candles—she will talk about these for hours when she gets home. Moreover the riverside there is thronged with junks working their way upstream, with dozens of boatmen busy loading and unloading. And these vessels, so much larger and more exciting than their barge, have a vivid place in her recollections too.

2

Chatung stands wedged between the river and mountains, its wall in the rear coiling like a snake on the hillside. By the wharves outside the front section of the wall a host of small craft lie at anchor. These go downstream laden with *tung* oil, rock salt or the galls used in dyeing; and upstream with raw cotton, cotton yarn, textiles, miscellaneous goods or sea products. On the frontage between the wharves space is so limited that most houses are built on stilts overhanging the water. In spring the river rises imperceptibly till families living on the front throw long ladders from their roofs to the city wall and, swearing and shouting, lugging bundles, bedding and big rice containers, cross by these ladders into town. When the water recedes, they come out through the city gate. At times the river rises so suddenly that some houses on the front are swept away before the blank eyes of the watchers on the city wall, including the flood victims themselves, who take this loss as phlegmatically as any other natural calamity they are powerless to avert. Watchers on the wall can see houses, oxen, sheep and big trees washed down from the mountains on the swirling, foaming water which has overflown its banks. So men often wait in sampans where the current flows less strongly, in front of the Customs Boat, for instance; and as soon as an animal, tree, empty boat or one with a woman or child crying in it come into sight, they row off furiously to intercept it, and having lassoed it pull it back to the shore. These stout fellows are typical of the locality, being both profit-seeking and good-hearted. Whether out to save lives or salvage goods, they risk their necks cheerfully with a courage and resourcefulness beyond all praise.

This river, famed in history as the Yu, is now known as the White River. After reaching Chenchow where it mingles with the River Yuan, its waters grow turgid. But if you sail upstream, you can see clear to the bottom of pools thirty to fifty feet deep, so transparent is the water. In sunlight, even the white pebbles on the river bed and the veins on the cornelian pebbles stand out distinctly. The fish darting to and fro seem floating in air. The mountains on either side, covered with the tapering bamboos from which paper is made, are a deep, vivid emerald the whole year round. Most homesteads near the water are set among peach and apricot trees, so that in spring wherever there is blossom you can count on finding people, and wherever people are you can count on a drink. In summer the girls' purple tunics hung up to dry in the sun serve as flags to mark the whereabouts of men, while all through the middle reaches of the river in autumn and winter your eyes are caught by the cottages perched on crags over-hanging the water. With their brown mud walls, black tiles and perfect setting, they harmonize so completely with the surroundings that your heart leaps up in delight. Any traveller with the least feeling for poetry or painting could drift here without tiring for full thirty days in a small boat, for there are fresh marvels at every turn produced by man's labour and the bold skill of Nature which hold you utterly spellbound.

The White River rises on the Szechuan border, and in spring when the water is high small vessels can push up as far as Mount Hsiu in Szechuan. But Chatung is the last port on the Hunan border. Though the river is half a *li* wide here, in autumn and winter when the water falls it dwindles to a mere two hundred feet across, flowing through an expanse of black rocks. Since boats can go no further, all goods coming into Szechuan or leaving it are unloaded or loaded here. Coolies with carrying-poles of mulberry wood bring goods here for shipment east, while freight brought in is made up into loads here for porters to take on.

The town is garrisoned by a battalion reorganized from the old Green Battalion. There are about five hundred military households, some of which own fields in the hills or *tung* oil presses; some are small capitalists who have invested in oil, rice or cotton yarn; but most are soldiers' families drafted here. There is a revenue bureau too in the small temple at the end of the waterfront outside the city wall, which generally has a long notice posted up. The director of the bureau lives in the town. The old military yamen serves as barracks, but the soldiers' presence would probably pass unnoticed if not for the sentries who practise bugling every day on the wall. If you go into town during the day in winter, you see clothes and vegetables drying before every door, sweet potatoes hanging with trailing vines from the eaves, as well as sacks full of chestnuts, hazel-nuts or the like. Poultry cluck cheerfully. Men saw wood in front of their doors or chop firewood to stack in the yard, while middle-aged women in starched blue cotton clothes and flowered aprons chat to each other in the sunlight as they bend over their work. Peace reigns supreme and the townsfolk spend all their days in an unspoiled solitude hard to imagine. Tranquillity makes them reflect more deeply on life, makes them dream more. Naturally every soul in this little town in his allotted span of days has his private hopes and is torn by love and hate. Exactly what fills their minds it is hard to say. Those living high up in the town can watch the river from their doorsteps, the boats plying to and fro and the endless lines of towmen on the further bank. Some towmen from downstream bring superior cakes and foreign confectionery to sell in town when their junk moors: that is what a boat's arrival means to most children. As for the older folk, they raise a brood of chicks or a couple of pigs for the boatman in exchange for gold ear-rings, a few yards of strong blue material, a vat of good soyabean sauce or a handsome paraffin lamp—these are the chief concern of the housewives.

For all its quiet tranquillity, this little town is a centre of trade and communications for east Szechuan, and therefore the small waterfronts have a character all their own. There are inns where merchants put up, barbers' establishments, not to mention restaurants, general stores, oil and salt depots and draper's shops. There are ship-chandlers too, and "wharf-rats" who make a living by recruiting boatmen. The long tables in front of the modest eating houses often bear crisp brown carp fried with beancurd and garnished with slivers of red paprika in shallow dishes next to bamboo holders filled with scarlet chopsticks. For a few cents anyone can sit down at the table and pull out a pair of chopsticks. Then a woman with plucked eyebrows and a powdered face will come to ask: "Would you care for sweet wine or rice wine, master?" A spirited man who likes to tease will retort: "Sweet wine? What do you take me for—a child?" Then rich yellow wine is ladled out of the vat into an earthen bowl and brought promptly to the table. This potent, fragrant brew can knock a strong man out if he drinks too much. The general stores sell paraffin, paraffin lamps, candles and paper. The oil depots purchase *tung* oil. The salt merchants store the dark rock salt from Szechuan's salt wells. The drapers stock white cotton yarn, cloth, cotton and black silk headscarves. The ship-chandlers have everything a junk can need down to anchors weighing a good hundred catties displayed outside to tempt the customers in. The doors of the "wharf-rats" on the waterfront remain open all day long as in and out troop jolly boatmen or boat-owners in dark satin jackets over long gowns. These places are like tea-houses where no tea is sold. They are not opium dens, yet you can smoke opium there. Although men come here on business, from the boat-owners down to the oarsmen and towmen they make it a rule never to mention figures. Most of them drop in here to have a good time. They discuss local happenings, the state of trade in both provinces, and news from down-river. Meetings and financial transactions take place here too, not to mention dicing and gambling. But the two main items of business are deals in boats and in wives.

As trade in a town develops, so do parasites. And to cater for the merchants and boatmen, the shanties on the waterfront of the small town begin to house women of a special type who come in from the surrounding countryside or whose husbands, Szechuanese soldiers, have been drafted to Hunan and never returned. These women wear artificial silk tunics, flowered print trousers, and have long, arched eyebrows, big, lavishly scented chignons. They pass the day seated on stools at their doors embroidering red and green phoenixes on their slippers or waistbands for their lovers, one eye on the passers-by. Or they stare down from their windows at the junks being loaded and unloaded, or listen to the boatmen's chants as they swarm up the masts. At dusk they set to work in earnest, entertaining merchants and boatmen one after another.

Border ways are so simple that even these girls remain honest. Before entertaining a stranger, they ask for their money and count it before closing the door and getting down to business. But in the case of an old customer, the matter of payment is left up to him. Whereas most of the women's income comes from merchants, it is usually the boatmen who win their hearts. Two lovers at parting bite their lips and swear to go steady during their separation. For six or seven weeks maybe, the man on his boat and the girl on the waterfront wait for the long days to go by, the hearts of each with the loved one far away. The girls, especially, love so well that if one's sweetheart fails to return by the time appointed, she dreams of his boat putting in to shore and sees him bound down the gangway to run to her side. If she has begun to doubt him, she dreams of him singing to another woman, forgetting her. Then weaker spirits jump into the river or swallow opium in their dreams, while the bolder seize a chopper to take revenge. Although outside the pale of normal society, their love affairs too are attended by tears and laughter, and love and hate loom so large in their lives that passion can easily blind them to all around. Where they differ from other young people is simply in intensity of feeling—call it greater folly, if you like. Short-term engagements, long-term "marriages", or a temporary retirement—none of the simple folk there think any the worse of prostitutes for such behaviour, not using the standards of educated men to condemn them. Prostitutes they may be, yet setting such store by right, so little by profit, they are often more to be trusted than those gentlemen in the city who talk of nothing but morality and conscience.

The wharf-master, Hsun Hsun, served under the Ching dynasty banner before becoming an officer in the celebrated 49th Detachment of the revolutionary army in 1911. Whereas other officers made a name during the revolution or lost their heads, he went home with a game leg and invested his modest savings in a six-oared boat which he hired out to a poor boat-owner to ship goods between Chatung and Chenchow. His luck held for two years, and with the money he made he married a fairly well-to-do, good-looking widow. A few years later he had four boats, large and small, a wife and two sons.

Fortune smiled on this open-handed, easy-going man; but being a sociable fellow, quick to help those in distress, he never made a pile like some oil merchants. Having roughed it himself in the army, he knew the hardships of life on the road and could sympathize with the misfortunes of others; thus he gave unstinted help to boat-owners bankrupt through wrecks, demobilized soldiers on their way home, or needy scholars. This was how he disposed of the money he made on the river. In spite of his game leg he could still swim; and although he walked with a limp, he was straight as a die in his dealings. The regulation of the river traffic is a simple business, based on established custom. If two boats collide or one gets in another's way, there are time-honoured methods of settling the matter. But the arbitration has to be done by an elderly man whose integrity is beyond question. One autumn the old wharf-master died, and Hsun Hsun took his place. He was only fifty but so shrewd, honest and easy to get on with, so little interested in money, that no objections were raised on the score of his age.

Hsun Hsun's elder son is eighteen now, the younger sixteen. Strong as a pair of young oxen, good boatmen, swimmers and walkers, they excel in all the activities that village youngsters go in for. The elder takes after his father, being manly and open, impatient of meaningless conventions. The younger is quieter, more like his good-looking mother. One glance at his fine features and you can see that here is an intelligent, sensitive lad.

To toughen his sons, now that they are no longer boys, Hsun Hsun sends them out in turn on trips. They travel downstream on his boats sharing the discomforts and pleasures of the crew. Rowing, they pull the heaviest oar; towing, they head the team. Their food is salted fish, paprika and pickled vegetables; their bed the hard deck. At other times they trudge in straw sandals to east Szechuan with goods to sell at Mount Hsiu, Lungtan and Yuyang. Whatever the weather, cold, sweltering, wet or snowy, they have to make each stage on time. They carry knives so that, if set upon, they can draw to defend themselves, settling the dispute with blood if necessary. Knives are indispensable in these parts for dealing with enemies or for swearing friendship. And these youngsters lose no chance of using them. They have learned trading, the laws of hospitality, how to fit into a new place, and how to defend themselves and their good name. This upbringing is designed to teach them courage and give them a sense of values. As a result, Hsun Hsun's two lads are strong as tigers but pleasant-spoken and modest, with nothing in them of the loafer, braggart or bully. Indeed, they and their father are highly thought of in all the region round Chatung.

When the boys were young, Hsun Hsun realized that his first-born took after him and would have no trouble making his way in the world, while the younger boy was cast in a finer mould. He had a soft spot in his heart for the younger, giving him the name No-sung, his brother that of Tien-pao. And No-sung was such a fine-looking boy that the Chatung boatmen nicknamed him Yueh Yun.① For everyone's first impression of No-sung was that here was a Yueh Yun in white helmet and armour just off the stage.

3

The military commander in this area has succeeded so well in preserving the peace that for ten years and more there has been no serious disturbance at the border. Trade by land and water has not been disrupted by fighting or banditry. Order reigns and men live well content with their lot. The loss of a buffalo, the capsizing of a boat or a death in the family will plunge them into sorrow; for the rest, however, they seem quite untouched by the unhappy struggles going on elsewhere in the country.

The liveliest days in this border town are the Dragon Boat Festival, the Mid-Autumn Festival and the Spring Festival. The whole of Chatung makes as merry on these occasions as fifty years ago, and the local people have the time of their lives.

On the Dragon Boat Festival in the fifth month, women and children put on new clothes and paint the character for "king" on their foreheads with a mixture of realgar and yellow wine. Fish and meat are eaten by every family. The whole town sits down to lunch round about eleven, then doors are locked and they go out to watch the boatrace. Those with friends on the waterfront may go there; the rest flock to the wharves or the door of the Customs House. The race starts downstream just off Changtan and finishes at the Customs House. So today all the notables of the town, including army officers and customs officials, gather there to watch the fun. Preparations have been made well in advance, different groups choosing their strongest, ablest young men to practise rowing. The dragon boats are longer and narrower than ordinary sampans, with curved ends and sides painted with

---

① 译者注：Son of Yueh Fei, a brave patriotic general of the Sung dynasty, who fought against invaders. Yueh Yun is presented on the stage as a handsome and courageous young fighter.

vermilion stripes. They are stored in dry caves by the river for the rest of the year. Each boat seats twelve to eighteen oarsmen, a cox and two men to beat drums and gongs. Each rower has a short oar and the beat of the drum regulates their speed while the red-turbaned cox in the stern signals with two small flags the course to take. Generally the drum and gong are in the middle, and when the race reaches a critical stage they raise a din like thunder which, added to the roar of cheers and boos on the bank, reminds you of some epic river battle of old. The winning crew receives prizes at the Customs House: red silk and a small silver badge to be sported by one of the oarsmen as a sign of their stamina and co-ordination. To greet the victorious boat, the bluff army officers let off five hundred fire-crackers at the river's edge.

After the race, the notables enjoy themselves with the humble folk and add to the excitement of the day by getting soldiers to throw into the river thirty green-headed drakes with red cloth tied round their long necks. The best swimmers, soldiers or civilians, chase these birds, and whoever catches one keeps it. This provides a new spectacle—a river dotted with drakes chased by good swimmers.

The boatrace and the race between drakes and men continue till dusk falls.

Wharf-master Hsun Hsun was a champion swimmer who never failed to catch a drake. But No-sung, the year that he was ten, bagged a bird by swimming under water to it, after which Hsun Hsun told his sons, half in jest: "I can leave this to you now. No point in my competing with the two of you." So he no longer takes part in these races, though when it comes to saving someone from drowning he thinks nothing of jumping into the water. Even if he lives to be eighty, you may be sure Hsun Hsun will go through fire or flood to rescue someone in danger.

Tien-pao and No-sung are two of the best rowers and swimmers in these parts.

Now the Dragon Boat Festival is at hand again. The race will take place on the fifth. So on the first a meeting is held on the waterfront, and it is decided to lower the waterfront's boat that very morning. As it happens, Tien-pao has to set out today with some merchants to deliver festival goods to Lungtan; so it is left to No-sung to take part. Sixteen youngsters, strong as young oxen, carrying candles, fire-crackers and a big oxhide drum painted with a red diagram of the *yin* and *yang*,① march through the hills to where their boat is kept and, lighting the candles, carry it down to the water. Once aboard, they let off their firecrackers and with a great burst of drumming fly off like a featherless arrow downstream to Changtan.

That happens in the morning. After noon the fisherfolk on the further shore launch their dragon boat too and both crews begin training for the race. The first roll of drums on the water brings home to all who hear it the happy realization that the festival is at hand. The thoughts of the women on the waterfront who are waiting and longing for their lovers fly to the men far away. Many junks will hasten back for the festival, others will have to spend it far from home; and this makes it a time for rejoicing as well as for grieving. Some eyes in the little town shine with joy while others are dimmed with disappointment.

When the roll of drums carries over water and hills to the ferry, the first to hear it is Brownie. Barking wildly, he dashes round the house. Next time passengers are ferried across, he follows them up the east bank and races up the hill overlooking town, yapping frantically.

Emerald, seated on the rock outside their hut, has been plaiting locusts and centipedes out of palm leaves while Brownie slept in the sun. When he comes back from dashing round like a mad creature she scolds:

"Now then, Brownie! Behave yourself!"

But presently she too catches the distant drumming and starts racing round the house, then crosses the river with her dog to stand listening on the next hill, letting the intoxicating sound carry her back in fancy to a previous year.

---

① 译者注：A Taoist sign.

4

Two years before this, on the fifth of the fifth month, her grandfather found someone to mind the ferry while he took Brownie and Emerald into town to watch the dragon-boat race. The bank was thick with people as four long vermilion boats came rowing upstream. The river had just begun to rise and in the sunlight the water was pea-green. As the drums rolled, Emerald bit her lips, happier than words could tell. So many eager spectators were milling round that she did not notice when her grandfather disappeared, leaving her with Brownie.

Her eyes on the boats, she thought: "Grandad will soon be back." But as time went by she began to be rather worried. The day before he had asked: "If you went alone to see the boatrace tomorrow, would you be afraid of the crowds?" "No, I wouldn't," she said. "But it's no fun all alone." At that he bethought himself of an old friend in town and went in that same night to ask him to see to the ferry for one day, so that he could give Emerald a good time. Since this friend lived all alone without even a dog, they invited him to a meal and to drink some yellow wine with a pinch of realgar. The meal at an end and the job handed over, the others set off. On the road, her grandfather said: "There's a fearful crowd there, lass. It's a regular bedlam. Dare you watch from the bank alone?" "Of course I dare," she said. "But it's dull on your own." Once by the river, the boats claimed all her attention. The ferryman thought, "There's still a good three or four hours to go. My friend oughtn't to miss this. I'll go back and change with him." He told Emerald: "There's such a mob here, don't move away. I've something to do, but I'll be back for sure to take you home." Intent on two boats now abreast, she agreed without thinking. And knowing that Brownie would guard her, the old man left.

He found his friend at the foot of the white pagoda straining his ears to catch the sounds in the distance.

He called him to bring the boat over, and they crossed back to stand by the pagoda together. The ferryman explained his return, concluding, "Don't trouble to come back if you're enjoying yourself. Just tell Emerald to come home when everything's over. If she's scared, you might bring her back." His old crony had no wish to watch the race, however, preferring to sit and drink a few cups by the stream. The old man gladly fetched out a gourdful of wine and shoved it towards him. So they drank, talking over festivals long gone by, till his friend fell into a drunken sleep on the rock.

A drunken man could not go to town and the ferryman did not like to leave his post. Meanwhile Emerald down by the river started to fret.

After the race, some army officers sent out sampans to drop ducks into the water; but still there was no sign of her grandfather. On the chance that he was waiting somewhere else, she and Brownie searched through the crowd, but all in vain. It would soon be dusk. The soldiers who had brought out benches were carting them home again. Only a few drakes were still at large on the river, while the number of their pursuers was dwindling too. As the setting sun fell on the girl's home upstream, a fearful thought crossed her mind: "Can grandad be dead?"

He had told her to stay where she was, and to disprove her wild notion she assured herself that some friend must have kept him drinking. Since this was highly likely, she decided against going home with Brownie before it was really dark. Instead she stood there waiting on the wharf.

Presently the two dragon boats from the further bank rowed into a backwater and disappeared. Most of the spectators had scattered. Lights had been lit in the brothels, where girls were singing to the accompaniment of tambourines and guitars. From other houses came shouts of men in their cups playing the finger-game.① On some boats moored near by supper was being prepared: greens and turnips hissed and spluttered in boiling fat. Daylight

---

① 译者注：A traditional Chinese game played at drinking feasts. The two contestants stretch out a hand each indicating any number between zero and five and call out a number up to ten supposed to be the sum total of the two hands. The one who calls the correct total wins and the loser must drink a cup as forfeit.

was fast fading on the river, where only one solitary white duck was floating, pursued by one solitary swimmer.

Still Emerald stayed where she was, sure that her grandfather would fetch her.

The singing in the houses grew louder, and a boatman on a junk close by remarked: "Chin-ting! Isn't that your girl singing to some fat Szechuanese while he swills his wine? Like to bet on it?" Another boatman retorted: "When she sings for other fellows, she thinks of me. She knows I'm here."

"Get on! When she's in another man's arms, she thinks of you? Prove it!"

"All right. I will."

He whistled a few notes, and almost at once the singing upstairs stopped. The two boatmen roared with laughter. They went on to discuss that particular woman in language so coarse that it grated on Emerald's ears, but she could not go away. When one remarked that the prostitute's father had been murdered seven years earlier on Cotton Hill, slashed with seventeen knives, Emerald's mind was troubled again with the strange notion: "Can grandad be dead?"

The two boatmen went on talking while the white duck floated slowly towards Emerald's wharf and she thought, "If you come any closer, I'll grab at you!" She waited quietly till the duck was about thirty feet from the bank when the boatmen were hailed with a laugh by a swimmer in the water who had caught the duck. They called back through the gloaming: "Good for you, Number Two! How many did you catch today—five?"

"This one was a cunning old bird." replied the swimmer. "But I bagged it in the end."

"You'll be just as good at bagging women one of these days!"

The swimmer made no reply but struck out to the wharf. As he climbed ashore, dripping, Brownie set up a great barking to indicate the presence of his young mistress, and the swimmer caught sight of Emerald. Apart from her the wharf was deserted.

"Who are you?" he asked.

"Emerald."

"Who's Emerald?"

"My grandad's ferryman at the Green Stream."

"This is no ferry. What are you doing here?"

"Waiting for grandad. He's going to take me home."

"He can't be coming. Must have gone to the barracks to have a drink, got drunk and been carried home."

"My granddad's not like that. If he said he'd come, he will."

"Well, don't wait here. Come to my house—that one with the lamps—and wait for him there."

Emerald's ears were still tingling from the boatmen's coarse talk so that she misunderstood this well-meant invitation and thought he wanted her to go to the building where a woman was singing. She had never flown out at anyone before, but now, troubled by her grandfather's long delay and afraid she was being insulted, she swore under her breath:

"To hell with this hooligan!"

Low as the words were, he caught them, and realized that she was no more than a girl. "Such language from a child!" he teased, chuckling. "If you stay here, mind a big fish doesn't bite you—don't expect me to rescue you!"

"Whether it bites me or not, that's none of your business!"

Brownie started barking again, as if aware that his mistress was offended. The young man shook the white duck in his hand at the dog. "Hey there! What's wrong with you?" Then he walked away. Brownie would have chased angrily after, but Emerald cried: "Quiet, Brownie! Never mind him!" She meant that a fellow like this was beneath their notice, but the young man took her words in good part and laughed heartily as he was lost to sight.

Presently a man with a torch made of old cordage approached from the waterfront, waving his torch and calling Emerald's name. But when he reached her the girl saw he was a stranger. He told her the ferryman couldn't come for her but had sent a message asking her to go straight home. Since he brought word from her grandfather, Emerald let him lead the way with his torch while Brownie circled round the pair of them as they skirted the city wall and made for the ferry. Emerald asked how he had known where she was. He said Number Two had told him. He worked in Number Two's house and would have to go back as soon as he had seen her to the ferry.

"How did Number Two know where I was?"

"He saw you on the wharf when he came back from catching ducks. Said he asked you to wait in our house, but only got cursed for his pains! And your dog took him for a bad lot and kept on barking!"

"Who is Number Two?" she asked in astonishment.

"Don't you know Number Two?" It was his turn to be astonished. "No-sung, of course. The Yueh Yun of the waterfront. He told me to see you home."

No-sung's name was so well-known in Chatung that Emerald, abashed to have sworn at him, said no more but followed the torch-bearer in silence.

Soon they rounded the hill and saw the lights in the hut across the stream. That same moment her grandfather saw the torch and promptly brought the boat over, calling gruffly: "Emerald! Is that you, Emerald?" His grand-daughter made no answer, but whispered to herself: "No, it's not Emerald. Emerald's been eaten by the big fish in the river." Once she was aboard, the man with the torch turned back. Pulling on the hawser, her grandfather demanded, "Why don't you say anything, lass? Angry with me?"

She just stood in the stern without a word. But once home her indignation melted away when she saw the other old man in a drunken stupor. Some secret reflections, though, kept her quiet and thoughtful the whole of that evening.

5

Two years have passed since then.

Both years saw moonless Mid-Autumn Festivals, so that the young folk could not stay up all night, as the custom in this border region is, to watch the moon and sing; and accordingly both festivals made little impression on Emerald. Each Spring Festival, though, lion dances and processions of dragon lanterns were arranged by the garrison and villagers from the countryside around; gongs and drums made a cheerful din at the ceremony to welcome spring, while on the evening of the fifteenth the troops, stripped to the waist, performed dragon and lion dances and were welcomed everywhere by fire-crackers and fireworks. In the barracks, the residence of the chief of Customs and some of the larger shops on the waterfront, they prepared fireworks by cutting lengths of bamboo or hollowing out the stems of coir palms and filling eight hundred or a thousand of these tubes with nitre, sulphur and charcoal. Bold soldiers bent on pleasure marched in a gay procession with lanterns and drums, while bundles of fire-crackers on long poles rained down upon their naked arms and shoulders, and the frenzied beating of gongs and drums added to the general excitement. After a burst of fire-crackers, they lit the fuses of the big fireworks tied to the legs of stools in the square. Then sizzling white streaks of light shot up two hundred feet with a roar like thunder, to sprinkle the whole sky with sparks as they came down. The spectators ducked nervously yet joyfully. But the soldiers paraded their lanterns through the shower of sparks most splendidly unperturbed. Emerald and her grandfather watched and shared in the excitement; yet the impression left on her was less vividly sweet than her recollection of that earlier Dragon Boat Festival.

Under the spell of this memory, she went to the river to watch the last dragon-boat race; but just when everything was most exciting, it started to rain and everybody was soaked. To shelter from the rain the ferryman took her and Brownie to Hsun Hsun's house, where they found themselves a corner. Someone walked past carrying a stool, and Emerald recognized the man who had escorted her back with a torch.

"Grandad!" she whispered. "That's the man who saw me home that year. He led the way with a torch like an outlaw from the hills."

Her grandfather said nothing, but next time the man passed he seized him and called with a laugh:

"Hey, there, outlaw! You wouldn't come in and have a drink with me. Afraid I'd poison a big man like you, eh?"

When the other recognized the ferryman, he grinned. "You've grown, Emerald," he remarked. "Number Two said the big fish in our river would eat you. Now none of our fish here could swallow you."

The girl said nothing but dimpled.

Number Two was nowhere to be seen, however. From the men's conversation, Emerald learned that he was spending this festival six hundred *li* away at Green Wave Rapids in the middle reaches of the Yuan. She met his elder brother, though, and the celebrated Hsun Hsun. Number One brought home a duck he had caught in the river, and when the old ferryman remarked on its plumpness, Hsun Hsun told his son to give the bird to Emerald. Moreover, knowing that she and her grandfather lived in too humble a way to make *tsung tzu*① for the festival, he gave them a great bundle of pointed *tsung tzu*.

While the famed wharf-master and her grandfather were talking, Emerald kept her eyes on the river; but this did not stop her from catching every word. Observing that she had grown into a lovely girl, Hsun Hsun asked her age and whether she were betrothed. Her grandfather, in high good humour, spoke of Emerald in glowing terms but said nothing about her marriage, as if this could be no concern of anyone else.

Going home, he carried the duck and other things while she led the way with a torch. They skirted the city wall, walking by the river. "Hsun Hsun's

---

① 译者注：Glutinous rice wrapped in palm leaves, often stuffed with sweetmeats, always eaten during the Dragon Boat Festival.

one of the best," said her grandfather. "Open-handed. And Number One is a good youngster too. It's a fine family!"

"Do you know the whole family?"

He missed the point of this question and because he was in such good spirits asked impulsively: "If Number One wanted you, lass, and sent over a go-between, would you have him?"

"Are you out of your mind, grandad? Don't talk such nonsense!"

The old man kept silent, but he was obviously turning over this ridiculous notion in his head. In her annoyance Emerald raced on in front, swinging the torch from side to side.

"Steady on, child! If I fall into the river, this duck will get away."

"Who wants their duck?"

Knowing why she was annoyed, the old man sang the shanty of oarsmen shooting the rapids. Though his voice was gruff, he sang clearly. Emerald listened, then halted suddenly to ask:

"Grandad, is your boat going down the Green Wave Rapids?"

Instead of answering, he went on singing. Both knew that Number Two was at Green Wave Rapids, but neither guessed what was in the other's mind. Without further speech the old man and girl made their way home. At the ferry, his substitute had the boat waiting. They crossed to the hut and stripped off the wrappings round the *tsung tzu*. After the meal the other man rose to leave, and Emerald made haste to light a torch for him. When they had crossed the stream, she and her grandfather stood in the boat while their friend climbed up the hill.

"Grandad!" said Emerald. "Watch the outlaw climb the mountain!"

The old man, his hand on the hawser, kept unseeing eyes on the mist rising from the stream, and a soft sigh escaped him. Having pulled the barge gently back to the other side, he told Emerald to go on in while he waited there, for during this festival there were bound to be villagers coming back in the dark after watching the race in town.

三

荷花淀——白洋淀纪事之二①

孙　犁

月亮升起来，院子里凉爽得很，干净得很，白天破好的苇眉子潮润润的，正好编席。女人坐在小院当中，手指上缠绞着柔滑修长的苇眉子。苇眉子又薄又细，在她怀里跳跃着。

要问白洋淀有多少苇地？不知道。每年出多少苇子？不知道。只晓得，每年芦花飘飞苇叶黄的时候，全淀的芦苇收割，垛起垛来，在白洋淀周围的广场上，就成了一条苇子的长城。女人们，在场里院里编着席。编成了多少席？六月里，淀水涨满，有无数的船只，运输银白雪亮的席子出口，不久，各地的城市村庄，就全有了花纹又密、又精致的席子用了。大家争着买：

"好席子，白洋淀席！"

这女人编着席。不久在她的身子下面，就编成了一大片。她象坐在一片洁白的雪地上，也象坐在一片洁白的云彩上。她有时望望淀里，淀里也是一片银白世界。水面笼起一层薄薄透明的雾，风吹过来，带着新鲜的荷叶荷花香。

但是大门还没关，丈夫还没回来。

很晚丈夫才回来了。这年轻人不过二十五六岁，头戴一顶大草帽，上身穿一件洁白的小褂，黑单裤卷过了膝盖，光着脚。他叫水生，小苇庄的

---

① 中文选自：孙犁．荷花淀．北京：人民文学出版社，1979；英译文选自：Sun，L. *The Blacksmith and the Carpenter*. Gladys Yang（trans.）. Beijing：Chinese Literature Press，1982.

游击组长，党的负责人。今天领着游击组到区上开会去来。女人抬头笑着问：

“今天怎么回来的这么晚？”站起来要去端饭。水生坐在台阶上说：

“吃过饭了，你不要去拿。”

女人就又坐在席子上。她望着丈夫的脸，她看出他的脸有些红涨，说话也有些气喘。她问：

“他们几个哩？”

水生说：

“还在区上。爹哩？”

女人说：

“睡了。”

“小华哩？”

“和他爷爷去收了半天虾篓，早就睡了。他们几个为什么还不回来？”

水生笑了一下。女人看出他笑的不象平常。

“怎么了，你？”

水生小声说：

“明天我就到大部队上去了。”

女人的手指震动了一下，想是叫苇眉子划破了手，她把一个手指放在嘴里吮了一下。水生说：

“今天县委召集我们开会。假若敌人再在同口安上据点，那和端村就成了一条线，淀里的斗争形势就变了。会上决定成立一个地区队。我第一个举手报了名的。”

女人低着头说：

“你总是很积极的。”

水生说：

“我是村里的游击组长，是干部，自然要站在头里，他们几个也报了名。他们不敢回来，怕家里的人拖尾巴。公推我代表，回来和家里人们说一说。他们全觉得你还开明一些。”

女人没有说话。过了一会，她才说：

“你走，我不拦你，家里怎么办？”

水生指着父亲的小房叫她小声一些。说：

“家里，自然有别人照顾。可是咱的庄子小，这一次参军的就有七个。庄上青年人少了，也不能全靠别人，家里的事，你就多做些，爹老了，小华还不顶事。”

女人鼻子里有些酸，但她并没有哭。只说：

“你明白家里的难处就好了。”

水生想安慰她。因为要考虑准备的事情还太多，他只说了两句：

“千斤的担子你先担吧，打走了鬼子，我回来谢你。”

说罢，他就到别人家里去了，他说回来再和父亲谈。

鸡叫的时候，水生才回来。女人还是呆呆的坐在院子里等他，她说：

“你有什么话嘱咐我吧！”

“没有什么话了，我走了，你要不断进步，识字，生产。”

“嗯。”

“什么事也不要落在别人后面！”

“嗯，还有什么？”

“不要叫敌人汉奸捉活的。捉住了要和他拼命。”这才是那最重要的一句，女人流着眼泪答应了他。

第二天，女人给他打点好一个小小的包裹，里面包了一身新单衣，一条新毛巾，一双新鞋子。那几家也是这些东西，交水生带去。一家人送他出了门。父亲一手拉着小华，对他说：

“水生，你干的是光荣事情，我不拦你，你放心走吧。大人孩子我给你照顾，什么也不要惦记。”

全庄的男女老少也送他出来，水生对大家笑一笑，上船走了。

女人们到底有些藕断丝连。过了两天，四个青年妇女集在水生家里来，大家商量：

“听说他们还在这里没走。我不拖尾巴，可是忘下了一件衣裳。”

“我有句要紧的话得和他说说。”

水生的女人说：

“听他说鬼子要在同口安据点……”

“那里就碰得那么巧，我们快去快回来。”

“我本来不想去，可是俺婆婆非叫我再去看看他，有什么看头啊！”

于是这几个女人偷偷坐在一只小船上，划到对面马庄去了。

到了马庄，她们不敢到街上去找，来到村头一个亲戚家里。亲戚说：你们来的不巧，昨天晚上他们还在这里，半夜里走了，谁也不知开到哪里去。你们不用惦记他们，听说水生一来就当了副排长，大家都是欢天喜地的……

几个女人羞红着脸告辞出来，摇开靠在岸边上的小船。现在已经快到晌午了，万里无云，可是因为在水上，还有些凉风。这风从南面吹过来，从稻秧上苇尖吹过来。水面没有一只船，水像无边的跳荡的水银。

几个女人有点失望，也有些伤心，各人在心里骂着自己的狠心贼。可是青年人，永远朝着愉快的事情想，女人们尤其容易忘记那些不痛快。不久，她们就又说笑起来了。

“你看说走就走了。”

“可慌(高兴的意思)哩，比什么也慌，比过新年，娶新——也没见他这么慌过！”

“拴马桩也不顶事了。”

“不行了，脱了缰了！”

“一到军队里，他一准得忘了家里的人。”

“那是真的，我们家里住过一些年轻的队伍，一天到晚仰着脖子出来唱，进去唱，我们一辈子也没那么乐过。等他们闲下来没有事了，我就傻想：该低下头了吧。你猜人家干什么？用白粉子在我家映壁上画上许多圆圈圈，一个一个蹲在院子里，托着枪瞄那个，又唱起来了！”

她们轻轻划着船，船两边的水哗，哗，哗。顺手从水里捞上一棵菱角来，菱角还很嫩很小，乳白色。顺手又丢到水里去。那棵菱角就又安安稳稳浮在水面上生长去了。

“现在你知道他们到了哪里？”

“管他哩,也许跑到天边上去了!”

她们都抬起头往远处看了看。

“唉呀！那边过来一只船。”

“唉呀！日本,你看那衣裳!”

“快摇!”

小船拼命往前摇。她们心里也许有些后悔,不该这么冒冒失失走来;也许有些怨恨那些走远了的人。但是立刻就想,什么也别想了,快摇,大船紧紧追过来了。

大船追的很紧。

幸亏是这些青年妇女,白洋淀长大的,她们摇的小船飞快。小船活象离开了水皮的一条打跳的梭鱼。她们从小跟这小船打交道,驶起来,就象织布穿梭,缝衣透针一般快。

假如敌人追上了,就跳到水里去死吧!

后面大船来的飞快。那明明白白是鬼子！这几个青年妇女咬紧牙制止住心跳,摇橹的手并没有慌,水在两旁大声哗哗,哗哗,哗哗哗!

“往荷花淀里摇！那里水浅,大船过不去。”

她们奔着那不知道有几亩大小的荷花淀去,那一望无边际的密密层层的大荷叶,迎着阳光舒展开,就象铜墙铁壁一样。粉色荷花箭高高的挺出来,是监视白洋淀的哨兵吧!

她们向荷花淀里摇,最后,努力的一摇,小船窜进了荷花淀。几只野鸭扑楞楞飞起,尖声惊叫,掠着水面飞走了。就在她们的耳边响起一排枪!

整个荷花淀全震荡起来。她们想,陷在敌人的埋伏里了,一准要死了,一齐翻身跳到水里去。渐渐听清楚枪声只是向着外面,她们才又扒着船帮露出头来。她们看见不远的地方,那宽厚肥大的荷叶下面,有一个人的脸,下半截身子长在水里。荷花变成人了？那不是我们的水生吗？又往左右看去,不久各人就找到了各人丈夫的脸,啊！原来是他们!

但是那些隐蔽在大荷叶下面的战士们,正在聚精会神瞄着敌人射击,半眼也没有看她们。枪声清脆，三五排枪过后，他们投出了手榴弹，冲出了荷花淀。

手榴弹把敌人那只大船击沉，一切都沉下去了。水面上只剩下一团烟硝火药气味。战士们就在那里大声欢笑着，打捞战利品。他们又开始了沉到水底捞出大鱼来的拿手戏。他们争着捞出敌人的枪枝、子弹带，然后是一袋子一袋子叫水浸透了的面粉和大米。水生拍打着水去追赶一个在水波上滚动的东西，是一包用精致纸盒装着的饼干。

妇女们带着浑身水，又坐到她们的小船上去了。

水生追回那个纸盒，一只手高高举起，一只手用力拍打着水，好使自己不沉下去。对着荷花淀吆喝：

"出来吧，你们！"

好象带着很大的气。

她们只好摇着船出来。忽然从她们的船底下冒出一个人来，只有水生的女人认的那是区小队的队长。这个人抹一把脸上的水问她们：

"你们干什么去来呀？"

水生的女人说：

"又给他们送了一些衣裳来！"

小队长回头对水生说：

"都是你村的？"

"不是她们是谁，一群落后分子！"说完把纸盒顺手丢在女人们船上，一泅，又沉到水底下去了，到很远的地方才钻出来。

小队长开了个玩笑，他说：

"你们也没有白来，不是你们，我们的伏击不会这么彻底。可是，任务已经完成，该回去晒晒衣裳了。情况还紧得很！"

战士们已经把打捞出来的战利品，全装在他们的小船上，准备转移。一人摘了一片大荷叶顶在头上，抵挡正午的太阳。几个青年妇女把掉在水里又捞出来的小包裹，丢给了他们，战士们的三只小船就奔着东南方向，箭一样飞去了。不久就消失在中午水面上的烟波里。

几个青年妇女划着她们的小船赶紧回家，一个个象落水鸡似的。一路走着，因过于刺激和兴奋，她们又说笑起来，坐在船头脸朝后的一个噘着嘴说：

“你看他们那个横样子，见了我们爱搭理不搭理的！”

“啊，好象我们给他们丢了什么人似的。”

她们自己也笑了，今天的事情不算光彩，可是：

“我们没枪，有枪就不往荷花淀里跑，在大淀里就和鬼子干起来！”

“我今天也算看见打仗了。打仗有什么出奇，只要你不着慌，谁还不会趴在那里放枪呀！”

“打沉了，我也会浮水捞东西，我管保比他们水式好，再深点我也不怕！”

“水生嫂，回去我们也成立队伍，不然以后还能出门吗！”

“刚当上兵就小看我们，过二年，更把我们看得一钱不值了，谁比谁落后多少呢！”

这一年秋季，她们学会了射击。冬天，打冰夹鱼的时候，她们一个个登在流星一样的冰船上，来回警戒。敌人围剿那百顷大苇塘的时候，她们配合子弟兵作战，出入在那芦苇的海里。

Lotus Creek

Sun Li

It was a summer night in the year 1940. The moon had risen and the little courtyard was delightfully fresh and clean. The rushes split during the day were damp and supple, just waiting to be woven into mats. A woman was sitting in the yard plaiting the long soft rushes with nimble fingers. The thin, fine strands leaped and twisted in her arms.

Baiyangdian lies in the middle of the province of Hebei and is known all over China for its reeds and rushes. I can't tell you the exact area grown with them nor the yearly output. All I know is that each year when the rush flowers blow in the breeze and the leaves turn yellow, the whole crop is cut and stacked in the squares round Baiyangdian like a Great Wall of reeds. The women plait mats in their threshing-fields or courtyards, vast quantities of silvery, snow-white mats. And in June, when the water in the creek is high, countless boats ship them away, until soon towns and villages in all parts of the country have these finely woven mats with their lovely designs.

"Baiyangdian mats are best," is quite an axiom.

The young woman in the yard was plaiting a mat, seated on the long stretch of it already accomplished where she seemed enthroned on virgin snow or on a fleecy cloud. From time to time she strained her eyes towards the creek, another world of silver white. Light, translucent mist had risen over the water, and the breeze was laden with the scent of fresh lotus leaves.

The gate was still open—her husband wasn't home yet.

It was very late before her husband came home. He was twenty-five or twenty-six, a barefoot young fellow in a large straw hat, a spotless white shirt and black trousers rolled up over his knees. His name was Shusheng and he was chief of the anti-Japanese guerrillas in Lesser Reed Village, as well as the leader of the Communist Party branch there. Today he had taken his men to the district town for a meeting. His wife looked up with a smile as he came in.

"What kept you so long today?"

She stood up to fetch him some food. Shusheng sat on the steps.

"Never mind about that—I've eaten."

She sat down on the mat again. Her husband's face was rather flushed and he seemed out of breath.

"Where are the others?" she asked.

"Still in town. How's Dad?"

"Asleep."

"And Xiaohua?"

"He was out half the day with his grandad shrimping and went to bed hours ago. Why haven't the others come back?"

Shusheng gave a forced laugh.

"What's wrong with you?"

"I'm joining the army tomorrow," he said softly.

His wife's hand twitched as if a reed had cut it, and she started sucking one finger.

"The district committee called this meeting today. Very soon now, they say, the Japs are going to try to set up more bases. If they manage to get a base at Tongkou—which is only a few dozen *li* away—that will alter our position here completely. The meeting decided to form a district brigade to keep the Japs out. I was the first to volunteer to go."

His wife lowered her head and muttered:

"Always a step ahead of the others, aren't you?"

"I'm chief of our village guerrillas and one of the cadres: of course I have to take the lead. The others volunteered too. They didn't dare come home, though, for fear their folk would try to hold them back. They chose me to come back and explain things for them to their families. Everyone felt you had more sense than most wives."

His wife digested this in silence.

"I won't try to stop you," she said presently. "But what about us?"

Shusheng pointed to his father's room and told her to keep her voice down.

"You'll be taken care of, naturally. But our village is small and seven fellows are joining the army this time. That doesn't leave many young men at home. We can't look to others for everything: the main burden will fall on you. Dad's old and Xiaohua's too young to do much."

His wife felt a lump in her throat but held back the tears.

"So long as you know what we're up against, that's all."

Shusheng wanted to comfort her but time was short. He still had many things to do before leaving.

"You shoulder the load while I'm away. When we've driven the Japs out and I come home, I'll make it up to you."

With this, Shusheng set off for some neighbours' houses, promising to come back and explain matters to his father.

He didn't come back till cock-crow. His wife was still sitting like a statue in the yard, waiting.

"What instructions have you got for me?"she asked.

"Nothing really. Mind you go on making progress while I'm away. Work hard and learn to read and write."

"Uh-huh."

"Don't fall behind the others."

"Uh-huh. What else?"

"Don't let the Japs or traitors take you alive. If you're caught, fight to the finish." This was the main thing he had to say, and his wife assented in tears.

When day broke she made a little bundle of a new cotton suit, a new towel, a new pair of cloth shoes. The other wives had similar bundles for

Shusheng to take. The whole family saw him off. His father, holding Xiaohua's hand, said:

"You're doing the right thing, Shusheng, so I won't stop you. Go with an easy mind. I'll look after your wife and boy for you, don't worry."

The whole village, men and women, young and old, turned out to see him off. Shusheng grinned at them all, stepped into a boat and rowed off.

But there must be something of the clinging vine about women. Two days after Shusheng left, four young wives gathered in his house to talk things over.

"Apparently they're still here: they haven't gone yet. I don't want to cause problems, but there's a jacket I forgot to give him."

"I've something important to say to him."

Shusheng's wife said:

"I heard that the Japs want to set up a base at Tongkou...."

"There's not a chance of our running into them, not if we pay a flying visit."

"I didn't mean to go, but my mother-in-law insists that I ought to see him. What for, I'd like to know?"

Without breathing a word to anyone, the four of them took a small boat and paddled to Ma Village across the river.

They dared not look for their husbands openly there but went to a relative's house at one end of the village.

"You've just missed them," they were told. "They were still here yesterday evening but left some time in the night. No one knows where they've gone. You've no call to worry, though. I hear Shusheng was made a vice-platoon leader straight off: they're all in tremendous spirits."

Shame-faced and blushing, the women took their leave and rowed off again. It was nearly noon, without a cloud in the sky, but on the river was a breeze from the paddy fields and rushes in the south. Theirs was the only boat afloat on this endless expanse of water like rippling quicksilver.

Disappointed and rather upset, each woman was secretly laying the blame on her heartless brute of a husband. But young people are incurably optimistic and women have a special knack of forgetting their troubles. Very soon they were laughing and chattering again.

"So they just up and left!"

"I'm sure they're having the time of their lives. This means more to them than New Year or getting married."

"They're like wild horses: they won't stay tied up in a stable."

"No, they all break away."

"Take it from me, that man of mine hasn't given one thought to his home since he joined the army."

"That's true. Some young soldiers once stayed in our house. Singing from dawn to dusk they were. We've never larked like that! I was fool enough to think that once they had nothing to do, they'd start looking glum. But what do you suppose? They painted a whole set of white circles on our courtyard wall, and squatted down one by one for target practice, still singing all the time!"

They paddled easily along while water gurgled on each side of the boat. One of them scooped up a water chestnut, still tiny and milky white. She threw it back into the river. The water chestnut floated placidly there, where it would grow.

"I wonder where they've gone."

"He can go to the end of the earth for all I care!"

"Look! A boat!"

They all raised their heads and gazed into the distance.

"Why, they're Japanese soldiers—see that uniform!"

"Quick!"

They rowed on for dear life. One started wishing they had never taken such a risk, another blaming the husbands who had deserted them. But in no time they put these thoughts out of their heads. They must row fast—the larger boat was coming after them.

The Japanese were going as swiftly as they could.

It was lucky that all these young wives had grown up by the river: their boat went like the wind. It shot forward like some flying fish, hardly skimming the water. They had been in and out of boats since they were children, and could paddle as fast as they could spin or sew.

If the enemy overtook them, they would drown themselves in the river.

The large boat was making quick headway. No doubt about it, those were Japanese. The young women clenched their teeth and fought down their panic. They did not let their hands tremble. The oars plashed loudly, steadily through the water.

"Head for Lotus Creek! It's too shallow for a boat that size."

They raced for the creek, a good many *mu* in extent, where as far as eye could see massed lotus leaves reached towards the genial sun like a solid wall of bronze. Their pink buds, thrust up like arrows, seemed sentinels watching over Baiyangdian.

They rowed for the creek and with one final effort drove their small craft in among the lotus. Some wild ducks flapped their wings and flew off with shrill cries, whirring low over the water. A volley of shots rang out!

Pandemonium broke loose. Sure that they had fallen into an enemy ambush with no hope of escape, they jumped all together into the water. But presently, realizing that all the shots were aimed towards the river, they caught hold of the boat's side and peered cautiously out. Not far away under a broad lotus leaf they saw a man's head—the rest of him was submerged. It was Shusheng. Looking right and left, each soon discovered her husband—so this was where they were!

But the men under the lotus leaves were too busy aiming at the enemy to so much as glance at their wives. Quick shots rang out, and after four or five volleys they threw hand-grenades and rushed forward.

The grenades sank the enemy boat with everything on board, leaving nothing but smoke and fumes of saltpetre on the surface. With shouts and laughter, the men started salvaging trophies. They dived as if they were after fish. They raced to retrieve enemy rifles, cartridge belts, and sack after sack of dripping flour and rice. Shusheng swam with a great splashing after a carton of biscuits bobbing on the waves.

Soaked to the skin, the wives climbed back into their boat.

Holding the biscuits high in one hand and paddling hard with the other, Shusheng shouted towards them:

"Come out of that, you!"

He sounded angry.

They rowed out—what else could they do? Without warning a man popped up from under their bows, and Shusheng's wife was the only one to recognize him. It was the captain of the district brigade. Wiping the water from his face, he demanded:

"What are you doing here?"

Shusheng's wife answered:

"We were taking them some more clothes."

The captain turned to Shusheng:

"Are they all from your village?"

"That's right. A bunch of backward elements!" He hurled the biscuits into their boat and disappeared with a splash, reappearing some distance away.

The captain laughed.

"Well, your trip wasn't wasted. If not for you, our ambush wouldn't have been so successful. But now you've completed your mission, you'd better hurry home and dry your clothes. The situation is still pretty serious."

By now the men had loaded all their trophies on their boats and were ready to move on. Each of them had plastered a large lotus leaf on his head to keep off the midday sun. The women rescued their bundles which had fallen into the water and threw them over. Then the men's three boats made off quickly towards the southeast, to be swallowed up soon in the heat haze over the river.

The women lost no time in starting back, bedraggled as drowned rats. But all the excitement they had been through soon set them laughing and chattering again. The one in the stern made a face over her shoulder.

"Did you ever see the like? Just couldn't be bothered with us!"

"As if we'd lost face for them!"

They laughed, knowing that they hadn't exactly covered themselves with glory. Still:

"We haven't got rifles. If we had, we could take on the Japs without hiding in the creek."

"Well, so at last I've seen fighting! What's so wonderful about it? As long as you don't lose your head, anybody can squat there and let off a gun."

"When a boat sinks I can dive to collect stuff too. I promise you I'm a better swimmer than they are—I can go down deeper than that."

"Let's set up a unit when we go back, or we'll never be able to leave the village again."

"Looking down on us the moment they join the army! In another two years they won't think us worth talking to, but are they all that much better?"

That autumn they learned to fire rifles. When winter came and the time to catch fish in the ice, they took it in turn to take out the sleigh and whizz back and forth over the ice, patrolling the village. When the enemy attempted to "mop up" the marshlands, they worked hand in glove with the army, slipping fearlessly in and out of the sea of reeds.

四

杨梅烧酒[①]

郁达夫

病了半年，足迹不曾出病房一步，新近起床，自然想上什么地方去走走。照新的说法，是去转换转换空气；照旧的说来，也好去祓除祓除邪孽的不祥；总之久蛰思动，大约也是人之常情，更何况这气候，这一个火热的土王用事的气候，实在在逼人不得不向海天空阔的地方去躲避一回。所以我首先想到的，是日本的温泉地带，北戴河，威海卫，青岛，牯岭等避暑的处所。但是衣衫褴褛，饘粥不全的近半年来的经济状况，又不许我有这一种模仿普罗大家的阔绰的行为。寻思的结果，终觉得还是到杭州去好些；究竟是到杭州去的路费来得省一点，此外我并且还有一位旧友在那里住着，此去也好去看他一看，在灯昏酒满的街头，也可以去和他叙一叙七八年不见的旧离情。

象这样决心以后的第二天午后，我已经在湖上的一家小饭馆里和这位多年不见的老朋友在吃应时的杨梅烧酒了。

屋外头是同在赤道直下的地点似的伏里的阳光，湖面上满泛着微温的泥水和从这些泥水里蒸发出来的略带腥臭的汽层儿。大道上车夫也很少，来往的行人更是不多。饭馆的灰尘积得很厚的许多桌子中间，也只坐有我们这两位点菜要先问一问价钱的顾客。

---

① 中文选自：郁达夫．郁达夫小说集（下册）．浙江：浙江文艺出版社，1983：549-556；英译文选自：Yu，D. F. Arbutus Cocktails. In Yu，D. F. *Nights of Spring Fever and Other Writings*. Gladys Yang（trans.）. *Chinese Literature*，1984：83-91.

他——我这一位旧友——和我已经有七八年不见了。说起来实在话也很长，总之，他是我在东京大学里念书时候的一位预科的级友。毕业之后，两人东奔西走，各不往来，各不晓得各的住址，已经隔绝了七八年了。直到最近，似乎有一位不良少年，在假了我的名氏向各处募款，说："某某病倒在上海了，现在被收留在上海的一个慈善团体的××病院里。四海的仁人君子，诸大善士，无论和某某相识或不相识的，都希望惠赐若干，以救某某的死生的危急。"我这一位旧友，不知从什么地方，也听到了这一个消息，在一个月前，居然也从他的血汗的收入里割出了两块钱来，慎重其事地汇寄到了上海的××病院。在这××病院内，我本来是有一位医士认识的，所以两礼拜前，他的那两元义捐和一封很简略的信终于由那一位医士转到了我的手里。接到了他这封信，并且另外更发见了有几处有我署名的未完稿件发表的事情之后，向远近四处去一打听，我才原原本本的晓得了那一位不良少年所作的在前面已经说过的把戏。而这一曲实在也是滑稽得很的小悲剧，现在却终于成了我们两个旧友的再见的基因。

他穿的是肩头上有补缀的一件夏布长衫，进饭馆之后，这件长衫却被两个纽扣吊起，挂上壁上去了。所以他和我都只剩了一件汗衫，一条短裤的野蛮形状。当然他的那件汗衫比我的来得黑，而且背脊里已经有两个小孔了，而我的一件哩，却正是在上海动身以前刚花了五毫银币新买的国货。

他的相貌，非但同七八年前没有丝毫的改变，就是同在东京初进大学预科的那一年，也还是一个样儿。嘴底下的一簇绕腮胡，还是同十几年前一样，似乎是刚剃过了三两天的样子，长得正有一二分厚，远看过去，他的下巴象一个倒挂在那里的黑漆小木鱼。说也奇怪，我和他同学了四五年，及回国之后又不见了七八年的中间，他的这一簇绕腮胡，总从没有过长得较短一点或较长一点的时节。仿佛是他娘生他下地来的时候，这胡须就那么地生在那里，以后直到他死的时候，也不会发生变化似的。他的两只似乎是哭了一阵之后的肿眼，也仍旧是同学生时代一样，只是朦胧地在看着鼻尖，淡含着一味莫名其妙的笑影。额角仍旧是那么宽，颧骨仍旧是高得很，颧骨下的脸颊部仍旧是深深地陷入，窝里总有一个小酒杯好摆的样子。他的年纪,也仍旧是同学生时代一样,看起来,从二十五岁到五十二岁止的中间,无论哪一个年龄都可以看的。

当我从火车站下来,上离车站不远的一个暑期英算补习学校——这学校也真是倒霉,简直是象上海的专吃二房东饭的人家的两间阁楼——里去看他的时候,他正在那里上课。一间黑漆漆的矮屋里,坐着八九个十四五岁的呆笨的小孩,眼睛呆呆的在注视着黑板。他老先生背转了身,伸长了时时在起痉挛的手,尽在黑板上写数学的公式和演题,屋子里声息全无,只充满着滴滴答答的他的粉笔的响声。因此他那一个圆背和那件有一大块被汗湿透的夏布长衫,就很惹起了我的注意。我在楼下向他们房东问他的名字的时候,他在楼上一定是听见的,同时在这样静寂的授课中间,我的一步一步走上楼去的脚步声,他总也不会不听到的。当我上楼之后,他的学生全部向我注视的一层眼光,就可以证明,但是向来神经就似乎有点麻木的他,竟动也不动一动,仍在继续着写他的公式,所以我只好静静的在后一排学生的一个空位里坐落。他把公式演题在黑板上写满了,又从头至尾的看了一遍,看有没有写错,又朝黑板空咳了两三声,又把粉笔放下,将身上的粉末打了一打干净,才慢慢的转身来。这时候他的额上嘴上,已经盛满了一颗颗的大汗。他的红肿的两眼,大约总也已满被汗水封没了吧,他竟没有看到我而若无其事的又讲了一阵,才宣告算学课毕,教学生们走向另一间矮屋里去听讲英文。楼上起了动摇,学生们争先恐后的奔往隔壁的那间矮屋里去了,我才徐徐的立起身来,走近了他,把手伸出向他的粘湿的肩头上拍了一拍。

"噢,你是几时来的?"

终于他也表示出了一种惊异的表情,举起了他那两只朦胧的老在注视鼻尖的眼睛。左手捏住了我的手,右手他就在袋里摸出了一块黑而且湿的手帕来揩他头上的汗。

"因为教书教得太起劲了,所以你的上来,我竟没有听到。这天气可真了不得。你的病好了么?"

他接连着说出了许多前后不接的问我的话,这是他的兴奋状态的表示,也还是学生时代的那一种样子。我略答了他一下,就问他以后有没有课了。他说：

"今天因为甲班的学生，已经毕业了，所以只剩了这一班乙班，我的数学教完，今天是没有课了。下一个钟头的英文，是由校长自己教的。"

"那么我们上湖滨去走走，你说可以不可以？"

"可以，可以，马上就去。"

于是乎我们就到了湖滨，就上了这一家大约是第四五流的小小的饭馆。

在饭馆里坐下，点好了几盘价廉可口的小菜，杨梅烧酒也喝了几口之后，我们才开始细细的谈起别后的天来。

"你近来的生活怎么样？"开始头一句，他就问起了我的职业。

"职业虽则没有，穷虽则也穷到可观的地步，但是吃饭穿衣的几件事情，总也勉强的在这里支持过去。你呢？"

"我么？象你所看见的一样，倒也还好。这暑期学校里教一个月书，倒也有十六块大洋的进款。"

"那么暑期学校完了就怎么办哩？"

"也就在那里的完全小学校里教书，好在先生只有我和校长两个，十六块钱一月是不会没有的。听说你在做书，进款大约总还好吧？"

"好是不会好的，但十六块或六十块里外的钱是每月弄得到的。"

"说你是病倒在上海的养老院里的这一件事情，虽然是人家的假冒，但是这假冒者何以偏又要来使用象你我这样的人的名义哩？"

"这大约是因为这位假冒者受了一点教育的毒害的缘故。大约因为他也是和你我一样的有了一点知识而没有正当的地方去用。"

"嗳，嗳，说起来知识的正当的用处，我到现在也正在这里想。我的应用化学的知识，回国以后虽则还没有用到过一天，但是，但是，我想这一次总可以成功的。"

谈到了这里，他的颜面转换了方向，不再向我看了，而转眼看向了外边的太阳光里。

"嗳，这一回我想总可以成功的。"

他简直是忘记了我，似乎在一个人独语的样子。

"初步机械二千元,工厂建筑一千五百元,一千元买石英等材料和石炭,一千元人夫广告,嗳,广告却不可以不登,总计五千五百元。五千五百元的资本。以后就可以烧制出品,算它只出一百块的制品一天,那么一三得三,一个月三千块,一年么三万六千块。打一个八折,三八两万四,三六一千八,总也还有两万五千八百块。以六千块还资本,以六千块做扩张费,把一万块钱来造它一所住宅,嗳,住宅,当然公司里的人是都可以来住的。那么,那么,只教一年,一年之后,就可以了。……"

我只听他计算得起劲,但简直不晓得他在那里计算些什么,所以又轻轻地问他:

"你在计算的是什么?是明朝的演题么?"

"不,不,我说的是玻璃工厂,一年之后,本利偿清,又可以拿出一万块钱来造一所共同的住宅,吓,你说多么占利啊!嗳,这一所住宅,造好之后,你还可以来住哩,来住着写书,并且顺便也可以替我们做点广告之类,好不好?干杯,干杯,干了它这一杯烧酒。"

莫名其妙,他把酒杯擎起来了,我也只得和他一道,把一杯杨梅已经吃了剩下来的烧酒干了。他干下了那半杯烧酒,紧闭着嘴,又把眼睛闭上,陶然地静止了一分钟。随后又张开了那双红肿的眼睛。大声叫着茶房说:

"堂倌!再来两杯!"

两杯新的杨梅烧酒来后,他紧闭着眼,背靠着后面的板壁,一只手拿着手帕,一次一次的揩拭面部的汗珠,一只手尽是一个一个的拿着杨梅在往嘴里送。嚼着靠着,眼睛闭着,他一面还尽在哼哼的说着:

"嗳,嗳,造一间住宅,在湖滨造一间新式的住宅。玻璃,玻璃么,用本厂的玻璃,要斯断格拉斯。一万块钱,一万块大洋。"

这样的哼了一阵,吃杨梅吃了一阵了,他又忽而把酒杯举起,睁开眼叫我说:

"喂,老同学,朋友,再干一杯!"

我没有法子,所以只好又举起杯来和他干了一半,但看看他的那杯高玻璃杯的杨梅烧酒,却是杨梅与酒都已吃完了。喝完酒后,一面又闭上眼

睛,向后面的板壁靠着,一面他又高叫着堂倌说:

“堂倌!再来两杯!”

堂倌果然又拿了两杯盛得满满的杨梅与酒来,摆在我们的面前。他又同从前一样的闭上眼睛,靠着板壁,在一个杨梅,一个杨梅的往嘴里送。我这时候也有点喝得醺醺地醉了,所以什么也不去管它,只是沉默着在桌上将两手叉住了头打瞌睡,但是在还没有完全睡熟的耳旁,只听见同蜜蜂叫似的他在哼着说:

“啊,真痛快,痛快,一万块钱!一所湖滨的住宅!一个老同学,一位朋友,从远地方来,喝酒,喝酒,喝酒!”

我因为被他这样的在那里叫着,所以终于睡不舒服。但是这伏天的两杯杨梅烧酒,和半日的火车旅行,已经弄得我倦极了,所以很想马上去就近寻一个旅馆来睡一下。这时候正好他又睁开眼来叫我干第三杯烧酒了,我也顺便清醒了一下,睁大了双眼,和他真真地干了一杯。等这一杯似甘非甘的烧酒落肚,我却也有点支持不住了,所以就教堂倌过来算账。他看见了堂倌过来,我在付账了,就同发了疯似的突然站起,一只手叉住了我那只捏着纸币的右手,一只左手尽在裤腰左近的皮袋里乱摸;等堂倌将我的纸币拿去,把找头的铜元角子拿来摆在桌上的时候,他脸上一青,红肿的眼睛一吊,顺手就把桌上的铜元抓起,锵丁丁的掷上了我的面部。扑搭地一响,我的右眼上面的太阳穴里就凉阴阴地起了一种刺激的感觉,接着就有点痛起来了。这时候我也被酒精激刺着发了作,呆视住他,大声地喝了一声:

“喂,你发了疯了么,你在干什么?”

他那一张本来是畸形的面上,弄得满面青青,涨溢着一层杀气。

“操你的,我要打倒你们这些资本家,打倒你们这些不劳而食的畜生,来,我们来比比腕力看。要你来付钱,你算在卖富么?”

他眉毛一竖,牙齿咬得紧紧,捏起两个拳头,狠命的就扑上了我的身边。我也觉得气极了,不管三七二十一就和他扭打了起来。

白丹,丁当,扑落扑落的桌椅杯盘都倒翻在地上了,我和他两个就也滚跌到了店门的外头。两个人打到了如何的地步,我简直不晓得了,只听见四面哗哗哗哗的赶聚了许多闲人车夫巡警拢来。

等我睡醒了一觉，渴想着水喝，支着鳞伤遍体的身体在第二分署的木栅栏里醒转来的时候，短短的夏夜，已经是天将放亮的午前三四点钟的时刻了。

我睁开了两眼，向四面看了一周，又向栅栏外刚走过去的一位值夜的巡警问了一个明白，才朦胧地记起了白天的情节。我又问我的那位朋友呢，巡警说，他早已酒醒，两点钟之前回到城站的学校里去了。我就求他去向巡长回禀一声，马上放我回去。他去了一刻之后，就把我的长衫草帽并钱包拿还了我。我一面把衣服穿上，出去去解了一个小解，一面就请他去倒一碗水来给我止渴。等我将五元纸币私下塞在他的手里，带上草帽，由第二分署的大门口走出来的时候，天已经完全亮了。被晓风一吹，头脑清醒了一点，我却想起了昨天午后的事情全部，同时在心坎里竟同触了电似地起了一层淡淡的忧郁的微波。

“啊啊，大约这就是人生吧！”

我一边慢慢地向前走着，一边不知不觉地从嘴里却念出了这样的一句独白来。

Arbutus Cocktails

Yu Dafu

For six months I lay ill, confined to my room. Naturally, once up and about again I felt the urge to travel. "A change of air" is the term we use today for what used to be called "throwing off noxious influences". At all events, it is only human nature to want to move after long inactivity. Besides, we were in the middle of a heat-wave which made you eager to escape to wide open spaces. My thoughts turned first to the warm springs in Japan, then to Chinese resorts: Beidaihe, Weihaiwei, Qingdao, Guling.... But the last few months had reduced me to such a state of shabbiness and near-starvation that I had to lay aside these ambitious plans. In the end I decided to pay a visit to Hangzhou. The fare would cost less, and I had an old friend there. I should be able to see him and stroll through those dimly lit streets redolent of wine, talking over all we had done in the seven or eight years since we parted.

The afternoon after this decision was reached found me with the friend I had not seen for so long in a small restaurant beside the West Lake,① sipping the arbutus cocktails then in season.

Outside blazed a mid-summer sun, fierce as in the tropics. From the tepid, muddy water of the lake rose a faint odour of decay. There were few rickshaws on the road and not many pedestrians either. My friend and I, who had to ask the price of each dish we ordered, were the only customers

① 译者注：The well-known scenic spot in Hangzhou.

sitting there among empty tables thickly coated with dust.

We had not met for seven or eight years. To cut a long story short, we had both taken the same preparatory course at the university in Tokyo but gone our different ways after graduation and been completely out of touch ever since. Recently, however, a young sharper had raised money in my name by sending out a circular stating that I had fallen ill in Shanghai and been admitted into X Hospital run by a charitable organization. He appealed to all men of good will and philanthropists, whether they knew me or not, to make a contribution and help save my life. Word of this had somehow reached my old friend, with the result that a month previously he had sent two hard earned dollars to X Hospital in Shanghai. As it happened, I knew one of the doctors there; and consequently, a fortnight earlier, this doctor had passed on to me the two-dollar donation along with a very brief letter. The receipt of this letter and discovery of a certain unfinished manuscript published under my name made me investigate until I got to the bottom of the trick played by the aforementioned young sharper. But at least this little tragicomedy had brought my friend and myself together again.

He was wearing a linen gown patched on the shoulders. Once inside the restaurant, he hung this up by two buttons on the wall. That left both of us barbarously attired in nothing but vests and pants. Needless to say, his vest was dirtier than mine and I spotted two small holes in the back. My own was a native product on which I had expended fifty cents just before setting out from Shanghai.

Not only was he completely unchanged by the last seven or eight years, I found him exactly the same as the year he entered the university in Tokyo and took the preparatory course. The short beard on his chin looked just as it had a dozen years ago—as if he had just trimmed it two or three days ago. In fact, seen from a distance, his lower jaw reminded you of a small black-lacquered wooden fish① hung upside-down. Strange as it may seem, in our

---

① 译者注：A skull-shaped block on which Chinese Buddhist priests beat time when chanting.

four or five years as classmates and in the seven or eight years since our returning to China, during which time we had not met, this growth on his chin had not varied by one iota. You could swear the fellow had been born with it and was doomed to sport it until his dying day. His eyes, puffy as if from weeping, were also the same as in his student days, focused vaguely on the tip of his nose and holding the hint of a bewildered smile. His forehead was as broad as ever, his cheekbones just as prominent, and the cheeks below them equally scored and hollow. And he looked no older than in his student days. You could take him for any age between twenty-five and fifty-two.

I had gone straight from the train to the summer school not far from the station where English and mathematics were taught. It was a wretched hole of a place, that school, one room upstairs and one down, like the tenements sublet in Shanghai. I arrived while he was in the middle of a lesson. Eight or nine young duffers of fourteen or fifteen were sitting in the dark, poky room staring blankly at the blackboard to which he kept turning and stretching out trembling fingers to write mathematical problems and formulae. The only sound in the room was the squeak of his chalk. This being the case, I centred my attention on his bent back and the sweat stain on his linen gown. When I had asked for him downstairs he must have heard his name up here, and the classroom was so quiet that he could not have failed to hear me mounting the stairs. Witness the fact that when I reached the top all his students turned to stare at me; yet he, whose reactions had always been rather slow, went on stolidly copying out his formulae. I had to edge into an empty place in the back row of the class. Having copied out all the formulae and problems, he checked through them carefully from beginning to end, coughed a couple of times, put down the chalk, dusted off his gown and then at last turned slowly away from the blackboard. Sweat beaded his forehead and upper lip and must have blinded his puffy red eyes as well, for he failed to see me and went on talking for a while as if all were as usual, before sending his students to the other room for English. The floor shook as they rushed out, jostling, to the other poky room. Then I quietly stood up and went over to pat his damp shoulder.

"Oh! When did you get here?"

At last he evinced some surprise, raising his lacklustre eyes from the tip of his nose. Gripping my fingers in his left hand, with his right he pulled a damp, grimy handkerchief from his pocket and started mopping his head.

"I was so absorbed in my teaching, I didn't hear you come up. What a scorching day! Well, are you really better?"

This incoherent way of talking when excited was another carry-over from his student days. After a perfunctory answer, I asked if he had any more classes.

"Grade A has graduated, so there's only Grade B left," he said. "I'm through with my maths today. The head's taking them for English now."

"Suppose we go down to the lake, then?"

"A good idea. Let's go right away."

So down we went to the lake, to this small fourth or fifth-rate restaurant.

Having sat down and ordered a few cheap but tasty dishes, we sipped our arbutus cocktails and started chatting.

"How are you making a living nowadays?" was his first question.

"I've no job and am permanently hard up, but I manage to make ends meet. How about you?"

"You can see the shape I'm in, but it's all right. This month's teaching in the summer school will bring me in an extra sixteen dollars."

"And after that?"

"I'll go on teaching in the primary school. There are only two teachers, the head and myself, so there's no danger of losing that sixteen dollars a month. I hear you've been writing. Do your books bring in much money?"

"Not much. Anything between sixteen and sixty dollars a month."

"That fellow who said you were in an old people's home in Shanghai, why should he use the name of somebody like us?"

"Probably because he's poisoned by a little education. Because, like us, he has a little knowledge but no proper use for it."

"The proper use of knowledge—that's what's occupying me now. I've not used my knowledge of chemistry for a single day since coming back to China. But this time, I really think it's coming off."

He turned his face away to look at the sunlight outside.

"Yes, this time I think I'll pull it off."

Oblivious of my presence, he was talking to himself.

"Two thousand dollars for the first lot of machines, 1,500 for the factory premises, 1,000 to buy quartz, lime and other materials, 1,000 for wages and advertisements—can't do without advertisements, you know. That totals 5,500. A capital investment of 5,500. Then we go into production, and even if we only produce a hundred a day, that means 3,000 in a month. In a year, 36,000. Knock off twenty per cent and that still gives you 25,800 dollars. Six thousand to pay back the capital, 6,000 to expand the plant, 10,000 to build housing. Of course, all members of the firm will be able to live there. Yes, I need only one year, after one year things will be all right...."

I had not a clue as to the meaning of these hurried calculations.

"What are you working out?" I asked softly. "An exercise for tomorrow morning?"

"No, no, a glass works. In one year capital and interest will be repaid and I'll be able to spend ten thousand on building a hostel—I'm on to a good thing this time! Ha, once that hostel's built, you're welcome to move in and write there. You can draft a few advertisements for us too, how about it? Drink up, now! Finish that glass!"

Still day-dreaming, he raised his glass and I had to do the same. I had eaten the arbutus and now gulped down the liquor. After drinking he clamped his lips together and closed his eyes, remaining silent for a moment. Then he opened his puffy bloodshot eyes and called:

"Here, waiter! Two more glasses!"

When two fresh cocktails arrived, he closed his eyes and leaned back against the wooden partition. With one hand he mopped his perspiring face, with the other he picked the fruit out of his glass and put it into his mouth.

Leaning back, eating with closed eyes, he went on muttering:

"Yes, we'll build a house, western-style, overlooking the lake. Glass, we'll use the glass from our works, stained glass. Ten thousand dollars. Ten thousand silver dollars...."

Some minutes passed while he muttered to himself and ate. Then he raised his cup abruptly again, opening his eyes to say:

"Here, old classmate! Drink, my friend!"

There was nothing for it but to swallow half my drink. He, however, finished all the fruit and liquor in his tall glass. Then once more he closed his eyes, leaned back against the partition and shouted:

"Waiter! Two more glasses!"

Two more brimming glasses were put down in front of us. Just as before he leaned back with closed eyes, popping arbutus after arbutus into his mouth. Since I was feeling quite tipsy by this time, I paid no attention but rested my head on my arms and prepared to sleep. I was dozing off when I heard a buzz in my ears:

"That's it! Ten thousand dollars! A house by the lake. An old classmate's come all this way.... We must drink, my friend! Drink up!"

I could not sleep through this noise. But exhausted by two glasses of liquor on a broiling day, on top of a tiring train journey, all I wanted was to find a hotel and rest. Just then, however, opening his eyes again, he proposed another toast. Waking up, I too opened my eyes and drank with him. When the sweet, burning liquid reached my stomach, my head started reeling and I called for the bill. The moment the waiter handed it to me, however, my friend sprang up like a madman, seized my right hand which was holding some notes, and with his left fumbled desperately in his wallet. The waiter took my money and came back with copper change, which he placed on the table. At that, livid, a murderous look in his bloodshot eyes, my friend snatched up the coins and threw them in my face. Something cold struck my right temple, which started to sting. Inflamed by drink myself, I glared back and roared:

"Are you crazy? What's the idea!"

His irregular features were ghastly, contorted with rage.

"To hell with you! Down with all capitalists! Down with you parasites! Here, let's see who's the stronger! Who asked you to pay? —Flaunting your money in my face!"

Scowling and gritting his teeth, he charged at me with clenched fists. In my fury I fought back.

Crash! Tables, chairs, glasses and dishes overturned, and the two of us rolled out into the street. How long we fought I do not know. Idlers, rickshawmen and police crowded round us, shouting.

I woke up parched with thirst, bruised and aching, behind wooden bars in the No. 2 Police Station. Summer nights are short, and now at nearly four in the morning it would soon be light.

Only when I had taken a good look round and asked the policeman on duty outside what I was doing in the lock-up, did some recollection of the previous day come back to me. When I inquired about my friend, the policeman told me he had sobered up two hours earlier and gone back to the school by the station. I urged him to get permission from the superintendent for me to leave, and he came back soon enough with my gown, Panama and wallet. I put on my gown and begged for a cup of water. By the time I had slipped a five-dollar note into his hand, put on my hat and left the police station, day had already dawned. The early morning wind cleared my brain, bringing back the memory of all that had happened the previous afternoon. A pang like a mild electric shock ran through me. And as I walked slowly on, I found myself muttering:

"Well, such is life!"

第五编

戴乃迭女性文学英译

一

百合花[①]

茹志鹃

一九四六年的中秋。

这天打海岸的部队决定晚上总攻。我们文工团创作室的几个同志，就由主攻团的团长分派到各个战斗连去帮助工作。大概因为我是个女同志吧！团长对我抓了半天后脑勺，最后才叫一个通讯员送我到前沿包扎所去。

包扎所就包扎所吧！反正不叫我进保险箱就行。我背上背包，跟通讯员走了。

早上下过一阵小雨，现在虽放了晴，路上还是滑得很，两边地里的秋庄稼，却给雨水冲洗得青翠水绿，珠烁晶莹。空气里也带有一股清鲜湿润的香味。要不是敌人的冷炮，在间歇地盲目地轰响着，我真以为我们是去赶集的呢！

通讯员撒开大步，一直走在我前面。一开始他就把我撂下几丈远。我的脚烂了，路又滑，怎么努力也赶不上他。我想喊他等等我，却又怕他笑我胆小害怕；不叫他，我又真怕一个人摸不到那个包扎所。我开始对这个通讯员生起气来。

嗳！说也怪，他背后好像长了眼睛似的，倒自动在路边站下了。但脸还是朝着前面，没看我一眼。等我紧走慢赶的快要走近他时，他又登登的

---

① 中文选自：茹志鹃，等. 百合花. 北京：人民文学出版社，1958:1-14；英译文选自：Ru，Z. J. Lilies. Gladys Yang（trans.）. *Chinese Literature*，1959(2)：29-38.

自个向前走了，一下又把我甩下几丈远。我实在没力气赶了，索性一个人在后面慢慢晃。不过这一次还好，他没让我撂得太远，但也不让我走近，总和我保持着丈把远的距离。我走快，他在前面大踏步向前；我走慢，他在前面就摇摇摆摆。奇怪的是，我从没见他回头看我一次，我不禁对这通讯员发生了兴趣。

刚才在团部我没注意看他，现在从背后看去，只看到他是高挑挑的个子，块头不大，但从他那副厚实实的肩膀看来，是个挺棒的小伙，他穿了一身洗淡了的黄军装，绑腿直打到膝盖上。肩上的步枪筒里，稀疏地插了几根树枝，这要说是伪装，倒不如算作装饰点缀。

没有赶上他，但双脚胀痛得象火烧似的。我向他提出了休息一会后，自己便在做田界的石头上坐了下来。他也在远远的一块石头上坐下，把枪横搁在腿上，背向着我，好象没我这个人似的。凭经验，我晓得这一定又因为我是个女同志的缘故。女同志下连队，就有这些困难。我着恼的带着一种反抗情绪走过去，面对着他坐下来。这时，我看见他那张十分年轻稚气的圆脸，顶多有十八岁。他见我挨他坐下，立即张惶起来，好象他身边埋下了一颗定时炸弹，局促不安，掉过脸去不好，不掉过去又不行，想站起来又不好意思。我拚命忍住笑，随便地问他是哪里人。他没回答，脸涨得象个关公，呐呐半晌，才说清自己是天目山人。原来他还是我的同乡呢！

“在家时你干什么？”

“帮人拖毛竹。”

我朝他宽宽的两肩望了一下，立即在我眼前出现了一片绿雾似的竹海，海中间，一条窄窄的石级山道，盘旋而上。一个肩膀宽宽的小伙，肩上垫了一块老蓝布，扛了几枝青竹，竹梢长长的拖在他后面，刮打得石级哗哗作响。……这是我多么熟悉的故乡生活啊！我立刻对这位同乡，越加亲热起来。我又问：

“你多大了？”

“十九。”

“参加革命几年了？”

"一年。"

"你怎么参加革命的?"我问到这里自己觉得这不象是谈话,倒有些象审讯。不过我还是禁不住地要问。

"大军北撤时①我自己跟来的。"

"家里还有什么人呢?"

"娘,爹,弟弟妹妹,还有一个姑姑也住在我家里。"

"你还没娶媳妇吧?"

"……"他飞红了脸,更加忸怩起来,两只手不停地数摸着腰皮带上的扣眼。半晌他才低下了头,憨憨地笑了一下,摇了摇头。我还想问他有没有对象,但看到他这样子,只得把嘴里的话,又咽了下去。

两人闷坐了一会,他开始抬头看看天,又掉过来扫了我一眼,意思是在催我动身。

当我站起来要走的时候,我看见他摘了帽子,偷偷的在用毛巾拭汗。这是我的不是,人家走路都没出一滴汗,为了我跟他说话,却害他出了这一头大汗,这都怪我了。

我们到包扎所,已是下午两点钟了。这里离前沿有三里路,包扎所设在一个小学里,大小六个房子组成品字形,中间一块空地长了许多野草,显然,小学已有多时不开课了。我们到时屋里已有几个卫生员在弄着纱布棉花,满地上都是用砖头垫起来的门板,算作病床。

我们刚到不久,来了一个乡干部,他眼睛熬得通红,用一片硬拍纸插在额前的破毡帽下,低低的遮在眼睛前面挡光。他一肩背枪,一肩挂了一杆秤;左手挎了一篮鸡蛋,右手提了一口大锅,呼哧呼哧地走来。他一边放东西,一边对我们又抱歉又诉苦,一边还喘息地喝着水,同时还从怀里掏出一包饭团来嚼着。我只见他迅速地做着这一切。他说的什么我就没大听清。好象是说什么被子的事,要我们自己去借。我问清了卫生员,原来因为部队上的被子还没发下来,但伤员流了血,非常怕冷,所以就得向

---

① 原作者注:一九四五年日本投降后,共产党为了全国人民实现和平的愿望,和国民党进行和平谈判,并忍痛撤出江南。但时隔不久,国民党竟背信撕毁"双十协定",又向中原、苏中等解放区大举进攻。

老百姓去借。哪怕有一二十条棉絮也好。我这时正愁工作插不上手,便自告奋勇讨了这件差事,怕来不及就顺便也请了我那位同乡,请他帮我动员几家再走。他踌躇了一下,便和我一起去了。

我们先到附近一个村子,进村后他向东,我往西,分头去动员。不一会,我已写了三张借条出去,借到两条棉絮,一条被子,手里抱得满满的,心里十分高兴,正准备送回去再来借时,看见通讯员从对面走来,两手还是空空的。

"怎么,没借到?"我觉得这里老百姓觉悟高,又很开通,怎么会没有借到呢?我有点惊奇地问。

"女同志,你去借吧!……老百姓死封建。……"

"哪一家?你带我去。"我估计一定是他说话不对,说崩了。借不到被子事小,得罪了老百姓影响可不好。我叫他带我去看看。但他执拗地低着头,象钉在地上似的,不肯挪步。我走近他,低声的把群众影响的话对他说了。他听了,果然就松松爽爽的带我走了。

我们走进老乡的院子里,只见堂屋里静静的,里面一间房门上,垂着一块蓝布红额的门帘,门框两边还贴着鲜红的对联。我们只得站在外面向里"大姐、大嫂"的喊,喊了几声,不见有人应,但响动是有了。一会,门帘一挑,露出一个年轻媳妇来。这媳妇长得很好看,高高的鼻梁,弯弯的眉,额前一溜蓬松松的留海。穿的虽是粗布,倒都是新的。我看她头上已硬挠挠的挽了髻,便大嫂长大嫂短的向她道歉,说刚才这个同志来,说话不好别见怪等等。她听着,脸扭向里面,尽咬着嘴唇笑。我说完了,她也不作声,还是低头咬着嘴唇,好象忍了一肚子的笑料没笑完。这一来,我倒有些尴尬了,下面的话怎么说呢!我看通讯员站在一边,眼睛一眨不眨地看着我,好象在看连长做示范动作似的。我只好硬了头皮,讪讪地向她开口借被子了,接着还对她说了一遍共产党的部队,打仗是为了老百姓的道理。这一次,她不笑了,一边听着,一边不断向房里瞅着。我说完了,她看看我,看看通讯员,好象在掂量我刚才那些话的斤两。半晌,她转身进去抱被子了。

通讯员乘这机会,颇不服气地对我说道:

“我刚才也是说的这几句话,她就是不借,你看怪吧! ……”

我赶忙白了他一眼,不叫他再说。可是来不及了,那个媳妇抱了被子,已经在房门口了。被子一拿出来,我方才明白她刚才为什么不肯借的道理了。这原来是一条里外全新的新花被子,被面是假洋缎的,枣红底,上面撒满白色百合花。她好象是在故意气通讯员,把被子朝我面前一送,说:“抱去吧。”

我手里已捧满了被子,就一努嘴,叫通讯员来拿。没想到他竟扬起脸,装作没看见。我只好开口叫他,他这才绷了脸,垂着眼皮,上去接过被子,慌慌张张地转身就走。不想他一步还没走出去,就听见“嘶”的一声,衣服挂住了门钩,在肩膀处,挂下一片布来,口子撕得不小。那媳妇一面笑着,一面赶忙找针拿线,要给他缝上。通讯员却高低不肯,挟了被子就走。

刚走出门不远,就有人告诉我们,刚才那位年轻媳妇,是刚过门三天的新娘子,这条被子就是她唯一的嫁妆。我听了,心里便有些过意不去,通讯员也皱起了眉,默默地看着手里的被子。我想他听了这样的话一定会有同感吧! 果然,他一边走,一边跟我嘟哝起来了。

“我们不了解情况,把人家结婚被子也借来了,多不合适呀! ……”我忍不住想给他开个玩笑,便故作严肃地说:

“是呀! 也许她为了这条被子,在做姑娘时,不知起早熬夜,多干了多少零活,才积起了做被子的钱,或许她曾为了这条花被,睡不着觉呢。可是还有人骂她死封建。……”

他听到这里,突然站住脚,呆了一会,说:

“那! ……那我们送回去吧!”

“已经借来了,再送回去,倒叫她多心。”我看他那副认真、为难的样子,又好笑,又觉得可爱。不知怎么的,我已从心底爱上了这个傻呼呼的小同乡。

他听我这么说,也似乎有理,考虑了一下,便下了决心似地说:

“好,算了。用了给她好好洗洗。”他决定以后,就把我抱着的被子,统统抓过去,左一条、右一条地披挂在自己肩上,大踏步地走了。

回到包扎所以后,我就让他回团部去。他精神顿时活泼起来了,向我敬了礼就跑了。走不几步，他又想起了什么，在自己挎包里掏了一阵，摸出两个馒头，朝我扬了扬，顺手放在路边石头上，说：

“给你开饭啦!”说完就脚不点地地走了。我走过去拿起那两个干硬的馒头，看见他背的枪筒里不知在什么时候又多了一枝野菊花，跟那些树枝一起，在他耳边抖抖地颤动着。

他已走远了，但还见他肩上撕挂下来的布片，在风里一飘一飘。我真后悔没给他缝上再走。现在，至少他要裸露一晚上的肩膀了。

包扎所的工作人员很少。乡干部动员了几个妇女，帮我们打水，烧锅，作些零碎活。那位新媳妇也来了，她还是那样，笑咪咪地抿着嘴，偶然从眼角上看我一眼，但她时不时地东张西望，好象在找什么。后来她到底问我说：

“那位同志弟到哪里去了?”我告诉她同志弟不是这里的，他现在到前沿去了。她不好意思地笑了一下说：“刚才借被子，他可受我的气了!”说完又抿了嘴笑着，动手把借来的几十条被子、棉絮，整整齐齐地分铺在门板上、桌子上(两张课桌拼起来，就是一张床)。我看见她把自己那条白百合花的新被，铺在外面屋檐下的一块门板上。

天黑了，天边涌起一轮满月。我们的总攻还没发起。敌人照例是忌怕夜晚的，在地上烧起一堆堆的野火，又盲目地轰炸，照明弹也一个接一个地升起，好象在月亮下面点了无数盏的汽油灯，把地面的一切都赤裸裸地暴露出来了。在这样一个“白夜”里来攻击，有多困难，要付出多大的代价啊！我连那一轮皎洁的月亮，也憎恶起来了。

乡干部又来了，慰劳了我们几个家做的干菜月饼。原来今天是中秋节了。

啊！中秋节，在我的故乡，现在一定又是家家门前放一张竹茶几，上面供一副香烛、几碟瓜果月饼。孩子们急切地盼那炷香快些焚尽，好早些分摊给月亮娘娘享用过的东西，他们在茶几旁边跳着唱着：“月亮堂堂，敲锣买糖，……”或是唱着：“月亮嬷嬷，照你照我，……”我想到这里，又想起我那个小同乡，那个拖毛竹的小伙，也许，几年以前，他还唱过这些歌吧！……我咬了一口美味的家做月饼，想起那个小同乡大概现在正趴在工事里，也许在团指挥所，或者是在那些弯弯曲曲的交通沟里走着哩！……

一会儿，我们的炮响了，天空划过几颗红色的信号弹，攻击开始了。不久，断断续续地有几个伤员下来，包扎所的空气立即紧张起来。

我拿着小本子，去登记他们的姓名、单位，轻伤的问问，重伤的就得拉开他们的符号，或是翻看他们的衣衿。我拉开一个重彩号的符号时，“通讯员”三个字使我突然打了个寒战，心跳起来。我定了下神才看到符号上写着×营的字样。啊！不是，我的同乡他是团部的通讯员。但我又莫名其妙地想问问谁，战地上会不会漏掉伤员。通讯员在战斗时，除了送信，还干什么，——我不知道自己为什么要问这些没意思的问题。

战斗开始后的几十分钟里，一切顺利，伤员一次次带下来的消息，都是我们突击第一道鹿砦，第二道铁丝网，占领敌人前沿工事打进街了。但到这里，消息忽然停顿了，下来的伤员，只是简单地回答说“在打”，或者“在巷战”。但从他们满身泥泞，极度疲乏的神色上，甚至从那些似乎刚从泥里掘出来的担架上，大家明白，前面在进行着一场什么样的战斗。

包扎所的担架不够了，好几个重彩号不能及时送后方医院，耽搁下来。我不能解除他们任何痛苦，只得带着那些妇女，给他们拭脸洗手，能吃得的喂他们吃一点，带着背包的，就给他们换一件干净衣裳，有些还得解开他们的衣服，给他们拭洗身上的污泥血迹。

做这种工作，我当然没什么，可那些妇女又羞又怕，就是放不开手来，大家都要抢着去烧锅，特别是那新媳妇。我跟她说了半天，她才红了脸，同意了。不过只答应做我的下手。

前面的枪声，已响得稀落了。感觉上似乎天快亮了，其实还只是半夜。外边月亮很明，也比平日悬得高。前面又下来一个重伤员。屋里铺位都满了，我就把这位重伤员安排在屋檐下的那块门板上。担架员把伤员抬上门板，但还围在床边不肯走。一个上了年纪的担架员，大概把我当做医生了，一把抓住我的膀子说：“大夫，你可无论如何要想办法治好这位同志呀！你治好他，我……我们全体担架队员给你挂匾！……”他说话的时候，我发现其他的几个担架员也都睁大了眼盯着我，似乎我点一点头，这伤员就立即会好了似的。我心想给他们解释一下，只见新媳妇端着水站在床前,短促的“啊”了一声。我急拨开他们上前一看,我看见了一张十分年轻稚气的圆脸,原来棕红的脸色,现已变得灰黄。他安详地合着眼,军装的肩头上,露着那个大洞,一片布还挂在那里。

“这都是为了我们,……”那个担架员负罪地说道,“我们十多副担架挤在一个小巷子里,准备往前运动,这位同志走在我们后面,可谁知道狗日的反动派不知从哪个屋顶上撂下颗手榴弹来,手榴弹就在我们人缝里冒着烟乱转,这时这位同志叫我们快趴下,他自己就一下扑在那个东西上了。……”

新媳妇又短促地“啊”了一声。我强忍着眼泪,给那些担架员说了些话,打发他们走了。我回转身看见新媳妇已轻轻移过一盏油灯,解开他的衣服,她刚才那种忸怩羞涩已经完全消失,只是庄严而虔诚地给他拭着身子,这位高大而又年轻的小通讯员无声地躺在那里。……我猛然醒悟地跳起身,磕磕绊绊地跑去找医生,等我和医生拿了针药赶来,新媳妇正侧着身子坐在他旁边。

她低着头,正一针一针地在缝他衣肩上那个破洞。医生听了听通讯员的心脏,默默地站起身说:“不用打针了。”我过去一摸,果然手都冰冷了。新媳妇却象什么也没看见,什么也没听到,依然拿着针,细细地、密密地缝着那个破洞。我实在看不下去了,低声地说:

“不要缝了。”她却对我异样地瞟了一眼,低下头,还是一针一针地缝。我想拉开她,我想推开这沉重的氛围,我想看见他坐起来,看见他羞涩地笑。但我无意中碰到了身边一个什么东西,伸手一摸,是他给我开的饭,两个干硬的馒头。……

卫生员让人抬了一口棺材来,动手揭掉他身上的被子,要把他放进棺材去。新媳妇这时脸发白,劈手夺过被子,狠狠地瞪了他们一眼。自己动手把半条被子平展展地铺在棺材底,半条盖在他身上。卫生员为难地说:“被子……是借老百姓的。”

“是我的——”她气汹汹地嚷了半句,就扭过脸去。在月光下,我看见她眼里晶莹发亮,我也看见那条枣红底色上洒满白色百合花的被子,这象征纯洁与感情的花,盖上了这位平常的、拖毛竹的青年人的脸。

Lilies

Ru Zhijuan

Mid-autumn, 1946.

When our coastal command decided to launch a general offensive against the Kuomintang forces, some of us in the concert group were sent by the commander of the leading regiment to lend a hand in different combat companies. Probably because I was a woman, the commander kept me till one of the very last before finally assigning me to a first-aid post near the front. I put on my rucksack and followed the messenger sent to show me the way.

It had rained that morning, and though the weather had cleared the road was still slippery, and the crops on either side sparkled fresh and green in the sunlight. There was a moist freshness in the air. If not for the sporadic booming of the enemy artillery which was firing at random, you could have imagined you were on your way to a fair.

The messenger strode along in front of me. Straight off, he put a distance of about a dozen yards between us. Because my feet were blistered and the road was slippery, try as I might I could not catch up with him. If I called to him to wait, he might think me a coward; but I couldn't hope to find the post alone. He began to annoy me.

The funny thing was that he seemed to have eyes in the back of his head, for presently he stopped of his own accord. He didn't look at me, though, just stared ahead. When I had nearly struggled up to him, he strode off again, promptly leaving me a dozen yards behind. Too exhausted to catch up, I plodded slowly along. But it was all right. He neither let me fall too far behind nor get too close to him, keeping at a distance of a dozen yards. When I quickened my step, he swung along with big strides; when I slowed down, he started sauntering too. Oddly enough, I never caught him looking back at me. I began to feel curious about this messenger.

I had barely glanced at him at regimental headquarters. Now I saw he was a tall young fellow, but pretty strong judging by his strapping shoulders. He was wearing a faded yellow uniform and puttees. The twigs in the barrel of his rifle seemed put there more for ornament than camouflage.

Though I couldn't overtake him, my feet were swollen and smarting. I called out, suggesting that we stop to rest, and sat down on a boundary stone. He sat on another stone further on, his gun across his knees and his back to me, ignoring my existence completely. I knew from experience that this was because I was a girl. Girls always had trouble like this with bashful young fellows. Feeling rather disgruntled, I went over and sat down defiantly opposite him. With his young, ingenuous round face, he looked no more than eighteen at the most. My closeness flustered him. He didn't know what to do. He hardly liked to turn his back on me, but it embarrassed him to look at me and he couldn't very well get up either. Trying hard to keep a straight face, I asked where he was from. Flushing up to his ears, he cleared his throat and told me:

"Tienmushan."

So we were from the same district!

"What did you do at home?"

"Helped haul bamboo."

I glanced at his broad shoulders, and through my mind flashed a picture of a sea of vivid green bamboo, with a narrow stone path winding up and up. A broad-shouldered lad with a square of blue cloth over his shoulders was hauling young bamboos whose long tips rattled on the stones behind.... That was a familiar sight in my home village. At once I felt drawn to my young fellow countryman.

"How old are you?" I asked.

"Nineteen."

"When did you join the army?"

"Last year."

"Why did you join?" I couldn't help asking the questions, though I realized this sounded more like a cross-examination than a conversation.

"When the army withdrew to the north①, I came along with it."

"What family do you have?"

"Mum, dad, a younger brother and sisters, an aunt who lives with us."

"Are you married?"

"...."He flushed and fumbled with his belt, looking more sheepish than ever. With his eyes on the ground, he laughed awkwardly and briskly shook his head. It was on the tip of my tongue to ask if he had a fiancée, but I bit the question back.

After we had sat there, tongue-tied, for a while, he looked at the sky and then at me, as if to say: "Time to move on!"

It was two in the afternoon by the time we reached the first-aid post. This was set up in a primary school three *li* from the front. Six buildings of different sizes were grouped roughly in a triangular formation, and the weeds in the yard between showed that classes has stopped for some time. We arrived to find several orderlies there preparing dressings, and the rooms filled with doors taken off their hinges and laid across bricks to serve as beds.

Presently a cadre from the local government came in, his eyes bloodshot from working late at night. To shade his eyes from the light, he had stuck a cardboard visor under his old felt hat. He had a gun over one shoulder, a scale over the other, and was carrying a basket of eggs and a large pan. He walked in, panting, put down these things, and between sips of water and bites at a ball of cooked rice produced from his pocket apologized for the state things were in. I was so fascinated by the speed with

---

① 译者注:After the Japanese surrender in 1945, in an attempt to give the whole country peace, the communist party conducted peace talks with the kuomintang and withdrew from the south of the Yangtse. Not long after, the kuomintang went back on its word and launched fierce attacks on the liberated areas.

which he did all this that I hardly heard what he was saying, simply catching something about bedding which we would have to borrow. I found out from the orderlies that as the army quilts had not arrived but casualties who had lost blood were extremely susceptible to the cold, we had better borrow quilts from the villagers. Just one or two dozen mattresses would be better than nothing. Anxious to be of some use, I volunteered for the job; and because it was urgent asked my young fellow countryman to help me before he left. After a second's hesitation he agreed.

We went to a nearby village, where he turned east, I west. Before long I had handed out three receipts for two mattresses and one quilt. Heavily laden as I was, my heart was light, and I had decided to deliver these and come back for more when the messenger walked over—empty-handed.

"What happened?" The people here were so solidly behind the party and so hospitable that I couldn't understand why they had refused to lend him bedding.

"You go and ask them, sister.... These feudal-minded women!"

"Which house? Take me there." He must have said the wrong thing and annoyed someone. Getting one quilt less didn't matter, but offending the local people would have serious consequences. He stood there as if nailed to the ground till I reminded him quietly how important it was not to offend the masses and what a bad effect this was likely to have. At once he led the way.

No one was stirring in the hall of the house we entered. A blue curtain with a red border on top hung over the door of the inner room, and on both sides were pasted in bright red characters: "Happiness". Standing there, I called several times; but no one answered though we heard movements inside. Presently the curtain was raised and a young woman appeared. She was very pretty with fine features, arched eyebrows and a fluffy fringe. Her clothes were homespun, but new. Since she had done her hair like a married woman, I addressed her as Elder Sister-in-law, apologizing if the messenger had said anything to annoy her. She listened with a slightly averted face, biting her lips and smiling. When I had finished, she simply hung her head and went on biting her lips as if to keep from laughing. I scarcely knew how to bring out my request. But the messenger was watching me intently, as if I were a company commander about to demonstrate some new drill. Putting on a bold front, I asked bluntly for a quilt, explaining that the Communist Party's soldiers were fighting for the common folk. She listened to this without smiling, glancing from time to time back into her room. Then she looked first at me and next at the messenger, as if to weigh my words. The next moment she went in to fetch a quilt.

The messenger seized this chance to protest:

"Well, I never! I told her the same thing just now, but she wouldn't listen."

I threw him a warning glance, but it was too late. She was already at the door with the quilt. At last I understood why she hadn't wanted to lend it. It was a flowered quilt, completely new. The cover was of imitation brocade, with countless white lilies on a rich red ground. As if to provoke the messenger, she held the quilt out to me, saying:

"Here you are!"

Since my hands were full, I nodded to the lad. He pretended not to see. When I called him he pulled a long face, and with downcast eyes took the bedding and turned to rush off. There was a ripping sound—his jacket had caught on the door and torn at the shoulder. Quite a large rent it was. With a smile, the young woman went in to fetch needle and thread, but he wouldn't hear of her mending it. He went off with the quilt.

We hadn't gone far when some one told us that the young woman was a bride of three days' standing, and this quilt was all the dowry she had. That upset me, and the messenger looked unhappy too as he stared in silence at the quilt in his arms. He must have felt as I did, for he muttered to me as we walked:

"How could we know we were borrowing her wedding quilt? It's too bad...."

To tease him, I said solemnly: "Yes. To buy a quilt like this, ever since she was a girl she must have got up at dawn and gone to bed late, doing all sorts of extra jobs to make a little money. Think how much sleep she may have lost over it! Yet I heard someone call her feudal-minded. . . . ”

He halted suddenly.

“Well—let’s take it back!”

“You’d only hurt her feelings, now that she’s lent it.” I was amused and touched by the earnest, unhappy look on his face. There was something extraordinarily lovable about this simple young countryman of mine.

He thought that over and evidently decided I was right, for he answered:

“All right. Let it go. We’ll wash it well when we’ve done with it.” Having settled this in his mind, he took all the quilts I was carrying, slung them over his shoulders and strode quickly off.

Back at the first-aid post, I told him to rejoin regimental headquarters. He brightened up immediately, saluted me and ran off. After a few steps he remembered something, and fumbled in his satchel for two buns. He held these up for me to see, after which he put them on a stone by the road, calling:

“Dinner’s served!” Then he flew off. As I walked over to pick up the two stale buns, I noticed that a wild chrysanthemum had appeared in his rifle barrel to sway with the other twigs behind his ear.

He was some distance now, but I could still see his torn jacket flapping in the wind. I was very sorry I hadn’t mended it for him. Now his shoulder would be bare all evening at least.

There were not many of us in the first-aid post. The man from the local government found some village women to help us draw water, cook and do odd jobs. Among them was the bride, still smiling and pouting. She glanced at me from time to time, and kept looking round as if in search of someone. At last she asked:

“Where has that comrade gone?”

When I told her he had gone to the front, she smiled shyly and said, “Just now when he came to borrow bedding, I treated him rather badly.” Then smiling she set to work neatly spreading the mattresses and quilts we had borrowed on the improvised beds made of door-boards and tables(two tables put together is one bed). She put her own quilt on a door-board under one corner of the eaves outside.

In the evening a full moon rose. Our offensive still hadn't started. As usual the enemy was so afraid of the dark that they lit a host of fires and started bombarding at random, while the flares that went up one after the other to hang like paraffin lamps beneath the moon made everything below as bright as day. To attack under these conditions would be very hard and would surely entail heavy losses. I resented even that round, silver moon.

The man from the local government brought us food and some home-made moon cakes. Apparently it was the Moon Festival!

That made me think of home. At home now, for the festival, there'd be a small bamboo table outside each gate, with incense and candles burning beside a few dishes of sunflower seeds, fruit and moon cakes. The children would be waiting impatiently for the incense to burn out so that they could share the good things prepared for the goddess of the moon. Skipping round the table, they would sing: "The moon is so bright; we beat gongs and buy sweets...." or "Mother moon, please shine on me...." My thoughts flew to the lad from Tienmushan who had hauled bamboos. A few years ago he had probably sung the same songs.... I tasted a delicious home-made cake, and imagined the messenger lying in a dugout, or perhaps at regimental headquarters, or walking through the winding communication trenches.

Soon after that our guns roared out and red tracer bullets shot across the sky. The offensive had begun. Before long, casualties started trickling in, and the atmosphere grew tense in the first-aid post.

I registered the names and units of the wounded. The lighter cases could tell me who they were, but when they were heavily wounded I had to turn back their insignia or the lapels of their jackets. My heart missed a beat when under the insignia of one badly injured man I read: "Messenger". But I found he was a battalion messenger. My young friend worked in regimental headquarters. I resisted a foolish impulse to ask if casualties ever got left on the field, and what messengers did during combat apart from delivering dispatches.

For an hour or so after the offensive started, everything went swimmingly. The wounded men, as they came in, reported that we had broken through the first stockade, then the barbed wire entanglement, occupied the first fortifications, and started fighting in the streets. But at that point the news stopped. In answer to our questions, incoming casualties just told us briefly: "They're still fighting...." "Fighting in the streets." But from the mud which covered them, their utter exhaustion and the stretchers which looked as if dug out of the mire, we could imagine the fierceness of the battle.

Soon we ran out of stretchers, so that not all the heavily wounded could be sent straight to the hospital in the rear. There was nothing I could do to alleviate the men's pain, except get the village women to wash their hands and faces, give a little broth to those able to eat, or change the clothes of those who had their packs with them. In some cases we had to take off their clothes to wash away the blood and filth in which they were covered.

I was used to work like this, but the village women were shy and afraid to attempt it. They all wanted to cook instead. I had to persuade the young bride for a long time before, blushing furiously, she would consent. She only consented, though, to be my assistant.

The firing at the front was spasmodic now. I thought it must soon be dawn, but actually it was only the middle of the night. The moon was very bright and seemed higher than usual. When the next serious casualty was brought in, all the beds inside were occupied and I had him put under the eaves outside. After the stretcher-bearers laid him there, they gathered around and wouldn't go. One old fellow taking me for a doctor caught hold of my arm and said earnestly: "Doctor, you've got to think of a way to cure him! If you save him our stretcher-bearers' squad will give you a red flag!" The other bearers were watching me, wide-eyed, as if I had only to nod to cure the soldier. Before there was time to explain, the bride came up with water, and gave a smothered cry. I pushed through the bearers to have a look, and saw a young, round ingenuous face which had been ruddy but now was deathly pale. His eyes were peacefully closed, and the torn flap in the shoulder of his uniform was still hanging loose.

"He did it for us," said the old stretcher-bearer remorsefully. "Over ten of us were waiting in a lane to go forward, and he was just behind us when the bastards threw a hand-grenade down from a roof. The grenade was smoking and whizzing about between us. He shouted to us to drop flat, and threw himself on the thing. . . ."

The bride drew in her breath sharply. I held back my tears while I said a few words to the bearers and sent them off. When I turned back again, the bride had quietly fetched an oil lamp and undone the messenger's jacket. Gone was all her previous embarrassment, as she earnestly gave him a gentle rub down. The tall young messenger lay there without a sound. . . . I pulled myself together and raced off to find the doctor. When we got back to give him an injection, the bride was sitting at his side.

Bending over her work, stitch by stitch she was mending the tear in his uniform. The doctor made a stethoscope examination, then straightened up gravely to say: "There's nothing we can do." I stepped up and felt the lad's hand—it was icy cold. The bride seemed to have seen and heard nothing. She went on sewing neatly and skilfully. I couldn't bear to watch her.

"Don't do that!" I whispered.

She flashed me a glance of surprise, then lowered her head to go on sewing, stitch by stitch. I longed to take her away, to scatter this atmosphere of gloom, to see him sit up and laugh shyly. At that moment I felt something in my pocket—the two stale buns the messenger had given me.

The orderlies brought a coffin, and removed the quilt. The bride suddenly turned pale. Snatching up the quilt, she spread half of it on the bottom of the coffin, leaving half to cover him.

"That quilt belongs to one of the villagers," an orderly said.

"It's mine!" She turned away. Her eyes were bright with unshed tears in the moonlight. I watched as they covered the face of that ordinary country lad, who had hauled bamboo, with this red quilt dotted with white lilies—flowers of true purity of heart and love.

二

玫瑰色的晚餐[①]

谌　容

酒打开了，汽水打开了！酒是殷红的，汽水是橙黄的。孩子们欢呼了！蝴蝶结在飞舞，小酒窝儿夹在皱折的面孔中，乌黑的小脑袋和庄严的白发交映在一起。两张桌子拼起来，围坐着一大家子人。这久已失散，而今又重新聚在一起的亲骨肉。幸福之神啊，你真在人间遨游吗？请降临这星期六的晚餐，来参加这家庭的华宴吧！

"玫瑰、玫瑰、红玫瑰，我心中的玫瑰……"新买的收音机放在崭新的酒柜上。女歌唱家仿佛含着微笑在为这家人高歌。玫瑰的歌声，为这团聚的晚餐增添了欢乐的色彩。啊，音乐，永远是人生旅途中不可缺少的伴侣。无论是在远古，还是在现代；无论是在苦中，还是在乐时。

看来，今天还是应该来！苏宏正襟坐在桌前。左边是自己五岁的小女儿，右边是自己的妻子。女儿跪在椅子上喊："奶奶，我一人喝一瓶汽水！"孩子毕竟是孩子，一下子就熟了。谁能相信，她结识自己的奶奶还不到一小时。妈妈笑了，妈妈是慈祥的、高兴的，好象早在梦中就等待着这一声叫喊。妻子也在叫："妈！您手艺真好！这猪肝是怎么卤的？"她的声音多甜，多腻！她笑得多难看！她怎么叫得出口！多少年了，她没有叫过；连提也没提过他们，好象她根本没有婆婆，没有公公。

恶梦过去了，醒来又是清晨。你们总算回来了，从荒野的山中回到繁

---

① 中文选自：谌容．谌容小说选．北京：北京出版社，1981：399-416；英译文选自：Shen，R. *At Middle Age*. Gladys Yang（trans.）. Beijing：Chinese Literature Press，1987.

华的城市，从中世纪的野蛮回到现代的文明中来。北京，是个人人羡慕的好地方啊！颐和园、参考电影、昆明湖上的轻舟、回音壁前的神秘、中央精神、北京烤鸭、四川榨菜，开不完的专业会议，看不尽的传统节目……多少人托了关系，得不到调令，报不上户口，挤不进来。而你们，不管怎么说，回来了。在这新生的首都，大楼愈来愈高。住在十三层上算什么？有电梯。在高高的弯弯曲曲的空中走廊上散步，俯视街上的行人车辆象玩具模型，多有意思，多有情趣！人生恰似流水，逝去的再也无法找回来。向前看，这是最明智的。准备晚年吧！儿女都大了，不要你们的钱。十二吋的黑白电视可以换成十九吋的彩色电视。电冰箱、洗衣机到处都有，连山货铺都出售，不用走后门。收录机买得好，四个喇叭、立体声的。闭目静坐，听一晚上莫扎特、斯特劳斯。美妙的旋律会带走你心中的郁闷，连同那过去的恶梦。

“来，来，都喝一杯！”妈妈的声音从什么时候起变得沙哑了，好象是从鼻子里发出来的。她是在笑？还是在哭？只见一个灰白的头一闪，她变得多么苍老了啊！他记得，她的头发是乌黑的、浓密的，她的声音是清脆的、圆润的。

一只只杯子朝她面前伸了过去，一张张笑脸都仰了起来。红红的、浓浓的汁液，流向透明的杯中。这是醉人的酒，还是医治创伤的药？“玫瑰、玫瑰、红玫瑰……”

父亲坐在首席。他老了，雪白的头低垂着，好象已经在这轻快的歌声中睡去。不，他醒着。他冷着脸，埋在浓眉下的一双眼睛谁也不看。

妈妈斜睨了父亲一眼，那目光是在责备他的冷漠。这顿晚饭是她精心筹划的，是她通知的。她要儿子、女儿、孙子、孙女儿、外孙子都来，吃一顿团圆饭。不是年，不是节，可比过年过节还要值得庆贺啊！那二十个春节，二十个中秋，他们是在怎样的凄风苦雨中渡过！

妹妹和妹夫，带着他们的小淘气，单眼皮儿，小眼睛，在椅子上滚来滚去象个小猴儿。弟弟满面春风，笔挺的制服，雪白的衬衣，高昂起头，一脸的笑，低声向他的未婚妻献着殷勤。姑娘真漂亮，水灵灵的眼睛，深不可测，仿佛是两把小小的火苗在燃烧。这一对眼睛真亮，有点象……真象！

象她，那永远埋藏在他心底的她。她那最后的一瞥，可怜的一瞥啊！“玫瑰、玫瑰、红玫瑰，我心中的玫瑰……”

“关上吧！”喑哑的声音，父亲终于说话了，眼皮仍然没抬起来。好象他不是这新居的主人；好象这丰富的晚餐不是为了庆祝他、庆祝他二十年的错案得到纠正；好象他不知道他已重返画坛；好象他并不高兴“苏半舍画展”、《苏半舍画册》将重见天日。他象一匹疲惫不堪的老马，跑完了长长的路程。他象一个孤寂惯了的老人，厌恶这热闹场中的噪音。啊！不，他谁也不厌恶，只厌恶我。妈妈在笑着，沙哑地笑着。她装作没有听见那命令，她不去关收录机，竭力想让大家都高兴。她要造成和谐的空气。啊，妈妈，妈妈呀，泼出去的水收不回来，破镜不能重圆，破碎的心怎能捏到一起？

厌恶我吧！咒骂我吧！恨我吧！我是这家庭的叛徒。我在这里是不受欢迎的人。我为什么要来？我根本不该来！女儿听说要到爷爷、奶奶家，瞪大了眼问：“我有爷爷吗？我有奶奶吗？”她是从来没有听说过呀！妻子听说妈妈打了电话来，表现出异乎寻常的积极。穿什么衣服去呀，带什么礼物去呀，忙忙叨叨，典型的小市民！看她那烫成小卷的头，乱糟糟的；看她那咧着的嘴，笑的那个样子，好象她早就惦记着来给婆婆请安，好象她跨进了这个重新兴旺的家庭，就进入了一个新的世界。怨她，都怨她，她为什么一定要来？不来，就不会有这种尴尬和烦恼了。

难道能全怪她？不，这也不公平。我也是想来的。毕竟是自己的爸爸，六十多岁了，活不了几年了，怎么说我也是他的大儿子，曾经是他最宠爱的大儿子啊！啊！童年，无忧无虑的童年，梦幻一般的童年，金子一样的童年。江流在峡谷中奔泻；小舟在逆浪中挣扎；纤夫在河滩上匐行；夕阳把川江粼粼的波光和船夫汗涔涔的脸照得通红。扒在那宽大的案头，看着爸爸的笔移来移去，一切都出现在宣纸上了，多美妙啊！

“宏宏，你的杯子呢！”妈妈还在张罗着。宏宏！这一声喊，他想哭。一个什么东西从他流血的心上爬过。

“你吃你的吧！”喑哑的声音、冷冷的声音从上方传来，好象打在他的手腕上。苏宏举起的杯子放下了。立刻，他伸出另一只手：“来，妈，我自己来,我自己来!”他抬起身,伸出臂,嘴角努力翘上去,笑着。很好,只是自己的声音在发抖似的。他惶惑,瞥了一眼左边的弟弟,感到一股冷嗖嗖的光射向自己。是啊,弟弟应是这家的宠儿。在他们困难的时候,没吃的时候,挨斗的时候,只有他在身边。他还小,他是狗崽子,跟他们去了山里。他从几百里地外给他们背过南瓜,救过他们的命。

所有的酒杯都举起来了,碰在一起,叮叮当当地响着。“祝爸爸妈妈身体健康!”弟弟的声音多么悦耳,他未婚妻那银铃样的声音也在喊着“爸爸、妈妈”,“健康”。妹妹尖声在喊,妹夫在笑。小淘气站在椅子上,“祝爷爷奶奶身体健康,”妹夫教他喊的。孩子们都跟着嚷。女儿也笑着,叫着,露出缺了门牙的珍珠般的白牙齿。“玫瑰、玫瑰、红玫瑰……”

苏宏也举起杯来,举起这沉重的酒杯。他的嘴唇碰到了杯沿,冰凉的。这感觉,多么熟悉,那是在什么时候?什么时候?

一叠叠的宣纸,一方方的砚台,一支支的毛笔。朱砂、石绿、大红、大块的墨。好大的砚台。两只小手儿捧住墨,使劲儿地磨。爸爸要画了!“小书童,好儿子!”满墙的画啊,满屋的人,都听爸爸讲。“骨法用笔”、“意到笔不到”。多有趣,白白的一张纸上,突然飞来了鸽子,游来了大虾。梅花开了,菊花香了。爸爸有一支神奇的笔。他简直是魔术师。“宏宏,给爸爸倒杯酒来!”快,给爸爸倒酒去,他要酒,才画得好。宏宏端来酒,小手儿捧得紧紧的,怕洒了。爸爸总是弯下腰来,先把酒杯搁到宏宏的嘴边。“来,好儿子,喝一口,甜的。”是甜的啊,甜蜜的童年。这甜,是爸爸的爱,不是酒。酒是辣的,香的,呛人的。当他皱着眉,闭着唇,挤着眼,脸上做出怪相时,爸爸总是开怀大笑,用那扎人的胡茬子蹭着他的小脸蛋儿,用那双巨大的手把他高高举起。举得真高呀,伸手能摸到房顶了……啊,再也不会来了。再也不会来了。从那个可怕的时候起,一切都逝去了,象无情的流水,象飘忽的行云,父亲的柔情一去不复返了!一切都变得那么冰冷,父子俩仿佛是陌生人。他哆嗦了一下,跟着吵吵闹闹嘻嘻哈哈的一桌子人,举起了杯,呷了一口。酒,是苦的,一直苦到心底。

跟前是道道金光,金光里只见千万花朵在旋转。那时候,他的生活铺满阳光和鲜花。幽静的清华园,红色工程师的摇篮,流体力学,未来的专家，登上科学高峰的学者，后补党员，又红又专。令人欣喜的朦朦胧胧的爱情，水灵灵的眼睛，一汪清水样纯洁的心，玫瑰色的脸颊，林中小河边的漫步……忽然，天旋地转，希望之厦倾倒了，生活的灵光熄灭了。“你爸爸是右派！”“你要站稳立场，划清界限！”“是跟党站在一起，还是跟右派站在一起，两条道路由你选！”天哪！怎么会有这样的事情？怎么办？

“你为什么当右派？”

在笑语欢声中，一个声音顽固地来到耳边。多么可笑，说这样的话！这样问自己的父亲！父亲没有回答，无法回答的啊！他不敢抬头去望那张冰冷的脸，他却看见一双手在膝盖上怎样地颤抖！妈妈的沙哑的笑声从上方传来，她哪是在笑，她明明是在哭，在说：“宏宏，不要这样问你爸爸，他受不了！”她用身子挡住那坐着的人，哭泣着……

他感到一个什么东西堵在喉头，是泪水，就要涌出来的泪水。此时此刻，千万不能……他悄悄地不动声色地拿起酒瓶，又为自己倒满一杯。他笑着，把嘴角翘上去，苦着脸喝下去。“玫瑰、玫瑰、红玫瑰……”红的，玫瑰的红真好看，不是刺眼的大红，不是俗气的粉红，是那么一种雅致的、深沉的、泛着淡淡哀伤的红色，温柔的红色，和这整个的屋子一样的颜色。这间房好新啊！墙是白的，玻璃是亮的，门是新漆的，电镀的家具那么亮。一抹夕阳斜射，红光扑来，一切都染成了喜洋洋的玫瑰的颜色。一切全是新的，没有污垢，没有疵瑕，新起的炉灶新安的家。旧的好似被大水冲去了。大水啊，你为什么不能把人的心灵冲刷？让过去死掉，让今朝重生。一切都重新开始，世界该是多么美好！

冲刷不掉了。白纸黑字地印在那里。他第一次在报纸的铅字里找到了答案。“右派画家苏半舍一贯思想反动，他对党对社会主义有着刻骨的仇恨。在他的画里，祖国的天空阴沉，大地灰暗，社会主义如同一只破船，人民或在水中挣扎，奄奄一息；或在舟中跌倒，惊慌失措。这是多么险恶的用心啊！”这是结论，这是最后的审判！

当然要划清界线，家，再也不能回去了。没有必要回去了。是人民的乳汁哺养了我，是党培养了我。党就是家。丢掉那些小资产阶级情调吧，做一个心如铁、志如钢的革命者。

白色的油鸡,深色的松花,绛色的猪肝,红色的香肠,绿色的泡菜。家乡的泡菜,妈妈回来才泡的。一双双筷子,一张张笑脸。殷勤的劝酒,莫名其妙的笑声,令人作呕的献媚。她笑什么呢?虚伪,做作,小市民,怎么能同这样的人生活在一起?竟和她同床共枕二十年?这是命运的安排,还是历史的作弄?啊,当初怎么会走到这一步?

"玫瑰、玫瑰、红玫瑰,我心中的玫瑰……"我心中的玫瑰在哪儿?她到哪儿去了?她那纯真的脸,姣好的身姿,象爸爸画室里那散花的天女。那幅画,抄家时被烧毁了。

她应该永远享有幸福。尘土玷污她的肌肤简直就是犯罪,世俗纷扰她的宁静也是对艺术的亵渎。他怎么能,怎么能用自己有罪之身去损害这无辜的人儿!看她的双眸已经蒙上了忧郁的羽纱,看她的步履已经不似往日那样轻盈。斩断那恼人的情思,该做出决断了,放她到自由的天空中去!她应象一只自由的鸽子,飞到她该去的地方。让她享有幸福,这就是我的爱情!

爱情,爱情,什么是爱情?他把"爱情"献给了图书管理员。在那古老的藏书楼上,在浩如烟海的书卷中,她象一只色彩斑斓的玩具鸭,呱呱地叫着,花枝招展地打扮着,扰乱着那些孜孜不倦的求知者。他象老鹰似地扑向她,使她受宠若惊。他挽着她招摇过市,到处展示他的爱情,在他的鸽子面前显示。死了心吧,我的心已经死了!

她惊讶,她惶恐,她忧伤。那一封封烫人的长信啊!她的眼睛低低地垂下去,睫毛盖住了就要溢出的一池秋水。真傻啊!自以为扮演得很成功。然而,他演得是多么笨拙!毕业典礼完了,掌声过去了,该告别清华园了。不,该告别青春的梦了。小河,河边那棵垂柳,她应该站在那里的,在月光下,多少次,她站着。她真的来了,走吧,赶快逃开去,可是,他不能。这是最后的一面了。最后的,最后的,让一切都结束吧!难道可以这样地忍心离去?他走过去,迎着她,他们相视而行,愈走愈近了,象是什么?象莎士比亚悲剧里的角色。悲剧,怎么不是悲剧?她的眼里有多少忧伤?多少愁苦?真想用一个热吻替她抹去!

"你,不该这样。你在欺骗自己,你在欺骗我,你也在欺骗她……"

他震动了！向她忏悔吧，把心中的苦水向她倾吐吧，只有她能了解。啊！不，我一个已经够了，划清界线并没有把自己从厄运中拯救出来。专业被调换了，不再属于尖端保密项目了。后补期延长了，“对右派父亲还存在着温情主义”，连留校当一名助教的资格都没有了。天涯海角，何处是归宿？我带着优异的成绩，将要在人生的茫茫大海中去撞荡。等待着我的不是静静的小溪，而是惊涛，而是骇浪。我的小船还不知划向哪里，怎么能带着这应属于天国的女神，在尘世的硝烟中彷徨？

“我跟她，已经有了……”

话未完，她已转身走去。急急的脚步，又一步一步地放慢了，停住了，她回过头来，朝他看，睁着梦幻般的大眼睛，凄凉的眼神，可怜的眼神，她在等着……

错，错，错，无可挽回的错啊！

又是弟弟在笑，他的美人也在笑。舒心的笑，刺耳的笑！孔雀喜欢展示自己的羽毛。姑娘们爱俏。情人们爱笑。啊！他们是在偷偷地碰杯，悄声祝福他们的未来。祝福吧，牛车到火车，风筝到火箭，粗布衣到的确凉，钻木取火到宇宙飞船。幸福，人类追寻了多少代？从盘古开天地到永无休止的未来。

爱情，幸中之幸，福中之福，这幸福之王啊！爱情，自私的东西，不愿被别人窥见。他和他们的目光相遇，恰恰是不该相遇的时候。弟弟的笑容立刻消失了，脸象冰结成的。那一张漂亮的脸，为什么也露出轻蔑？她凭什么看不起我？难道只有你们才配得到爱情？弟弟把什么都告诉她了，一定的。

你们笑吧，你们得意吧，你们享受生活的美酒去吧！你们没有权利轻视我，你们懂得什么叫爱情？你们懂得什么叫牺牲？爱情是和牺牲连接在一起的，这才是真正的爱情！啊，想这些干什么，不要嫉妒他们，吞下自己这黄连般的爱情的苦酒吧！她现在在哪里？东北的松花江畔？西北的黄土高原？十年生死两茫茫，不，她该还活在这微笑的大地上！

他又伸手去拿酒瓶。

“你少喝点！”

一张宽宽的白脸。熟悉得很,却又象个生人似的脸。脸上射出不满的、关切的目光。他装作醉了。醉了的人都是醉眼朦胧,看起人来模模糊糊。你是我的妻子吗?我怎么好象不认识你!

真是同床异梦啊!怪不得她经常抱怨,唠唠叨叨。习惯,真是个可怕的东西。习惯了,天天下班回家,把自行车支在屋檐下,女儿跑来叫爸爸,现成的饭菜,衣服洗好了,裤子烫平了。妻子是无辜的。为什么她该是替罪羊?一天天的日子磨炼着,他变了些,她才尝到一点幸福。只是,他的心是冷的,他的自我谴责是有限的,他的施舍也是吝啬的。在一起过日子罢了,人都要结婚,都要生孩子,这是天经地义,这就是生活。

"玫瑰、玫瑰……"怎么总是放这个曲子呢?大概是收录机没有自动回转重播电路。弟弟为了取悦未婚妻,让它反复反复。她是玫瑰,当然,是他心中的玫瑰。他面前的路是用爱的鲜花铺成的,爸爸的爱,妈妈的爱,未婚妻的……这歌声简直叫人要发疯!

"关上!"爸爸又叫了一声,他终于忍不住了,自己站起来把女歌唱家赶出屋子了。歌声戛然而止,屋子突然一静,屋里这么多人,为什么显得空空的?啊,妈妈走了,她又去厨房端菜去了。她做了多少菜,大概排了两天队……

"鸭子,鸭子,大鸭子!"孩子们拍手叫起来了。

久违了,八宝鸭:黄灿灿,油浸浸,香喷喷,透亮透亮的。"吃吧,都来,多少年没做了,都忘了!"妈妈挽起袖子,把筷子和刀子一起戳向那只可怜的鸭子。

"宏宏,你吃吧,你顶爱吃的!"她夹了一箸鸭腿上的肉,用匙子接着滴滴答答的油汁,伸着双臂递了过来。赶快用碟子接住,妈妈怎么变得这么客气?他记得妈妈用筷子敲自己的头,那是哪一年?过春节,他抢鸭子吃,她不准他吃多了。他是顶爱吃,他还顶爱看妈妈做鸭子。他总是挤在厨房里,案桌旁,看她灵巧地把鸭子翻过来,把骨头剔掉,再装上火腿、香菇、糯米、百合,又变成了一只肥胖的鸭子。对,还有薏仁米。他也用小手抓了往里塞,妈妈用胳膊肘推他,撵也撵不走,等着吃鸭子。妈妈骂他:"馋相!"

眼望着碟子里的鸭子，还是做得那么好，那么地道，她从哪里弄来的薏仁米？一定是在药房买的。他只望着，提不起筷子，他怎么吃得下呢？“资产阶级右派分子的家庭生活，潜移默化地腐蚀过我。我要同这罪恶的家庭划清界线。”为表明自己的坚贞，他控诉过鸭子。真的，这不是笑话！“那不是八宝鸭！那是八毒鸭。”唉！多亏了这只八毒鸭，荒唐！当了四年预备党员之后，居然转了正。他怎么咽得下，又重新端来的鸭子？

爸爸也吃不下。他的脸黑沉沉的，嘴唇慢慢地嚅动着，他还剩有几颗好牙？他曾有一副结实的白牙齿，象弟弟现在的一样漂亮。“中国人的吃也是艺术，搞艺术的人而不懂得吃，他就搞不好艺术！”为这话，他挨过批。苏半舍的画值钱，可到月底妈妈就嚷没钱买米。爸爸能花钱，妈妈会做菜。稿费到手，画友酒友，叔叔阿姨，“奇珍阁”“萃华楼”，文人聚集的“康乐”，餐馆里的匾上是郭老的题字。加上大小家宴，三天五天，花个精光。“金钱乃身外之物，生不带来，死不带去”，是他的格言。爸爸大方得很，吃过他的人，揭发他时材料真多啊！

如今，他老了，酒量没有了，食量也没有了。他坐在这丰盛的餐桌旁，那神情好象在开会，简直象是让他交代问题，他已失去了享用的乐趣，他已厌倦了。他用漠然的眼光审视着八宝鸭，审视着围在他身边的大大小小的人。冷冷的空洞的目光掠过苏宏的脸，这目光里没有爱，甚至没有恨，只有一股浸人的冷淡，令人不寒而栗的冷淡！

苏宏低下了头，痴痴地凝望着空了的酒杯。酒杯空空的，心也空空的。啊！你为什么要把这样的目光投向我？我心里好受吗？如果我曾经伤害了你，做了一个儿子不该做的，也决不是我的本意。哪怕你骂我一顿，也比这好。不，你不会骂我了！你心中那个“好儿子”早已不存在了，就当没有生他！不，不，我不愿意这样，我从心里是……爱你的。当然，我不会说出口了，我什么也不愿对你说了。一切都搅乱了，理也理不清，说也说不明。我心里的苦，有谁知道？干嘛想这些，我应该笑，是在庆祝啊！难得的……

“玫瑰、玫瑰、红玫瑰……”收录机明明关了，怎么这声音仍象蚊子似的，在耳边叫着，赶也赶不走。我知道，你怪我，唉，这辈子是不会原谅了。

你发配去劳改时，妈妈通知了我。九点四十五的火车，我现在还记得清清楚楚。那时我坐在办公室，看着秒针走到那个时刻，我没有请假去送你，我不愿去吗？应该说，我不敢去。去请假，要说那么多话，作那么多解释，我……

那三封信，但愿你烧了才好。你给我的那唯一的一封信，我早已烧了，当时就烧了。但那三句话我记得："苏宏，你工作忙吧？我已摘了帽子。我和你妈妈都好。父字。"用钢笔写的，不是毛笔。你以前给人写信总是用毛笔。我回了信，从报上抄的话，别人看见也不要紧。我不能不谨慎。为了信，多少人挨了整啊！过了一年，我又给你写过一封，又过了一年，"文化大革命"以后，我连信也不敢给你写了。我知道，你会怪我。不，你不会怪我了！无所谓了！

命运为什么总是捉弄人？那一次我不去四川出差就好了。四川街上什么吃的也没有，真惨！你说我们家乡是"天府之国"，你说那地方"山清水秀出雅人"。你自命风雅，为这挨过批。你也是太天真了，太傻了，怪不得人家说你书呆子！没有想到去参观什么"大好形势展览会"，头头要去，我当然跟着。更没有想到你在那里帮忙。在走廊里，我只看见一个驼着背的老工人，背着梯子，提着黄色的颜料桶迎面过来，浑身是五颜六色的颜料，光着脚。我躲那梯子，一扭头才发现是你。我想张嘴，头头叫我快走。我走了，我打算另外找时间去看看你，可是，我没有去。我知道，你恨我。不，不，不，你也许忘了。忘了就好了，忘不了啊！

"宏宏，你怎么不吃呀！"妈妈沙哑的声音，笑着的声音，她是个聪明人，是体察入微的。为什么只叫我？我在这家里特殊！需要特殊的照顾。

"他醉了！"妻子笑嘻嘻地裂着嘴。有什么可笑的！醉了倒好，什么也不想，连意识也没有。

醉就醉吧！他面前的酒瓶已经空了。他伸手拿过妹妹那边的一瓶，公然地拿过来，大大方方地给自己倒上。喝吧，吃吧，什么也别想，什么也别说。他举起筷子，挟了一点菜放在嘴里。是鱼？是虾？是鸡？是鸭？"食而不知其味"，大概就是这个味道？这是鱼，新买的青花长瓷盘子装着。浓味的鱼上放着三朵花，胡萝卜刻的，青菜叶儿扎的，以示吉祥，为了好看。爸爸讲究“美食美器”，这是艺术！“君子不吃翻身鱼！”过年的时候，都撑饱了，妈妈捧上鱼，谁也吃不下了，爸爸总说这句话。一家子都是君子。君子？知识分子，多少年才绕到劳动者的队伍里。鱼活了，在宣纸上跳。现在这屋子怎么没有画？那间屋里有多少画啊！活的鱼，活的虾，过去了啊，一切！怎么老是胡思乱想，大概是喝多了点儿。

“我头疼，你们吃吧！”父亲终于耐不住，他抬身要走了。装作醉了，其实他没有醉，他根本没怎么喝。蜗牛躲进自己的躯壳里，带着箭伤的老鹿藏进丛林的深处。他驼着背走了，又回头瞥了一眼。啊，黑沉的脸，阴冷的目光，他恨我，他恨我！我不该来的！

“你们一家又团聚了！”机关的同志这么说，我只好笑着点头。可，他们永远不会知道，这是怎样的团聚啊！亲人不亲，不如不要。朋友可以选择，路人可以不理，亲人就是亲人。生活，不是一页稿纸。写错了，撕掉一页，再写一页。生活，是冷峻的，血和肉写成的历史。写在上面的一切，改不了，撕不掉，多可怕！

他们在笑些什么？他们在说些什么？跳舞？还跳五十年代的舞吗？太慢了，还是《魂断兰桥》的调调。八十年代了，“迪斯科”，会吗？跳给你看。又是他们俩，弟弟和她。“迪斯科”为什么不能跳？也挺文明，手都不挨。自己扭自己的，爱怎么扭怎么扭。一星期坐在办公室，跳一场也不错！不行了，跳不动了。学校的晚会总是通宵，她是舞会上的皇后。她大概也跳不动了。

红红的脸儿，喘嘘嘘地坐回到位子上。妈妈递过去手巾，擦擦头上的汗。妹妹从哪里学会的这一套，奉承话似乎准备好了，一套又一套的。她心里羡慕她们。她的婚姻是幸福的，还是不幸的？妹夫比她大得多，眼镜后面藏着一颗谁也看不见的心。那么瘦，那么贪吃。也许这是他吃到的最好的菜了。他又吃鱼了，他肯定不会跳舞。他只是叫小淘气儿吃，真是个好爸爸。他对她好象很体贴。妹妹和弟弟说得多热闹，哪来那么多话！他们不理我，装作在讨论跳舞。跳舞有什么可讨论的？谁爱跳就跳。天又不会塌下来？他们也恨我，我在这里是多余的。

妹妹什么都知道，她也跟着他们的，因为小，离不开。可她早早结婚了,还是离开他们了。她好象跟他们联系密切,给妈妈买了布去,给弟弟寄了鞋去。她做出一副宽容的样子,叫大哥了。不,我用不着你的宽容。我犯了什么罪? 我有什么错? 也许,我害怕了,我懦弱。对! 我只承认我懦弱。不过,开始时,我是真信啊! 怎么能反党?

一点也没有醉,这酒根本不醉人。我有酒量,这大概是遗传,我很清醒。妈妈坐下了,父亲离了桌,她好象精神松弛了,一下子垮了似的。她还在笑,叫别停筷子,又叫把收录机打开。"玫瑰、玫瑰……"怎么没有别的曲子? 屋里又显得热闹了,她怕冷场。"宏宏,吃呀!"沙哑的声音,妈妈在装假,她明明恨我。她装出笑脸,她装的。那天晚上她说过:"苏宏,你忘掉我们吧,我们也不连累你!"她说过,她忘不了,她恨我!

今天我根本就不该来!

"玫瑰、玫瑰、红玫瑰,我心中的玫瑰……"

玫瑰的歌声,绕在屋中;玫瑰的夕阳,停在桌上。一切都蒙上了这颜色。雅致的、深沉的、泛着淡淡的哀伤。我心中的玫瑰,你在哪儿?

A Rose-coloured Evening Meal

Shen Rong

The bottles of wine and soda-water are opened. Deep red wine, orange soda-water. The children cheer. Ribbons dance, dimples appear between wrinkled faces, and little black heads next to dignified white hair. The whole family sits round two tables put together. This is their first reunion after a long separation. Has the God of Happiness really come back to the earth? Please join in this Saturday evening's family feast.

"Rose, rose, red rose, the rose in my heart...." A newly bought tape-recorder stands on the brand-new wine cabinet. The soprano seems to be smiling as she sings for this family, her song adding to the festive atmosphere. Ah, no one can do without music, whether in ancient or modern times, whether in grief or joy.

It looks as if he was right to come. Su Hong sits straight by the table, his five-year-old daughter to his left, his wife to his right. The little girl kneeling on her chair is calling, "Granny, I'm going to drink a whole bottle of pop!" Being a child, she feels at home straight away. Who could believe that she's only known her grandmother for one hour. Mum laughs. Kindly, happy old lady, she seems to have dreamed of her grand-daughter calling her. His wife exclaims, "What a fine cook you are, Mum! How did you prepare this liver?" Her voice is nauseatingly sweet. Her smile is repulsive. How can she bring herself to say such things? All these years she's never mentioned his family, as if she had no in-laws.

The nightmare's over, a new day has dawned. At last you've come back from a rugged mountain to a prosperous city, from medieval barbarity to modern civilization. Everybody longs for Beijing: the Summer Palace, foreign films, boating on the Kunming Lake, the marvellous Echo Wall in the Temple of Heaven, the spirit of the Central Committee, Beijing roast duck, hot pickled mustard tubers from Sichuan, endless specialized conferences, a host of traditional performances.... Thousands of people pull strings yet fail to get transferred here, to squeeze their way in. And now you have come back, never mind how. In this revitalized capital the high-rise buildings are growing higher and higher. What does it matter living on the thirteenth floor? There's a lift. How fascinating it is, looking down from the balcony so high in the air at the toylike pedestrians and traffic below. Life, like a flowing stream, can never bring back what it has borne away. It's wisest to look to the future. Prepare for old age! Your children are grown up, you don't have to support them. You can buy a nineteen-inch colour TV in place of your twelve-inch black and white set. Refrigerators and washing machines are on sale everywhere, you needn't go through back doors. That's a good stereo tape-recorder you've bought, with four loudspeakers. You can sit with closed eyes all evening listening to Mozart and Strauss. The lovely music will carry away your cares, even your past nightmares.

"Come on, let's all drink a toast!" Mum's husky voice sounds rather nasal. Is she smiling or tearful? Her hair is grey, how she has aged. He remembers her with abundant jet-black hair and a sweet, mellow voice.

All glasses are held out towards her, each smiling face turns to her. Deep red liquid flows into their crystal glasses. Is this intoxicating wine or healing medicine? "Rose, rose, red rose...."

Father has the top seat. He has aged, his snow-white head is drooping as if the light music has lulled him to sleep. No, he's awake. His expression is cold. His small eyes under thick eyebrows aren't looking at anyone.

Mum shoots him a sidelong glance, deploring his coldness. She has gone to great pains to prepare this meal for them all, and invited her sons, daughter and grandchildren to this family reunion. This isn't any festival, but the occasion is more worth celebrating. The last twenty Spring Festivals and Mid-Autumn Festivals had been lonely times for them.

His younger sister and her husband have brought their Imp, a beady-eyed child who is fidgeting on his chair like a monkey. Younger Brother's face is shining. Wearing a spruce uniform and snow-white shirt, with his head held high, he is murmuring to his fiancée. A lovely girl, her limpid, unfathomable eyes are lit up like two little flames. Those bright eyes remind him... yes, remind him of the girl for ever hidden in his heart. Her last glance at him was so pathetic. "Rose, rose, red rose in my heart...."

"Turn it off!" Father has at last spoken, gruffly, not raising his eyes. He is not behaving like the master of this new flat, not as if this sumptuous meal is to celebrate his rehabilitation after twenty years in disgrace. He seems unaware that he has returned to the field of art, that his paintings are to be exhibited again and *Su Banshe's Art Album* republished. He looks like an old horse exhausted after a long gallop, like an old man so accustomed to isolation that this rowdy party revolts him. No, I'm the only one who revolts him. Mum's laughing, laughing huskily. Turning a deaf ear to his request she's leaving the tape-recorder on to make everybody happy. She wants to create a harmonious atmosphere. Ah, Mum, Mum, how can you recover spilt water, repair a broken mirror, or heal a broken heart?

He's disgusted with me. Curses me. Detests me. I'm this family's renegade. Persona non grata here. Why did I come? I shouldn't have come. When my daughter heard we were going to see her grandparents, she stared in surprise. "Have I a granny? A grandad?" She had never heard of them. When my wife knew that Mum had phoned, she was quite carried away. What should she wear, what presents should she bring? She bustled about like a typical petty bourgeois. Look how she's messed up her hair, having it waved in tight curls. Look at her broad grin. As if she's been longing to greet her mother-in-law, as if she's entering a new world by coming into this family which is prospering again. It's her fault, all her fault, why did she insist on coming? If she hadn't, I wouldn't be feeling so awkward and irritated.

Is it really all her fault? No, that's not fair. I wanted to come too. After all he's my dad, in his sixties, without much longer to live. Besides, I'm his elder son, once his favourite son. Childhood, carefree childhood, dream-like, golden childhood. The current races down the gorge, small boats struggle upstream, tow-men strain forward, bent double, the setting sun dyes red the glinting river and the boatmen's perspiring faces. Dad, stooping over his big desk, with a few strokes of his brush paints this enchanting picture.

"Honghong, your glass!" Mum is looking after us all. Honghong! He feels like crying. Something has lacerated his bleeding heart.

"Get on with your meal." The gruff voice sounding coldly from the head of the table seems to rap his wrist. Su Hong puts down the glass he has raised. At once he raises his other hand. "Here, Mum, let me help myself." He stands up, reaching out and forcing a smile. Good, only his voice is trembling.

Frantic, I glance at my brother on the left and sense the coldness of his look at me. Yes, he should be the favourite son. When they went through hard times, had nothing to eat and were under fire, he was the only one who stayed at their side. Still small, treated as a little cur, he went with them to the mountains. Saved their lives by lugging them a sack of pumpkins from hundreds of *li* away.

All glasses are raised, clinked together. "Here's to your health, Dad and Mum!" Brother has a pleasing voice, and his fiancée chimes in like a silver bell, "Dad, Mum, good health." Sister's voice is shrill, her husband grins. The Imp stands on his chair. "Here's to your health, grandad, grandma." His father has told him what to say. All the other children join in. My daughter smiles too and calls out, showing the gap in her pearly front teeth. "Rose, rose, red rose...."

Su Hong raises his glass too, this heavy glass of wine. Its rim feels cold to his lips. A familiar feeling. What does it remind him of?

Stacks of rice paper, square inkstones, brushes, cinnabar, malachite green, bright red, big ink-slabs. What an enormous inkstone. Two small hands clutching an ink-slab are grinding it hard, Dad's going to paint! "That's my good sonny!" Paintings cover the wall and everyone listens to Dad as he explains different techniques. What fun it is seeing a dove fly suddenly on to a sheet of white paper. A prawn swims over. Plum-blossom blooms. Chrysanthemums scent the air. Dad has a magic brush. He's a real magician. "Honghong, pour Dad a glass of wine." Quick, pour the wine, Dad paints best when he's drinking. Honghong holds the glass carefully, afraid to spill it. Dad always bends down to put the glass to his lips. "Here sonny, have a sip, it's sweet." Yes, it's sweet, honey-sweet childhood. What's sweet is Dad's love, not the wine. Wine is sharp, bitter, choking. When he frowns, shuts his mouth and makes a face, Dad always bursts out laughing and brushes his prickly moustache against his cheeks, then swings him up high in the air. So high that he can touch the ceiling.... Well, those days can never come back. Ever since that fearful time everything has passed away like a flowing stream or like a floating cloud. Father's tenderness has gone never to return. Everything has turned icy cold, father and son seem strangers. He coughs, raises his glass with the noisy laughing people around the table, and takes a sip. The bitter wine fills his heart with bitterness.

He sees shafts of golden light in which thousands of flowers are swirling. In those days his life was full of light and fresh flowers. The secluded college campus, cradle of engineers, future specialists, scholars scaling the heights of science, probationary Party members, both red and expert. Entrancing, dream-like love, limpid eyes, an innocent heart, rose-red cheeks, strolling in the wood by the brook.... Abruptly the earth spins round, his hopes are toppled, the light of life is extinguished. "Your father's a Rightist." "You must stand firm and make a clean break with him." "Make your choice: side with the Party or with a Rightist." Heavens, how could this have happened? What should he do?

"Why are you a Rightist?"

Amid the talk and laughter this question rings in his ears. What a ridiculous thing to ask his father. His father doesn't answer, cannot answer. He dares not raise his eyes to that icy face, but sees his hands trembling on his knees. Mum's husky laugh rings out, but her laugh is close to tears. "Don't ask your father that, Honghong, how can he bear it." Sobbing, she stands in front of the seated figure....

He feels a lump in his throat, tears spring to his eyes, but he must on no account shed them. He stealthily picks up the bottle to refill his glass. Forcing a smile he screws up his face and drinks. "Rose, rose, red rose...." His rose is a beautiful red, not a gaudy scarlet, not a vulgar pink, but a refined tender crimson suffused with faint melancholy. The same colour as this room. A brand-new room. White walls, glittering glass, a newly painted door, bright electroplated furniture. The red rays of the setting sun have dyed everything in their gay rosy light. Everything is new and spotless in this new home they have set up. The old seems to have been swept away by a flood. Why can't the flood scour our souls? To let the past die and embark on a new life. If we could start again from scratch what a fine world this would be.

It can't be done. Printed in black on white paper, he found the answer in the newspaper. "The Rightist artist Su Banshe with his reactionary outlook has an inveterate hatred for the Party and socialism. In his paintings our motherland's sky is overcast, the earth is grey, socialism is like a sinking ship with people at their last gasp struggling in the water or lying panic-stricken on the deck. What vicious insinuations!" That was the conclusion reached. The final verdict.

Of course he had to make a clean break, could never go home again. There was no need to go. It's the people who raised me, the Party that trained me. The Party is my home. Scrap those petty-bourgeois sentiments and be an iron-willed revolutionary.

White chicken, dark brown preserved eggs, deep red liver, pink sausage, green pickles. Mum made these hometown pickles on her return here. So many pairs of chopsticks, so many smiling faces. Toast after toast, senseless laughter, disgusting flattery. What is she laughing at? How can I live with such a petty-bourgeois hypocrite? Have I really slept with her for twenty years? Is this fate or a trick played on me by history? How could I ever have taken up with her?

"Rose, rose, red rose, the rose in my heart...." Where is the rose in my heart? Where has she gone? With her sweet face and graceful figure she was like the goddess scattering flowers in one of Dad's paintings. That painting was burnt when our house was raided.

She ought to be happy for ever. It would be a crime to let the dust defile her or worldly conventions upset her. How could he, a criminal, harm such an innocent girl? Her eyes are misted over, her step is no longer so light. Stop maundering like this and make up your mind to release her. She should be like a dove, free to fly wherever she pleases. Because I love her I want her to be happy.

Love, love, what is love? He had given his "love" to the librarian. In the old library among all those books, she had seemed a little duck quacking away and preening herself, distracting serious students. He had swooped on her like an eagle, sweeping her off her feet. Had taken her everywhere to flaunt his love, even to the one he loved. Give me up, my heart already numbed.

Amazed, fearful, wounded, she wrote him long passionate letters. Her eyes downcast, her lashes covered her eyes brimming over like autumn pools. What a fool he'd been, thinking he'd acted a part successfully when his performance had in fact been so crude. After the graduation ceremony, when the applause had died away, it was time to take leave of his college. No, take leave of his dreamlike youth. She should be standing by the brook under the weeping willows. How many times she had stood there in the moonlight. Yes, she had come. Go quickly to avoid her. But he couldn't. This was their last meeting, the last, last one, to end everything between them. How could they part like this? He went over to her. Gazing into each other's eyes they drew closer and closer together as they walked. Like characters in a Shakespearian tragedy. A tragedy? Yes, it was a tragedy. He longed with one ardent kiss to wipe away all the hurt, the grief in her eyes.

"You shouldn't do this. You're deceiving yourself, deceiving me and her too...."

This staggered him. Why not pour out to her all the bitterness in his heart? Only she could understand. No, his own wretchedness was enough. Making a clean break hadn't saved him. He had been switched from studying a most advanced, top-secret course. His admission to the Party had been postponed because he "still sympathized with his Rightist father". He wasn't even eligible to teach in the college as an assistant. Where in the wide world was there a place for him? With my fine academic record I must strike out for myself in the sea of life and battle with angry billows. Not knowing where to row my little craft, how can I involve this angel in such danger?

"She and I have already...."

She turned and quickly made off. Then slowed down and stopped to stare at him with her big dreamy eyes, her sad, expectant eyes….

What a ghastly, irretrievable mistake.

Brother is laughing again, his pretty fiancée too. Carefree laughter, piercing laughter. Peacocks like to flaunt their plumage. Girls like to dress up, lovers to laugh. Ah, they're quietly clinking glasses and drinking to their future happiness. Happiness. From ox-carts to locomotives, kites to rockets, homespun to dacron, kindling fire by rubbing wood to space ships, for how many generations has mankind sought for happiness? Ever since Pan Gu created the world and the search will continue till the end of time.

Love, the greatest happiness of all. Selfish love unwilling to be seen by others. He meets their eyes at an inopportune time for them. At once Brother's smile vanishes, his expression freezes. Why is there such contempt on her beautiful face? Why should she despise me? Are you the only ones fit to be in love? My brother must have told her everything.

Laugh, preen yourselves, enjoy the sweet wine of life. You've no right to despise me, what do you know about love? Do you know what sacrifice means? Love and sacrifice go together, that is the only true love. But why think of such things, don't envy them, swallow the bitter wine of your own love. Where is she now? By the Songhua River in the northeast? On the loess steppe of the northwest? For ten years we hovered between life and death, no, surely she's still alive on this smiling earth.

He reaches again for the bottle.

"Don't drink so much!"

A broad white face. All too familiar, yet like the face of a stranger. Looking at him with reproachful, anxious eyes. He pretends to be drunk. Drunkards with their bleary eyes can't see distinctly. Are you my wife? I don't seem to know you.

Yes, they were strange bedfellows. No wonder she was always complaining, nagging. Habit is a fearful thing. Habit made him come home from work every day and park his bicycle under the eaves as his daughter ran out calling daddy. His meals were cooked for him, his clothes washed, his trousers pressed. His wife was not to blame. Why make a scapegoat of her? As time passed he steeled himself, underwent a slight change, and she had known a little happiness. But his heart was like ice, there was a limit to his self-reproach. He was miserly too with his kindness. They lived together, that was all. Everyone must marry and have children, that was only right and proper. Such was life.

"Rose, rose...." Why does this tune go on and on? Probably this tape-recorder has an automatic replaying circuit. To please his fiancée Brother keeps it repeating itself. She is a rose. Of course, the rose in his heart. His road is strewn with the fresh flowers of love, father's love, mother's love, his fiancée's love.... This song is maddening!

"Turn it off," Father calls, finally losing patience. He gets up to drive the soprano out of the room. With the music turned off the room is suddenly quiet. With so many people there why should it seem so empty? Ah, Mum has gone to the kitchen to fetch another dish. She must have queued up for two days to prepare so many.

"Duck, duck, a big duck!" The children clap their hands. It's long since he's seen an Eight-treasure Duck, so yellow, succulent, savoury and translucent. "Come on everybody, eat. I forgot how to cook this after all those years." Mum rolls up her sleeves to attack the poor duck with a knife and chopsticks.

"Honghong, have this, it's one of your favourites." She offers him a leg, using a spoon to catch the fat dripping from it. Quickly hold out your plate. Why has Mum become so ceremonious? He remembers her rapping him on the head with her chopsticks. Which year was that? One Spring Festival, when he was wolfing down duck and she didn't want him to over-eat. He loved duck, loved the way Mum cooked it. He always squeezed into the kitchen, beside the table, to watch as she deftly turned and boned the duck, then stuffed it with ham, mushrooms, sticky rice and lilies. Yes, and Job's-tears. With his little hands he stuffed in a handful too. When Mum tried to elbow him aside he refused to go, waiting right there for the duck to be cooked. She scolded, "Greedy guts!"

The duck on his plate is just as well cooked, with all the old ingredients. Where did she manage to find Job's-tears? No doubt in a pharmacy. He looks, but doesn't pick up his chopsticks—how can he eat this? "Life in the family of a bourgeois Rightist imperceptibly corrupted me. I'm going to make a clean break with my guilty family." As a sign of determination he had denounced this duck, yes, seriously. "That wasn't Eight-treasure Duck but Eight-poison Duck." How utterly ludicrous. Because of this Eight-poison Duck he had been four years on probation before being admitted into the Party. How could he stomach this duck served up today?

Dad isn't eating either. His face is dark, his lips quivering. How many sound teeth has he left? He used to have strong white teeth as handsome as Brother's now. "Eating is an art in China. If an artist doesn't know how to eat, he can't be a good artist." He had been criticized for saying this. His paintings fetched high prices, but by the end of each month Mum complained that she had no money to buy rice. Dad was a spendthrift, Mum was a good cook. When he received money he invited his artist friends and drinking friends to one of the well-known restaurants frequented by men of letters, with inscriptions inside written by Guo Moruo. And every few days they entertained guests at home till all the money was spent. His maxim was: "Money is something we're born without, and it can't be taken with us when we die." Dad was very open-handed. Many, many of his former guests had denounced him.

Now he's old, has given up drinking and hasn't much appetite. He's sitting at this feast as if at a meeting where he has to come clean. He's lost his *joie de vivre*, is worn out, looking listlessly at the duck and at the grown-ups and children seated around him. His cold, blank glance sweeps over Su Hong's face with no love in it, no hate either, nothing but a fearsome coldness which seeps into people's bones.

Su Hong hangs his head, staring stupidly at his empty glass, as empty as his heart. Why look at me like that? Am I feeling good? If I hurt you, acting in a way no son should, it certainly wasn't because I wanted to. If you'd bawl me out it would be better than this. But you can't. Your "good sonny" disappeared long ago, pretend he was never born. No, no, not that.... I love you with all my heart. Of course I can't say so, I don't want to tell you anything. Things are too snarled up to be sorted out or explained. Who knows how wretched I am? Instead of dwelling on these things I should be smiling. This is a celebration, a special occasion....

"Rose, rose, red rose...." Why do I still hear that song, like a mosquito buzzing by my ears, when the tape-recorder's turned off? I can't drive it away. I know you blame me, know you can never forgive me. When you were sent away for labour reform, Mum notified me that the train left at 9 : 45. I remember that distinctly. I sat in my office then, watching the second hand creep to "9". I didn't ask for leave to see you off. Didn't I want to go? I didn't dare to. If I'd asked for leave I'd have had to make long explanations.

I hope you've burnt those three letters. I long ago burnt that one you wrote me, burnt it as soon as I got it. But I remember every word in it. "Su Hong, is work keeping you busy? I've been cleared. Your mum and I are both well. Father." You'd written with a fountain-pen, not a brush, though all your previous letters to me had been written with a brush. I wrote back copying phrases from the paper, so that it wouldn't matter who read my letter. I had to be careful. So many people had got into trouble over letters. A year later I wrote to you again. The year after that, when the "cultural revolution" started, I didn't even dare write. I knew you would hold it against me. No, you can't have. Nothing matters to you anymore.

Why does fate play such tricks on us? I shouldn't have gone to Sichuan that year on business. There was nothing to eat on sale, it was terrible. You'd said our native province was "the land of plenty". That its green hills and limpid streams produced men of good taste. For boasting of your good taste you were criticized. You were too ingenuous, too foolish, no wonder they called you a pedant. I hadn't intended to go to that exhibition, but as my boss went I had to. I hadn't expected you to be helping out there. In the corridor I spotted an old stooped workman, a ladder over one shoulder, approaching with a bucket of yellow paint. He was barefoot, his clothes stained with paint of different colours. Stepping out of the way of the ladder I saw that it was you. I wanted to speak but my boss told me to hurry. I went on, meaning to come back later to see you, but I never did. I know you resented that. No, no no, you may have forgotten. So much the better. I wish I could forget.

"Why aren't you eating, Honghong?" Mum's husky laughter. She's extremely observant. Why single me out? I'm someone special here, needing special consideration.

"He's drunk!" My wife chuckles, showing her teeth. What's funny? I only wish I were drunk, too drunk to think or be conscious of anything.

All right, get drunk. The bottle in front of him is empty. He reaches for the one by his sister and fills his glass. Drink up, eat, don't brood or talk. He picks up his chopsticks to help himself to some food. Is it fish? Prawn? Chicken? Duck? This must be what is meant by "eating without tasting". It's fish, set out on a new blue and white oblong porcelain dish. The tasty fish is decorated with three flowers cut out of carrots and Chinese cabbage to add a festive note. Dad liked "beautiful food, beautifully served". Called that art. "The superior man won't eat a fish that has been turned over." He said this at each Spring Festival when Mum brought in a fish and we were all too full to finish it. So we were all "superior men". Superior men? Then why had it taken intellectuals so long to join the ranks of the working class? Live fish frisk on rice paper. Why are there no paintings in this room? We used to have so many. Live fish, live prawns, all gone now. These speculations must come from drinking too much.

"My head aches, I'll leave you to it." His patience exhausted, Dad stands up, pretending to be tipsy. He's not, in fact, as he has drunk very little. A snail retreats into its shell, an old stag struck by an arrow hides deep in the forest. He walks away, stooping, then glances back. His face is dark, his glance cold, he hates me, hates me. I shouldn't have come.

"So your family's reunited." When colleagues say this I have to smile and nod. But they will never know the nature of this reunion. If kinsmen are unkind it's best to have none. You can choose your friends, can ignore the people you meet, but not your family. Life is not a sheet of paper; if you make a mistake you can tear it up and start again. Life is ruthless, a history written in flesh and blood. Nothing written there can be altered or torn up, how fearful.

What are they laughing at? What are they saying? Dance? The dances of the fifties were too slow, to tunes like *Auld Lang Syne*. It's disco in the eighties, can you dance this? I'll show you how. It's the two of them again, my brother and her. Why not dance disco? It's most civilized, you don't even hold hands. Just twist any way you please. After sitting in an office for a week it's good to dance for a while. But I can't do it. Our college parties used to last all night, she was the queen of those dances. Now she probably can't dance either.

With flushed cheeks, puffing, they sit down again. Sister hands them towels to wipe their perspiring faces. Where did she learn her stock of compliments? She must envy them. Is her marriage happy or not? Her husband's much older than she is, inscrutable behind his spectacles. So thin, so greedy. This may be the best meal he's ever eaten. He's eating the fish too. I'm sure he can't dance. Like a good father he's urging the Imp to eat. He seems very fond of Sister. She and Brother are chattering away. They ignore me, pretend to be discussing dancing. What's there to discuss? Let anyone dance who wants to. It won't make the sky fall down. They hate me too. I'm odd man out here.

Sister knows the whole story, she went with them too, being too small to leave them. But a long time ago she married and left them. She seems to have kept in close touch, buying cloth for Mum, sending Brother shoes. Posing as tolerant she greeted me as Elder Brother. I don't need your tolerance. What crime have I committed? Maybe I was afraid, weak. Yes, I admit I'm a weakling. But to start with I really believed I was right. How could I oppose the Party?

I'm not drunk, no one could get drunk on this wine. I inherited a capacity for liquor, I'm quite sober. Mum's sitting down looking limp, on the verge of collapse since Father left the table. She's still smiling, urging everyone to eat, and to put on the tape-recorder. "Rose, rose...." Is there no other cassette? The room's lively again, she doesn't like awkward silences. "Honghong, eat!" With her husky voice Mum's putting on a show; she obviously hates me. Her smile is a sham. That evening she told me, "Su Hong, forget us, and we won't involve you." That's what she said, she can't have forgotten. She hates me.

I shouldn't have come today.

"Rose, rose, red rose, the rose in my heart...."

The song of the rose circles round the room. The rosy sunset comes to rest on the table. Everything is veiled in its refined, deep colour tinged with grief. Where are you, rose in my heart?

三

沉重的翅膀(1-2 章)[①]

张　洁

让我们从这个普通人的，这句朴素的话里，得到超度吧：——实践，是检验客观真理的唯一标准。

一

令人馋涎欲滴的红菜汤的香味，从厨房里飘送过来。案板上，还响着切菜刀的轻快的节奏。

也许是因为身体已经恢复了健康，叶知秋的心情就象窗外那片冬日少有的晴朗的天空。这一刹那，她竟觉得自己好象恢复了学生时代那么贪吃的胃口，一口气可以吃得下五两干饭。这种难以寻觅的旧时情怀，引起她的一种渴望，使她起意要干一件与她的年龄极不相称的、学生时代的恶作剧才好。

唉，当然不能胡闹，她毕竟是一个头发已经开始花白的人了。况且，即使在自己的家里，她也不能太过地放肆，因为这种放纵自己的行为，如果成为一种习惯，然后不知不觉地带到办公室，或者是带到公共场合里去，那就会引起莫名其妙的指责或非议。即使她是这样地注意检点自己，在别人的眼睛里，她也将是一个行为荒诞，哪怕每天做十件好事也不会有

---

① 中文选自：张洁. 沉重的翅膀. 北京：人民文学出版社，1981；英译文选自：Zhang，J. *Leaden Wings*. Gladys Yang（trans.）. London：Virago Press，1987.

人记得，却会因为心不在焉的一个小小的疏忽，弄得人家怀恨在心的、不合时宜的人物。天知道！她不过是一个最简单的人，简单得象一个只有第一信号系统的低级动物一样。而人们的认识，经过十年“文化大革命”的陶冶，越是复杂的现象、越是谎言，倒越是显得正常，容易让人相信，容易让人理解。而越是简单的、越是真话，反倒显得不正常、不容易让人相信、不容易让人理解了。白白地活了四十几年，却还没有学会生活！冷静的时候，她好象也很明白自己的欠缺，等到激动起来，却仍然是浑然一片。

于是，她勉强着把自己这种快乐的冲动，压进一个中年的、中华民族的妇女所应该具有的风度的模式里去。也许因为她的压力还不很足，那冲动“嗞”的一下又冒出来了一点，她突然想起了久已忘记的法文，不禁高声地问了一句：“今天中午吃什么？”

莫征立刻在厨房里用法文接了上来：“红菜汤、腊肠和面包。”

这孩子真不赖，竟然没有忘记。这当然应该归功于他自小在那个有教养的家庭里所受到的训练。

有教养的家庭?! ——可他现在什么也没有了，真正地成了一个孤儿，就象她自己一样。

是的，莫征曾经有过一个温暖的、有教养的家庭。

可教养又是什么呢？在那几年，它是一种容不得的奢侈品，是资产阶级这个词汇的同义语。

人类真是一群疯狂的傻瓜，为什么要创造物质文明呢？要是都停留在洪荒时代，或是还用四肢在地上爬行，那么，一切大概都会简单得多。

莫征的父母，曾是一所名牌大学里的法文教授。五十年代中期，叶知秋做过他们的学生。那时，莫征只有三岁多。长得非常可爱，很象英国电影《雾都孤儿》里的那个可爱的小男孩奥利佛尔，穿着一套浅蓝色的法兰绒衣服，黑黑的眼珠，象两颗滚动着的黑宝石。每次开饭以前，总是把两只洗得干干净净的小手，平放在桌子上让妈妈检查，然后有礼貌地用法文问妈妈：“我可以吃饭了吗？”每每叶知秋到莫教授家里做客的时候，总是戏谑地管莫征叫奥利佛尔。当时，叶知秋绝没有想到，他以后的命运，竟是孤儿奥利佛尔的翻版。为这，叶知秋总觉得自已有点对不起莫征，没想到她这善意的玩笑竟成了一个巫婆的咒语，不然，何以会应验得如此准确呢？

问题还不只是他现在已经什么也没有，成了一个真正的孤儿。残酷的生活，使他失去了本应该是他所有的，却增添了许多不应当强加于他的。父母在“文化大革命”中双双死于非命之后，他成了靠偷窃过日子的小贼，象一只流落在街头的野狗。当叶知秋第一次把他从派出所领回来之后，他甚至也狠狠地咬了她一口，在她家里等于来了一次卷逃。这也许是一条野狗才会有的惨痛的经验，因为无数次的事实证明，每一只向它伸过去的手，几乎都是痛打它的手，它无论如何也不会想到还有一只想要抚慰它的手。从来没吃过糖的人，怎么能够想象“甜”是一种什么样的感觉呢？

叶知秋再一次把他从派出所领了回来。她也理不清自己到底为什么要这样做。

也许因为她自小也是一个孤儿，饱尝过世态的炎凉和寄人篱下的痛苦？这痛苦象一条天生的纽带把她和这个孩子联在了一起。

也许是因为她知道她这一生永远无法实现自己的母爱，她象一切女人一样，顽强地需要一个表现这女人的天性的机会。

对于一个女人来说，再没有比丑陋这件事更使她伤心的了。真的，那真是一种不幸。

说不出叶知秋脸上的每一个部件，究竟有什么明显的缺陷，可是这些部件凑在一起，毫不夸张地说，几乎使她成了一千个女人里也难以遇到的一个顶丑的女人。

那些很代表她的性格的头发，又粗、又多、又硬。头发的式样也非常古板，又不肯让理发师剪个稍稍时髦一点的发型，稍稍地削薄一点。于是，又短，又厚的头发，每一根都象放射线似地向四外支楞着，远远看去，活象头上戴了一顶士兵的钢盔。

浑身上下看不到一点儿女性的曲线和魅力。肩膀方方正正，就象伐木人用斧子砍倒一棵老树后的树桩——是砍倒而不是用锯锯倒的。

没有一个神经正常的男人，会娶这样一个女人做妻子的。

最坚强的心，也许是最脆弱的心。对于在各种逆境中，备受作践、蹂躏、摧残……从而变得残酷、冷漠的心灵来说，再没有比“温暖”这种东西更强大、更能征服他的力量了，它甚至超过原子弹、氢弹。因为他得到的太少、失去的太多，一旦得到，就很懂得珍惜。何况叶知秋给莫征的，决不只是一点点温暖，而是真正的、象母亲一样的爱。这两个被许多过着正常家庭生活的人们视为不可理喻的人，充分地享受着那些或许是正常的家庭享受不到的天伦之乐。

菜饭端进来了。

莫征，象饭店里老练的服务员，右手端着腾着热气的红菜汤，左手拿着两个分盛着腊肠和面包的盘子。两个盘子上还摆着一个小小的盛果酱的盘子。

腊肠切得很薄，一片片错落有致地向着一个方向，顺着盘子绕成环形，斜躺在盘底。面包切得很均匀，每片面包的厚度一样，简直象用尺子比着、量着切出来的。

每每看着莫征十分在行地抄起锅碗瓢勺在厨房里忙着做饭，以及他带着一种看不出来的、又猜不透含义的微笑，象饭馆里的大师傅那样，有意地用勺子在炒锅底上俏皮地敲两下的时候，叶知秋的心里，总泛起一种说不出是悲凉还是欣喜的复杂情绪——只是淡淡的。他的生存能力似乎比她们这一代人强。比如，直到现在她还不会做饭烧菜，如果没有莫征，她就不得不去吃那口味单调透顶的食堂。奇怪，食堂里烧的东西，别管是红烧肉还是黄焖鸡，永远是一个味儿，你就分不清它们到底有什么不同。她喜欢吃口味好的菜，可是要她为那种事分心她又舍不得时间，就算下了狠心抽出时间，她也不会做。她的生活安排得一塌糊涂…… 不，生存能力！当然她指的不是这个，不过她也不知道怎么会产生这样毫不相干的联想。实际上她想得更多的却是，只要他愿意，他可以干好任何一件事情，别管是做饭、弹钢琴、或是法文……他当然比她强得多！可是他为什么这样一副乐天知命的样子端着这几个盘子呢？不，也不是说端盘子有什么不好，她不是这个意思，而是……而是什么呢？她的思绪飘移开去……

汤大概很烫，放到桌子上之后，莫征立刻吹着自己的手指头尖。

那应该是一双艺术家的手。手指粗而长，手掌厚而宽，指关节和挠腕关节都生得十分结实。她知道，小的时候他学过几年钢琴。小小的人儿，脚还够不着踏板，却会在一片琴键的轰鸣中忘记了玩耍和吃饭……可现在，就是叶知秋心血来潮地，在他们家里那架落满尘土的钢琴上，用僵硬的、不听使唤的手指勉强弹上一曲的时候，他呢，却远远地躲进他自己房间的一个角落里，仿佛琴声里有什么让他感到害怕的东西……

什么叫做应该是呢？莫征早已不是那个穿着一套浅蓝色法兰绒衣服的小男孩。他已经变成又高又大的青年，穿着一件军绿色的棉布上衣，那是部队上的处理物资。衣服皱皱巴巴，原先的扣子早已掉光了，现在的五个扣子是有深有浅，大小不一。又肥又长的劳动布裤子，象没有盛满东西的口袋，挂在他那又瘦又长的腿上，裤脚上还有一个没有补缀上的三角口子。他所有的裤脚上几乎都有这样的口子，这大半和他干的工种有关系，整天和树枝、灌木丛打交道，灌水、剪枝、喷药……一不小心，就会被树枝刮破。但即使这样，他仍然是个让姑娘们一见倾心的人物——假如她们不知道他的过去的话——方方的下巴，棱角清晰的大嘴巴，黑而柔软的头发从中间分开，松松地披向脑后，仿佛修剪过的、那么不宽不窄的眉毛，整齐地、直直地伸向太阳穴，只是在眉梢有那么几根，微微地往上翘着，这使他在不动声色的时候，也给人一种神采飞扬的感觉。也许因为黑眼珠比平常的人稍大了一些，目光总显得凝重、迟缓，还有点儿淡漠。而这效果完全不同的眉毛和眼睛，给他造就了一个不能不引人注意的面孔。

莫征用脚勾出放在桌下的凳子，在那因为开榫已经摇摇晃晃的凳子上坐下，凳子立刻吱吱嘎嘎地呻吟起来，仿佛因为这突然增加的负荷而感到极大的痛苦。

一听见这声音，叶知秋总是不放心。她已经说过多少次，要么赶快拿出去修理，要么就丢掉它，不然，早晚有一天会摔坏人的。而莫征总是不以为然地、懒懒地说："没事儿，只要您记着别坐它就行了！"其实，他倒并不是懒，在他来说，摔一跤又算得什么了不起的、值得担心的呢？叶知秋只好随他。不过每每他往那个凳子上坐下去的时候,她的眼睛总会不由地对那凳子瞟上几眼。这会儿,她的眼睛也是那么不放心地瞟着。虽然是不动声色的,莫征也还是感觉到了。唉,太过于操心了。

然后,他仿佛是不经心地问道:“怎么样?味道还可以吧?”

叶知秋这才低头吹着汤勺里滚烫的汤,匆匆地呷了一口,笑了,满意地称许着:“不错,挺地道,象你的法文发音一样的地道。”

莫征的汤勺在半路上停住了。啊,为什么要提起那与旧日的生活有关系的回忆呢?莫征决不愿意去回想它。可为什么只要有一点点光亮,它立刻就会象影子一样出现,紧紧地跟随着他,纠缠着他,不肯和他分离。凭空地给他增添了许多的烦恼。其实,这烦恼也是多余的。他张开嘴巴,带着一种差不多是发狠的样子,咽下了那勺菜汤,好象把那烦恼和菜汤一起咽进了肚子里去。适才牵动他眉头的那根神经好象安定下来。接着,用自己那副白而坚实的牙齿撕下一块面包。

“哐当”一声。叶知秋一愣,一时以为莫征到底是翻倒了凳子。不,那声音是从天花板上传来的。一定是楼上有人碰翻了什么。随之而来的是小壮嚎啕的哭声、嚓嚓地响着的杂沓的脚步声和小壮的妈妈刘玉英压抑着的啜泣声。

莫征的脸上闪过一丝冷冷的微笑,说道:“高尔基笔下的人物的生活。”

叶知秋停下了吃饭。

莫征,还是带着那淡淡的、冷冷的微笑:“怎么啦?”

叶知秋不好意思地笑了。在比她似乎还老于世故、不易动情的莫征的面前,她觉得自己有时倒象个幼稚的、容易感情冲动的小女孩:“不知道为什么,在别人的哭声里,我咽不下饭去……”

“您简直象个基督教徒。”

她发气了:“莫征!”觉得他亵渎了自己的感情。然后站起身来,往外走去。莫征把他长长的腿往她面前一横,那弓着的腿,活象一个放在二百米跑道上的中栏:“您还是歇会儿吧!您管得了吗?过不了两天还得打。”

他说的是真话。楼上这一家,总是孩子哭大人骂的。那两口子都不是那种泼皮式的人物,两个孩子也都懂事听话,可是,他们的生活为什么过得那么沉重啊!

莫征和解地劝慰着她:“您还是再吃点吧,一会儿该凉了!”

叶知秋已经没有了胃口,饭前那阵美妙的情绪不知为什么已经消散得无影无踪,她摇摇头。

她无言地在写字台前坐下,顺手翻动着这些天因为生病没有细读过的报纸。习惯性地注意着哪些工程竣工投产、哪些企业已经超额完成今年的生产计划的报道……是的,这些报道都给她一种年终将近的气氛。还有一个多月,七九年就要过去了。她立即想起她病前就要急着写完的那篇报道,开始寻找她已经写好的那份提纲。

奇怪,那份提纲哪儿去了呢?她明明记得放在这一摞稿纸上嘛!没有!也许放在抽屉里了?

她依次拉开一个又一个抽屉,每个抽屉都是一样的混乱:日记本、信札、邮票、装着钞票的信封或钱包、工作证、眼镜盒(有好几个)、药瓶子(空的或是装着药的)……要是没有极大的耐心,谁也别想在这一大堆乱七八糟的东西里找到一件要找的东西。偏偏叶知秋就是一个顶缺乏这种耐心的人,所以每当她急急地在这里面找什么东西的时候,她都会下定最大的决心,什么时候一定要清理一下这些东西,没用的就把它扔掉,这里有很多没有用的东西:这些旧信,瞧,还有这个空药瓶子。“砰”的一声,她顺手把那空药瓶子扔到墙角里去。

可是,等到这阵骚乱一过,她便会忘掉自己的决心,那些废物便依旧安然无恙地躺在抽屉里。再说,那些旧信虽然都不是什么亲朋故旧寄来的,但她依然舍不得丢掉。它们好象是她的生活的记录:失败的,然而却是昂扬的。

因为她是记者,又因为她对每一个受了命运的不公平待遇的人的那种由衷的同情,对一切丑恶的现象的义愤——在那些年这种事情是那样地遍及每个角落,在她采访过的那些平凡的工人、基层干部中间,她简直就象个可以以心相托的朋友。她不自量力地干预了多少工作份外的事情哟!那些事情,照例地没有得到合理的解决,每每她象个没头苍蝇,乱碰一气，精疲力竭地回来，坐在桌前翻动这些信件的时候，她总是感到内疚，好象她也愚弄了那些善良而忠厚的人们，不过，他们并没有认为她是个不可信托的人。难呐！远方的客人往往会突如其来地降临：站在门口，一个劲儿地搓着一双骨节粗大的手，羞涩地微笑着，微微地涨红了脸，然后，牢骚一发就是大半夜。闹得莫征的房间简直象个客店。

这两年，信件的色彩有了明显的转变：谁谁家的，被谁谁的后门挤掉了大学报考名额的儿子终于考上了大学；谁谁的所谓叛徒问题终于澄清，恢复了工作；谁谁再也不穿小鞋了，因为那个靠帮派势力上台的党委书记撤了职……这些信，怎么舍得丢掉呢？

但是，提纲总得找到！

"莫征，看见我放在桌上的一张纸了吗？"她知道她用不着说什么提纲不提纲的，那对找到或找不到是完全没有一点儿帮助的。这孩子对她的工作总是不大以为然，从来不会朝她写过的那些东西看上一眼的。

"什么纸？我没在您桌子上拿过什么纸！"

"一张稿纸，上面写了字的！"

莫征这才想了起来："噢——前天小壮来玩儿，我在您桌子上拿了一张废纸给他包糖来着！"

叶知秋真正地痛心了："哎呀呀！那是我准备写的一篇今年工业完成情况的报道提纲，怎么是废纸！"

"我怎么知道什么提纲不提纲。"语调里竟没有一点不安或歉意。

"我跟你说过多少次，我写过字的纸，不要乱动，不要乱动！你全当成耳旁风！"

莫征终于显出一副懊悔的模样。倒不是他已经觉悟到自已撕掉了一篇提纲，而是因为叶知秋那副气急败坏的面孔和语调里那种懊丧的情绪。便诚心诚意地表示着自已的改悔："其实，有工夫您不如好好休息休息，急什么呢？那些报道什么的，不过是冠冕堂皇的官话！有人看吗？又有人信吗？"

"你怎么能这么说话。我看你脑子里的那些乱七八糟的东西可是越来越多了。"叶知秋拍桌子了。

莫征不再说话。他不愿意惹叶知秋生气。于是只顾低着头不紧不慢地吃着。房间里只有汤勺磕着碗盏,以及莫征那轻轻地、有节奏的嚼东西的声音。

他们经常发生争论,但往往让步的,却是莫征。他不愿意惹她生气。在他那荒漠似的心里,竟也还有一片浓密的绿荫,因为她是他在这个世界上唯一爱着的、给他温暖的、不记着他的过去的人。也还因为他有一种这一代人对上一代人的优越感。

有时他不能理解,他们之间不过差了二十个年头,在对客观事物的认识上,却有这样悬殊的差异。简直莫名其妙！难道他们那一代全是这个样子吗？差不多！唉,他们那一代,是多么善良、多么轻信、多么纯洁而又多么顽固地坚守着那一套陈腐的观念的一代啊！

这种争论,也常使叶知秋打心眼儿里感到委屈,她觉得她终归还不是一个没有头脑的女人。她的思想是新鲜的,感觉是敏锐的。她并不陈腐。陈腐这种印象是莫征这一代人强加在她头上的。在他们的眼睛里,大半凡是有了年纪的人,都是老朽的。

自从五六年大学毕业以后,她已经在新闻战线工作了二十多年。这工作使她的接触面十分广泛,对真实情况了解得也比较多一点、深一点。她早就对许多发生过的事物有她自己的看法,虽然她感到无可奈何,但是她总在心里告诫自己,叶知秋哟,你不管报道什么,千万不要有半点虚伪,可不能愚弄了养活我们的人民。就拿“文化大革命”那些年来说,她宁肯耍赖不写,也不肯跟着那些挂羊头卖狗肉的理论家们吹喇叭。她明白,这绝不是因为她勇敢,而恰恰是因为她幸好不是搞理论的。相反,她是懦弱的。但这能怪她吗？那是整整一个懦弱的时期。

她接触过不少战斗在工业第一线上的基层的同志。那都是些实打实的人和实打实的工作。那些在一般人看来都是干巴巴的数字,在她眼睛里都是一张张熟悉的脸、出炉的钢水、转动的机床、血管一样输送电流的送变电线路……每每想起这些,她总是感到安慰,毕竟还有脚踏实地的工作在干着。她因此而觉得她的工作也是脚踏实地的工作,是值得她忠诚地献出一切的工作。可是,听听莫征在说什么？

现在,她愈想愈气,连下巴都有点哆嗦,伸出长长的脖子,拿眼睛瞪着莫征,连她的眼镜也好象发了脾气,恨不得从鼻梁上跳下来,在莫征面前跺上几脚才解气。

这下莫征不吃了,他感到了问题的严重。她误解了他的意思。他收起了脸上那种淡漠的冷冷的笑,神情变得严肃起来。他说:"我不是说您的工作,我是说那些没完没了的数字。好些人都会以为那些个数字,是从基层到上面,一级一级按着统计表格的要求,个、十、百、千、万,一个算盘子儿、一个算盘子儿地扒拉出来的。其实,根据我的经验,没有什么是不可以伪造的,就连'最高指示'在内。报纸上总在写工业生产今年下半年比上半年超额完成百分之几,今年又比去年超额完成百分之几。扯淡!有什么意思。我也并不是说这些数字全是假的,我是说它没有意思。就拿咱们楼上老吴这个工人来说,他们家的生活情况是怎么样的呢?应该有人写一篇这样的文章:这许多年来,这些流汗出力的、脚踏实地给我们这个社会创造了财富,并且使我们得以生存下去的工人们的生活情况的真实报道。这样的报道才能真实地反映我们的工业生产发展了没有,发展得怎么样。您说那些数字有什么用?您想过没有?!"这回,倒是莫征难得地动了肝火,他越说越快,最后还使劲儿地把汤盘往前一推。菜汤洒了出来,向四周漾开,顺着桌子一角淌了下来,淌了莫征一裤腿。他掏出揉成一团的、已经脏得分不清到底是什么颜色的手帕,擦着湿了的裤腿。不停地,一下又一下……那动作早已失去了它本来的含义,那不过是在发泄着他极力压抑着的情绪。

莫征的话,象在她那憋足了气的心口上安了一个减压阀,使里面的压力渐渐地降了下来。他说的话,虽然带着孩子气的偏激,但是有他那一面的道理。她痛心地想起从五六年以后经济政策上的那些错误、失败。如果不是这么来回折腾,老百姓的生活总会稍好一些吧?但总之,不论如何比解放以前好得多了。

她不大有劲地说:"这些数字至少还是说明了我们的国民经济年年都在发展,比起解放前……"

莫征立刻停止擦腿,打断她的话说:"我就知道你又该这么比了。老这么比也不行呀！这是两个完全不同的社会呀！你不是社会主义吗？那是旧社会，没有可比基数嘛！”他露出一脸不屑再说下去的神气，把手里的手帕当成了抹布使劲往剩下的菜汤里一摔——大概也有点气昏了头，站起身来，拾掇起桌上的碗盏向厨房走去。到了门口，又回转身来，好象忽然来了一阵风，刮走了他脸上的那层乌云。满怀真情地对叶知秋说：“真的，您还是想想老吴一家子，为什么老是打架吧？”

那真情的语调出自莫征的嘴巴，自有一种揪人肺腑的力量。他是很少流露温情这种东西的。他觉得他是男人，而温情，是一种软弱的表现；实际上，他比谁都需要这个，因为他从人们那里得到的，往往都是戒备和提防。他曾经是个贼，谁知道他真的不偷了，还是假的？温情对于他，象奢侈品对贫困的人一样，只有不自量力的傻瓜才去巴望它！情感的分配，虽然不象物质的分配那样，可以任人随心所欲地转移或是靠强力去争夺，但是有些人更多一些忧虑和愁苦，有些人更多一些欢乐、温情和满足，它是可以随着权力、等级、金钱……派生的东西。莫征明白，他只有固执地抵御那对温情的渴望，才可以使他免于被这种可望而不可即的诱惑所伤害。

但是，青春啊，青春，不管你是怎样地冷静，怎样地想在一天之内成熟起来，你仍然充满那许多的真诚，那许多的忘我，那许多的激情，那许多的渴望！

老吴一家，是多少年的老邻居了。叶知秋还清楚地记得吴国栋曾是那么一个对妻子体贴入微的，英俊的小伙子。当刘玉英怀第一个孩子的时候，这栋楼里的住户，没有一个人不拿吴国栋那种过分的体贴开过玩笑。二楼的王奶奶经常说：“小吴啊，没事儿！女人生孩子，就跟母鸡下个蛋一样，别那么紧张，看吓着小刘哇！”说归说，叶知秋相信，只要没有人看见，他一定会整天小心翼翼地把小刘捧在手里，倒好象小刘是个刚下的鸡蛋而不是准备下蛋的母鸡。而小刘呢，又曾经是一个多么娇美的小媳妇啊，也不过是十几年的时间，可这一切全都哪儿去了呢？怎么完全变成了另一副模样：吴国栋怎么变得那么粗暴，两个鬓角也过早地秃了上去；而小刘的额头上又怎么那么快地就添上了许多皱纹啊!

二

头发的确烫得不错,很合夏竹筠的心意。波浪似地推向一个方向,很有一种雍容华贵的气派。她上了年纪,不能再象年轻的妇女那样弄得满头小卷。再说那也很俗气,好象那些小市民阶层的妇女,好不容易烫次头发,要不弄得满头是死死的小花,顶好一年不用再烫,就好象亏了本似的。

她对着前后的镜子,从从容容地打量了额前、脑后、两侧的头发,满意地微微笑着。向站在身后,举着另一面镜子的刘玉英点点头。

她想:这理发员的手艺不错,难怪人家向自己推荐。只是她的眼睛为什么显得那么愁苦?年纪不大嘛!怎么会有这么一副消沉的样子!让人看了觉得心里挺沉闷的。

夏竹筠轻轻地舒了一口气,等着理发员去拿她存放的提包和大衣。

银嵌的、深灰色的大衣很厚,但分量很轻,那一定是质地很好的纯毛料的。提包的式样也很少见,不是一般人常用的象饼干盒子的那一种,而是扁扁的,很宽,面上有压制出来的花纹。那是夏竹筠的老头子去年到英国考察时给她带回来的礼物。

这是老规矩,不管老头子上哪儿出差,总得带些礼物给她。逢到这时,她的脸上就会浮起皇后接受藩邦进贡时的那种微笑。可是,比方要是她知道老头子在杭州给她买龙井茶叶的时候,带着怎样一种淡淡的、揶揄的口气,学着保定府的口音对人家说:“送给我‘耐’(爱)人的!”她一定不会这么笑了。

刘玉英站在一旁,看着夏竹筠慢慢地穿上大衣,轻轻地蒙上头巾——小心不要压坏了刚才做好的发式——又慢慢地打开提包。这种缓慢,绝不是有意地做作出来的,这是那种有个有地位的丈夫,又长年地过着优裕的生活,受惯了人们的逢迎,知道自己的一举一动(哪怕就是掉了一张早已失去兴趣的、某种化妆品的使用说明),立刻会使一些别管有多么着急的事在等着办的人,耐着性儿,毕恭毕敬地守候着的,上了年纪的妇女才会有的缓慢。

夏竹筠从提包里拿出一个精致的皮钱夹，浅黄的皮革上，烫着咖啡色的花纹，配着两个金黄色的金属按钮。

皮夹里至少有五、六张十元钱一张的钞票，那几乎就是刘玉英一个月的工资，也许还要多。刘玉英也只有发工资的那一天，身上才会带着这么多的钱。平时，能拿得出来的，不会超过一元。

夏竹筠从钱夹里面抽出一张，食指和拇指用力地捻了一下，好象还能捻出来一张似的，然后递给了刘玉英。

在柜台前交帐的时候，小古看见刘玉英那因为愁苦而显得更加疲倦的面容，一面数着零钱，一面匆匆地看了看墙上的挂钟，说："五点半了，你该下班了！"

刘玉英知道，这是小古的关心。她朝小古笑了笑，心里想，下班又怎样呢？还不是一大堆烦心的事在等着她！

钱很脏，揉得皱皱巴巴的，特别是那些角票。夏竹筠嫌恶地用手指头尖儿轻轻地捏着，不过没有忘记清点一下找回的钱数。然后合上钱夹，那两个金属按钮，清脆的"咔嗒"一响。

夏竹筠再一次向镜子里瞥了一眼，然后向理发店门口走去。这时，她听见理发员在她身后轻声地说了句："再见！"才赶紧回过头去补了一句："再见！"心里泛起了一丝类似懊恼那样的情绪，倒不是因为她没有对理发员付出的劳累表示感谢(她不是已经付了钱吗！)而觉得有什么对不起那理发员的地方，而是懊恼自己怎么没想起先说声"再见"！显得她好没有教养。想不到，那么一个理发员，倒更懂得规矩。

走出理发馆大门，夏竹筠朝手腕上的小金表看了一眼。烫一回头发，花了差不多四个小时。可是她并不在乎时间，她只发愁如何打发时间。洗衣服、收拾房间、做饭有阿姨在管着。跟前剩下的这个女儿也大了，已经参加了工作。工作很理想，是个摄影记者。唯一操心的是，得给她找一个称心如意、门当户对的丈夫。

身体好、情绪好的时候，她也上上班。心脏不大舒服的时候，也可以在家休息一段日子。可也不能老是躺着睡觉哇！织毛衣吧，几年也织不好一件。老头子笑着说:“等你这件毛衣织好了,我的胡子该由白的变成绿的了。”

分不清他是开玩笑还是挖苦人。管他,反正那是一种消遣。

当然,她还可以看书、看报。订了许多的杂志、报纸,每天几乎有一大半时间在看书,看杂志,看报纸。她和那些高干的老婆可不一样,她上过大学,受过高等教育。但是,优裕的生活是一种腐蚀剂,它使她对人类精神生活的追求、理解、记忆等等的能力发生了退化。她记不住那些书上、杂志上、报纸上说了些什么!

到了晚上,老头子在部里开会,女儿在外面有活动,会客室的几张大沙发上就只有她一个人,守着一台 20 吋的日本彩色电视机。说她在看,又分明眯着眼睛,似睡非睡;说她没看,又明明在沙发上对着电视机坐着。真到了床上她又睡不着了。于是,便会找点事情来想想。她用不着吝惜晚上的睡眠,反正第二天早上她愿意睡到几点就睡到几点,用不着着急起床。她常想的是女儿的婚事:王副司令员的老二还没有对象,不过那孩子太吊儿郎当,没什么正经的本事;又想起俞大使的儿子,可那孩子身体不好,别中途夭折害了自己的女儿;又想起田部长的老三,长相不错,人也聪明,是个翻译,可不知有没有对象了……想着想着,她会爬起来去敲老头子书房的门。也不知道老头子果真是睡得那么死,还是知道她压根儿就没有什么了不起的大事情,有意地不睬她。反正,他没有起来给她开门。

当然,在她这样的年龄,花这样多的时间去装扮自己,早已不是为了讨什么人的喜欢,这不过是多年来养成的一种要讲究的、而且是能显示自己身份的习惯。她那位忙着上班、忙着开会、忙着深入基层、忙着打电话的丈夫,从来没有时间欣赏她的衣着和发式。他的电话为什么那么多,甚至在家里也不能逃脱,惹得她经常埋怨:“整天给你接电话!”他却说:“谁让你那么爱去接呢!”不让她接电话,那可不行。电话当然得由她来接,这是显示女主人的权力以及监督丈夫的重要一环。

五六年有一次她死命地拉着丈夫去北京饭店参加了一次舞会,第二天,她问他:“你觉得昨天晚上我穿的那件衣服合适吗?”

他确实认真地想了想,说:“不错,浅黄色很配你的皮肤!”

听了他那经过认真思索的回答，夏竹筠目瞪口呆了好一阵子，好象有谁给她施了定身法。然后，她气得大叫一声："天呐，我想你该不会突然地患了色盲症吧？我昨天穿的是一件紫红色的皱绸旗袍啊！"

他听了之后，却哈哈大笑："那么，你再做一件浅黄色的就是！"

等到她真做了一件浅黄色的绸衬衣穿给他看的时候，他早已忘记了自己说过的，浅黄色很配她的肤色这件事，却说："浅黄色？你穿起来好象不怎么合适！"

不过，除此之外，他没有什么可以让她挑剔的。年轻的时候，他人很漂亮，也很有风度，和他一起在街上走的时候，是足以使许多女人羡慕得眼红的。而且他很忠实，从来不对任何女人发生兴趣，就连她，也好象是他房间里一件可有可无的摆设。他们早就不住在一个房间里了。她曾暗自揣度，他是不是曾经懊悔为什么要找一个老婆来麻烦自己？也或许他们结婚的时候，他错把青年人的冲动当成了爱情。他是不是从来没有爱过她？以致他把自己没有实现过的热情全部给了工作？有时她埋怨他：总是工作，工作，工作，好象这个家，这两个女儿不是他的。要不是她出面张罗，小女儿能到那么一个理想的单位去工作？摄影记者，这工作又体面又轻松，接近的是上层人物，见识的是大场面。当然，还得张罗一套好房子，老头子恢复工作的时候，部里的房子一时紧张——怪事，部里年年盖房子，偏偏不想到给部长级的干部盖一些——只好在这套房子里住下了，这哪里象个副部长住的房子？五个房间，还是四层楼。瞧瞧别的副部长，有谁住这样的房子？当然，夏竹筠也并不是让部里花钱专门给盖一套，可换一套合适的，还是合情合理的吧？她有心脏病，老头子哮喘呐！这事靠老头子是不行的，还得由她出面。

顾客一走，好象把刘玉英撑着的那点劲儿也带走了，她立刻觉得全身象散了架一样。昨天晚上，整整一夜也没有合眼，早上连饭也没吃就出来了，中饭也没咽下去几口，一口气堵在嗓子眼里，她咽不下去。想起来她就伤心，可是她不愿意坐下来歇着。她必须分散自己的注意力，不然眼泪就会很快地掉下来。她拿起扫帚，打扫散落在地上的头发。

长这么大,不论爹,不论娘,别说碰自己一手指头,就连一声申斥也没有过。可昨天,她挨了一个嘴巴子。打她的,就是她恨不得连命都舍给他的自己的丈夫。为什么?不过是因为小壮打了一个暖水瓶。吴国栋也不问问孩子是不是烫着了,伸手就是一巴掌,她只是说了一句:“不就是一个瓶胆嘛,一元来钱的事儿,干嘛打孩子!”

听听吴国栋说了句什么哟:“听你说这话,好象你是个部长太太!一元来钱,你有几个一元来钱!”

一元来钱倒是有的,可要是到了月底,就是花一元来钱,也要颠过来、倒过去的盘算好几遍呐!谁要是没过过那种日子,谁就体会不到一元来钱是怎样地牵动着一个家庭主妇的心!

自从吴国栋得了肝炎,病休以后,每个月只拿60%的工资,也就是四十几元钱,她自己,加上辅助工资顶多五十来元钱。四口人,每个月还要给吴国栋老家里的父母寄十五元钱。吴国栋有病,需要加强营养,可是,能让两个孩子眼巴巴地看着吗?吴国栋也咽不下去啊!

自然,日子还是过得去的,比上不足,比下还是有余,只不过要让刘玉英使出好大的劲儿才行!

为了省几分钱,她从来不买切面或是挂面,哪怕在理发店里站了一天,脚背肿得多高,回到家里,也要自己擀。

为了省几分钱,她从来没有买过新鲜的时菜,总是到地摊上去买一角钱一堆的“处理菜”。大姐从新疆来信说,那里的青菜很贵。这么一比,北京还是不错,什么都有处理的卖:菜啦,鱼啦,布啦,鞋啦……刘玉英很熟悉在哪几个商场可以买到这样的便宜货。

为了省点洗衣粉,她充分地显示了她在计划学方面的才能:先洗浅色的衣服,后洗深色的,然后再刷两个儿子的鞋,最后还用这不起沫的黑汤洗拖把!

她把一个女人所能有的全部天才和智慧都用来打发这操心的日子了。在家当姑娘的时候,她哪过过这种日子,受过这种罪。不过,那时候情况不同呀!她怀念五八年以前的日子,那时候,家家的日子过得多富裕呀!六五年以后,这日子一天天地就难起来了!

难,可是她还怕爹妈知道,一是怕他们惦记,二是他们自己的日子也不宽裕。爹从厂子里退了休,弟弟也添了个小闺女。何必让他们揪心呢!每次回娘家看看,刘玉英总是尽心地把大人孩子收拾得整齐一点,还带上一盒子点心,不过都是七角多一斤的蛋糕,六角多一斤的桃酥。但这一切苦心都逃不过慈母的一双眼睛。做娘的也是千方百计地找个借口,老大、老二过生日啦,逢年过节啦,总要添补添补闺女,还琢磨着怎么才能不让女婿看出来,免得伤了女婿的自尊心。

这还不算,刘玉英放弃了一切作为一个女人天性里那种对于美的追求。前些日子,添了一件冬天的罩衣,本来,她很喜欢一块驼色的,上面有绿色和蓝色小麻点儿的棉的确良。一算,一件上衣得十来块钱,她下不了决心,在柜台前头转了好几个来回,最后,还是买了块布的。因为有那些钱,还不如给吴国栋买些营养品,再说,两个儿子也该添棉鞋了……

可这一切劳苦,全象她一个人应该受的,没有一句体贴的、知情的话,却遭到了这样的抢白,这样的奚落。刘玉英心里不由地想着:这也罢了,凭什么还要拿孩子们撒气呢?不是一次、两次了!孩子有什么罪!要是你没能耐撑住一个家,你就别结婚,既是有了家,你就得咬牙撑住它,那才叫个男人!要是你只会怨天怨地,打孩子骂老婆,拿他们撒气,那你还叫男人嘛!那叫窝囊废!她越想越冤,越想越气,就说了一句更让吴国栋火上浇油的话:"谁让你不是部长!"

"你当初怎么不找个部长嫁去!"

谁也不饶谁,谁都觉得自己有一肚子的委屈,一肚子的苦水,谁都觉得对方不怜惜自己。于是,你一刀、我一枪,话赶着话,越吵越厉害。自然,小壮又成了借题发挥的对象,吴国栋往死里打,刘玉英就坚决不答应,本来是在孩子身上做文章,打着打着,吴国栋往刘玉英脸上来了一巴掌。他自己也被自己的行为吓懵了。他这是怎么啦!

刘玉英突然不吵了,也不哭了,只是定定地瞅着他,好象共同生活了十几年,头一次才认识了他!

这几年来,他们经常吵架,却从来没发生过这样的事情。这究竟是怎么搞的,又应该怪谁啊?

这一巴掌倒好象把吴国栋自己打清醒了，他这才感到，刘玉英是家里的功臣，要是没有她，这个家可怎么撑得下去呢？他问过她凭着那点收入怎么把日子过下来的吗？没有。他想过她的什么小小的需要了吗？没有。她，毫无怨尤地献出了自己的一切。就是她，用她那柔弱的肩膀，默默无言地、坚忍地担着这副力不胜任的担子。

女人，也许是比男人更为坚忍，更为顽强，更富于自我牺牲精神的！

但是，不知他中了什么邪，却不能立即说出一句赎罪的话。也许他觉得那句话并不足以表示他的心情；也许他觉得那么一来，这一切更象儿戏；也许他想那么一来，不但不会得到她的原谅和理解，反而会更加激怒了她！

而在那一瞬间，刘玉英想了很多、很多。她想过，不如立刻死掉，让吴国栋后悔一生一世。但是，撇下的孩子谁来管呢？也许他们会摊上一个苛刻的后娘！她想起小时候听过的，那许多后娘怎样虐待前房孩子的凄惨的故事，眼泪止不住地淌了下来，好象她真地死了似的。不行！死不得！她想过和吴国栋离婚，可离婚象什么话，那会让人觉得她不正经，好象她干了什么丢脸的事儿。不是吗？人们不就是用那种鄙夷和猜疑的目光看待那些离过婚的妇女吗？不行，她可不能让人家指自己的脊梁背。她想过，一卷铺盖卷回娘家去，不行，家里哪有地方让她住。再说，两位老人又该多着急……想来想去，从早上到现在，她也没想出来什么好办法来惩罚吴国栋。

天呐，她想：为什么她的命是这样地苦啊！比起刚才那位顾客，她们的生活该有多么的不同啊？她一定幸福、知足、快乐，丈夫别说打她，就连一句重话都不会说的啊！

想到这里，她的眼泪又涌了上来，她生怕别人瞅见，赶紧用手背抹去了。

下雪了，一片片茸茸的、洁白的、轻飘飘的雪花，在寒风里欢快地飞舞着，这是今年的第一场雪。这让她想起了自己做姑娘时的生活，也是这么轻盈、这么新鲜、这么清凉凉地。多好啊！

从外面又进来一男一女两个青年人。姑娘的脸蛋被冷风吹得绯红，越发显得眼睛亮晶晶的、活泼泼的。

小伙子手里拎着两个很大的提包，里面满塞着一个个印有各个商场名称的纸包。一进门就站在那里，傻傻地笑着，并不是因为有什么可笑的事情，只是因为他觉得幸福，他不能不笑。

刘玉英接待过各式各样的顾客，她知道，眼前这俩人，是准备办喜事的一对儿。

姑娘对刘玉英说："同志，我想找这里的刘师傅……"

"你找她有什么事呢？"

小伙子清清嗓子，大约是为了使人知道，他将要谈到的事情是多么地重要："我们想请她给烫个头，听说她的手艺顶好！"

开票的小古插嘴说："找谁烫不行，我们这里的师傅，手艺都不错！"她觉得刘玉英今天的脸色尤其不好，她是不是病了？病了也不休息一下。这人太要强，也太好心，只要指名要她做活的，她没有不答应的。

小伙子窘了。打这样的交道，在他的一生中，当然还是第一次。他不知道怎样才能让人们明白，这件事对他，对他未来的妻子都是多么的重要："是这样……"他找不到恰当的语言了。

刘玉英明白，现在，对他来说，一切与他未来的妻子有关的，哪怕是微不足道的小事，都成了天底下顶重要的事了。她很累，她心烦，她一肚子的委屈，可是那小伙子的傻里傻气的劲头里，有一种动人的东西。她不由地说："我姓刘！"

小古说："好吧，好吧，那就开票吧！"然后小声地埋怨刘玉英："瞧瞧你的脸都肿了！"

姑娘把钱递给小古："冷烫！"

小古立刻把钱塞了回去，看看墙上的挂钟说："哟，冷烫可来不及了。"

那两个被幸福冲击得有点昏头昏脑的小傻瓜，这才知道世界上所有的事物，并不是都以他们那个点为圆心的。他们面面相觑地站着，不知道该怎么好。

姑娘说："明天哪儿还能抽出时间来呢？来不及了……"

刘玉英朝小古使了个眼色。小古才象发了大慈大悲："好吧，好吧，给你们开个票就是。你们可得好好谢谢这位刘师傅!”

姑娘站在挂着各种发型的镜框面前,看了一会儿,带着茫然的微笑,回过头去问小伙子:“烫个什么式样的好呢?”

小伙子也带着同样的微笑,鹦鹉学舌似地重复着:“烫个什么式样的好呢?”然后,象是忽然来了做丈夫的灵感:“刘师傅,您看吧,您看哪个合式那就准行!”

姑娘也好象有了主意:“对,准行!”

刘玉英说:“好吧,既是你们相信我,我就看着办啦!”她拿起姑娘的小辫,刚要下剪子,不由地朝小伙子望了一眼。她在他眼睛里,看到了一种十分复杂的情绪。

他在想什么?也许他在想,辫子,辫子,剪了这辫子,她就要跨进另一个门坎。这会儿,是不是应该由他来牵着她迈过这门坎儿呢?

刘玉英停住了手,忽然对小伙子说:“也许这一剪子该由您来剪才合适?”

他们没有想到,他们心里还在朦胧着的、没有剖析清楚的、对于彼此那种神圣的责任感,纯真的信赖感,却被这个有着一双愁苦的眼睛、一张爬满了皱纹的浮肿的面孔的,也许是没有更多的知识的中年妇女,勾勒得那么清楚、那么贴切。她怎么会具有这样的能力呢?这当然不在于人的文化水平,而在于有些人,天生地具有一颗专为体会美好事物的心。光凭这样一颗心,就应该得到人们的尊敬啊!

小伙子几乎下不了剪子。大凡善良的人,在看到一朵美丽的花,而又不得不亲自摘下它的时候,都会有这种矛盾的心情吧?他拿着两条剪下来的辫子看了很久,然后小心翼翼地装进了一个小塑料口袋。这一切情景,刘玉英觉得好象都是十几年前她和吴国栋经历过的一样。她想,她今天这是怎么啦?怎么什么事都会和吴国栋和她自己联系起来呢?

刘玉英拿着吹风机,最后再把那姑娘的发式修饰一下。

镜子里映出的是两张多么不同的面孔。在那张绯红的面孔、亮晶晶的眼睛旁边,她的面孔更显得苍老、灰暗。她从前不是也曾有过这样绯红的面孔和这样亮晶晶的眼睛么？看着眼前这张年轻而美丽的面孔，刘玉英心里不由地生出了由衷的祝愿："哦，姑娘，希望你永远这样美丽，这样新鲜啊！"

吹风机嗡嗡地响着，刘玉英用手托着姑娘耳后的头发，于是两个发卷绕过耳后，往脸颊前面弯了过去，立刻给那姑娘的脸上添了一种少妇的妩媚。姑娘不好意思地瞟着自已映在镜子里的那个显得陌生了的面庞，羞涩地微笑着。她还不习惯自己的这个新形象。

两个年轻人不知怎么都意识到了，他们婚前的这个晚上，在这个理发店里所经过的这并不奇特的一切，以及遇见的这个并不奇特的理发师傅，必将会在他们将要度过的几十年的共同生活中，发生一种长远的影响。

小伙子在一阵激动和慌乱之中，在提包里掏出一个纸袋，递给刘玉英："刘师傅，请您收下，这是——这是我们的喜糖！"

刘玉英执意不肯接受："哪能这样，我心领了就是了！"

推来推去，盛情难却。刘玉英只好打开纸袋，挑了两块包着红色箔纸、印有"囍"字的乳糖，然后又把纸袋塞进他们的提包，送他们出了理发馆。

路上的行人已见稀落，地上的雪也已积了薄薄的一层。刘玉英就那么站在雪地里，久久地望着他们远去的、幸福的背影，又再一次地在心里默祝那姑娘："愿你永远这样美丽！"

直到他们的背影消失在夜色里，她才掉转头来。忽然，她看见，在理发店门口的一棵树干上，靠着吴国栋。他一定站了很久了，旧棉帽上、两个肩膀头上、围巾上全都积了一层薄薄的雪花。刘玉英用力地攥住了手里的那两块喜糖，看着吴国栋一步步地向她走过来。

Leaden Wings(Chapters 1—2)

Zhang Jie

Our Salvation lies in this simple saying of an ordinary individual: Practice is the sole criterion of truth.

1

An appetizing smell of beetroot soup came wafting from the kitchen, with it the rhythmic sound of chopping.

Perhaps because Ye Zhiqiu—Autumn—had got over her illness, her heart felt light on this fine winter day. She felt as if she had recovered the appetite she once had as a student, when she could wolf down five ounces of rice at one meal. She was in a mood to play some prank out of keeping with her age.

But of course she mustn't; her hair was turning grey. Even at home she had to watch her step, because if she let herself go there and it became a habit, she might do the same in her office or in public, scandalizing everyone. As it was, though she tried to hold herself in check, some people considered her a ridiculous misfit because of her inadvertent carelessness. Heavens! She was just the simplest of beings. But since the ten years of turmoil, the more complex or fantastic anything was, the more normal and rational it seemed to people. Simple, truthful statements struck them as abnormal and difficult to understand. She was over forty now, yet still had not learned how to cope with life.

So she tried to repress her elation, to behave like a middle-aged Chinese woman. Perhaps she didn't try hard enough, for a little of it came bubbling out as she called in her rusty French, 'Qu'est-ce qu'on mange au déjeuner?'

Mo Zheng promptly called back from the kitchen, 'De la soupe au potiron, de saucisson et du pain.'

Good lad, he hadn't forgotten his French. That came of his upbringing in a cultured family.

A cultured family? But now he had nothing. Like her he was an orphan.

Once, sure enough, he had a warm, cultured home.

But what was culture? For some years it had been an intolerable luxury, a synonym for "bourgeois".

What fools human beings were to have created material civilization. If they had stayed as they were at the time of the flood, life would have been much simpler.

Mo Zheng's parents had taught French at a top university. During the fifties Autumn had been their student. Mo Zheng had only been three then, an adorable child dressed in light blue flannel who reminded her of little Oliver Twist in the English film. His black eyes had flashed like gems. Before every meal he would wash his hands and put them on the table to show his mama, then ask respectfully, "Est-ce que je peux manger?" Whenever Autumn called on Professor Mo, she would tease the child by calling him Oliver. Her joke had later turned into a witch's curse, and like Oliver Twist he had ended up an orphan.

It wasn't just that he was destitute. Life had robbed him of his birthright and forced things on him that he should never have known. After his parents were killed in the Cultural Revolution the boy had roamed the streets like a homeless cur, living on what he could steal. The first time that Autumn had fetched him home from the police station, he had savagely bitten her hand. How could a vagrant, who only knew hands stretched out to hit him, conceive of a helping hand?

Autumn had fetched him from the police station again, not even aware herself why she did so.

Perhaps it was because she too had been an orphan, had suffered the pain of living in a home that was not her own. This pain created a bond between them.

Perhaps it was because she knew she would never have any other outlet for her maternal love.

Nothing is more agonizing for a woman than ugliness.

There was nothing grotesque about any of Autumn's features, but taken together they made her one of the ugliest women alive. Her hair, in keeping with her character, was a thick, wiry mane. It looked old-fashioned too, as she refused to have it thinned out or styled. It stuck out in all directions, and from a distance looked like a soldier's helmet.

She had no feminine curves or charm either. Her square shoulders were like a tree stump hewn with an axe.

No man in his right senses would marry such a woman.

The strongest characters may be the weakest. Always prepared to be trampled upon or destroyed, in the end they grow callous and cold. Then nothing has greater power over them than warmth, for having received so little of it they treasure it. And Autumn had treated Mo Zheng not simply with warmth but with a mother's love. The two of them were probably happier together than people in most normal families, but that was not understood by such people.

Lunch was brought in.

Like an experienced waiter, Mo Zheng held two steaming bowls of soup in his right hand, two plates of bread and sausage in his left. On each plate was also a tiny dab of jam. The fine slices of sausage were laid out in a circle. The neatly cut slices of bread might have been measured with a ruler.

Each time she watched Mo Zheng preparing a meal so efficiently in the kitchen, a faint mysterious smile on his face as he scraped the scoop on the bottom of the pan, Autumn's feelings were mixed. He seemed better equipped to survive than her generation. For instance, she still couldn't cook. But for him, she would be reduced to eating in the canteen where everything tasted the same. She liked tasty food but begrudged spending time on cooking. Her life was too disorganized. She often thought that Mo Zheng could make a success of anything he turned his hand to, whether cooking, playing the piano or learning French.

The soup was so hot that, after putting it down, Mo Zheng blew on the tips of his fingers. He had the hands of an artist: long fingers, broad, thick palms, strong knuckles and wrists. He had played the piano for several years as a child, when he was still too small to reach the pedals, forgetting his food and games as he pounded away. Now, however, whenever she felt the urge to play the dusty piano with her stiff, refractory fingers, he would retreat to a corner of his room as if afraid of the sound.

Mo Zheng was no longer the little boy in light blue flannel. He was a tall young man in a crumpled and padded PLA jacket from an army surplus sale. He had replaced the original buttons with five of different sizes and colours. The cuffs of his long baggy trousers were usually torn, as his job was pruning, watering and spraying trees and shrubs. Even so, girls who didn't know his history were attracted by his square jaw, full lips, soft hair parted in the middle and combed loosely back, and arching eyebrows the tips of which curved down, so that even when still he struck people as animated. The pupils of his eyes were unusually large, and he would look slowly around, seriously and coolly. This contrast between his eyebrows and his eyes was what made his face so striking.

With one foot Mo Zheng hooked out a stool from under the table. It creaked when he sat on it, as if unable to bear his weight.

That creaking worried Autumn. Time and again she had urged him to take the stool to be repaired before it collapsed and somebody got hurt. Be he always shrugged this off. "It's nothing. Just remember not to sit on it yourself!" It wasn't that he was lazy, but to him a fall was nothing to worry about. She had to let it go at that, but she couldn't help eyeing the stool each time it creaked.

Now he asked as if casually, "Well? Do you like the flavour?"

Autumn blew on a spoonful of soup, then tasted it. She smiled. "Not bad. The real thing—like your French accent."

Mo Zheng's spoon stopped in mid air. Why did she have to rake up the past? He disliked recalling it, yet could never free himself from it. He gulped down a spoonful of soup as if to swallow his own anger. Then with his strong white teeth he bit into a slice of bread.

There was a crash, and for a second she thought his stool had collapsed. But no, the sound came from upstairs. Something must have been knocked over. Then they hear Little Zhuang howling, heavy footfalls and his mother Liu Yuyin—Jade—sobbing.

Mo Zheng smiled rather grimly. "Like people out of Gorki."

Autumn stopped eating.

"What's wrong?" he asked, still smiling faintly.

She looked sheepish. The wordly-wise, phlegmatic Mo Zheng made her feel like an ingenuous little girl, too easily upset. "I don't know why, but I can't eat when I hear crying."

"Like a real Christian."

"Mo Zheng!" she protested, feeling he could see through her. She stood up to go out. He barred the way with one of his long legs. "Take it easy! What can you do about it? They'll be rowing again within a couple of days."

He was right. The children upstairs were always crying and their parents always quarrelling. They were not a cantankerous couple and the two children were well-behaved, so why was life getting them down?

Mo Zheng urged her to finish her soup before it got cold, but Autumn's appetite had gone, along with her earlier high spirits. She shook her head.

She sat down silently at her desk and leafed through the last few days' papers. She noted, as always, which new factories had started production, which enterprises had over-fulfilled their quotas. These reports reminded her that the year was drawing to an end. In just over a month it would be 1980. At once she remembered the article she had been about to write before her illness, and started looking for her draft of it.

Strange, where had it gone? She distinctly remembered putting it on this pile of documents. It wasn't there. Had she slipped it into a drawer?

She opened her drawers one by one. Every one was a mess. Diaries, stationery, old letters, stamps, envelopes of money, empty medicine bottles... all lay in complete confusion. And she lacked the patience to make a careful search. She tossed an empty bottle into a corner.

She could not bring herself to throw away those old letters. Although not from friends, they were a record of her life, of her gallant failures.

She was a reporter who sympathized with the victims of injustice and waxed indignant over all abuses of which there had been so many in recent years. The ordinary workers and grassroot cadres whom she interviewed trusted her. She had overreached herself intervening in problems which were none of her business and often failed to solve them. These letters had made her feel guilty, as if she had deceived those good, honest people, yet they still looked to her for help. It was hard. Visitors from far away would turn up on her doorstep, rubbing their big-jointed hands, smiling bashfully and looking rather red in the face, then pour out their grievances till the middle of the night. Mo Zheng's room was like an inn.

The last couple of years had seen a marked change in her correspondence. She had received letters from families who had been cleared, whose sons, formerly excluded by people with pull, had now got into college; from people once labelled as renegades but now rehabilitated; from others no longer persecuted because the Party secretaries who had risen to power by joining some clique had now been dismissed. She hadn't the heart to throw away such letters.

But she had to find that draft.

"Mo Zheng, did you see a sheet of paper on my desk?" She knew it was useless to tell him it was a draft: the boy thought so little of her job, he never read what she wrote.

"What paper?"

"A sheet of lined paper with writing on it."

"Oh, when Little Zhuang came here to play the day before yesterday I wrapped some sweets up for him in a sheet of waste paper from your desk."

“That wasn’t waste paper, it was the draft of a report I’m writing on this year’s industrial output.”

“How was I to know?” He didn’t sound at all contrite.

“I’ve told you often enough not to touch my writing! You pay not a blind bit of notice.”

Mo Zheng looked sorry now. Not for tearing up her draft, but for upsetting her. He said, “But what’s the hurry? You need a good rest. Besides, who reads those reports with all that pompous official nonsense? Who believes them?”

“What a thing to say! Your ideas are getting wilder and wilder.” She pounded the desk.

Mo Zheng kept quiet and went on eating. The only sounds in the room were the clinks of his spoon against the bowl and his soft munching.

In their frequent clashes he was usually the one who backed down, not wanting to upset her. She was the only person in the world who loved him, who didn’t hold his past against him. Anyhow, he thought his generation superior to hers.

He could not grasp why, with only twenty years between their ages, there was such an amazing difference in their understanding of life. Were all her generation like her? More or less. In their purity of heart and credulity they clung stubbornly to their obsolete ideas.

Their arguments often rankled in Autumn’s mind. She didn’t consider herself a brainless woman. She had original ideas and keen insight. It was only his generation who thought all older people fuddy-duddies.

She had worked as a reporter for twenty-odd years since graduating from college in 1956, coming into touch with all sorts of people and getting a good grasp of the way things really were. She had her own views, and had resolved never to write false reports. In the Cultural Revolution she had found excuses for writing nothing rather than joining the chorus of those dishonest theoreticians.

She knew a lot of people working in industry. It comforted her to find that there were still some doing an honest job. And she loved to collect figures of increased output, which were not just dry statistics to her. She threw herself whole-heartedly into her work. How could Mo Zheng malign it like that?

Her jaw quivering with anger, she glared at him and tamped her foot.

Mo Zheng stopped eating, realizing that she had misunderstood him. He wiped the faint smile off his face and said seriously, "I wasn't talking about your work but about those endless statistics. Some people imagine they're sent up from below, worked out by abacus. In fact there's nothing that can't be faked, including Chairman Mao's 'supreme instructions'. The papers always claim that our industrial output is going up. Rubbish! I'm not saying all those figures are false, but I see no point in them. Take Old Wu upstairs. How does his family manage? Someone ought to write a truthful report on how the workers who sweat to create society's wealth live. That would show whether our industry has really developed. What use are your statistics? Have you ever thought about that?" For once Mo Zheng had lost his temper. He shoved his bowl aside so that the soup slopped on to his trousers. Then he pulled out a dirty, crumpled handkerchief to mop his trouser legs and work off his feelings.

Slowly her resentment died down. There was some sense in what he said, immature though it was. She thought bitterly of the mistakes, the chops and changes in the economic policy since 1956. But for all that the people would surely have a higher standard of living. Still, they were better off than before Liberation.

She said feebly, "At least these figures show that our economy has grown every year. Compared with before Liberation..."

"I knew you'd say that," he cut in. "You can't go on making that comparison for ever. How can you compare the old days with socialism?" Unwilling to carry on with the argument, he chucked his handkerchief into what was left of the soup, and sprang up to clear the table. At the kitchen door he turned, and it seemed as if a gust of wind had blown the dark clouds off his face. "You really ought to think about Old Wu's family, and why they keep having rows."

She felt the force of his sincerity. He seldom showed warmth, thinking tender-heartedness a weakness in a man, a luxury that he could not afford, was not fool enough to expect...

But no matter how cold-hearted he tried to appear he was filled with genuine feeling, selflessness and aspirations. Old Wu's family had been their neighbours for years. Autumn remembered how devoted he had been to his wife Jade. During Jade's first pregnancy everyone in the building had teased him for the way he cosseted her. Granny Wang on the second floor used to say, "Don't worry, Young Wu. Having a baby is like a hen laying an egg. If you get so worked up you'll scare her." Still he looked after his wife very carefully. Jade had been a charming bride and he had been a handsome young man, yet in a dozen years things had changed completely. Wu Guodong was so rough now, balding prematurely, and his wife's forehead was lined.

2

Not bad at all, this perm, just what Xia Zhuyun—Bamboo—had wanted. Really stylish. At her age it wouldn't do to wear her hair in tight curls like a girl. That looked vulgar, cheap, as if you could only afford a perm once a year.

She surveyed herself complacently in the two mirrors. Then standing up she nodded at Jade who was holding the mirror behind.

Bamboo thought: She knows her job, no wonder she was recommended to me. But why does she look so unhappy? She's still young. What's on her mind?

She relaxed as she waited for her handbag and coat. It was a thick, dark grey coat, yet very light, made of good worsted. The handbag was special too, flat and wide with an embossed design, a gift from her husband after his last visit to England.

Wherever he went on business, he always brought her back a present. Then she would smile like an empress receiving tribute.

Jade stood watching as Bamboo slowly put on her coat and headscarf, taking care not to spoil her new hairdo, then slowly opened her handbag. Her slowness was not deliberate but second nature. For, this middle-aged wife of a highly-placed official had lived in affluence for years, accustomed to being waited on by others.

From her handbag Bamboo took out an elegant leather purse with two gold-coloured metal clasps. In it were half a dozen ten-yuan notes, as much if not more than Jade's monthly salary.

Bamboo extracted one note and twisted it between her thumb and first finger before handing it over.

Jade took it up to the counter. At the sight of her worried, careworn face, Little Gu glanced at the clock. "Half-past five, time for you to knock off."

Jade smiled at her for her kind thought, but remembered the troubles waiting for her at home.

The notes in the change were dirty and crumpled. Bamboo took them superciliously, but didn't forget to count them before she clicked her purse shut.

She left, glancing at her small gold wristwatch. The perm had taken nearly four hours. That did not worry her; her problem was how to kill time. Her maid saw to all the laundry, cleaning and cooking. Their only daughter still at home was grown-up and had a very good job as a press photographer. Her sole worry was how to find the girl a suitable husband.

When she felt so inclined she would go to her office. If her heart was troubling her she rested at home. But she couldn't spend the whole day sleeping. Knitting helped to pass the time, though she never finished anything. And of course she could always read. They subscribed to many magazines and papers, and she spent hours reading. Unlike so many wives of high officials she had graduated from university, but her affluent life had corroded her mental faculties. Whatever she read she forgot.

In the evenings her husband had meetings and her daughter went out, so she sat alone on a sofa watching their twenty-inch Japanese colour TV.

She often closed her eyes and dozed off, so that when she went to bed she couldn't sleep and had to find something to occupy her mind. Often she thought about her daughter's marriage. Deputy-commander Wang's second son wasn't engaged, but he was too feeble and had no real talent. Ambassador Yu's son was sickly—she didn't want her daughter to be an early widow. Minister Tian's third son wasn't bad-looking and was bright, he worked as a translator, but perhaps he already had a girlfriend?... Sometimes she got up to knock on her husband's door, but he never opened it, either because he was sound asleep or because he knew that it was never anything that mattered.

Of course, at her age she didn't spend all that time on her appearance to make herself attractive; she just wanted to be smart, in keeping with her status. Her husband, busy with endless meetings, visits to the grass roots or telephone calls, had no time to admire her clothes or her hair-styles.

Once in 1956 she had dragged him to a dance in Beijing Hotel. The next day she asked, "Did it suit me, that dress I wore yesterday?"

He thought hard. "Not bad. Yellow goes well with your complexion."

Bamboo gaped at him. "What! Are you colour-blind? I was wearing a purple silk gown!"

He roared with laughter. "Well, why not get yourself a yellow one made?" Yet when she had a yellow silk dress made he said, "Yellow? Doesn't suit you."

Apart from this she had no complaints about him. He had been such a handsome, dashing young man that many girls had envied her when they went out together. He had never shown any interest in other women. In fact he treated even her as an ornament he could easily dispense with. They had long slept in separate rooms. She wondered if he regretted having married. Had he ever really loved her? He immersed himself so thoroughly in his work that his home and two daughters seemed to mean nothing to him. If she hadn't pulled strings their younger girl would never have found such an ideal job. It carried a high status but wasn't strenuous, and it brought her in touch with all sorts of important people. Of course she would have to fix up a good flat for her family too. When her husband regained his old post the ministry's housing shortage had forced them to accept this flat. A vice-minister deserved something better than five rooms on the third floor. Especially since she had a weak heart and her old man had asthma. She'd have to see to it, he wouldn't do a thing.

When Bamboo left the hairdresser's Jade felt completely limp. She hadn't slept a wink last night, had left home without breakfast and had been too upset to eat lunch. She didn't want to sit down and rest, though. She had to find something to do to keep from crying. She started sweeping the floor.

Her parents had never spanked or scolded her. But yesterday she'd been struck by her husband for whom she would have laid down her life. Why? All because Little Zhuang had broken a thermos flask. Wu Guodong had slapped the child without even asking if he had scalded himself. All she'd said was, "A flask only costs one yuan. What did you have to hit him for?"

"You're talking like a minister's wife," he had retorted. "How many one yuan do you have?"

It was true: towards the end of the month she had to count every cent.

Since Wu had gone on sick leave with hepatitis he drew only sixty per cent of his monthly pay, just over forty yuan, while she made fifty at most. Four mouths to feed, and every month they had to send his parents fifteen yuan. He needed nourishing food too, and they couldn't let the children go without.

There were others even worse off, and they could just make ends meet, but Jade had her work cut out to manage.

To save a few cents she never bought ready-made noodles. She kneaded dough and cut her own, even though her ankles were swollen after standing in the shop all day.

She never bought fresh vegetables, only the cheap ones that were sold off at ten cents a pile. Her elder sister wrote from Xinjiang① that greens were expensive there. Beijing was better—you could always find cut-price things.

To economize on detergent, she washed light-coloured clothes first, then dark ones, then the two boys' shoes,② and finally the mop.

Things had been different when she was a girl. She looked back wistfully on the years before 1958 when everyone had been better off. And since 1965 things had gone from bad to worse.

She hid her hardships from her parents, not wanting to worry them as they weren't having an easy time themselves. Her dad had retired, and her younger brother now had a baby daughter. Each time she went to see them, Jade spruced up the kids and took a box of cheap cakes. This didn't fool her mother. On the boys' birthdays or at festivals she helped her daughter out with a little money in ways which wouldn't hurt her son-in-law's pride.

A few days ago Jade had been going to make a winter jacket, and some beige dacron took her fancy. But it would have cost over ten yuan. She hesitated for a while by the counter, then bought some cotton instead. Better save the money to buy Guodong some nourishing food. And the boys both needed new padded shoes.

She spared no pains yet received not a word of thanks. Instead her husband swore at her and took things out on their sons even when they had done nothing wrong. In her resentment she had snapped at him, "Why aren't you a minister?"

"Why didn't you marry one?"

Neither would back down, each felt so wronged. They went for each other hammer and tongs. And when Jade tried to stop him hitting Little Zhuang, he had slapped her in the face. The next moment he

---

① 译者注：A border province in north-west China.

② 译者注：Chinese cloth shoes.

stood aghast at his own behaviour.

Jade hadn't cried, but just stared at him steadily, as if only now, after all these years, had she realized what he was really like.

They had often had rows before but this was the first time they had ever come to blows. Who was to blame?

That slap had brought Wu to his senses and made him realize that Jade was the mainstay of the family. Without her they could never have kept going. Had he ever asked her how she managed on so little money? No. Had he shown any concern for her? No. She had taken the heavy burden on her weak shoulders without a word of complaint.

Perhaps women are tougher and more self-sacrificing than men.

But he had not been able to bring himself to apologize. Perhaps it was because an apology would not have been enough. It might have made her even angrier.

In that instant Jade had thought, why not die and be done with it? Let him regret it for the rest of his life. But then who would look after the children? They might have a cruel stepmother. The thought made her weep. No, she could not die. What about a divorce? No, people would think she'd done something disgraceful. Divorcees were always despised, talked about behind their backs. And she couldn't go home to her mother: they had no room for her. Besides, that would only worry the old couple... She had been wondering all day how to punish her husband.

Why was fate so cruel to her? What a different life that last customer must have. Her husband would never beat her or say a harsh word.

She brushed away the tears with the back of her hand before anyone could see them.

It was snowing. Fluffy white snowflakes swirled gaily in the wind—the first snowfall this year. They reminded her of her happy girlhood.

A young man and a girl came in. The cold wind had brought colour to the girl's cheeks and made her eyes sparkle. The young man was carrying two big shopping-bags stuffed with purchases. He stood there beaming.

Jade sized them up at once as a couple about to get married.

The girl said, "Comrade, I'm looking for a hairdresser named Liu..."

"What for?"

The young man cleared his throat, as if to stress the importance of his statement: "We want her to do a perm. People say she's very good."

"Any of our stylists can give you a good perm," Little Gu put in. She thought Jade needed a rest. She was too kind-hearted to refuse if asked for by name.

The young man looked flummoxed. This was the first time in his life he had tried to do anything like this. Couldn't they grasp how important it was to him and his bride-to-be?

Jade understood. To him, his fiancée mattered more than anything else on earth. Tired out and wretched as she was, she felt touched.

"I'm Liu," she admitted.

"All right then," Little Gu sighed. "I'll give you a ticket for her." She whispered reproachfully to Jade, "Your face is swollen."

The girl handed over some notes. "A cold perm."

Little Gu pushed the money back looking at the clock. "It's too late for a cold perm."

The young couple stared at each other in dismay.

"I shan't have any time tomorrow," said the girl.

Jade glanced at Little Gu, who relented: "Very well. Liu's doing you a great favour."

The girl looked at the photographs of different hair styles, then asked her fiancé, "Which would suit me best?"

"Ask the stylist," he suggested.

Jade said, "All right, leave it to me." Just about to cut off the girl's plaits, she glanced at the young man and saw mixed feelings in his eyes. "Would you prefer to cut them off yourself?" she asked.

It came as a surprise to them, the intuition of this middle-aged woman with her lined, swollen face. No wonder people spoke so well of her.

The young man took the scissors, cut off the plaits, looked at them for a long time, then put them carefully into a small plastic bag. He reminded Jade of her husband years ago.

Jade gave the final touches to the girl's hair with the drier. The mirror reflected two very different faces. Next to that rosy face with sparkling eyes, Jade looked old and washed out. She thought, "I hope you'll always look as fresh and lovely."

The girl gazed bashfully at her unfamiliar reflection, the waved hair giving her the look of a young married woman. She smiled shyly.

The two young people somehow felt that everything, commonplace though it might be, that happened here on the eve of their wedding, including their meeting this commonplace hairdresser, would influence the whole of their married life.

In a flurry the young man produced a paper bag and handed it to Jade. "Please take some of our wedding sweets!"

"I couldn't", said Jade. "But thank you all the same."

When he insisted, she took out two sweets. They were wrapped in red paper with the character for "Double happiness". She then thrust the rest back into his shopping-bag and saw them out.

There were few people in the snow-covered street. Jade stood and watched the happy young couple walking away.

When they had disappeared from sight she turned and suddenly saw her husband leaning against a nearby tree. He must have been there for some time: his old padded cap, shoulders and scarf were white with snow. Clutching the sweets she watched him come over to her.

四

天堂里的对话

残　雪①

昨天夜里我又出去了。你曾劝告过我，不要在夜里出去游逛，以免遇到意想不到的伤害。我记得你的警告，但我还是出去了，象有鬼使神差一样。我脚一抬，就轻飘飘地下了楼梯。我的眼前白茫茫的，我穿过幢幢高楼，穿过"哗哗"作响的树林，穿过古老的崖石，这些东西都放射出一种冷漠的、没有色调的光，象被记忆遗忘了的某个地方，古旧而虚幻。有一只全身灰白的夜鸟在我旁边和我一道飞，但我知道那并不是一只鸟，那是很久以前，我在厨房里折的一只纸鹤，它将伴随我直到我的末日。

我从小就很能飞，这个秘密只有我自己知道，因为在我飞的时候，别人是看不见的。假如有可怕的东西追来了，我只要双脚轻轻一踮，就到了电线杆之上。我吻着那些屋脊，恐惧而又得意，假如我要转弯和改变方向，那也十分容易，我只要将一只手臂升高或放低，就能达到这个目的。我十分灵巧，敏捷，从来也没被抓住过，一次也没！昨夜出了点毛病，我出门后不久，毛毛雨就下起来了，天虽然还是白的，但我的眼前更加迷蒙，这一定又是该死的感冒引起的，我抓住一根老树的枝条，暂时栖息在那上面喘一口气。我想起了你。那一天我躺在你怀里，一边叹息一边抚摸你的头发和脸颊，忽然看见你躲在远处的小树林里。其实我发现的只是一张彩照，一张很大的立体彩照，那照片里的你时隐时现，而且能够运动，一下

---

① 中文选自：残雪．天堂里的对话．天津文学，1988(6)：35-37；英译文选自：Can，X．Dialogue in Heaven．Gladys Yang（trans.）．*Chinese Literature*，1989（Winter）：57-60．

躲到这棵树后面，一下又躲到那棵树后面，并且你的面孔也不断地变幻，一下子变成我的舅舅，一下子变成我的表哥，一下子又变成似是而非的你自己。我听说现在有一种照片，能有录相的效果，这是我在某一天在一间假设的空房里听人说起的，这个印象永远抹杀不掉。也许这就是那种照片？我正打算把我看到的告诉抱着我的你，但我一张嘴，发现你并不在，原来是我躺在草地上自己跟自己玩游戏呢！然而彩照确确实实是真的。秋天的落叶“沙沙”作响时，你坐在那堆很高的圆木上，用手支着下颌，一个钟形玻璃罩罩住你的全身。那一次，我曾用脑袋去撞击墙壁，发出炸弹爆炸一样的声音。一次，我暗暗下定决心，我一定要找到我的舅舅，将这件事问它个水落石出：世上究竟有没有这种照片？为什么从懂事那天我就总是看到它？我要告诉他这是一个了不得的谜语，每次在我看到它时，我就找到了准确的答案，而一旦它消失，又重新成为一个谜，于是找到的答案也遗忘得干干净净。问题就在于：它并不是喊来就来的，只是在你完全忘记了它时，又才赫然出现在你的眼前。至于照片里的人物，也绝不是随心所欲的，它有时是那个人，有时又是某个意想不到的、早就断了联系的人，那个人的出现与我的急切盼望毫无关系，你不招自来。我问了我的舅舅，但我没法证实，我语无伦次地说了一通瞎话，打了无数不着边际的比喻，使他十分惊奇，如此而已。

该死的毛毛雨，冷得很呢。我不敢就这样回去，因为有雨的天气会导致我失去平衡。每次你不由自主地吻了我的嘴唇，我就说：“亲爱的。”只要我说了这句话，我马上变得苍白而冰凉，然后左右环顾，躲开想象中的黄蜂。所以我后来变得小心翼翼，我不再说：“亲爱的。”我把这句话留在喉咙里，默默地用手指梳理你的头发。但这也一样，你能感觉得到，你知道我把这句话留在什么地方了，你依然苍白、颤抖，象面具一样凝固了你的表情，无声地说：“我的左腿患有萎缩症，你把我错认成某个黄昏蹲在河边扔石子的男人啦。这样的错误你一生中至少犯过两次以上。”你暗示我，别以为自己飞来飞去，就能穿透一切啦，我穿不透，比如说你，因为你是一个比照片之谜更大得多的谜语，就连你的存在都是一个问题，我根本不应该对你的存在这样有把握，因为你说不定会在一天早上消失在人流中,成为无数陌生面孔中的一个;也说不定我并不走开,只是我认出了你不是黄昏扔石子的那个人,于是走开,那时我就会清晰地发现自己的轻狂,并痴痴地笑起来。

这雨一下子不会停了,我记得出了树林就有一座石塔,我可以到那里面去休息。“桔红色的游艇在海上从容不迫地行驶,拖出一条细细的红线,一个老头咳了一声嗽。你那么确信真奇怪。”你坐在钟形玻璃罩里没有表情地说。出了树林之后才知道并没有塔,那座塔不是在林边,却是在海涛里,塔顶有盏绿灯,我是在十岁那年看见的,一见之下终生难忘,就象那些彩照。第一张彩照是我八岁时出现在床头柜上的,照片的背景是一片黄绿的草地,正中有一个穿着天蓝色绣花短裤的男孩,正在踢足球。我用手拨了一拨照片,他就一眨眼,调皮地飞起一脚。那一回真把我看呆了。我在空地上不断地转圈子,因为有很多小东西来来回回在地面游走,那里面也有野猪和豹子,我不敢贸然降落。我忽上忽下地滑行,居然还认出了我和你躺过的那块崖石。从上面看去,那崖石成了一个黑糊糊的圆斑,象生在灰白躯体上的一个坏疽。

你的手掌温暖而柔和,这是我躺在崖石上感觉到的。当时阳光将你的唇须染成了棕红色,你沉重的辗转使得崖石裂开了几条缝,数不清的雀子惊慌地窜入云霄。我把我这种感觉向你说了,你那么吃惊,立刻就捡起一块鹅卵石,捏了个粉碎。“一切都并不存在的。”你抬起手臂划了一个很大的、不确定的弧形,一只又一只透明的粉蝶从你背后懒洋洋地、斜斜地飘过。“我能飞。”我又打起精神想和你抗争:“你的手的确很美。我折纸鹤的时候,哭起来了。”你神秘地挤了挤眼说:“那也一样。有很多人为的东西证实我们是不存在的,我们只不过是那些飘忽不定的粉蝶。当你感觉到我的手掌时,也许它压根儿就是另外一个人的,而那个人早就消失在人群里了。那种感觉长时间留在你的脸颊上,这件事与那个人完全无关。你也许会去找,但永远也无法确定。他有时在黄昏的河边扔石子,有时出现在塔顶,有时又在船头撒网,每次都不是同一个人。你不得不将使你心脏悸动的形象附着在一个又一个人的身上,而每一次都是真实而生动的。那些人将血肉和魅力赋予这个模特,使它令人销魂,青春永注,而你……”

“你干吗吻我?”你没有回答我的问题,你那些幽雅的指头在我的掌心变成了皮筋一类的东西,我将手掌握起来,一根怒跳的血管破裂了,血液慢慢渗出,如一条鲜红的蚂蟥在手臂上慢慢爬动。

十五岁那年,我摔伤了腿,躺在床上折了几千只纸鹤。一天早上,我将细瘦发绿的颈脖伸出窗外,霜风透骨,窗下熙熙攘攘的人群喧哗着,我一直呆到天黑,被冰霜紧紧地粘在窗台上了。那一次我的手臂差点闹到要截肢的地步。我记得那些纸鹤有各种美丽的颜色(我想象的色彩),玲珑雅致。终于有一天,一个模样和你相似的青年走进我的房间,看见了扔在地上的那些纸鹤,他沉默了好久,最后弯下腰,似乎要捡起那些小东西。我连忙用脚踏住他要捡的那一只,我们对视的眼光碰出一排星星,我看见他的鬓角有一道疤。他正是那个人,我对这张有一道疤的脸熟悉极了。我讲的这些,就是你过去的经历,我们从前多次相会,我曾经是折纸鹤的少女,这当然一点也看不出来了。

雨停了,我就要飞回去。在假设的空房间里,在坏疽般的崖石上,我将再次和你不期而遇,你会不由自主地吻我的嘴唇,而我,下一次一定要说:

“你就是他,我是那个女人,在河边,在灯塔,在船头,在中午烈日下的沙滩上,在黄昏的桂花林里。南方温暖的蒙蒙细雨中,红玫瑰的花苞就要绽开,一个雪白的人影在烟色的雨雾中伫立。”

Dialogue in Heaven

Can Xue[①]

Last night I went out again. You warned me not to wander about at night for fear of an accident. And I remembered your warning, but still I slipped out like a wraith, rising in the air to flit downstairs. Before my eyes was a vast expanse of white. I crossed tower-blocks, soughing woods and old cliffs from which emanated a cold, colourless light, as if these were forgotten places, hoary and illusory. Beside me flew a pale grey night-bird, but I knew this was no bird, it was a paper crane I had made long ago in the kitchen, which would accompany me till the end of my life.

I have been a good flier since childhood, a secret known only by me, because no one can see me flying. If I'm chased by something scary, I have only to rise lightly on my toes and I'm up on a telegraph pole. I kiss the roof-tops, afraid yet pleased, and if I want to change course that's very easy. I have only to raise or lower an arm and it's done. I am so nimble that I've never been caught, not once! Last night something went slightly wrong; I hadn't been gone long when it started to drizzle, and though the sky was still white my view was blurred, no doubt because of my tiresome cold. I grabbed hold of the branch of an old tree and perched there for a while to catch my breath. I thought of you. Lying in your arms that day I'd sighed as

① 译者注：Can Xue, born in 1953 in Changsha, Hunan, began to publish stories in 1985, and her works have been translated into English, French and Japanese. This is her third story.

I stroked your hair and face, till I suddenly saw you hide in a distant wood. Actually what I saw was simply a coloured photograph, very big and stereoscopic, in which you appeared, disappeared and moved about, hiding behind first one tree then another. Your face kept changing too, first into that of my uncle, then my cousin, then into what seemed—yet wasn't—your real self. I've heard that nowadays there is a kind of photograph that's like a video cassette. I heard that one day in an imaginary empty room, and it made an unforgettable impression. Maybe this was a photograph like that. I was meaning to tell you what I'd seen as you held me in your arms, but as I opened my lips I found you'd gone and I was lying on the grass playing make-believe with myself! But that coloured photograph really exists. When the fallen leaves rustle in autumn, you sit on that high pile of logs, your chin in your hands, and your whole body enclosed in a bell-shaped glass globe. Once I butted my head against the wall, which sounded like a bomb exploding. Another time I made up my mind to find my uncle and ask him to tell me the truth: Does this type of photograph actually exist? Why had I been seeing it as far back as I could remember? I'd tell him: This is an extraordinary riddle; each time I see it I find the correct answer, but as soon as it disappears it becomes a riddle again, and the answer I'd found has completely slipped my mind. The problem is: it won't come when called; only when completely forgotten will it appear imposingly before you. And the people in the photograph are definitely not the ones you'd choose. It may be him or someone you hadn't been thinking of, with whom you'd long lost touch. Whoever appears it has nothing to do with my longing. He comes without being called. I asked my uncle, but I had no proof, speaking incoherently with endless irrelevant comparisons, so that he was astounded—that was all.

This tiresome drizzle is freezing. I dare not go back like this, because wet weather throws me off balance. Each time you impulsively kissed my lips, I said, "Darling." And then I promptly turned pale and icy cold, looking right and left to avoid imaginary wasps. So later I took care not to say "darling" again. I swallowed it back, silently smoothing your hair with my fingers. But you could sense it all the same, you knew what I had in mind, and you still turned pale and trembled, your expression frozen like a mask. And wordlessly you said: "My left leg is atrophied, yet you've mistaken me for a man crouching by the river at dusk to play ducks and drakes. You've made this mistake more than twice." You implied that I shouldn't imagine that by flying I could penetrate through anything—I couldn't. Take yourself for instance. Because you were a much bigger riddle than the photograph, and as even your existence was in question I shouldn't be so sure that you existed; for one morning you might vanish into the crowd, becoming one of countless strange faces; and I might not go away, just realizing that you weren't the man playing ducks and drakes at dusk. Then I'd go, well aware of my own flightiness and laughing foolishly.

This rain wouldn't be stopping yet awhile; I remembered a stone tower outside the wood where I could go and rest. "An orange pleasure-boat cruises over the sea, trailing a thin red thread, and an old man coughs. Your conviction is really strange." Sitting in a bell-shaped glass globe you spoke impassively. After leaving the wood I realized that there was no tower; it wasn't by the wood but in the sea, with a green light on top. I had seen it when I was ten and found it as hard to forget as that coloured photograph. The first photograph had appeared on the cabinet by my bed when I was eight; in its background was a green meadow; in the middle a boy in sky-blue embroidered shorts was playing football. When I flicked the picture he winked and kicked out mischievously. I couldn't take my eyes off him. I circled round and round the open ground because many little creatures were moving to and fro there, among them boars and panthers, and I didn't dare alight rashly. Gliding hastily up and down, I recognized the cliff where the two of us had lain. Seen from above it was a round black splodge, like gangrene on a pale grey body.

As I lay on the cliff I felt your palms, soft and warm. The sunlight had turned your moustache a reddish brown. Tossing heavily about, you made cracks in the cliff, and countless sparrows soared up in fright to the clouds. When I told you my feelings you were so startled you snatched up a pebble and crushed it into pieces. "Nothing exists." You raised one arm and swung it in an enormous arc, while transparent butterflies, one after another, fluttered lazily, slantingly, from behind your back. "I can fly." I aroused myself again to debate with you. "Your hands are really beautiful. When I made paper cranes I cried." You winked cryptically and said, "It's the same. Many man-made things confirm that we don't exist, we're simply butterflies flitting about at random. When you feel the palms of my hands, they may actually belong to someone else who has long since disappeared into the crowd. That feeling stays for a long time on your face, but this has nothing to do with that man. You may search for him but can never be sure you've found him. Sometimes he plays ducks and drakes by the river at dusk, sometimes appears on a tower, sometimes casts his net from the prow of a boat—each time it's someone different. You have to attach the image which captivates you to one person after another, and each time it is realistic and moving. Those men give their flesh, blood and spirit to this model, so that it is soul-stirring, forever young. But you...." "Why kiss me?" You didn't answer; your delicate fingers on the palms of my hands gripped them like rubber bands till an angrily pulsing blood-vessel broke, and blood trickled out to crawl slowly like a bright red leech over the back of my hand.

The year that I was fifteen I fell and injured my leg. While in bed I folded several thousand paper cranes. One morning I stuck my thin, greenish neck out of the window. The frosty wind pierced me to the bone, but the noisy bustling crowds outside kept me watching until dark, and ice and frost riveted me to the window sill. I nearly had to have my arms amputated. I remembered those paper cranes were of various lovely colours (my imaginary colours), dainty and stylish. Finally one day a young man looking like you came into my room, saw the paper cranes tossed on the floor and after a long silence bent down as if he wanted to pick them all up. I hastily trod on the one he was reaching for. Our glances, clashing, sparked off a row of stars, and I saw a scar at the corner of his temple. He was me: how well I knew that scarred face. All I've said is your past history; we've met many times; I was the girl who made the paper cranes; of course this isn't in the least apparent.

The rain has stopped; I must fly back. I shall meet you again by chance in an imaginary empty room or on the gangrenous cliff. You will impulsively kiss my lips, and next time I shall certainly say:

"You are he, I am that girl, on the river bank, the light-house, the prow of a boat, on the beach under the fierce midday sun, or in the grove of fragrant osmanthus at dusk. In the warm drizzle of the south red rosebuds will open, a snow-white figure will stand in the smoke-coloured mist."

附录一　戴乃迭译事年表

1919 年

1 月 19 日，出生于北京。

1937 年

入读牛津大学走读生学院（Society of Home Students），攻读法国文学。

经中文教授休斯先生介绍加入中国学会并担任秘书，结识该学会主席杨宪益，帮助杨宪益组织中国学会的会议。

从法国文学专业转读中国文学，随休斯研读《诗经》《论语》《易经》、唐代传奇和佛教书籍等。

1938 年

与杨宪益合译《离骚》。

1940 年

从牛津大学毕业，获二等荣誉学位，成为牛津大学中国文学荣誉学位第一人。

经国立中央大学校长罗家伦推荐，往重庆中央大学柏溪分校任教，受聘为英语系讲师。

1941 年

与杨宪益赴贵阳师范学院任教,受聘为英文系教授。

1943 年

与杨宪益一同接受国立编译馆聘任,开启夫妻二人携手合作的职业翻译生涯。

开始与杨宪益合译《资治通鉴》。

1944 年

开始与杨宪益合译《老残游记》。

与杨宪益合译陶渊明诗歌、唐五代诗歌、唐变文、南北朝佛学论争文、苗族创世诗等,但当时未出版发行。

与杨宪益合译艾青、田间诗,郭沫若、阳翰笙戏剧等,但当时未出版发行。

1947 年

与杨宪益合译《老残游记》(*Mr. Decadent*)由南京独立出版社出版。

1948 年

与杨宪益合译《老残游记》,由英国乔治·艾伦-昂温出版公司(George Allen & Unwin Ltd.)出版,英译者署名 G. M. Taylor(戴乃迭婚前英文名字)。

1949 年

受聘中央大学(后来的南京大学)外文系英文组教授。

1950 年

11 月 25 日,在南京大学校刊委员会编印的《南大生活》上发表文章

《对目前抗美援朝运动的看法》。

独译《原动力》(*The Moving Force*)①出版。

1951 年

5 月 11 日,在《南大生活》发表文章《我要以实际行动来表示对新中国的热爱》。

独译“朝鲜前线通讯 4 篇”在 1951 年第 1 期《中国文学》杂志上发表。

1952 年

与杨宪益合译宋庆龄著作《为新中国奋斗》(*The Struggle for New China*)由外文出版社出版。

1953 年

独译《李家庄的变迁》《雪峰寓言》由外文出版社出版。

与杨宪益合译《离骚》《阿 Q 正传》由外文出版社出版。

1954 年

与杨宪益合译《柳毅传——唐代传奇选》《王贵与李香香》《太阳照在桑干河上》《白毛女》《渡荒》《周扬文艺论文集》《鲁迅短篇小说选》等由外文出版社出版。

1955 年

与杨宪益合译《长生殿》、《屈原》(五幕剧)由外文出版社出版。

独译《阿诗玛》在 1955 年第 3 期《中国文学》杂志上发表。

---

① 《原动力》一书为女作家草明(原名:吴绚文)创作的新中国第一部反映工人阶级精神风貌的经典作品,1949 年 5 月初版,英译本于 1950 年推出,并未署名。本信息来源自 1951 年 5 月 11 日,戴乃迭发表在《南大生活》的文章《我要以实际行动来表示对新中国的热爱》。

1956 年

与杨宪益合译《鲁迅选集》(1 卷)、《柳荫记》、《打渔杀家》由外文出版社出版。

独译《罗才打虎》与新疆青年作家小说 2 篇分别在 1956 年第 1、4 期《中国文学》杂志上发表。

1957 年

与杨宪益合译《鲁迅选集》(2 卷)、《中国古代寓言选》、《儒林外史》、《杜十娘怒沉百宝箱——宋明平话选》、《十五贯》(昆曲)、《白蛇传》(京剧)由外文出版社出版。

独译《阿诗玛》《三里湾》由外文出版社出版。

独译《在冬天的牧场上》《三里湾》分别在 1957 年第 2、3 期《中国文学》杂志上发表。

1958 年

与杨宪益合译《搜书院》(粤剧)、《秦香莲》(评剧)、《汉魏六朝小说选》、《关汉卿杂剧选》、《中国古典文学简史》、《中印人民友谊史话》由外文出版社出版。

独译《大林和小林》(张天翼)由外文出版社出版。

独译朱自清散文 5 篇、《哥哥下乡去了》分别在 1958 年第 1、5 期《中国文学》杂志上发表。

1959 年

与杨宪益合译《鲁迅选集》(3 卷)、《中国小说史略》(鲁迅著)由外文出版社出版。

与人合译《毛泽东诗词》由外文出版社出版。

独译《红旗谱》《百合花》《莫干山纪游词》《捣米》《宝葫芦的秘密》《张天翼和他的小读者》等各类作品近 20 篇在 1959 年第 1—12 期《中国文学》

杂志上发表。

1960 年

独译毛泽东诗 3 首、闻一多诗 4 首、张永枚诗 2 首、新民歌 13 首、康朗甩诗 2 首等诗歌近 40 首在 1960 年第 1—11 期《中国文学》杂志上发表。

1961 年

与杨宪益合译《老残游记》由香港复兴出版社出版。

与杨宪益合译《鲁迅选集》(4 卷)、《故事新编》、《不怕鬼的故事》(程十发绘图)等由外文出版社出版。

《史记》翻译工作完成(或为 1962 年)①。开始翻译《红楼梦》。

独译《红旗谱》由外文出版社出版。

独译《绿林行》、《你追我赶》、《童年的悲哀》、《惠嫂》、《三家巷》(节选)、闻捷诗 2 首、罗淑小说 2 则等文学作品 13 篇(首)在 1961 年第 3—11 期《中国文学》杂志上发表。

1962 年

与杨宪益合译《刘三姐》、《海市》(刘白羽、阳朔等著)由外文出版社出版。

独译《葛梅》《鱼的艺术——和它在人民生活中的应用及发展》《微神》《山地回忆》《东方之珠》等各类作品 9 篇在 1962 年第 2—12 期《中国文学》杂志上发表。

1963 年

独译《老社员》《鄂伦春组曲》《祖国,我生命的土壤》《〈呼兰河传〉序》《红色娘子军》等各类作品 20 篇在 1963 年第 1—12 期《中国文学》杂志上发表。

---

① 因历史原因,译毕很长一段时间未能刊印,70 年代初,杨宪益被告知译稿遗失,据说“文化大革命”期间被某位编辑卖给或送给香港,并在香港印制发行,并没有署杨宪益夫妇的名字。

1964 年

独译《旷野上》《沉船》《迎接朝霞》《迎冰曲》《“奴隶村”见闻》《难忘的人》等各类作品 22 篇在 1964 年第 1—12 期《中国文学》杂志上发表。

1965 年

《红楼梦》翻译工作停止。其他翻译工作停止。

与人合作改写、注释的简写本《青春之歌》译本由商务印书馆出版。

独译《农奴》《姑嫂》《修房曲》《草原纪事》《青年马龙》《特殊性格的人》等各类作品 23 篇在 1965 年第 1—12 期《中国文学》杂志上发表。

1966 年

独译《赤道战鼓》(七场话剧)由外文出版社出版。

独译《游乡》(独幕剧)、《新型的小喜剧》、《我们的工程师》、《雪路云程》、《竹鸡坡纪事》等各类作品 13 篇在 1966 年第 1—7 期《中国文学》杂志上发表。

1970 年

与詹纳(W. J. F. Jenner)合作编选、翻译鲁迅等人著《现代中国小说选》(*Modern Chinese Stories*)由牛津大学出版社出版。

1972 年

在“文革”中受到冲击。1968 年 4 月 27 日,和杨宪益双双被捕,在狱中度过 4 年。1972 年 5 月,出狱。继续翻译《红楼梦》,此后几年一直从事该书翻译工作。

1973 年

编选、翻译《无声的中国:鲁迅作品选》(*Silent China*: *Selected*

Writings of Lu Xun)①由牛津大学出版社出版。

1974 年

与杨宪益合译《野草》由外文出版社出版。

1975 年

与杨宪益合译《史记选》由香港商务印书馆出版。

1976 年

《红楼梦》译毕。

与杨宪益合译《朝花夕拾》由外文出版社出版。

1978 年

与杨宪益合译《红楼梦》(第一卷)由外文出版社出版。

1979 年

与杨宪益合译《红楼梦》(第二卷)、《史记选》由外文出版社出版。

独译《宝葫芦的秘密》由外文出版社出版。

独译《坚强的人——访问巴金》、《奴隶的心》、《从森林里来的孩子》、《含羞草》、艾青诗、黄永玉诗等各类作品 30 余篇(首)在 1979 年第 6—12 期《中国文学》杂志上发表。

1980 年

与杨宪益合译《红楼梦》(第三卷)由外文出版社出版。

独译《萧萧》《丈夫》《桂生》《太阳下的风景——沈从文与我》在 1980 年第 8 期《中国文学》杂志上发表。

---

① 因当时的社会环境,国外出版社与中国内地沟通不畅,所选文稿均为杨宪益、戴乃迭合译鲁迅作品,但书作上仅署戴乃迭一人。

1981 年

与杨宪益合译《呐喊》《彷徨》由外文出版社出版；与杨宪益合译《三部古典小说节选》《聊斋故事选》等由中国文学出版社出版。

与杨宪益合译《鲁迅小说全集》由美国印第安纳大学出版社出版。

与杨宪益合译《明代短篇小说选》由香港三联书店有限公司出版。

独译《边城及其它》《春天里的秋天及其它》《新凤霞回忆录》由中国文学出版社出版。

独译《蝴蝶》《自言自语》《新凤霞回忆录》《关于鲁迅的讽刺诗》《同路易·艾黎的对话》《鲁迅与宋庆龄》等各类作品15篇在1981年第1—11期《中国文学》杂志上发表。

1982 年

独译《湘西散记》《北京的传说》《李广田散文选》，与他人合译《当代女作家作品选》《黑鳗》《孙犁小说选》《三十年代短篇小说选1》《三十年代短篇小说选2》《三十年代小说选》由中国文学出版社出版。

独译《风云初记》由外文出版社出版。

独译《纪念鲁迅学术讨论会》《〈湘西散记〉序》《关于〈九叶集〉》《花鸟舅爷》《老渡船》《评〈阅微草堂笔记〉》《北京的传说》等各类作品22篇在1982年第1—12期《中国文学》杂志上发表。

1983 年

与杨宪益合译《老残游记》《诗经选》由中国文学出版社出版。

与杨宪益合译《中国古典文学史大纲》由香港三联书店有限公司出版。

与人合译《王蒙小说选》由中国文学出版社出版。

独译《单口相声故事选》《芙蓉镇》由中国文学出版社出版。

独译《单口相声故事5则》《单口相声故事2则》《以苦为乐》《南湾镇逸事》在1983年第1、2、5、8期《中国文学》杂志上发表。

1984 年

与杨宪益合译《唐宋诗文选》由中国文学出版社出版。

与人合译《五十年代小说选》《郁达夫作品选》由中国文学出版社出版。

独译《浮屠岭》《条件尚未成熟》《“九十九堆”礼俗》《血红的九月》《矛盾交响曲》《银风筝下的伦敦》《寓言 16 则》在 1984 年《中国文学》杂志夏、秋、冬季刊上发表。

1985 年

与人合译《古华小说选》《绿化树》《茹志鹃小说选》《老舍短篇小说选》由中国文学出版社出版。

独译《绿化树》、《祖母绿》、《烟壶》、《高女人和她的矮丈夫》、《北京人》(选)在 1985 年《中国文学》杂志春、夏、秋、冬季刊上发表。

1986 年

与杨宪益合译《汉魏六朝诗文选》《明清诗文选》《唐代传奇选》由中国文学出版社出版。

与人合译《北京人》《邓友梅小说选》《张洁小说选》由中国文学出版社出版。

独译《鸭巢围的夜》(节选)在《中国翻译》1986 年第 2 期发表。

独译《北京人》(选)、《单家桥的闲言碎语》、《树王》在 1986 年《中国文学》杂志春、秋、冬季刊上发表。

1987 年

独译《沉重的翅膀》(*Leaden Wings*)由英国首家专门针对女性读者的出版社维拉戈出版社(Virago Press)出版。

与人合译《人到中年》《冯骥才小说选》《叶圣陶作品选》《茅盾作品选》由中国文学出版社出版。

独译《减去十岁》《人人之间》在 1987 年《中国文学》杂志春、冬季刊上发表。

1988 年

与人合作编译《龙的传说》《流逝》《玛拉沁夫小说选》由中国文学出版社出版。

独译《一个不正常的女人》《清高》在 1988 年《中国文学》杂志春、秋季刊上发表。

合译张洁中短篇小说集《只要无事发生,任何事都不会发生》(*As Long As Nothing Happens, Nothing Will*)由英国维拉戈出版社出版,1991 年,由美国格罗夫出版社(Grove Press)刊印发行。

1989 年

与人合译《蒃竹山房》《村仇》《中国优秀短篇小说选 1949—1989》由中国文学出版社出版。

独译《菜园》《知识》《一个爱国的作家》《杨柳》《蜀道奇遇记》《天堂里的对话》《谈〈天堂里的对话〉》在 1989 年《中国文学》杂志夏、秋、冬季刊上发表。

1990 年

与人合译《闻一多诗文选》由中国文学出版社出版。

独译《黄豆芽,绿豆芽》在 1990 年《中国文学》杂志冬季刊上发表。

1991 年

独译《窑工老吕》《家丑》《转运汉巧遇洞庭红》在 1991 年《中国文学》杂志春、夏、冬季刊上发表。

1999 年

11 月 18 日,在北京阜外医院因病辞世,享年 80 岁。

附录二　戴乃迭独译作品总目①

表 1　出版社发行的单行本作品目录

序号	原作名称	英文名	作者	出版社/杂志	出版时间
1	《原动力》	*The Moving Force*	草　明	*Cultural Press*	1950
2	《李家庄的变迁》	*Changes in Li Village*	赵树理	外文出版社	1953
3	《雪峰寓言》	*Feng Hsueh-feng Fables*	冯雪峰	外文出版社	1953
	《雪峰寓言》	*Fables by Feng Xuefeng*	冯雪峰	外文出版社	1983
4	《阿诗玛》	*Ashma*	公刘等整理	外文出版社	1957
	《阿诗玛》	*Ashima*	李广田整理	外文出版社	1981
5	《三里湾》	*Sanliwan Village*	赵树理	外文出版社	1957/1964
6	《大林和小林》	*Big Lin and Little Lin*	张天翼	外文出版社	1958/1965
7	《唐小西在"下一次开船港"》	*Next-Time Port*	严文井	外文出版社	1958
8	《搜书院》	*The Runaway Maid: A Cantonese Opera*	广东粤剧团	外文出版社	1958
9	《宝葫芦的秘密》	*The Magic Gourd*	张天翼	外文出版社	1959/1979
10	《红旗谱》	*Keep the Red Flag Flying*	梁　斌	外文出版社	1961/1964/1980
11	《赤道战鼓》(七场话剧)	*War Drums on the Equator (a play of seven scenes)*	李　恍、张风一等	外文出版社	1966

① 附录二将戴乃迭译品分为两大类：出版社发行的单行本和发表在 1955 到 1991 年间《中国文学》杂志各期次上的译文。对于再次刊印发行而出版信息有变化的独立发行译作，不单列条目，仅列在首译后供参考查证。其中，1999 年中国文学出版社和外语教学与研究出版社联合推出"英汉对照 · 中国文学宝库 · 现/当代文学系列"，将戴乃迭此前所译作品按照作家结集出版发行(计 19 部)，单独列在出版社发行译作的后部，戴乃迭译沈从文作品"《鸭窠围的夜》(节选)"发表在《中国翻译》1986 年第 2 期，列在《中国文学》杂志各期次译文之后。

续表

序号	原作名称	英文名	作者	出版社/杂志	出版时间
12	《边城及其它》	*The Border Town and Other Stories*	沈从文	中国文学出版社（熊猫丛书）	1981
	《边城：英汉对照》	*The Border Town*	沈从文	译林出版社	2009/2011/2013/2015/2017
13	《新凤霞回忆录》	*Xin Fengxia Reminiscences*	新凤霞	中国文学出版社（熊猫丛书）	1981
14	《北京的传说》	*Beijing Legends*	金受申	中国文学出版社（熊猫丛书）	1982/2005
15	《李广田散文选》	*A Pitiful Plaything and Other Essays*	李广田	中国文学出版社（熊猫丛书）	1982/1990
16	《湘西散记》	*Recollections of West Hunan*	沈从文	中国文学出版社（熊猫丛书）	1982
	《湘西散记》	*Recollections of West Hunan*	沈从文	外文出版社	2009/2014
	《湘西散记：英汉对照》	*Recollections of West Hunan*	沈从文	译林出版社	2009
17	《风云初记》	*Stormy Years*	孙　犁	外文出版社	1982
18	《荷花淀》	*Lotus Creek and Other Stories*	孙　犁	外文出版社	1982
19	《单口相声故事选》	*Traditional Comic Tales*	张寿臣等	中国文学出版社（熊猫丛书）	1983
20	《芙蓉镇》	*A Small Town Called Hibiscus*	古　华	中国文学出版社（熊猫丛书）	1983/1987/1990
21	《古华小说选》	*Pagoda Ridge and Other Stories*	古　华	中国文学出版社（熊猫丛书）	1985
22	《沉重的翅膀》	*Leaden Wings*	张　洁	*London*: *Virago*	1987
23	《华君武漫画选》	*Satire and Humor from a Chinese Cartoonist' s Brush—Selected Cartoons of Hua Junwu* (*1983—1989*)	华君武	今日中国出版社	1991

表 2 杂志上发表的译文目录

序号	原作名称	英文名	作者	杂志名	出版时间
1	朝鲜前线通讯 4 篇： 《谁是最可爱的人》 《战士和祖国》 《冬天和春天》 《汉江南岸的日日夜夜》	*Reports from the Korean Front*	魏 巍	中国文学	1951(1)
2	《阿诗玛》	*Ashma*	公刘等整理	中国文学	1955(3)
3	《罗才打虎》	*Lo Tsai the Tiger-Hunter*	李南力	中国文学	1956(1)
4	新疆青年作家小说 2 篇： 《红旗》 《他找到自己的道路》	*Stories by Young Writers from Sinkiang*： *Layli and Seit* *The Right Road*	吐尔洪·阿勒玛斯 阿·麦斯伍德	中国文学	1956(4)
5	《在冬天的牧场上》	*A Blizzard on the Steppe*	安柯钦夫	中国文学	1957(2)
6	《三里湾》	*Sanliwan Village*	赵树理	中国文学	1957(3)
7	朱自清散文 5 篇： 《匆匆》 《房东太太》 《荷塘月色》 《温州的踪迹》 《背影》	*Fleeting Time*； *My Landlady*； *The Lotus Pool by Midnight*； *Memories of Wenchow*； *My Father's Back*	朱自清	中国文学	1958(1)
8	《下一次开船港》	*Next-Time Port*	严文井	中国文学	1958(2)
9	《长江上的白鸥》	*The White Gulls of the Yangtse*	江 波	中国文学	1958(2)
10	《哥哥下乡去了》	*Li-ming Goes to Work on the Land*	王西彦	中国文学	1958(5)
11	《红旗谱》	*Keep the Red Flag Flying*	梁 斌	中国文学	1959(1—5)
12	《百合花》	*Lilies*	茹志鹃	中国文学	1959(2)
13	《莫干山纪游词》	*A Visit to Mount Mokan(a poem)*	陈 毅	中国文学	1959(3)
14	《文成公主》	*The Envoy of the Princess of Tibet(a folk tale)*	佚 名	中国文学	1959(3)
15	《捣米》	*Hulling Rice (a poem)*	张 长	中国文学	1959(4)
16	《宝葫芦的秘密》	*The Magic Gourd*	张天翼	中国文学	1959(6)
17	《张天翼和他的小读者》	*Chang Tien-yi and his Young Readers*	袁 鹰	中国文学	1959(6)
18	《桥上》	*On the Bridge*	王鲁彦	中国文学	1959(6)

续表

序号	原作名称	英文名	作者	杂志名	出版时间
19	《海滨杂诗》	*By the Sea* (*a poem*)	臧克家	中国文学	1959(7)
20	《藏族民间故事一则》	*The Story of MuchiKyku* (*a Tibetan folk tale*)	佚　名	中国文学	1959(7)
21		*Tibetan Folk Music and Songs*	Gongpo Gyaltstan Huang Ping-shan	中国文学	1959(7)
22	《草原雨景》	*Rain on the Grassland* (*a poem*)	王书怀	中国文学	1959(7)
23	《故乡》	*My Home* (*a poem*)	戈壁舟	中国文学	1959(7)
24	《手》	*Hands*	萧　红	中国文学	1959(8)
25	《蚕姑》	*The Silkworm Maid*	董钧伦 江　源	中国文学	1959(8)
26	《亲人》	*One Family*	王愿坚	中国文学	1959(9)
27	严阵诗 2 首： 《月下练江》 《夜曲》	*Two Poems* *The River Lien in Moonlight* *A Midnight Call*	严　阵	中国文学	1959(9)
28	《架线工人之歌》	*The Electrician's Song* (*a poem*)	李幼荣	中国文学	1959(9)
29	《每当我印好一幅新地图的时候》	*Each Time I Print a New Map* (*a poem*)	李学鳌	中国文学	1959(10)
30	《飘动的篝火》(小说)	*The Flickering Camp Fires*	朱家胜	中国文学	1959(10)
31	《荷花淀》	*Lotus Creek*	孙　犁	中国文学	1959(10)
32	《沙漠里的春天》	*Spring Comes to the Desert* (*a poem*)	竹　人	中国文学	1959(10)
33	《在暴风雪中》	*Out in the Storm*	玛拉沁夫	中国文学	1959(10)
34	《茶园朝雾》	*Morning Mist in the Tea Plantations* (*a poem*)	治　芳	中国文学	1959(10)
35	《肯盖里工人新村》	*The Worker's Village* (*a poem*)	满　锐	中国文学	1959(10)
36	《一千八百担》	*Eighteen Hundred Piculs*	吴组缃	中国文学	1959(11)
37	《两代人》	*Mother and Daughter*	李　准	中国文学	1959(12)
38	《颂歌》	*My Country, I Sing Your Praise* (*a poem*)	田　间	中国文学	1959(12)

续表

序号	原作名称	英文名	作者	杂志名	出版时间
39	毛泽东诗词 3 首： 《蝶恋花 · 答李淑一》 《七律 · 送瘟神》(二首)	*Poems—Mao Tse-tung* *The Immortals* *Written for Li Shu-yi* *Farewell to the God of Plague*	毛泽东	中国文学	1960(1)
40	《义和团的传说故事》3 则	*Folk Tales of the Boxers Uprising*	佚　名 张士杰	中国文学	1960(1)
41	闻一多诗 4 首： 《红烛》 《死水》 《洗衣歌》 《这个名字》	*Poems* *Red Candle* *The Stagnant Ditch* *The Laundryman's Song* *This Name*	闻一多	中国文学	1960(2)
42	《闻一多诗词》	*The Poetry by Wen Yi-to*	臧克家	中国文学	1960(2)
43	《太阳刚刚出山》	*The Sun Has Risen*	马　烽	中国文学	1960(2)
44	《草原之路》	*The Path on the Steppe (a poem)*	Chiao Wei-shen Yeh Feng	中国文学	1960(2)
45	张永枚诗 2 首： 《轻巧的牛皮鞋》 《抬起头来》	*Two Poems* *The Yak-hide Coracle* *Raise Your Heads*	张永枚	中国文学	1960(2)
46	《多收了三五斗》	*A Year of Good Harvest*	叶圣陶	中国文学	1960(4)
47	《新民歌 13 首》	*New Folk Songs*	佚　名	中国文学	1960(4)
48	康朗甩诗 2 首： 《见到恩人毛主席》 《孔雀呀，飞向北京》	*Poems* *I Have Seen Chairman Mao* *Fly, Peacock, to Peking!*	康朗甩	中国文学	1960(6)
49	《在党培养下成长起来的傣族诗人——康朗甩》	*Hanan-chou, a Tai Poet*	陈贵培	中国文学	1960(6)
50	《梁斌〈红旗谱〉创作谈》	*How Liang Pin Came to Write "Keep the Red Flag Flaying"*	Fang Ming	中国文学	1960(7)
51	《包身工》	*Contract Labour*	夏　衍	中国文学	1960(8)
52	《三门峡——梳妆台》	*Sanmen Gorge (a poem)*	贺敬之	中国文学	1960(8)
53	《上甘岭》	*The Battle of Sangkumryung*	陆柱国	中国文学	1960(9)
54	《日出》	*Sunrise*	刘白羽	中国文学	1960(11)

续表

序号	原作名称	英文名	作者	杂志名	出版时间
55	《水乡探胜》	*A Visit to a People's Commune in Kwangtung*	陈残云	中国文学	1960(11)
56	《绿林行》	*A Tale of the Green Woods*	梁　斌	中国文学	1961(3)
57	《你追我赶》	*The Contest (a story)*	沙　汀	中国文学	1961(3)
58	《童年的悲哀》	*The Sorrows of Childhood*	王鲁彦	中国文学	1961(3)
59	《惠嫂》	*Aunt Hui (a story within a story)*	王宗元	中国文学	1961(4)
60	《三家巷》(节选)	*Three Families Lanes*	欧阳山	中国文学	1961(5—6)
61	闻捷诗 2 首： 《婚期》 《新村》	*Poems* *The Wedding*; *The New Village*	闻　捷	中国文学	1961(5)
62	《黑海笛音》	*Fluting by the Black Sea (a poem)*	李显荣	中国文学	1961(5)
63	《春暖时节》	*The Warmth of Spring*	茹志鹃	中国文学	1961(7)
64	《沙滩上》	*The Dunes*	王汶石	中国文学	1961(8)
65	《樱花雨》	*A Shower of Cherry Blossom*	杨　朔	中国文学	1961(9)
66	罗淑小说 2 则： 《生人妻》 《桔子》	*Two Stories* *Twice-married Woman* *The Oranges*	罗　淑	中国文学	1961(11)
67	《葛梅》	*Ko Mei*	管　桦	中国文学	1962(2)
68	《鱼的艺术——和它在人民生活中的应用及发展》	*The Fish Motif in Chinese Art*	沈从文	中国文学	1962(2)
69	《微神》	*A Vision*	老　舍	中国文学	1962(6)
70	《山地回忆》	*Recollections of the Hill Country*	孙　犁	中国文学	1962(9)
71	《芦花荡》	*The Marshes*	孙　犁	中国文学	1962(9)
72	《关于孙犁作品的片断感想》	*Some Thoughts on Sun Li's Writings*	黄秋耘	中国文学	1962(9)
73	《珍珠》	*Pearl of the Orient (an essay)*	刘白羽	中国文学	1962(9)
74	《边城》	*The Border Town*	沈从文	中国文学	1962 (10—11)

续表

序号	原作名称	英文名	作者	杂志名	出版时间
75	《哈德尔的故事》(《多浪河边》1、3、4、5章)	*The Tale of Kader (an excerpt from a novel)*	周　非	中国文学	1962(12)
76	《老社员》	*The Old Stager (a story)*	马　烽	中国文学	1963(1)
77	《鄂伦春组曲》	*The Olunchuns (travel notes)*	玛拉沁夫	中国文学	1963(1)
78	《祖国，我生命的土壤》	*Motherland, Native Soil (a poem)*	铁衣甫江·艾里也夫	中国文学	1963(1)
79	《呼兰河传》选译	*Harelip Feng (an extract from "The Hulan River")*	萧　红	中国文学	1963(2)
80	《〈呼兰河传〉序》	*Preface to "The Hulan River"*	茅　盾	中国文学	1963(2)
81	《北游》	*Journey to the North*	冯　至	中国文学	1963(3)
82	《诗人冯至》	*Feng Chih the Poet*	Lu Chien	中国文学	1963(3)
83	《同志之间》	*Comradeship*	茹志鹃	中国文学	1963(3)
84	《红色娘子军》	*It Happened in Hainan (a film story)*	梁　信	中国文学	1963(4)
85	《澄河边上》	*On the Banks of the Cheng*	茹志鹃	中国文学	1963(7)
86	《茹志鹃其人》	*A Woman Writer of Distinction*	Fang Wen-jen	中国文学	1963(7)
87	《雨中登泰山》	*Climbing Mount Taishan in the Rain*	李健吾	中国文学	1963(7)
88	《牡丹园记》	*Peony Park*	严　阵	中国文学	1963(7)
89	《风云初记》(节选)	*Stormy Years (excerpts from the novel)*	孙　犁	中国文学	1963 (8—9)
90	《桑金兰错》	*Shearing Time*	赵燕翼	中国文学	1963(10)
91	秦牧散文2篇： 《巧匠和竹》 《广州盆景》	*Essays* *Master Craftsmen and Bamboo* *Miniature Gardens*	秦　牧	中国文学	1963(10)
92	《麦仁粥》	*Barley Kernel Gruel*	李　准	中国文学	1963(11)
93	《杨梅烧酒》	*Arbutus Cocktails*	郁达夫	中国文学	1963(12)
94	《出奔》	*Flight*	郁达夫	中国文学	1963(12)
95	《旷野上》	*A Night in the Open*	管　桦	中国文学	1964(1)
96	《沉船》	*Shipwreck*	王统照	中国文学	1964(1)

续表

序号	原作名称	英文名	作者	杂志名	出版时间
97	闻捷诗 2 首： 《向导》 《猎人》	*Two Poems* *Our Guide* *The Hunter*	闻　捷	中国文学	1964(1)
98	《梅恩莎》	*Miansa*	杨　苏	中国文学	1964(4)
99	《迎接朝霞》	*The New Technician*	崔　璇	中国文学	1964(5)
100	《迎冰曲》	*Fighting the Ice*	肖育轩	中国文学	1964(6)
101	《"奴隶村"见闻》	*A Visit to "Slave Village" (a sketch)*	玛拉沁夫	中国文学	1964(6)
102	《难忘的人》	*An Unforgettable Character*	马　烽	中国文学	1964(7)
103	《鞋》	*Straw Sandals*	肖　马	中国文学	1964(7)
104	《亲人》	*Our Own Folk*	赖维记	中国文学	1964(8)
105	《虎竹山下脱险记》	*A Narrow Escape*	钟春山	中国文学	1964(8)
106	《在费总理的客厅》	*Director Fei's Reception Room*	许地山	中国文学	1964(9)
107	《铁鱼的鳃》	*The Iron Fish with Gills*	许地山	中国文学	1964(9)
108	《小黑》	*Young Chen*	李　准	中国文学	1964(10)
109	《凶手》	*Murderer*	沙　汀	中国文学	1964(10)
110	《老烟的故事》	*The Story of Old Droopy*	沙　汀	中国文学	1964(10)
111	《李准短篇小说的特色和作家的道路》	*Li Chun's Short Story*	陈丹晨	中国文学	1964(10)
112	《沙汀小传》	*Sha Ting the Novelist*	Pin Chih	中国文学	1964(10)
113	《四月花泛》	*The Flowers That Bloom in May (a story)*	徐怀中	中国文学	1964(12)
114	《草原夜话》	*Night on the Grassland*	刘白羽	中国文学	1964(12)
115	《张翠霞》	*The Most Marvellous Day in Her Life*	刘白羽	中国文学	1964(12)
116	《农奴》	*Serfs (a film story)*	黄宗江	中国文学	1965(1)
117	《姑嫂》	*Sisters-in-law*	浩　然	中国文学	1965(2)
118	《修房曲》	*Her House Has to Wait*	张峻	中国文学	1965(2)
119	《草原纪事》	*On the Grasslands (a poem)*	巴·布林贝赫	中国文学	1965(2)
120	《和田》	*Khotan (a poem)*	严　辰	中国文学	1965(2)
121	《三声笛》	*Three Whistles*	李声义	中国文学	1965(3)

续表

序号	原作名称	英文名	作者	杂志名	出版时间
122	《青年马龙》	*Young Ma Lung*	宫克一	中国文学	1965(3)
123	《特殊性格的人》	*A Man of Unusual Character*	胡万春	中国文学	1965(4)
124	《我是如何走上写作之路的》	*How I Took up Writing*	胡万春	中国文学	1965(4)
125	王书怀诗5首: 《第一座小房》 《紫燕》 《收牧》 《轻轻的桦皮船》 《这铺炕》	*Poems* *The First Cottage*; *Swallows*; *Home from the Pastures*; *White-birch Canoes*; *This "Kang"*	王书怀	中国文学	1965(4)
126	《机场上的故事》	*The Making of a Pilot*	官伟勋	中国文学	1965(6)
127	《喜期》	*The Eve of Her Wedding*	浩　然	中国文学	1965(6)
128	《赤道战鼓》	*War Drums on the Equator* (*a play in seven scenes*)	李恍、张风一等	中国文学	1965(7)
129	《老猎人的见证》	*An Old Hunter Bears Witness*	邓　普	中国文学	1965(8)
130	《红色子弟》	*Brisk Encounter*	林　雨	中国文学	1965(9)
131	《风雪新记》	*Our Weather Station*	马　力	中国文学	1965(9)
132	《光荣》	*Honour*	孙　犁	中国文学	1965(10)
133	《野火春风斗古城》	*In an Old City*	李英儒	中国文学	1965 (11—12)
134	《野火春风斗古城》	*An Episode from the Years of War*	李英儒	中国文学	1965(12)
135	《游乡》(独幕剧)	*Taking Goods to the Countryside* (*a short comedy*)	赵淑忍	中国文学	1966(1)
136	《新型的小喜剧》	*Short Comedies*	胡　余	中国文学	1966(1)
137	《我们的工程师》	*Our Engineer*	王慧芹	中国文学	1966(2)
138	《昆仑采玉》	*Kunlun Jade* (*travel notes*)	梁鸣达	中国文学	1966(2)
139	《映山花》	*Azaleas* (*a story*)	孙健忠	中国文学	1966(3)
140	《雪路云程》	*Journey Through Snow and Clouds*	碧　野	中国文学	1966(3)

续表

序号	原作名称	英文名	作者	杂志名	出版时间
141	《竹鸡坡纪事》	*It Happened on Pheasant Hill*	彭伦乎	中国文学	1966(4)
142	维吾尔族寓言诗 4 首： 《骆驼和羊》 《勇士和狮子》 《红柳和白杨》 《雨点和河》	*Uighur Fables* *The Camel and the Lamb*; *The Strong Man and the Lion*; *The Tamarisk and the Poplar*; *The Raindrop and the River*	佚　名	中国文学	1966(4)
143	《我们的连长》	*Our Company Commander (a story)*	林　雨	中国文学	1966(5)
144	《一个老矿工的遭遇》	*An Old Miner's Story*	袁发茂 张大喜	中国文学	1966(5)
145	《家》	*A Home from Home (a story)*	韩统良	中国文学	1966(7)
146	《艾青诗 12 首》	*Selection of Ai Qing's Poems*	艾　青	中国文学	1979(6)
147	《关于写诗》	*On Poetry*	艾　青	中国文学	1979(6)
148	《坚强的人——访问巴金》	*A Man Who Conquered Fate—An Interview with Ba Jin*	杨　苡	中国文学	1979(8)
149	《奴隶的心》	*The Heart of a Slave*	巴　金	中国文学	1979(8)
150	《从森林里来的孩子》	*The Music of the Forests*	张　洁	中国文学	1979(9)
151	《含羞草》	*A Bouquet for Dajiang*	张　洁	中国文学	1979(9)
152	《女作家张洁》	*Zhang Jie, a New Woman Writer*	郭林祥	中国文学	1979(9)
153	访德作诗 3 首： 《墙》 《访马克思故居》 《慕尼黑》	*Poems Written During a Visit to West Germany*	艾　青	中国文学	1979(12)
154	黄永玉诗 3 首： 《曾经有过那种时候》 《希望之花》 《献给妻子们》	*Three Poems*	黄永玉	中国文学	1979(12)
155	《萧萧》	*Xiaoxiao*	沈从文	中国文学	1980(8)

续表

序号	原作名称	英文名	作者	杂志名	出版时间
156	《丈夫》	*The Husband*	沈从文	中国文学	1980(8)
157	《贵生》	*Guisheng*	沈从文	中国文学	1980(8)
158	《太阳下的风景——沈从文与我》	*A Sunlit Landscape*	黄永玉	中国文学	1980(8)
159	《蝴蝶》	*The Butterfly*	王　蒙	中国文学	1981(1)
160	《自言自语》	*Soliloquies*	鲁　迅	中国文学	1981(1)
161	《新凤霞回忆录》	*Reminiscences*	新凤霞	中国文学	1981(4)
162	《关于鲁迅的讽刺诗》	*About Lu Xun's Lampoons*	吕　剑	中国文学	1981(4)
163	《同路易·艾黎的对话》	*An Interview with Rewi Alley*	白　夜	中国文学	1981(5)
164	《漫谈工笔重彩画》	*China's Meticulous Painting*	潘絜兹	中国文学	1981(5)
165	《罕见的阴山岩画》	*Rare Cliff Engravings of Yinshan*	盖山林	中国文学	1981(5)
166	《悲哀的玩具》	*A Pitiful Plaything*	李广田	中国文学	1981(6)
167	《野店》	*A Country Inn*	李广田	中国文学	1981(6)
168	《山之子》	*Son of the Mountain*	李广田	中国文学	1981(6)
169	《没有太阳的早晨》	*A Sunless Morning*	李广田	中国文学	1981(6)
170	《小草对阳光这样说》	*What the Grass Said to the Sun*	胡　风	中国文学	1981(6)
171	《我走过的道路》(节选)	*The Road I Travelled (extract)*	茅　盾	中国文学	1981(7)
172	《鲁迅与外国文学》	*Lu Xun and Foreign Literature*	王　瑶	中国文学	1981(9)
173	《鲁迅和宋庆龄》	*Lu Xun and Soong Ching Ling*	李何林	中国文学	1981(11)
174	《坚持鲁迅的文化方向 发扬鲁迅的战斗传统》	*Persist in Lu Xun's Cultural Direction and Develop Lu Xun's Militant Tradition*	周　扬	中国文学	1982(1)
175	《纪念鲁迅学术讨论会》	*Symposium on Lu Xun*	纪　鲁	中国文学	1982(1)

续表

序号	原作名称	英文名	作者	杂志名	出版时间
176	《湘西散记》3 篇： 《雪晴》 《巧秀和冬生》 《传奇不奇》	*Recollections of West Hunan* *After Snow*; *Qiaoxiu and Dongsheng*; *Truth Is Stranger than Fiction*	沈从文	中国文学	1982(2)
177	《〈湘西散记〉序》	*Preface to "Recollections of West Hunan"*	沈从文	中国文学	1982(2)
178	《关于〈九叶集〉》	*Introducing "The Nine Leaves Anthology"*	袁可嘉	中国文学	1982(4)
179	《花鸟舅爷》	*Flower-and-Bird Uncle*	李广田	中国文学	1982(4)
180	《老渡船》	*An Old Ferry-Boat*	李广田	中国文学	1982(4)
181	《评〈阅微草堂笔记〉》	*On "Notes of Yuewei Hermitage"*	邵海清	中国文学	1982(4)
182	《北京的传说》(5 则)	*Beijing Legends*	金受申	中国文学	1982(6)
183	《雁翼的诗》	*Yan Yi's Poetry*	艾　青	中国文学	1982(6)
184	《关于鲁迅的随笔三则》	*Notes on Lu Xun*	姜德明	中国文学	1982(7)
185	《澳大利亚印象》 《哈！那个澳大利亚人》 《口袋》	*Impression of Australia*: *Look! An Australia*; *Pouches*	黄永玉	中国文学	1982(8)
186	《羊角哀舍命全交》	*Yang Jiaoai Gives His Life to Save His Friends*	冯梦龙编	中国文学	1982(10)
187	《我与文学》	*How I Became a Writer*	古　华	中国文学	1982(12)
188	《单口相声故事 4 则》	*Four "Xiangsheng" Stories*	张寿臣	中国文学	1983(1)
189	《单口相声故事 3 则》	*Three "Xiangsheng" Stories*	张寿臣	中国文学	1983(2)
190	《以苦为乐》	*Finding Happiness in Hardships*	新凤霞	中国文学	1983(5)
191	《南湾镇逸事》	*It Happened in South Bay*	古　华	中国文学	1983(8)
192	《浮屠岭》	*Pagoda Ridge*	古　华	中国文学	1984 (summer)
193	《条件尚未成熟》	*The Time Is Not Yet Ripe*	张　洁	中国文学	1984 (autumn)

续表

序号	原作名称	英文名	作者	杂志名	出版时间
194	《"九十九堆"礼俗》	*Ninety-Nine Mounds*	古　华	中国文学	1984 (winter)
195	《血红的九月》	*Blood-Red September*	萧　乾	中国文学	1984 (winter)
196	《矛盾交响曲》	*A Symphony of Contradictions*	萧　乾	中国文学	1984 (winter)
197	《银风筝下的伦敦》	*London Under Silver Kites*	萧　乾	中国文学	1984 (winter)
198	《寓言 16 则》①	*Fables*	鲁迅等	中国文学	1984 (winter)
199	《绿化树》	*Mimosa*	张贤亮	中国文学	1985 (spring)
200	《祖母绿》	*Emerald*	张　洁	中国文学	1985 (summer)
201	《烟壶》	*Snuff-Bottles*	邓友梅	中国文学	1985 (autumn)
202	《高女人和她的矮丈夫》	*The Tall Woman and Her Short Husband*	冯骥才	中国文学	1985 (winter)
203	《北京人》(选)	*Chinese Profiles*	张辛欣 桑　晔	中国文学	1985 (winter) 1986 (spring)
204	《单家桥的闲言碎语》	*Shan Family Bridge*	潮　清	中国文学	1986 (autumn)
205	《树王》	*King of Trees*	阿　城	中国文学	1986 (winter)
206	《减去十岁》	*Ten Years Deducted*	谌　容	中国文学	1987 (spring)
207	《人人之间》	*Between Themselves*	王安忆	中国文学	1987 (winter)
208	《一个不正常的女人》	*A Freakish Girl*	谌　容	中国文学	1988 (spring)
209	《清高》	*Other-Worldly*	陆文夫	中国文学	1988 (autumn)

① 其中鲁迅、冯雪峰、张天翼等人的 6 首寓言系戴乃迭所译。

续表

序号	原作名称	英文名	作者	杂志名	出版时间
210	《傻二舅》	*Daft Second Uncle*	苏叔阳	中国文学	1989 (spring)
211	《送你一束夜来香》	*A Gift of Night Fragrance*	谌容	中国文学	1989 (spring)
212	《菜园》	*Vegetable Garden*	沈从文	中国文学	1989 (summer)
213	《知识》	*Knowledge*	沈从文	中国文学	1989 (summer)
214	《一个爱国的作家》	*A Patriotic Writer—in memory of my teacher Shen Congwen*	汪曾祺	中国文学	1989 (summer)
215	《杨柳》	*Willows*	丰子恺	中国文学	1989 (autumn)
216	《蜀道奇遇记》	*Strange Encounter in Sichuan*	丰子恺	中国文学	1989 (autumn)
217	《天堂里的对话》	*Dialogue in Heaven*	残　雪	中国文学	1989 (winter)
218	《谈〈天堂里的对话〉》	*On "Dialogue in Heaven"*	王　蒙	中国文学	1989 (winter)
219	《黄豆芽,绿豆芽》	*Soybean Sprouts and Mungbean Sprouts*	王金力	中国文学	1990 (winter)
220	《窑工老吕》	*Old Lü the Potter*	朱小平	中国文学	1991 (spring)
221	《家丑》	*A Family Scandal*	张　宇	中国文学	1991 (summer)
222	《转运汉巧遇洞庭红》	*The Tangerines and the Tortoise Shell*	凌濛初	中国文学	1991 (winter)
223	《鸭窠围的夜》①(节选)	*A Night at Mallard-Nest Village*	沈从文	中国翻译	1986(2)

① 《中国翻译》译稿上将原文标题误为《鸭巢围的夜》，此处更正。

中華譯學館·中华翻译研究文库

许　钧◎总主编

第一辑

中国文学译介与传播研究(卷一)　许　钧　李国平　主编
中国文学译介与传播研究(卷二)　许　钧　李国平　主编
中国文学译介与传播研究(卷三)　冯全功　卢巧丹　主编
译道与文心——论译品文录　许　钧　著
翻译与翻译研究——许钧教授访谈录　许　钧　等著
《红楼梦》翻译研究散论　冯全功　著
跨越文化边界:中国现当代小说在英语世界的译介与接受　卢巧丹　著
全球化背景下翻译伦理模式研究　申连云　著
西儒经注中的经义重构——理雅各《关雎》注疏话语研究　胡美馨　著

第二辑

译翁译话　杨武能　著
译道无疆　金圣华　著
重写翻译史　谢天振　主编
谈译论学录　许　钧　著
基于“大中华文库”的中国典籍英译翻译策略研究　王　宏　等著
欣顿与山水诗的生态话语性　陈　琳　著
批评与阐释——许钧翻译与研究评论集　许　多　主编
中国翻译硕士教育研究　穆　雷　著
中国文学四大名著译介与传播研究　许　多　冯全功　主编
文学翻译策略探索——基于《简·爱》六个汉译本的个案研究　袁　榕　著
传播学视域下的茶文化典籍英译研究　龙明慧　著

第三辑

关于翻译的新思考　许　钧　著
译者主体论　屠国元　著
文学翻译中的修辞认知研究　冯全功　著
文本内外——戴乃迭的中国文学外译与思考　辛红娟　刘园晨　编著
古代中文典籍法译本书目及研究　孙　越　编著
《红楼梦》英译史　赵长江　著
改革开放以来中国当代小说英译研究　吴　赟　著
中国当代小说英译出版研究　王颖冲　著
林语堂著译互文关系研究　李　平　著
林语堂翻译研究　李　平　主编
傅雷与翻译文学经典研究　宋学智　著
昆德拉在中国的翻译、接受与阐释研究　许　方　著
中国翻译硕士教育探索与发展(上卷)　穆　雷　赵军峰　主编
中国翻译硕士教育探索与发展(下卷)　穆　雷　赵军峰　主编

图书在版编目(CIP)数据

文本内外：戴乃迭的中国文学外译与思考 / 辛红娟，刘园晨编著. —杭州：浙江大学出版社，2021.5

(中华翻译研究文库 / 许钧总主编)

ISBN 978-7-308-21221-2

Ⅰ.①文… Ⅱ.①辛… ②刘… Ⅲ.①中国文学—英语—文学翻译—研究 Ⅳ.①H315.9

中国版本图书馆 CIP 数据核字(2021)第 055567 号

中華譯學館 莫言題

文本内外——戴乃迭的中国文学外译与思考

辛红娟 刘园晨 编著

出 品 人 褚超孚
总 编 辑 袁亚春
丛书策划 张 琛 包灵灵
责任编辑 陆雅娟
责任校对 董齐琪
封面设计 程 晨
出版发行 浙江大学出版社
(杭州市天目山路 148 号 邮政编码 310007)
(网址：http://www.zjupress.com)
排 版 浙江时代出版服务有限公司
印 刷 杭州高腾印务有限公司
开 本 710mm×1000mm 1/16
印 张 33
字 数 625 千
版 印 次 2021 年 5 月第 1 版 2021 年 5 月第 1 次印刷
书 号 ISBN 978-7-308-21221-2
定 价 98.00 元

版权所有 翻印必究 印装差错 负责调换

浙江大学出版社市场运营中心联系方式 (0571)88925591；http://zjdxcbs.tmall.com